Introduction to Counseling

Introduction to Counseling

James R. Engelkes
Michigan State University

David Vandergoot
Human Resources Center

Houghton Mifflin Company
Boston Dallas Geneva, Illinois
Hopewell, New Jersey Palo Alto London

Photo credits: Hanna Schreiber/Photo Researchers, Inc. (p. 2); Raimondo Borea/Gartman Agency (p. 12); Burk Uzzle/Magnum Photos, Inc. (p. 22); Richard Kalvar/Magnum Photos (p. 29); H. Armstrong Roberts (p. 40); Spencer Blank/Freelance Photographer's Guild (p. 56); Ellis Herwig/Stock, Boston (p. 62); Alice Kandell/Photo Researchers, Inc. (p. 70); Freelance Photographers Guild/Vannucci Foto-Services (p. 84); Bohdan Hrynewych/Stock, Boston (p. 100); Barry Kirk (p. 110); The Bettmann Archive, Inc. (p. 114); Owen Franken/Stock, Boston (p. 128); Institute for Rational Living (p. 141); The Bettmann Archive, Inc. (p. 162); Deke Simon/Real People Press (p. 172); Bohdan Hrynewych/Stock, Boston (p. 194); Hella Hammid/Rapho/Photo Researchers, Inc. (p. 201); Van Bucher/Photo Researchers, Inc. (p. 220); Peter Southwick/Stock, Boston (p. 228); Ed Lettau/Photo Researchers, Inc. (p. 232); Photographie De Sazo-Rapho/Photo Researchers, Inc. (p. 254); Tim Carlson/Stock, Boston (p. 266); Barry Kirk (p. 275); Barry Kirk (p. 302); Paul M. Schrock Photos/Freelance Photographer's Guild (p. 313).

Printed in the U.S.A.

Library of Congress Catalog Card Number: 79-7419

ISBN: 0-395-30800-3

Contents

Preface

Underlying every counselor's ideas, techniques, and behavior is a philosophy about people, particularly about how people can change. The authors of this book view counseling as a learning experience that facilitates the growth of counselees who want to change some aspect of how they think and behave. This requires counselors to be sensitive to what counselees want and need. As training and other lifelong learning experiences of counselors contribute to the skills they need to help people create change in their lives and in their institutions, the profession of counseling will become an even more respected component of the human services our society provides.

As counselors and authors, we have tried to express our philosophy throughout this book. A central belief guiding the selection of content is that the study of the counseling process and its effects should be grounded in a consistent theoretical background that can generate testable hypotheses about what counselors can do to create change. Creating desired changes in persons' lives seems to be an overall goal of a majority of counseling theories.

This emphasis on change is based on two main assumptions. The first is that permanent change is the chief indicator of learning. Therefore, counseling is an educative process where what people learn is seen in the results of counseling. Second, these learned changes, reflected in how people think and behave, are subject to observation, prediction, and control. This implies that counseling is deliberate; that guesswork is removed or reduced as much as possible; and that people can gain more control of their lives and how they view life when they participate in counseling. Both within and outside of the profession, there are more calls for accountability to counselees and society in general.

This book has been organized so that the beginning counselor can obtain the basic knowledge necessary for selecting values, theories, and practices. It is assumed that change brought about by counseling is a direct result of the counselor's intervention. The more a counselor knows, the more instrumental he or she can become in affecting change.

The counselor never ceases to learn and change. This growth must be grounded in an awareness of the realities of counseling, its history and theories, and those skills that have been shown to be most facilitative of good counseling.

This book has been organized to develop this sense of awareness. Chapter 1 contains an overview of the essential elements that make up counseling. Counselor values and counselee needs are discussed.

Chapter 2 provides a historical perspective of how counseling developed in the United States. Important events, people, organizations, and pertinent legislation are reviewed. Chapters 3 to 5 provide an up-to-date look at counseling today. Several models of counseling systems are examined in Chapter 3, and an overview of the functions and responsibilities of counselors is given in Chapter 4. Chapter 5 looks at the organizational contexts of counseling, for counselors and the counseling process can be viewed as components of larger systems. As a way of introducing systems theory, Chapter 5 describes systems based on the organizational dynamics and the behavior of individuals within organizations. Examples drawn from counseling organizations are used to illustrate the theory.

Chapters 6 through 9 contain an overview of some of the major theoretical concepts of counseling practice. Counseling as communication is elaborated upon in Chapter 6, which also contains a brief historical review of the research that supports this concept.

As a derivative of psychology, counseling has concentrated on the psychological makeup of people—their personality characteristics and how they think and behave. Chapters 7 and 8 contain counseling theories that describe what people are like and how they change in general ways. Chapter 7 centers around cognitive theories, in which people are viewed as being capable of consciously managing their own lives through rational thought processes. Chapter 8 reflects how people are influenced by unconscious emotional forces, which may be hard to control.

As with any attempt to classify concepts or theories that are interrelated, the division of counseling theories into cognitive and affective domains is simplistic. These counseling theories present the major directions the field has taken and provide a broad view of some of the major systems that have influenced counseling.

The behavior of individuals and how they learn is determined by more than their cognitive abilities and emotional qualities. Individuals are also members of groups. They are born into families and interact with groups of various kinds for most of their lives. Counseling theories have been extended to accommodate group processes. Chapter 9 describes the possibilities of group counseling.

Chapters 10 and 11 elaborate on the types of problems dealt with in counseling. These are presented from a perspective akin to the counselee's viewpoint rather than that of the professional counseling theorist. Both viewpoints are essential. Chapter 10 provides a scheme for classifying and understanding the problems and concerns that lead people to seek counseling. This scheme enables the counselor to sort out factors that underlie the needs of counselees and help them to offer appropriate strategies for answering these needs. Chapter 11 provides cases that illustrate the types of counseling concerns addressed in Chapter 10.

Chapters 12 and 13 provide information on how counselors manage their activities. Chapter 12 contains suggestions on how counseling services can be coordinated and administered. Chapter 13 is a review of program evaluation, research issues, and techniques that allow counselors to access their accountability. Program evaluation can provide the mechanism for managing information so that it is responsive to the demands made upon counselors. Research enables counselors to improve the technology that allows them to make changes in order to meet these demands.

J.R.E.
D.V.

Introduction to Counseling

1

Perception of counseling

1 So you're thinking about becoming a counselor

The bases of successful counseling are a positive attitude, a value system consistent with the mainstream of American society, and a strong desire to help others.

1 So you're thinking about becoming a counselor

Key terms

counseling
counselor
counselee
counseling outcomes
existential-humanistic theory
client-centered theory
behavior-modification theory
psychobehavioral theory
counselor burnout

Introduction

Although counseling has been a profession for about 100 years, what it is, who does it, and what it is supposed to accomplish are still issues that are subject to debate. One may say with certainty, however, that the very nature of counseling—two people attempting to resolve something—requires creativity and individuality. Probably, counseling exists because life is replete with uncertainties. Counseling becomes appropriate when people are unsure of how to raise their children, what educational or vocational training to pursue, how to develop better friendships, or how to become more skillful. Recognizing an uncertain situation earmarks an opportunity to learn, a challenge to change and grow. Such uncertainty may prompt individuals to seek information to help them make their own decisions. Problems and decision making, from this point of view, can become exciting, as well as being the first step toward a new, positive way of thinking and behaving.

Doing the investigative work required to obtain new information is not always an easy task. It may require meeting new people, uncovering hard-to-find sources, and, particularly, when counseling is involved, a potentially difficult period of self-searching. Removing uncertainties involves costs that are both monetary and psychological. Also, if information is obtained and alternatives become available, the individual must make a decision that can lead to a change, perhaps even a new situation, which has its own uncertainties. It is not surprising then that counseling, or any change-producing situation, given these costs, is approached with a certain apprehension. Most people, then, think that counseling is fine as long as it is for somebody else. But elements of counseling are a part of everyone's life, whether or not formal counseling ever occurs.

The situation facing someone in an introductory counseling course who is contemplating a future in counseling is similar to that of a counselee uncertain about any future course of action. There are no right or wrong choices or actions. People can make only inexact estimates of costs and benefits, using their own sets of values. This book should make the information search easier, the alternatives and their consequences more obvious, and the eventual decisions made regarding counseling careers fruitful ones. It is the effort of the reader, however, that may lead him or her to an exciting and valuable counseling career. New counselors expressing new ideas will continue the tradition of counseling as a growing, innovative, yet still undefinable, field. For counselors already practicing their profession, it is never too late to begin something new.

Need for counseling

Counselors as agents of change

Counseling is a particularly human experience in a world that seems to become less human every day. In an age of ideologies and technologies, the counseling profession helps maintain the importance of our humanness. Counseling permits people to work together for their common good. It is an opportunity for people to share their hopes and fears, but most important, they can share their humanity. It is easy, then, to understand why counseling is a valuable resource for our society, since it is often associated with helping people solve problems. As people overcome those barriers that inhibit them, society as a whole will benefit.

As we shall point out, counseling is directed at the concerns of individuals. In some aspects, individuals "own" their problems and have a personal responsibility to solve them in their own way. Counselors can help with this resolution, and historically, they have done so.

Types of counseling

In other aspects of life, though, obviously individuals are not able to control all the social, political, and cultural forces that affect their lives. Can counselors muster the insight and capability to serve as change agents of these institutional pressures? This is a new challenge that counselors are being urged to face: the need to help others accept and tolerate, or even act upon, these forces.

Traditionally, counselors have helped people deal with their concerns about vocations. Today, employers are coming to counselors to discuss the possibility of creating a more satisfying work place for employees and a more productive one for the employer. This has been called the "quality of work-life" movement. Counselors are being employed to counsel troubled employees and to consult on how best to build work environments that are sensitive to the needs of all concerned.[1]

In school settings, particularly at the secondary school level, counselors have traditionally helped students select educational and vocational directions and courses for their future. Although counselors still fulfill this function, they are facing the new challenge of helping students integrate their learning from elementary school to post-high school experience. This integration covers not only the learning-vocational link but also the learning-living link. School counselors are being asked to help prepare the school environment

1. Therese S. Cristiani and Michael F. Cristiani, "The Application of Counseling Skills in the Business and Industrial Setting," *Personnel and Guidance Journal* 58 (1979): 166–69.

so that it is more conducive to the overall psychological well-being and maturity of students. This challenge has been heightened with the passage of the amendment to the federal Education of the Handicapped Act in 1975.[2] The act has inspired the concept of mainstreaming, which prepares the way for schools to accommodate the educational needs of students whose disabilities have previously prevented them from sharing the learning experience of nondisabled students. This, too, has the potential for helping society eliminate another deep-seated prejudice, discrimination against the handicapped.

Along with this need to integrate students with disabilities into the educational mainstream is the need to link the counseling the schools offer to these students with that offered by rehabilitation counselors. The transition from school to work has been a difficult one for this group, and counselors need to pay attention to this problem. Rehabilitation counselors are also faced with the new challenge of helping individuals who have been confined to their homes, if not to their beds, in joining the mainstream of society. Typically, rehabilitation counselors have directed their efforts at the vocational needs of the counselees. Now, with the Rehabilitation Amendments of 1978, the entire scope of a disabled person's life comes within the focus of a rehabilitation counselor's purview. The purpose of the amendments is "independent living," which requires that people with disabilities have equal access to all the opportunities society offers. To reach this goal includes not only a career but also the freedom of movement, leisure experience, and access to educational opportunity that is available in our society.

In the early 1960s, the community mental-health movement received national attention from the Kennedy administration. This was another challenge for counselors to face. Mental health centers were established to provide assistance to those who were experiencing personal struggles in dealing with life's events. These people brought before counselors problems that differed in scope from the educational and vocational concerns counselors were used to dealing with. Marriage and family problems, personal adjustment to illness or death, grief, stress, and other needs were brought before counselors and other mental health providers much more often than in previous years. The success of meeting this challenge can be understood by witnessing the rapid growth of a variety of community agencies that employ counselors to help people with their concerns. Centers have been dedicated to helping youth deal

2. N. A. Sproles, E. E. Panter, and J. E. Lanier, "PL94-142 and Its Impact on the Counselor's Role," *Personnel and Guidance Journal* 57 (1976): 210 and 212.

with substance-abuse problems. Centers for alcoholics have been developed. Juvenile delinquency is addressed in others. Resources have been devoted to helping people deal with suicide.[3] Counselors attend to hot lines round the clock to be of service. A recent upsurge has occurred in programs for the aging. Counselors are an integral part of helping people adjust physically and emotionally to growing older and leading a productive life in their later years. The new focus on preretirement counseling[4] enables counselors to engage in a preventive approach with the aging. Another recent development is the attention given to child abuse. Centers have been set up to coordinate medical and legal help, and counselors are in the forefront of finding ways to bind and restore emotional cuts and bruises.

Other programs that have been developed depend heavily on counselors to provide emotional support and practical counseling to rehabilitate offenders in the correctional system. Promising new steps have been taken in developing programs in the community to foster the transition of offenders from behind prison walls into the community.[5] Counselors have taken an active role in conceptualizing programs, helping the local communities accept these programs and people, and establishing the climate and resources for preparing offenders for community life.

A counselor's challenge

What has been described illustrated how counselors have been in the forefront helping individuals and institutions achieve their potential as well as overcome their problems. As Herr has challenged the counseling profession:

> *The existence of guidance and counseling argues that in a complex society, such as the United States, individual rights and the development of full potential do not occur randomly. Most persons need information, support, and other forms of guidance and counseling to become their best selves, to know what possibilities exist for them, to plan. In short, talent must be cultivated; freedom and responsibility must be nurtured. Personal realities need to be considered and understood.*[6]

Many roles for counselors

This certainly challenges the counseling profession to do more than just address problems. In the 1970s, counselors were asked to be proactive as well as reactive. Initiating ways of attacking our per-

3. E. Lee, "Suicide and Youth," *Personnel and Guidance Journal* 57 (1978): 200–204.

4. *Business Week,* August 20, 1979, "Inflation Forces Retirees into New Careers."

5. Richard Ward and David Vandergoot, "Correctional Officers with Case Loads," *Offender Rehabilitation* 2 (1977): 31–38.

6. Edwin L. Herr, *Guidance and Counseling in the Schools* (Falls Church, Va.: American Personnel and Guidance Association, 1979), p. 27.

sonal and social ills in a preventive way and assuring that our resources can be expanded are now responsibilities of the counseling profession.

Can counselors manage all this? Over the last 20 years, the effectiveness of counselors has been challenged.[7] Although counseling can be helpful, it can also be harmful.[8] It is important to take this caution seriously, since counseling deals with basic human needs. Recently, a more global review of psychological counseling suggested that the evidence supports the general effectiveness of counseling.[9] Therefore, counselors can proceed with confidence to address old and new challenges alike.

The counselor

Some questions about counselors

It is very difficult to discuss just who counselors are. There are many different ways to approach the question. Depending upon one's interests, different questions could be asked that would provide various pieces of the puzzle. Possibly, an initial question could be "What are counselors like?" Usually, answers to this question have been given in terms of the personality characteristics, attributes, and qualities of counselors. These types of qualities usually have been studied by researching counseling outcomes achieved by counselors who possess varying degrees of these qualities. Yet, as will be pointed out shortly, this question is not as easily answered as it might seem.

A second question asked might be "What should counselors be like?" This question is often asked by persons considering a counseling career. It seems that there should be ideal counselor models. The building of ideal models, however, has been fraught with many difficulties. Ideal models grow from theoretical notions, which often seem to be determined more by personal preferences and values rather than by an objective assessment of what makes for good counseling.

Another appropriate question is "What do counselors do?" This is perhaps the easiest question to answer. Observing a counselor per-

7. Hans J. Eysenck, "The Effects of Psychotherapy," *Journal of Psychology* 1 (1965): 97–118.

8. Robert R. Carkhuff and Bernard G. Berenson, *Beyond Counseling and Therapy* (New York: Holt, Rinehart and Winston, 1967).

9. Mary L. Smith and Gene V. Glass, "Meta-analysis of Psychotherapy Outcome Studies," *American Psychologist* (1977): 752–60.

form a day's activities is relatively simple.[10] Also, studies have been done that describe the typical activities of counselors and the amount of time devoted to these activities. But it is hard to know whether what counselors are doing is relevant. And relevancy is an issue that underlies all these questions about counselors.

The relevance of counseling and counselors depends on the results counselors achieve for counselees and society. There is very little concensus regarding what counseling is supposed to achieve. There has been much debate among counselors about this problem, and it has been a particularly thorny issue for counseling researchers. One answer is that counseling outcomes are probably diverse and should be measured in a variety of ways.[11] A second answer is that counseling outcomes should be specific to each individual situation and reflect the goals of individual counselees on a case-by-case basis.[12]

These answers are not without problems. Counselors will still need to select some outcomes and exclude others. Counselors will influence the types of goals their counselees will want to obtain. The theoretical orientations and values of counselors will determine to a large extent what they want to achieve and how they will go about getting these results. Counseling is not yet a scientific process. Subjectivity is a major substance of what counseling is made of. In this sense, counselors are like "gods." This is a great responsibility since research has suggested that people can be helped by counseling, but they can also be hurt or remain unchanged.

What should counselors be like?

Two things seem to be required of persons who would be counselors. The great responsibility associated with counseling demands that counselors carefully consider the consequences of their actions. The second, related to the first, is that counselors must seek to reduce the uncertainty and risk involved in counseling. This can be done by carefully studying the consequences of what they do in order to better understand relationships between processes and outcomes and by supporting the development of a climate conducive to careful research of the processes and outcomes of counseling.

---

10. Shirley Jones, Jack McIntyre, and Ann LaForge, "A Week in the Life of a Counselor," *Journal of the American Vocational Association* 54 (1979): 31–38.

11. Allen E. Bergin, "The Evaluation of Therapeutic Outcomes," in *Handbook of Psychotherapy and Behavior Change*, ed. A. E. Bergin and S. L. Garfield (New York: John Wiley & Sons, 1971).

12. Bergin, "The Evaluation of Therapeutic Outcomes."

In spite of the fact that there is little agreement in the field regarding counselors and what they are all about, it is useful to review some of the literature on this topic. Two questions will be considered. The first question, "What should counselors be like?" will be addressed in this section. (The second, "What do counselors do?" will be the topic of Chapter 4.) This information can help those interested in counseling sort out their own value systems and clarify in their own minds the type of counselor they would like to be. To do this, various theoretical points of view will be presented to highlight the contrasts within the field of counseling.

Strupp, in a recent review of his career in counseling research, pointed out that studies have indicated that the experience and theoretical orientations of counselors influence the judgments they make about how to go about counseling and what they expect their counselees can achieve in counseling.[13] With this in mind, several prominent spokespersons for various theoretical orientations are reviewed regarding what they feel are important counselor attributes.

Existential-humanistic perspective

Arbuckle is an exponent of what he calls an existential-humanistic view.[14] Briefly, this is a system that takes society to task for imposing its will on people and thereby limiting personal freedom. Rather than experiencing the value of their personal selves on a moment-to-moment basis, people have allowed past occurrences and future fears to run their lives. According to Arbuckle, counselors who view the predicament of individuals from this framework should have these values:[15]

1. An intellectual flexibility that is not threatened by the ideas and beliefs of others and that does not adhere stubbornly to any one intellectual system, theory, or ideology.
2. A recognition that beliefs are ideas that cannot be proven right or wrong but are expressions of faith. Thus, it is better to believe that human nature has the potential for positive growth rather than that it is basically evil.
3. A personal conviction that values exemplifying personal freedom and integrity are important counselor characteristics that can provide strength to a struggling counselee.

Client-centered perspective

Carkhuff and Berenson are exponents of a point of view that has evolved from the client-centered perspective. This view is similar to

13. Hans H. Strupp, *Psychotherapy: Clinical, Research, and Theoretical Issues* (New York: Jason Aronson, 1973).

14. Dugald S. Arbuckle, *Counseling and Psychotherapy* (Boston: Allyn and Bacon, 1975).

15. Arbuckle, *Counseling and Psychotherapy*, pp. 392–95.

the existential-humanistic point of view in that it too believes strongly in the growth potential of each individual. In their book *Beyond Counseling and Therapy,* Carkhuff and Berenson maintain that counseling effectiveness is relatively independent of a counselor's theoretical orientation and techniques.[16] Rather, effective counselors offer certain levels of facilitative conditions. These conditions include empathy, respect, genuineness, and concreteness. They believe that any help-giver, whether a counselor or not, will have these qualities. Chapter 6, which explores the counseling relationship, will take a closer look at how this line of thought has influenced the field of counseling.

Truax, a fellow researcher of Carkhuff, has cited research that he feels supports the view that effective counseling can result if at least two of the above conditions are in evidence during counseling. Truax recognizes three important conditions, which he has labeled genuineness, nonpossessive warmth, and accurate empathic understanding.[17] These approximate Carkhuff's and Berenson's conditions with the exception of concreteness.

Behavior modification perspective

O'Leary and Wilson are exponents of behavior modification, which is concerned less with the essential ingredients of human nature and more with the processes of human learning. As such, counselors who are associated with behavior modification are concerned with buttressing the counseling relationship with expert application of techniques that have been developed from learning principles. In their book *Behavior Therapy,* they have outlined what they feel are important counselor characteristics.[18] These include:

1. An empathic understanding that is particularly important in the initial stages of counseling.
2. A capability of arousing a positive set of expectations on the part of counselees.
3. A therapeutic attraction that is appropriate and consistent with the context in which counseling occurs.
4. A capability of assuming various role models, depending on the needs of the counselee.

Craighead, Kazdin, and Mahoney, in their book on behavior modification, suggest an additional posture for counselors who are in-

---

16. Robert R. Carkhuff and Bernard G. Berenson, *Beyond Counseling and Therapy* (New York: Holt, Rinehart and Winston, 1967).

17. Charles B. Truax and M. Mitchell Kevin, "Research on Certain Therapist Interpersonal Skills in Relation to Process and Outcome" in *Handbook of Psychotherapy and Behavior Change* (New York: John Wiley & Sons, 1971).

18. K. Daniel O'Leary and G. Terence Wilson, *Behavior Therapy* (Englewood Cliffs, N.J.: Prentice-Hall, 1975), pp. 342–45.

clined to use behavior-modification principles.[19] They contend that counselors should approach each counseling case with a scientific methodology that seeks to uncover relationships between the different behaviors and thoughts of counselees. It is hoped that such an approach would permit the counselor and counselee to understand what contributes to a problem situation and thus gain control over it. Such mastery is expected to lead to greater personal freedom, the same value espoused by existential-humanists. It is interesting to note the similarities in values of persons who adhere to theoretical systems supposedly quite different from one another.

Other theorists have sought what is presumed to be a middle ground between the existential-humanist and behavioralist points of view.

Lazarus has suggested that counselees bring their own expectations to counseling regarding what counseling should be like.[20] A counselor should be able to quickly ascertain these expectations and then be capable of providing a variety of approaches on the basis of what the counselee would find most desirable. The counselor who is incapable of providing a compatible style should refer the counselee to someone who can.

Psychobehavioral perspective

Woody has developed what he calls a psychobehavioral approach.[21] In his view, a professional counselor should exhibit two essential qualities. The first is self-understanding, particularly in relation to knowing one's impact on other people. The second is a strong sense of responsibility, including the careful and expert selection of those counseling activities that hold the greatest value for the counselee.

Practically every book on counseling recommends that counselors assume certain characteristics, possess certain qualities, or learn certain skills. Research in this area is quite voluminous. In a succinct review of this research, however, Rowe and his colleagues make the point that since there is little consensus regarding what effective counseling is, it is hard to know which recommended set of characteristics, qualities, and skills to accept.[22] The student of counseling is left with the challenge to develop her/his own point of

19. W. Edward Craighead, Alan E. Kazdin, and Michael J. Mahoney, *Behavior Modification* (Boston: Houghton Mifflin, 1976).

20. Arnold A. Lazarus, *Behavior Therapy and Beyond* (New York: McGraw-Hill, 1971).

21. Robert H. Woody, *Psychobehavioral Counseling and Therapy* (New York: Appleton-Century-Crofts, 1971).

22. Wayne Rowe, Harry B. Murphy, and Robert A. DeCsipkes, "The Relationship of Counselor Characteristics and Counseling Effectiveness," *Review of Educational Research* 45 (1975): 231–246.

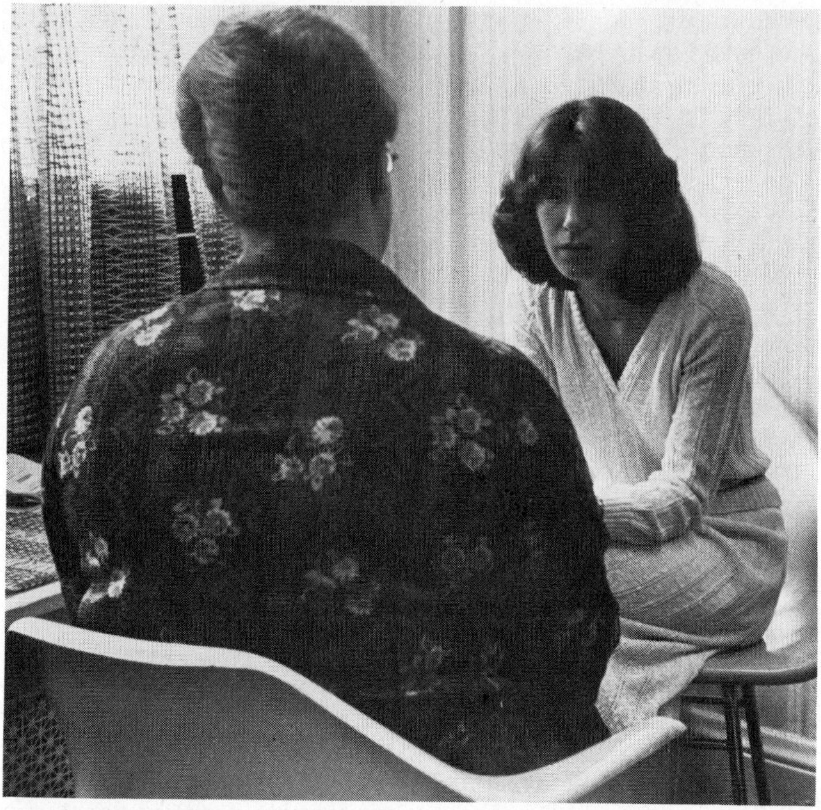

Counselors work in a variety of settings. This counselor, who works in a hospital, helps patients cope with illness-related issues.

view. A thorough knowledge of how others define their role and style of counseling is an important ingredient that must be built into counselor training.

Employment opportunities for counselors

For anyone contemplating a certain career direction, an important concern probably is whether or not one will be able to get a job after all the necessary entry requirements are met. This section of the chapter will offer data from which trends regarding the employment of counselors might be forecasted.

A directory of colleges and universities providing counselor education programs is published periodically. A recent edition indicates that the number of institutions preparing counselors continues to increase.[23] A total of 33 programs was added during the three years

23. Joseph W. Hollis and Richard A. Wantz, *Counselor Education Directory 1977* (Muncie, Ind.: Accelerated Development, 1977).

since the previous directory was published. In 1977 this directory estimated that there were about 500 programs providing counselor education. Of these, 453 supplied information to the directory. It was further estimated that these programs had been able to graduate almost 19,000 counselors with master's degrees, as well as others with doctorate and undergraduate degrees.

Employment settings

This directory also indicated the initial employment settings of these counselors. The following listing shows the employment settings of counselors with master's and specialist degrees, ranked from the most heavily employed setting to the least.

1. Junior or senior high schools
2. Elementary or middle schools
3. Mental health clinics
4. Community or junior colleges
5. Universities or colleges
6. Rehabilitation agencies
7. Correctional institutions
8. Vocational or technical schools
9. Employment agencies
10. Hospitals, including Veteran's Administration hospitals
11. Pastoral counseling agencies
12. Diagnostic centers
13. State departments of education

Also, new areas are being opened up. Business and industry, as well as unions, are beginning to provide counseling services. The burgeoning development of community agencies has created a need to hire counselors who attend to the special needs of the aging, families, children, husbands and wives, and the dying. Also, the rate at which counselors are going into business for themselves has been increasing. This trend can be expected to continue as more and more states are considering licensing or certifying counselors. All of these factors reflect the career diversity available to those in the counseling profession.

The *Occupational Outlook Handbook* is published every two years by the Bureau of Labor Statistics of the U.S. Department of Labor. All counselors should become familiar with the book as it provides information about hundreds of major occupations in the United States. It is interesting to compare the estimates of counselors employed in various settings taken from two recent editions. Table 1–1 was developed from the 1976–1977 and 1978–1979 editions of the *Occupational Outlook Handbook.* In each of the settings, except rehabilitation, the estimates have indicated a decrease in the number of employed counselors. Since evidence for

Table 1-1
Estimates of counselors employed by settings

	1974	1976
School counselors	44,000	43,000
Job service counselors	3,500	3,400
Other employment counselors	3,500	3,000
Rehabilitation counselors	19,000	19,000
College career and placement counselors	4,100	3,900

only a few of the many potential settings is available, however, this table should be considered cautiously.

Future demand for counselors

The forecasts of future demand are also cautious because public funds are usually used to employ counselors. In an uncertain economy, it is difficult to predict what will happen to occupations supported by public funds. Forecasts do generally conclude that most new openings will occur due to a need to fill existing positions. This prediction may seem to indicate that counseling as a profession is viewed by society as valuable but not necessary. But this is not really an accurate assessment. It is up to counselors to disprove this idea by achieving professional accountability. They need to show to the public the value of counseling, predictable techniques and processes, economic efficiency in terms of the costs and benefits associated with counseling, and the credibility of counseling as a profession. The discussions, theories, processes, and techniques described in this book are offered with this in mind. Counselors also need to support the advancement of research and evaluation of data in order to help people understand the social importance of counseling as a profession.

Recipients of counseling services

The individual counselee

Usually, the counseling system is composed of a counselor and a counselee and a situation that permits their communication. Up to this point, the chapter has focused on the counselor. It is more difficult to describe the counselee. One of the underlying philosophies of this book is that there is no "typical" counselee (or counselor for that matter). Psychology, concerned with the study of individual differences, dictates that counseling is a unique interaction each time an individual comes to a counselor. This is not to say that counseling is beyond the ken of scientific study. There seems to be a generalized way of how people learn and behave. Learning and behaving can become more predictable and, therefore, controllable to a certain degree. What is understood about the complexity of every individual's life and the interactions that constantly affect each of us are too uncertain to conclude that one counselee's concern and outcome is similar to that of another. What is needed is appropriate research and experience that will help counseling become a more accountable procedure with predictable costs and benefits.

There are some generalizations concerning the problems counselors face in their professional activities. Information about counselors in different counseling settings can help prospective or current counselors who are concerned with a counseling career.

In school settings, particularly college and secondary academic environments, the problems students see as appropriate for counseling are as expected. Their concerns are mainly with current academic pursuits and future career directions. Leviton, in a survey study of tenth, eleventh, and twelfth graders, found that they expected counseling programs to help them with such concerns as academic planning, academic weaknesses, study skills, and teacher relationships. Also ranked highly were post-high school planning and career education.[24]

Another survey study of high school students used a factor analysis to empirically categorize over 50 items concerning students' responses to what they would like their school and guidance department help them achieve.[25] A total of 10 meaningful factors appeared. Six of these reflected various current and future concerns, particularly in relationship to career development. Two factors described a concern for current school adjustment. One very important factor reflected a concern for self-understanding and self-acceptance. A final factor concerned a desire for information regarding substance abuse.

Needs of college students for counselors

Similar patterns appeared in a recent study involving college students.[26] Students indicated that they preferred that college counseling centers provide them with vocational and academic support as well as personal-adjustment support. The following list

24. Harvey S. Leviton, "Consumer Feedback on a Secondary School Guidance Program," *Personnel and Guidance Journal* 55 (1977): 242–44.

25. Richard H. Byrne and David Vandergoot, "Guidance Assessment Survey," unpublished manuscript, University of Maryland, 1977.

26. Charles J. Gelso, Janice M. Birk, Patrick W. Utz, and Anne E. Silver, "A Multigroup Evaluation of the Models and Functions of University Counseling Centers," *Journal of Counseling Psychology* 24 (1977): 338–48.

shows students' ranking of the appropriateness of functions, beginning with the most important function.

1. Educational-vocational counseling
2. Personal counseling/therapy
3. Study skills counseling
4. Short-term counseling
5. Counseling for normal personal-social problems

The authors of this study, which included the perceptions of counselors and other college staff groups, concluded from this and previous research that:

> *Everyone thinks vocational counseling is "a good thing," something central to the specialty, and something we ought to be doing a lot of; at the same time, that function is not something practitioners are eager to do. . . . The present findings, taken together with other recent research and position papers, suggest that the role of educational-vocational counseling and related activities in counseling psychology and counseling centers is badly in need of reassessment.*[27]

In a recent survey of clientele of a state rehabilitation agency, the preferences strongly favored the vocational-counseling function of rehabilitation counselors. Personal and family concerns were also cited but not nearly as much as vocational concerns. Interestingly, for personal and family problems, the counselees preferred to consult with friends or family members rather than with any other helping person, including the counselor.[28]

In summary, the major constituents of academic and rehabilitation counseling, namely counselees, recognize the value of counseling in terms of their own educational and vocational concerns. Prospective counselors should gain more understanding of their counselee's needs, however, as illustrated by two recent research studies that demonstrated that counselors did not accurately perceive the vocational needs or vocational readiness of their counselees.[29]

---

27. Gelso, Birk, Utz, and Silve, "A Multigroup Evaluation of the Models and Functions of University Counseling Centers," p. 347.

28. Charles H. Gregg, Leonard A. Miller, and Ralph R. Roberts, *A Study of Help Seeking Among Rehabilitation Counseling Bulletin* 19 (1976): 496–99.

29. Michael J. McGraw and James A. Bitter, "Counselor Perceptions of Client Vocational Needs," *Rehabilitation Counseling Bulletin* 18 (1974): 83–89; David Vandergoot and James R. Engelkes, "An Application of the Theory of Work Adjustment to Vocational Counseling," *Vocational Guidance Quarterly* 26 (1977): 45–53.

Other recipients and constituents

Although counselees are the primary concern of counseling services, many other groups can be affected by counseling. When counseling is supported by public funds, which is typically the case in many counseling settings, society has mandated certain benefits to be derived from counseling services. Government regulations accompany this support and demand accountability. In this way, society at large becomes a constituent of counseling services. This is a powerful constituent that cannot be overlooked.

Miller and Evgin have constructed a futuristic scenario in which counselors are required to pass strict competency-based recertification examinations.[30] The current trends toward certification or licensure for counselors working in all settings, as well as a push for competency-based accreditation procedures for academic training programs, suggests that such a scenario might become a realistic possibility sooner than even the authors expected.[31]

Generally, it makes sense to expect that significant others in the lives of counselees will be affected by any changes they make. Chapter 5 provides an overview of systems theory. The theory suggests that individuals can be viewed as subsystems of larger systems, in the way that a family or a work group is part of the larger society. These subsystems are dynamically related to one another; therefore, a change in one individual can be expected to have an impact on the entire system. Counselors need to attempt to anticipate these impacts and help the counselees prepare for them. Change is often resisted and lack of support from one's family, peer, or work group also can work against lasting change. It is hoped that social support can be gained through the efforts of the counselee and counselor. If not, the counselee can at least be prepared for possible confrontations.

Society as a counselor's constituency

Society in general and significant others of counselees are the constituents of counseling services in most counseling settings. Recent trends, however, have specified that unique settings have unique constituents. Constituents for elementary counselors include parents, teachers, school administrators, and community-based support persons.[32] Secondary counselors are perceived as having

30. Jane N. Miller and Ann W. Evgin, "Tomorrow's Counselor: Competent or Unemployed?" *Personnel and Guidance Journal* 54 (1976): 262–66.

31. Jerald Forster, "Counselor Credentialing Revisited," *Personnel and Guidance Journal* 56 (1978): 593–98.

32. Roger F. Aubrey, "Consultation, School Interventions, and the Elementary Counselor," *Personnel and Guidance Journal* 56 (1978): 351–54.

the basic capabilities of expanding their role and functions to include consultation activities affecting the total school environment.[33] A similar role is described for college counselors who have additional opportunities to work with other college staff, particularly student-affairs personnel, to deal with student problems that seem to stem from environmental rather than individual factors.[34]

Similarly, in rehabilitation, Molinaro has made a strong case for including employers as recipients of rehabilitation services.[35] He suggests that employer-related services could include:

1. Worker compensation assistance
2. Second-injury certification where applicable
3. Affirmative action consultation
4. Awareness training regarding disability-related factors involved in the work place
5. Selective placement
6. Worker-adjustment counseling (placement follow-up)
7. Troubled-employee assistance

Essentially, these services would reduce employer recruitment, hiring, and work-force retainment costs and presumably would make rehabilitants more attractive as employees.

Expanding the scope of rehabilitation services to include employers seems like a logical step. Employers are the real job developers in our society and linking them to rehabilitation in a direct way should generate better outcomes for all concerned. This step might also be advanced to include unions and the government sector, since these have a powerful influence on the labor market.

These attempts at broadening the target base of counseling services necessarily include new functions for counselors. These new functions may require new skills and knowledge as well as increased responsibilities. Nevertheless, it seems high time to recognize the rippling impact that counseling services have over a wide range of groups besides counselees. Systematic efforts at directing this impact is highly desirable and should be supported by research and training efforts.

---

33. Dan Carrington, Art Cleveland, and Clark Ketterman, "Collaborative Consultation in the Secondary Schools," *Personnel and Guidance Journal* 56 (1978): 355–58.

34. Franklin D. Westbrook, Mary M. Leonard, Frank Johnson, Vivian S. Boyd, Stanley M. Hunt, Michael T. McDermott, "University Campus Consultation Through the Formation of Collaborative Dyads," *Personnel and Guidance Journal* 56 (1978): 359–63.

35. David Molinaro, "A Placement System Develops and Settles: the Michigan Model," *Rehabilitation Counseling Bulletin* 21 (1977): 121–29.

Avoiding counselor "burnout"

The field of counseling is not without difficulties for those who pursue a career in it. Recently, attention has been directed at a phenomenon labeled counselor burnout.[36] It has been observed that frequently counselors will leave the field and begin a new career in a totally unrelated occupation. This is viewed as a personal as well as a social loss. In a working paper regarding the mobility patterns of social and rehabilitation workers, a listing of possible determinants of quit rates was suggested. Those that might apply to trained counselors include limited opportunity for advancement; excessive work loads; too many uncooperative, hostile, or inaccessible counselees; and a potential for a large amount of routine work that is seemingly peripheral to counseling.[37]

Job-related stress

It is important to consider that a counselor is confronted on a daily basis with the concerns and frustrations of other people. Sometimes, counselees appear to get in their own way, are "unmotivated," and challenge the counselor to "get me out of this mess." Counselors need to recognize that success is not attainable all the time. The most successful counselors, however, are persistent, skillful, professional, patient, and maintain a realistic set of expectations.

As with any professional occupation, stress can occur. In a general review of the literature, McGrath suggested six possible sources of work stress.[38] It is important for counselors to understand these sources so that stress can be taken in stride and appropriate countermeasures applied. McGrath's six areas include:

1. Task-based stress resulting from work load, ambiguity, difficulty, etc.
2. Role-based stress, particularly stemming from conflict
3. Stress resulting from the work setting, such as crowding or short staffing

36. Charles C. Warnath and John L. Shelton, "The Ultimate Disappointment: the Burned Out Counselor," *Personnel and Guidance Journal* 55 (1976): 172–75.

37. Raymond A. Katzell, Abraham K. Korman, and Edward L. Levine, "Determinants of Worker Job Mobility and Its Implications for Service Delivery," in *Working Papers No. I, National Study of Social Welfare and Rehabilitation Workers, Work, and Organizational Contexts,* Department of HEW, Social and Rehabilitation Services (Washington, D.C.: Author, 1971): 131–70.

38. Joseph E. McGrath, "Stress and Behavior in Organizations," in *Handbook of Industrial and Organizational Psychology,* ed. M. D. Dunnette (Chicago: Rand McNally, 1976): 1351–95.

4. Stress arising from the physical environment, such as lack of private, confidential counseling areas
5. Stress arising from interpersonal relations
6. Personal stress brought to the work setting

One means of reducing stress is to expect that it is a normal occurrence and to have the knowledge and skills to remove the stress-inducing circumstances. This book is directed at helping current and future counselors acquire realistic expectations about counseling careers and develop the basic tools to turn stressful situations into positive experiences.

Summary

Counseling is a profession that demands a high level of skill and knowledge. It has many challenges and more than sufficient rewards. It involves hard but interesting work. Individuals, groups, organizations, regulating authorities, other helping professionals, and interested publics all interact with the counselor to make variety almost infinite. It is a young profession, still identifying itself, achieving credibility, and developing technology. It has a potential for growth and welcomes those who want to grow along with it.

Questions

1. What is the major goal in most counseling theories?
2. Why is the counseling and guidance profession called a "helping" profession?
3. Are counselors today asked to assume more or fewer roles than twenty years ago? Explain your answer.
4. What are some reasons that counseling is difficult to define as a profession?
5. In what way is the existential-humanistic theory similar to the client-centered theory?
6. What is the main thrust of behavior modification?
7. Describe the various settings where counselors often work.
8. What is counselor "burnout"? What are some of the vulnerable areas where burnout often occurs?

Projects

1. Write a short paper explaining your image and definition of counseling. Save the paper so you can review how your attitudes have changed at the conclusion of the course.
2. Interview a counselor who has experienced burnout to learn how it happened and what might have been done to prevent it.
3. Interview several students to learn what their views of counseling services offered in their schools are.

2 Historical foundations of counseling and guidance

Papers read at professional meetings provide an opportunity to disseminate new research, theories, and data to large numbers of counselors.

Introduction

The counseling and guidance movement began in the 1890s in American schools. Since that time several individuals as well as movements have contributed substantially to the current status of counseling and guidance in the United States. As one reflects on the past, one can observe the importance of what has gone before as it relates to what is going on now, as well as what is likely to occur in the future.

Key Terms

vocational guidance
social gospel approach
psychometrics
school counseling
group-therapy movement
sensitivity training
encounter group
human-potential seminar
task-oriented group
developmental-counseling group
career education
accountability
outcome-oriented evaluation
professional associations

The origins of vocational guidance

During the 1890s, a man named Frank Parsons began to provide counseling and guidance to underprivileged youth in Boston. He is considered the father of vocational guidance.[1] Vocational guidance, in turn, was the springboard for other kinds of counseling and guidance in schools and other institutions. Parsons used two techniques. First, he facilitated students' study of occupational opportunities by providing them with information such as availability of jobs, entry requirements, and educational requirements. Next he provided a framework within which students could evaluate one or more possible jobs. The goal of this process was to place individuals into work settings that were appropriate to their skills and education. This process is still used today.

Parsons' techniques were prompted by his perception that many unskilled rural youth were migrating to the city of Boston. Upon their arrival, they experienced difficulty securing employment, largely due to their lack of skill in relation to employers' needs at that time.

Pioneers in counseling

Others were also involved in the counseling movement at its earliest stages. Another leader, Jessie B. Davis, was uncertain regarding his own career choice. He began a self-analysis regarding his own aptitudes, achievements, interests, and temperament. In addition, he made a study of the occupations available at that time. Finally, he matched himself to the teaching occupation. When he left Cornell University, he began teaching in Detroit, Michigan, and later in Grand Rapids, Michigan. Davis was an advocate of hard work, honesty in the work place and elsewhere, and the development of character and ambition through work. He instilled these values in the students with whom he had contact.[2] His sensitivity to the character

1. Frank Parsons, *Choosing a Vocation* (Boston: Houghton Mifflin, 1908).

2. Jessie B. Davis, *Moral and Vocational Guidance* (New York: Ginn and Company, 1914).

needs of his students led him to believe that one should feel a clear direction with regard to the choice of a career. He used the term *calling* to describe one's attraction to a vocation. To feel a calling seemed to enhance the individual's choice of a particular career as being the noblest way that person could serve society. Davis' concept of guidance had a religious fervor that reflected the times in which he lived. The concern with social problems of the 1890s, largely brought on by the Industrial Revolution and the changes it brought in human life, became a rallying point for the campaign to alter society so the value and goodness of each individual could be realized, and Davis' theories fit in well with this. Frequently, the work of Davis is referred to as the social gospel approach to counseling.

Another early leader in the guidance movement was Anna Y. Reed, who established guidance services in the schools of Seattle, Washington. Reed believed that individuals evolved in their social as well as biological forms from lower to higher levels through a competitive process of natural selection that allowed only the strongest and best to survive. She focused primarily on the system rather than on the individuals. She admired business philosophy and methods used to accomplish their objectives. Not only was the work ethic strong in the philosophy of Anna Reed but also the concept of morality to "build a better mousetrap." She thought that people needed to give their best effort to any task assigned in order to see themselves as successful. She believed in stiff competition for grades in school. She suggested that only complete success be expected in schools as it was in the business community. The role of the counselor was to guide students through this stiff competition with their colleagues.[3]

There were other early leaders in the vocational guidance movement, but their contributions were within the frameworks developed by the leaders just described. The first conference of vocational guidance was held in 1910; in 1911 the first school guidance program was organized in Cincinnati. The National Vocational Guidance Association was formed in Grand Rapids, Michigan, in 1913.

Developments in school counseling and guidance: 1890–1960

Several important developments and movements in related fields

3. Anna Y. Reed, *Vocational Guidance Report, 1913–1916* (Seattle: Board of School Directors, 1916).

contributed to the creation of the guidance and counseling profession as it is known today.

Influence of psychiatry and psychology

In the early 1900s, the theories and techniques from the newly emerging sciences of psychiatry and psychology lent much to the equally new guidance and counseling field. Sigmund Freud, the father of psychoanalysis, discovered the subconscious as a motivating force and explanation for human behavior. His theories concerning the functioning of the subconscious provided the underpinnings for many of the psychological and psychiatric theories that followed. Another movement that made a contribution to guidance and counseling was Carl Rogers' client-centered therapy, which he introduced in 1942 with the publication of his book *Counseling and Psychotherapy*.[4] Emphasis in counseling was now directed much more at the client. The client was no longer seen as someone on whom treatment was performed, but rather, was viewed for the first time as someone who entered into a therapeutic relationship that enabled him to change himself. Rogers' theories did much to humanize the guidance and counseling field.

The development of psychometrics

Psychometrics, the science of measuring psychological characteristics such as intelligence and aptitudes, emerged at this time. The publication in 1905 of the Binet Intelligence Scale is usually credited with being the first major effort in the field of psychometrics. Other related psychometrics efforts are those of Lahy (1913)[5] and Claparède (1922),[6] both of whom attempted to identify workers in various industries who were generally unsatisfactory due to being accident prone or due to other factors. Frank Parsons also maintained an interest in individual assessment as a means of facilitating a better self-understanding regarding the planning of one's future.

The psychometrics movement is based on the theory that individuals differ on a variety of characteristics. Understanding these differences could be helpful in planning present and future courses of action because individual differences suggest varying paths for individual personal and career development.

World War I fueled the psychometrics movement because a large influx of new recruits was taken into the armed forces. It was imperative that these new recruits be assigned quickly to a variety of posi-

4. Carl Rogers, *Counseling and Psychotherapy* (Boston: Houghton Mifflin, 1942).

5. J. M. Lahy, "Les conditions psychophysiologiques de l'aptitude au travail dactylographique," *Journal de physiologie et pathologie générale* 15 (1913): 826–34.

6. Edouard Claparède, "L'orientation professionnelle ses problemes et ses methodes (Geneva: International Labor Office, 1922).

tions to make the armed forces operative immediately. This need gave rise to the Army Alpha and Army Beta Intelligence Examinations. The large number of recruits also provided a sufficient data pool for understanding how well the examinations functioned as standards for assigning persons to different kinds of work. Considerable research to refine the instruments followed. Differentiating individuals based on psychological characteristics became a fundamental component of evaluating clients, with respect to educational and vocational placement.

The Wagner O'Day Act of 1932 authorized the establishment of the United States Employment Services, whose purpose was to facilitate the placement of the numerous persons unemployed during the Depression. This act then provided for ongoing vocational guidance and placement services to all unemployed Americans who wished to use the service. Psychometrics were used for this placement.

The rise of school counseling

Funding for school counseling

The National Defense Education Act, passed in 1958 and subsequently amended in 1968, provided funds for the establishment and strengthening of guidance services in local public schools. In addition, $7 million per year was provided for the operation of counselor-training institutes by universities. This act probably had more significance for the field of guidance than anything else. The Education Professions Development Act of 1968 continued federal funding for the preparation and employment of counselors but reduced the federal dollars spent specifically for guidance when compared to the NDEA program of 1958. Additional funding for guidance was provided by the 1968 amendments to the Vocational Education Act of 1963. These acts have served to stimulate and maintain the professional development of counseling and guidance specialists in the United States.

Community counseling

Other areas of nonpublic school counseling have resulted from the movement begun with Public Law 565 in 1954 regarding rehabilitation counseling. The law stimulated other laws that provided for new areas of service that included programs for the disadvantaged; community agencies, including clinics for child guidance and mental health; marriage and family counseling centers; pastoral counseling; crisis centers; and to a very limited extent, private practice.

Vocational rehabilitation

Funding for vocational counseling

The Rehabilitation Services Administration is a federal agency within the Department of Education charged with providing leadership and coordination of the basic rehabilitation services programs throughout the country. The National Institute of Handicapped Research is newly established as a separate agency from the Commissioner of the Rehabilitation Services Administration reporting directly to the Secretary. The institute is responsible for the research programs administered under the Rehabilitation Act of 1973 as amended in 1978. The most significant aspect of the rehabilitation counseling movement occurred with the adoption of Public Law 565 in 1954. Public Law 565 authorized funding for master's degree training in rehabilitation counseling by providing support for the teaching in such programs as well as a stipend for students enrolled. What began with ten federally funded programs now includes approximately 75 such programs around the country. Public Law 565 is probably the most significant nonschool related federal involvement in the counseling and guidance area.

New direction: 1960 to the present

The 1960s saw the rise of a plethora of psychological movements, some serious steps forward and others little more than passing fads. The group-therapy movement has made the most profound and enduring effect on the guidance and counseling field.

The second important development was that of career education as a specialty within guidance and counseling. As new technologies made many jobs obsolete and created other new jobs, additional information regarding the choice of a career—or careers, as it became more obvious that fewer and fewer persons would spend their entire lives working in one field exclusively—was needed.

Finally, as was fitting with the growing expertise and sophistication of the guidance and counseling field, accountability became and remains an important and pressing issue.

The group-therapy movement

Group guidance and counseling actually have existed for a long time in the world of education. Frank Parsons recognized that group involvement with regard to vocational guidance and vocational exploration was a reasonable and time-conserving approach to providing that kind of service. The nature of these early experiences was one of supplying information to large groups of individuals or that of sharing common concerns with regard to the planning of educational or vocational futures.

During the latter half of the 1960s, the group-therapy movement within the private sector of the United States literally swept the country. Group-therapy experiences were usually intensive, lasting anywhere from two days to three weeks. Individuals underwent close contact with others who shared common desires for understanding themselves better within a group. The majority of the group-therapy experiences were designed to aid in positive growth rather than to solve serious problems or bring about major personality changes on the part of the participants. Five basic types of groups dominated the group-therapy movement.

Types of group therapy

The first type is called sensitivity training. Individuals are given an opportunity to understand their behavior via feedback they receive from other individuals within the group. An attempt is made to focus on the heightening of an individual's awareness of the impact of his or her own behavior on others. The participants are further encouraged to try out new behaviors that allow them to be perceived more as they would like to be perceived by others. Usually, there are no rules associated with such groups, and each group is responsible for developing its own rules of interaction. In a sense, then, the "T-group," as these groups were known, becomes an opportunity for the participants to develop a microcosm of the larger social organization in which they function outside the group. The major focus of such groups is to help individual members learn more about the skills necessary to interact effectively with others.

A second type of group is the encounter group. It is meant to help normal individuals experience themselves and others in new ways and to learn from that experience. The major thrust of an encounter group is to facilitate individual members' attempts to become more aware of themselves at deeper levels; to help members attempt new, more spontaneous behaviors; to assist members in letting down defenses that act as barriers between themselves and others; and to help members develop new interpersonal skills. Encounter-group leaders tend to use nonverbal as well as verbal techniques to help individuals reach their full potential in their interaction with others as well as in experiencing themselves.

A third type of group is the human-potential seminar. The human-potential seminars place emphasis on group members' strengths and attributes rather than on their weaknesses. Participants are encouraged to set goals that are in line with their own values and to develop plans for action in line with these goals. Typi-

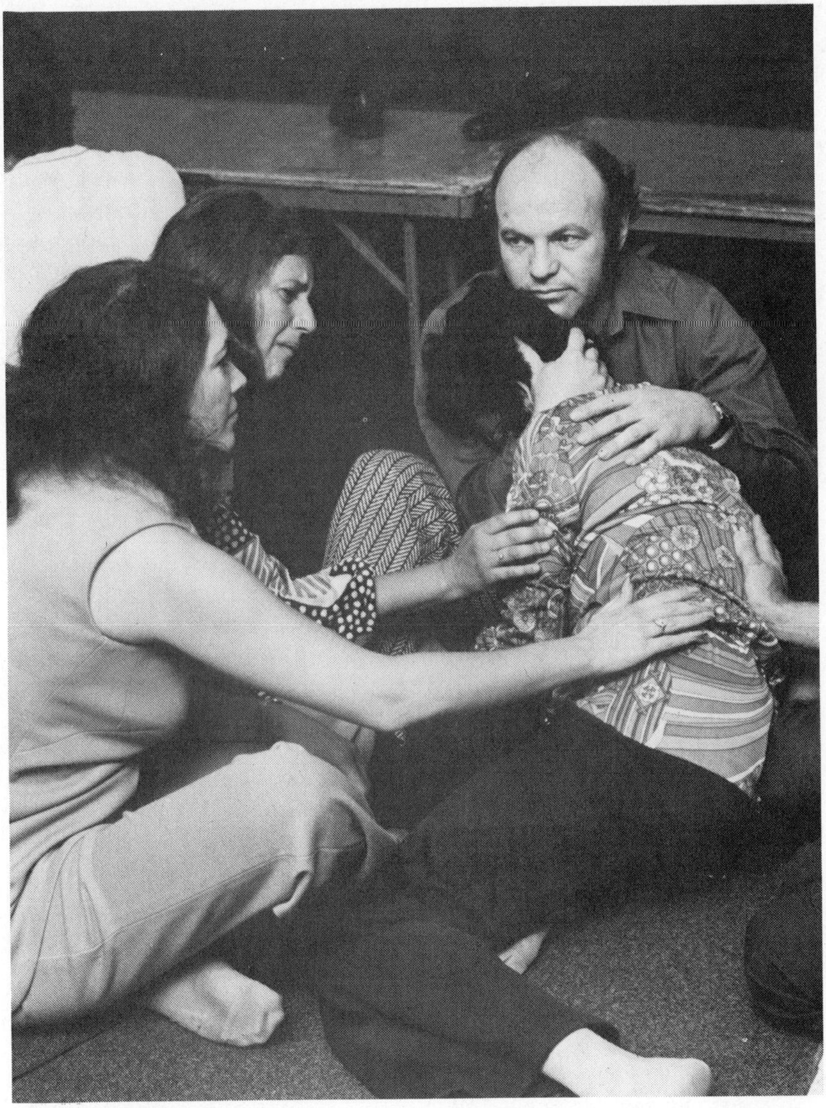

Encounter groups broke a taboo that began with the Freudians against offering physical, nonverbal aid to counselees. Here, group members offer comfort to a distressed participant.

cally, a seminar consists of a series of exercises that enable group members to increase their self-motivation, empathy toward others, self-assurance, and self-determination. The human-potential seminar is a fairly structured experience that maintains a focus on the positive strengths of an individual and how these can be developed beyond their current stage of development.

A fourth type of group is the task-oriented group. The task-oriented group is more specific regarding the behavior change on the part of participants. Each individual of the group establishes specific objectives that he or she wishes to accomplish via the group experience. Typically, some rules are defined by the group with respect to how they wish to facilitate the solving of individual member's problems. While the participants are working on their own objectives, they also gain experience in helping others, and they gain a perspective on the dynamics of group interaction.

The final type of group is the developmental-counseling group. In the developmental-group process, individuals explore their current feelings, values, behaviors, and attitudes with an eye for future change in these areas. The group works to outline steps for individual change. The role of the leader is to assist the group in establishing a trusting climate through which the members can provide help to one another.

The groups described all share a common theme of concern with increasing understanding of oneself and with meeting one's personal needs within a group context. Such groups may also represent the need on the part of individuals to explore new interpersonal behaviors and to experiment with ways of incorporating those behaviors into a group. Probably the single greatest contribution of the group movement has been to emphasize the need to achieve a comfort level within a group that enables individuals to gain mutual support from each other in regular social encounters.

Career education

Career education has been defined in numerous ways. The term *career education* was first used publicly by Sidney P. Marland, Jr., then Commissioner of Education, in 1971 during an address to the National Association of Secondary School Principals in Houston, Texas. Marland said:

> *Of those students currently in high school, only 30 percent will go on to academic, college-level work. One third of those will drop out before earning a baccalaureate degree. This means 80 percent of the present high school students should be getting occupational training of some sort. But only about a quarter of those students are getting such training. Consequently, half of our high school students, a total of approximately 1,500,000 per year, are being offered what amounts to irrelevant educational pap.*[7]

7. Sidney P. Marland, Jr., "Career Education Now," *School Shop* (May 1971): 27.

Validity of career education

Career education is the term used to describe the broadening of the typical education curriculum by the infusion of information regarding career development, preparation, and placement at appropriate levels within the educational system. Ideally, it uses all facets of the school and community in an attempt to provide a learning experience that is relevant to the individual career needs and goals of the students.[8] Since 1971 the United States Office of Education has given high priority to the concept of career education. Its conceptualization, implementation, and evaluation have been supported by a variety of grants to state departments of education, universities, and local school districts. The efforts in career education have been designed to address the lack of an occupational focus in the typical educational curriculum.

Career education also has been a response, perhaps in part, to the general public's lack of support for traditional education. It appears that more and more parents want their children to learn work-related skills in the classroom. At the same time, our society has more individuals than ever before who are making "second career" decisions that require a delicate interplay between one's work experience and one's education.

The concept of career education has given increased validity to the idea that not everyone should go on to college upon completing high school. Educators hope that as a result of career education not only will students be able to make the transition from school to work more easily, but at the same time, parents will feel that the schools are showing more accountability to their mission of preparing individuals to enter adulthood at several different educational levels.

Career education programs

Career education development incorporates knowledge as relating to the understanding of oneself, understanding of others, understanding of current and future environmental conditions that influence careers, and understanding of the skills and education required to enter and maintain a career that provides a maximum return to the individual. These are not new goals, but they have been given new interpretations, which have, in turn, resulted in considerable disparity among career education programs. Such disparities are of limited importance so long as each individual is given an opportunity to be exposed to the key elements in the process. These

8. Willa Norris, Raymond N. Hatch, James R. Engelkes, and Bob B. Winborn, *The Career Information Service,* 4th ed. (Chicago: Rand McNally, 1979), p. 8.

vary slightly from one program to another, but the following seem to constitute the basic elements of a good career-planning program:

1. A combination of experiences that ensure an objective self-concept. Such factors as one's value system, perception of self, and one's interpretation of interpersonal relationships to the environment are included.
2. An organized group of activities designed to provide the individual with an opportunity to understand others and to learn to relate to a broad spectrum of society.
3. A defined program of experiences that ensure comprehensive exposure to the characteristics of one's present and future environment.
4. A planned group of activities that provide each individual with an opportunity to explore personal strengths and preferences in relationship to environmental demands and opportunities.
5. A professional service of counseling to assist each individual in analyzing the alternatives of career choice and to aid in the establishment of appropriate career priorities.
6. A training program that maximizes the learning opportunities for the individual to pursue whatever career goal that has been selected.
7. An organized placement service designed to help the individual move from training experiences into a meaningful career.

Such a program provides individuals with educational, avocational, vocational, and social services consistent with their career goals. It is also a program that may be returned to whenever an individual's career goal must be redirected. The promise of such a program is to provide an opportunity for every member of society to develop a career that has been chosen in light of all available and relevant information.

Usually, a training program unique to one's needs is necessary to enhance progress in the individual's career choice. A program of this kind does not guarantee total satisfaction with the choices made, but it offers an opportunity for each person to develop a meaningful career, and at the same time, it provides each person with knowledge of the process of choice if a change becomes necessary.[9]

With the renewed focus upon the area of career-relevant activities in education, it is likely that the expansion and continued program support for career education will continue for some time to come.

9. Norris, Hatch, Engelkes, and Winborn, *Career Information Service*, pp. 19–20.

The issue of accountability

One of the most pressing issues facing the schools and human service programs of America is educational accountability, a movement that started in the 1960s and has refused to dissipate, although many had assumed it would by now have ceased to be an issue. Instead of being forgotten, though, the demand for greater accountability regarding the educational and service dollar is being made by more and more parents, taxpayers, and their representatives. The demand for accountability has now reached such proportions that public education and services at all levels face the choice of either proving the worth of their programs or suffering reduced monetary support.

Role of objectives

The most common means of achieving accountability is by defining and describing objectives. Implicit in the issuing of educational and service objectives, however, is the promise to attain those objectives. Criticism regarding unsatisfactory attainment of objectives often dramatizes a failure in accountability. Educators and service providers may choose to drop certain objectives, a move that society is apt to watch carefully, or move to improve accountability by creating programs that do achieve positive results. The entire subject of accountability has been explored in detail in countless volumes, and in all probability, interest in this controversial subject will only increase in the years ahead. Educational administrators in the public sector are becoming increasingly aware of the fact that voters are very consumer conscious as the cost of education and services continues to skyrocket at a time when inflation is taking its toll on each family budget. These dual conditions plus other social influences have set the stage for significant changes in American education.[10] Specifically regarding education, Hayes has pointed out, "The halo of faith in American education has become tilted and tarnished."[11]

Counselors and guidance specialists and educators all need to address the concept of accountability. Some professionals see accountability as an attempt to restrict their own activity. There appears to be some feeling that when a professional is required to state objectives and show evidence of movement toward obtaining those objectives, the flexibility to respond to needs as they arise is hindered. Another difficulty associated with accountability is the

---

10. Norris, Hatch, Engelkes, and Winborn, *Career Information Service,* pp. 31–32.

11. Donald G. Hayes, *The Organization of Pupil Personnel Programs—Issues and Practices,* ed. Raymond N. Hatch (East Lansing, Mich.: Michigan State University Press, 1974), p. 42.

need to clarify as specifically as possible the nature of the application of accountability. While it is relatively easy to measure certain specific behaviors or certain cognitive objectives involved in counseling, it is extremely difficult to quantify broader concepts and issues that may, in fact, be more effective measures of accountability.

Benefits of accountability

Although accountability may have some negative implications for counseling and guidance specialists, at the same time, it also may produce significant benefits. Professionals can be aided in their work by articulating the services they provide and by clarifying them through the use of stated objectives and goals. According to Caplan and Stoughton, the use of such objectives is also likely to incorporate counseling and guidance further into the mainstream of educational programs.[12] The clarification of objectives in counseling and guidance may also serve as the basis for better communications to the populations who are the consumers of such services. In that sense, accountability will even further the public-relations efforts of counseling and guidance specialists, enhance their professional status, increase support for their programs, and provide more personal satisfaction.[13]

Emphasis on outcome-oriented evaluation

The focus of accountability has been primarily in the area of outcome-oriented evaluation. This is because it is difficult to evaluate anything other than the outcome of a particular process or program of service. At the same time, though, it is important to measure the process variables within particular programs. When the content focus of a process is truly effective, for example, the potential control available through the use of process accountability may be as important as outcome-oriented evaluation. Without measuring process, it is difficult to know what parts of a program contribute in what measure to observed outcomes.

Handicapped children are the subject of yet another area of accountability that will be important in the coming decade. Public Law 94-142 has outlined the new areas of accountability toward handicapped children. The Appendix contains basic information and an understanding of the law, written in a question-and-answer format.

12. Lewis Caplan and Robert W. Stoughton, *Pupil Personnel Services Guidelines for Introducing and Developing a Program for Accountability* (Princeton, N.J.: National Association of Pupil Personnel Administrators, 1974).

13. John D. Krumboltz, "An Accountability Model for Counselors," *Personnel and Guidance Journal* 52, no. 10, 1974: 639–646.

The anticipated decrease in funding support for educational and human-service programs, whether due to inflation or actual monetary cuts, points to the need for ongoing refinement of an accountability model than can, in turn, facilitate good programming within a cost-containment context. Continued efforts to focus on accountability as a major tool for the counseling and guidance profession will undoubtedly be of growing importance in the 1980s. Chapter 13 contains more information on accountability.

Professional associations

Professional associations provide counseling and guidance specialists with a variety of services. First, they bring together colleagues with similar interests in various aspects of the counseling and guidance profession. Professional associations also provide national leadership, as well as a means of identifying critical issues within the profession. They provide a political strength that cannot be attained individually as professionals attempt to have an impact on legislative processes.

At least three major associations address the needs of the profession: the American Personnel and Guidance Association, the American Psychological Association, and the National Rehabiliation Association.

American Personnel and Guidance Association

The American Personnel and Guidance Association resulted from the merger in the early 1950s of the National Vocational Guidance Association, the Association of Counselor Educators and Supervisors, and the American College Personnel Association. Since that time, APGA has been the official national organization to speak for school counselors. Membership has expanded from 18,000 in 1965 to approximately 40,000 in 1978. There are 13 divisions of APGA at this time.[14] The divisions include school counselors, measurement and evaluation specialists in counseling and guidance, rehabilitation counselors, employment counselors, group workers, mental health counselors, and college-level counselors.

The American Personnel and Guidance Association publishes the *Personnel and Guidance Journal* on a monthly basis and the *Guidepost* on a biweekly basis. All but one of the 13 have their own

14. American Personnel and Guidance Association, *The Status of Guidance and Counseling in the Nation's Schools: A Series of Issue Papers* (Washington, D.C., 1978), p. 14.

quarterly publication. The following is a list of the divisions and their publications:

American College Personnel Association, *The Journal of College Student Personnel*

Association for Counselor Education and Supervision, *Counselor Education and Supervision*

National Vocational Guidance Association, *Vocational Guidance Quarterly*

Association for Humanistic Education and Development, *Humanist Educator*

American School Counselors Association, *The School Counselor* and *Elementary School Guidance and Counseling Journal*

The American Rehabilitation Counseling Association, *Rehabilitation Counseling Bulletin*

Association for Measurement and Evaluation Guidance, *Measurement and Evaluation in Guidance*

National Employment Counselors Association, *Journal of Employment Counseling*

Association for Non-White Concerns in Personnel and Guidance, *Journal of Non-White Concerns in Personnel and Guidance*

Association for Religious and Value Issues in Counseling, *Counseling and Values*

Association for Specialists in Group Work, *Journal for Specialists in Group Work*

Public Offender Counselors Association, no publication

American Mental Health Counselors Association, *American Mental Health Counselors Journal*

These divisions focus on the special areas of interest for the members of the American Personnel and Guidance Association. Information about activities of American Personnel and Guidance Association may be obtained by writing them at 2 Skyline Place, Suite 400, 5203 Leesburg Pike, Falls Church, Virginia 22041.

American Psychological Association

The American Psychological Association was founded in 1892 and incorporated in 1925 as the major organization representing psychologists in the United States. Currently, there are over 40,000 members in APA. The purpose of APA is to advance psychology as a science and as a profession that promotes human welfare. The APA has 33 divisions, which incorporate a variety of professional specialties.[15]

15. Biographical Directory of the American Psychological Association (Washington, D.C.: American Psychological Association, 1975).

Introduction

The rise in career education, the issue of accountability, and the application of systems technology are three major factors that have contributed to the development of counseling models now in use. These three movements were all born in the late 1960s and the early 1970s, so it is no surprise that this is the period that gave rise to most of the counseling models now in use. These models have undergone several waves of modification and further development. In addition, other new models are currently being developed, although for lack of space, only three of the more established models are discussed in this chapter.

Theoretical models are important not only because they parallel developments in education but also because of the way in which they work to organize the counseling profession. During the past fifty to seventy-five years, counseling has gone through several stages or orientations. Mostly, though, emphasis has been placed on the service aspects of counseling, and less attention has been paid to the management, integration, and articulation of counseling and guidance theories into functional models. With the development of models for the counseling profession, however, attention can be directed to these areas. Furthermore, paying attention to these areas does not mean that less attention will be paid to services, but rather, that services can now be planned, monitored, and evaluated in a way that will make them more effective.

Three models are presented in this chapter. They are Byrne's behavioral and systems-based counseling method,[1] the systematic model by Stewart et al.,[2] and a skill-based model of counseling developed somewhat independently by several researchers and theorists. These models offer easy comparison and analysis because they incorporate the same basic steps: overall assessment of the program, the establishment of priorities and/or goals, the articulation of objectives, the monitoring of activities, and comparison of the results.

Key terms

behavioral and systems-based model
goal accomplishment
performance objectives
performance outcomes
systematic model
functional analysis
learning objective
skill-based model
attending skills
facilitating skills
psychological listening
empathy
information-seeking skills
decision-making skills
problem-solving skills
confrontation

1. Richard Hill Byrne, *Guidance: A Behavioral Approach* (Englewood Cliffs, N.J.: Prentice-Hall, 1977).

2. N.R. Stewart; B. B. Winborn; R. G. Johnson; Herbert M. Burks, Jr.; and J. R. Engelkes, *Systematic Counseling* (Englewood Cliffs, N.J.: Prentice-Hall, 1978).

Behavioral and systems-based counseling model

Theory

Byrne's counseling model provides a good example of the way that a practical application can be implemented from a conceptual blueprint. Byrne's blueprint is strongly influenced by two theoretical frameworks. The first is systems theory, and the second is learning theory, also called behavior modification.

Role in school guidance

Because Byrne emphasizes that the guidance or counseling component is typically part of a larger educational structure or system, it is not surprising that he advocates a highly systematic approach to the development of counseling programs. Byrne's particular focus is on individual educational systems and the role of the guidance program within those systems. He feels the guidance program must mesh with the purposes of the school; it must help the school accomplish what it sets out to do. In determining the role of guidance, then, it is essential that one start with a clarification of the goals of the educational system. To accomplish this, Byrne has mapped out a procedure that consists of the following steps:

1. The identification of programs that contribute to goal accomplishment.
2. The identification or clarification of goals for each program.
3. The specification of competencies, or performance objectives, that demonstrate the accomplishment of goals.
4. The development of strategies that promise to reach these objectives.
5. The identification of appropriate personnel to conduct the strategies.
6. The observation of the level of goal accomplishment, usually achieved by measuring performance outcomes.

Basically, this part of Byrne's model is a process model derived from systems theory in which he illustrates how systems analysis provides a plan for specifying the necessary components and activities of a counseling program. Staff configurations and relationships as well as staff functions and tasks can also be addressed in this way. Since the development of these components and activities proceeds in a logical way from an initial starting point, the potential for developing a consistent program is high. The systems framework also provides a way to anticipate the kinds of information that must be collected, as well as the times to collect them. For example, observation and measurement of actual performances of students or staff provides information that is used to modify goals, staff patterns, and required performances. Figure 3-1 shows a systematic counseling model.

The functioning of the model

Byrne's insistence on specifying outcomes in terms of observable performance, which then become measures of competence, is evidence of behavior modification. This also results in behavioral descriptions of desired outcomes. One example of a behavioral description from the many that Byrne offers is: "Given a career stimulus, the student shall seek information from the school's Career Information Center and from other sources without stimulus from other persons to do so."[3]

Emphasis on performance outcomes

The use of behavioral descriptions of desired performance minimizes the amount of inference one must make in deciding whether a particular goal has been achieved. Seeing a student enter a room, request and locate, and then read a pamphlet about an occupation leads one to infer more strongly that a student knows how to find and use occupational information than if one were to ask a question on a written examination.

Byrne also uses behavior modification when he suggests that staff patterns and functions should be based on two things: first, the coping or developmental skills needed by the students, and second, the performance requirements, that is, the behaviors, expected of the staff.

Staff organization

Byrne also suggests the kind of personnel needed to implement the model. Due to the development of new technology related to behavior modification, he suggests the presence of a behavioral specialist. Such a person would not only handle the behavioral problems of students, but would also consult with the staff on the development of behavior change programs for individual students. In addition, this person would help to educate the staff with regard to new techniques.

Counselor roles in Byrne's counseling model

The second kind of staff person Byrne feels is essential to the success of the program is a counselor. The counselor's role would be to attend to normal behavior of students, helping them cope with routine problems related to the educational system. Byrne also sees a role for the counselors as a supplementary educator of the staff regarding the behavioral program.

A third staff person suggested by Byrne is a career development technician (CDT). This person would manage the information resource center, which would provide the necessary information for students to help plan careers. The CDT is not a librarian, but rather, is a specialist equipped to help teachers and other staff integrate appropriate career development knowledge and skills into the pro-

3. Byrne, *Guidance,* p. 123.

grams of the schools in addition to helping students. The CDT would need close ties to the local business community, so that the school could function as a source of job information based on local needs.

Byrne calls for other staff specialists, which might include a CDT assistant who would specifically manage the information service; a continuing education technician, who would specialize in helping students plan for education or training after they leave high school; teacher-advisers, who would actively use guidance principles in their education programs; counselors who would attempt to fulfill a school's obligations to dropouts; a registrar who would attend to many of the record-keeping chores typically ascribed to guidance; and finally, peer counselors, or trained students, who could interact with other students in a way that adults could not. Byrne recommends, in fact, that all students be trained as peer counselors because this training usually contributes to the development of interpersonal skills.

Byrne describes how these various staff persons could be trained and how they might coordinate their jobs within the guidance program. Byrne's model is at present visionary, since these components do not as yet exist in an integrated applied model anywhere. The value of Byrne's model is that it evolves from a systematic application of systems theory and behavior-change theory. It has much promise, particularly since many of its parts are supported by wide-ranging research.

Such conceptual work as Byrne's model helps to contrast what guidance has become through its historical development with what it might become if traditional practices were reevaluated and perhaps changed where they seem to be conceptually inconsistent. As changes are implemented, empirical evidence can be obtained to validate the conceptual applications. Byrne's process model is an important example of how theory can be used in program development. Continued conceptualizing is welcome, but it must be supported, in turn, by research that validates the theories. One without the other diminishes the capability of the counseling profession to develop its full potential. In comparing the models, we find that only Byrne's model defines staff roles within the overall system.

The systematic counseling model

Background

Beginning in the late 1960s, a group of counselor educators at Michigan State University began to develop a model that became known as the systematic counseling model. This model was first developed as a way to train students to become counselors. It was an attempt to form guidelines and instructional tools to help students gain an appreciation for the entire counseling process from the initial referral to the closing of the case. It was also intended to promote the understanding of how the seemingly discrete parts of the counseling process are actually interdependent. As the model was applied in actual counseling, it became apparent that it could also be used to guide the counselor and counselee through the counseling process to desired goals. Systematic counseling obviously could be more than just a learning tool. Its application in actual counseling also seemed to facilitate the achieving of counseling outcomes in an efficient manner. The educators most closely associated with systematic counseling were Norman R. Stewart; Bob B. Winborn; Richard G. Johnson; Herbert M. Burks, Jr.; and James R. Engelkes.

Theory

As with Byrne's behavioral approach, systematic counseling is more of a descriptive process than a theoretical examination of causality. Systematic counseling focuses on the counseling process itself and also incorporates a behavioral focus on how learning occurs.

Focus on counseling process

Systematic counseling borrowed heavily from systems theory in its early development. Systems theory provided the rationale and procedures for the construction of the model. Systems theory posits that a process can be viewed as a unit that has a specific goal. Analysis is then used to break down the process into its discrete components, each of which contributes to the achievement of the goal. These parts are then synthesized into a structure, flow, or sequence that best accomplishes the goal of the system. Finally, to recognize how the parts of the system are dependent on one another, and how the system itself is dependent on the environment that surrounds it, information-feedback devices are built throughout the system to ensure that it is flexible to the varied demands made upon it. This allows the system to handle routine circumstances and also to change itself when its environment changes the demands on the system.

The basic goal of systematic counseling is to achieve the outcome counselees and counselors have mutually developed and to implement it in the most efficient and accountable manner possible.

The functioning of the model

Figure 3–1 indicates one possible overall design for a systematic counseling model. Each of the rectangles represents a discrete phase in the counseling process that needs to be completed suc-

Figure 3–1 Systematic counseling model

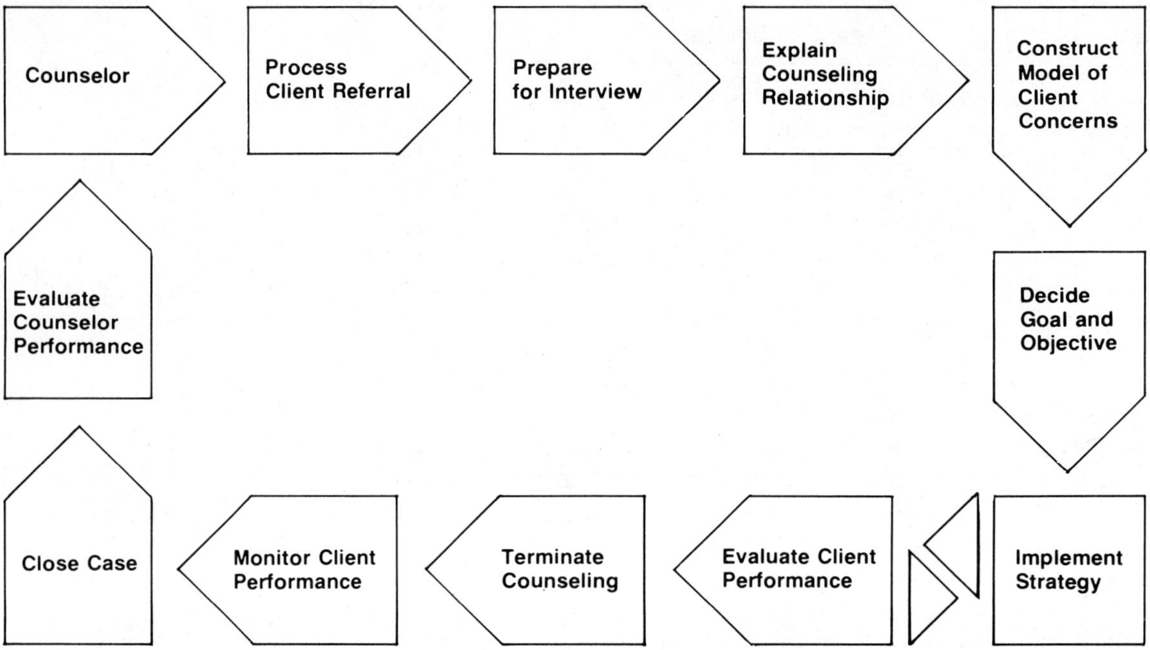

cessfully. Each of the parts must be accomplished in order to achieve a successful completion of counseling. The arrows indicate the process, or flow, of the model. In systems language, this design is called a flow chart.

You will note that the process begins and ends with the counselor. The counselor is the person responsible for the application of each step in the system, just as the counselor is the person held accountable for the flow of the counseling process. Although the counselor cannot control all the factors that determine the eventual outcome of counseling, the counselor is responsible for how counseling is implemented. The counselor can also ensure his or her continued professional development by carefully reviewing the feedback that is obtained regarding the relative effectiveness of counseling with each individual counselee at each step in the process. The first step in this model involves processing the client referral. This refers to activities the counselor should engage in prior to meeting with the counselee. These activities briefly include discussion with the referral source, gathering of information that will be needed in this particular counseling situation, and determination of the areas that will probably be explored during counseling. This does not mean that the counselor predetermines the issues that need exploration. Rather, it means that the counselor takes certain preliminary steps to prepare himself or herself professionally for the initial meeting. He or she obtains or reviews information that he or she feels will be needed in this situation based on what has been learned about the counselee. He or she should also at this stage consider and attempt to deal with any biases or preconceptions he or she may have regarding the counselee based on what is known about this person. Finally, he or she takes into account whether or not the person has had previous counseling and how to approach this issue with the counselee. These are all basic issues that will be dealt with in the first counseling session. Careful preparation at this stage will do much to ensure that all the ingredients for a successful counseling experience are attendant at the initial meeting.

Counselor roles in systematic model

Another important part of referral processing is to inform the referral source, if there is one, about the onset of counseling, what can be expected from the process, and what role the referral source might play as a counseling resource.

The next step is to prepare for the interview. This is simply a reminder to the counselor to schedule the first counseling interview efficiently and to prepare adequately for initiating counseling by carefully reviewing all the available information shortly before the meeting.

The next step, explanation of the counseling relationship, describes what typically must be accomplished during the first counseling session. Many counselees may have never been in a counseling relationship before, and they can be expected to be quite anxious. Popular notions of counseling often reflect the idea that persons who use counseling are less than competent or damaged emotionally. This idea must be dispelled before effective counseling can occur. The counselor can explain that counseling is a learning process that helps one live a more productive life. It is an effective way of dealing with the normal concerns of daily life, as well as the particularly stressful times.

Sometimes counselees are acquainted with counseling through the experiences of others or because they have personal experience with it. If this is the case, then the counselor needs to review with the counselee any attitudes he or she may be bringing to this experience. The counselor need not obtain a detailed history of previous experiences in counseling in every instance, but some idea of the counselee's past record must be obtained and evaluated.

At the initial meeting, some attempt should also be made to outline the responsibilities of counselor and counselee. Included in this discussion would be an affirmation of the confidentiality of counseling, as well as the voluntary and limited nature of counseling.

Although this is a general outline of the first meeting, the counselor should be aware that many counselees will be very anxious to discuss the problem they are seeking counseling for. Because of this, discussion of these issues may be ongoing in other early sessions, so the counselee can have the opportunity to discuss the issues that most concern him or her at the initial meeting. At some point early in counseling, however, these issues must be discussed in order to avoid problems and misunderstandings later.

Establishment of client concerns

The next step is to construct a model of client concerns. Before any strategies are developed, the counselor and counselee must mutually understand just what events, situations, and concerns are interfering with the counselee's life. Too often, upon identifying a counselee concern, counselors rush immediately into strategy development. This is too premature, and in the long run, this can cause counseling to become a trial-and-error process. Systematic counseling requires the careful development of a complete picture of what has brought the counselee to counseling. This will lead directly to a proper strategy building sequence that has a good likelihood of success.

Specifically, the counselor should solicit as many concerns as the counselee can identify. Even when there seems to be only one, the counselee should be urged to scrutinize the situation more carefully. During this phase, the counselor should use a blend of empathy and direct questioning that will help the counselee feel secure enough to explore and reveal all concerns. The counselor then helps the counselee decide which of the concerns will be dealt with first. This must be the counselee's choice to ensure the full cooperation of the counselee in the counseling process. Following the identification of one concern that is to be the immediate focus of counseling, the counselor needs to reassure the counselee that other concerns will be attended to at a later time or when they arise and that the most efficient procedure is to focus on one issue at a time.

Use of functional analysis to define counselee issue

The counselor and counselee then construct a model of the chosen issue. The suggested procedure is to break down the issue using functional analysis, which refers to the A–B–C approach described in the behavioral theory section in Chapter 7. Briefly, though, the behavior (B) of the counselee that is related directly to the concern is identified. The antecedents (A) and consequences (C) are discussed and tentatively identified. Often the counselee is urged to do "homework," that is, to observe and record these processes as they occur during the period between sessions. This often yields new insights into the issue, insights that differ from the ones that are developed during the counseling session. Following the homework assignment, these insights are pieced together and verified with the counselee.

The next step is to decide on a goal or objective for counseling. Before a strategy can be initiated, the ultimate goal must be decided on by counselor and counselee. The process of arriving at a counseling objective is one of elimination. The counselee first tries to identify what he views as the most idealistic outcome that can be hoped for as a result of counseling. The counselor then helps the counselee to recognize realistic limitations, if any, and to change expectations accordingly. Finally, the counselor then helps the counselee develop the learning objective or goal that will serve as the guide for strategy building. This process can be broken into three steps:

1. Describing the new counselee's desired behavior.
2. Describing the conditions that are present when the new behavior occurs.
3. Describing the criteria and evidence needed to indicate that the counselee has successfully learned the new desired behavior.

Development of learning objective

The goal should be stated plainly in the form of a learning objective. Every learning objective should consist of three parts: first, it should list the conditions or what must be done to prepare the environment for the new behavior; then it should state clearly the desired behavior; and finally, it should list the criteria for verifying the desired behavior. For example, if the counselee were an overweight person whose primary goal was to lose weight, then the learning objective might read as follows:

Given that all the right diet foods are purchased, and that a healthy exercise and eating schedule is set up, George will diet and exercise so well that he will reach the ideal weight for his height.

If the counselor feels that the goal is a reasonable and realistic one, as well as one that is within his or her counseling experience, then the stage is now set for beginning work on specific strategies.

Implementation of counseling strategy

The implementation of strategy is an activity where the counselor can use whatever expertise is available to help the counselee meet the objective. The results of this stage of counseling are dependent on what has gone on prior to this. Without the careful identification, selection, and description of a concern, and the helpful direction of a concrete objective, strategy becomes nothing more than trial and error. The development of strategies is a pragmatic rather than a theoretical process. Theories can provide helpful suggestions as to potential strategies, but they cannot replace the counselor's personal experience, shared experience with colleagues, and a thorough knowledge of the current counseling research literature. Any strategy or combination of strategies can be used at this point. Information seeking, decision making, or behavior-change methods from any variety of theoretical orientations can and should be considered. Even though this stage of counseling relies heavily on the expertise of the counselor, the counselee remains a partner in development and implementation of strategy. Often, after a careful study of the issue, the appropriate strategical steps become self-evident to the counselee. At this stage, careful attention should be given to the development of strategy-related tasks that are the counselee's responsibility. The counselor should not be solely responsible for developing and carrying out strategy steps. A final component of the strategy at this stage is to specify carefully each of the outcomes that can be expected if all the strategy tasks are successfully completed. This is necessary to provide a smooth transition for the next stage of counseling.

Termination process

Evaluation of client performance occurs after strategy implementation has been completed. The criteria used to measure success must be the same as those in the learning objective, and the data should also be comparable to what was defined in the learning objective. The data also provides the counselor and counselee with the necessary information to make decisions on what remains to be accomplished. If the information indicates that all the criteria of the learning objective have been met, then counseling can be terminated or a new concern can be explored. If the criteria have not been met after the first strategy, the counselee can continue to work with the counselor toward resolution of the concern.

Once all objectives have been accomplished, or in those cases where a concern cannot be resolved through counseling, provision has to be made for termination. Terminating a case is not just a matter of closing the file and saying good-bye. Counselor and counselee need to recognize that counseling must end if it is to really be effective. At times, the counselee will feel dependent on the relationship built with the counselor, and part of termination is recognizing these feelings and putting them in proper perspective. One way of easing this situation is for the counselor to speak openly about termination throughout the process so that it is an expected event. The counselor also can become attached emotionally to counselees. These feelings must be resolved in a way that also promotes counselee independence. An open discussion that reviews the entire learning process and ways that the method can be applied independently by the counselee is also necessary prior to termination. Finally, a plan must be established that enables the counselor to follow up with the counselee. The plan should indicate how the counselee can further use the counselor's services, if necessary. No meetings need to be scheduled but often phone checks at prearranged periods suffice.

The actual monitoring of counselee progress is the next step. This may last for as long as six months, if possible. Following the conclusion of this monitoring phase, if no further occasion for counseling occurs, the counselor can formally close the counselee's case by whatever method the counselor's agency requires.

One important final part of each counseling relationship is for the counselor to assess all aspects of the process for strengths and weaknesses in order to determine what occurred during the process that would be helpful in subsequent counseling situations. This evaluation process is the final step of the systematic counseling model. The integration of knowledge from the counseling process just completed to new or existing cases is perhaps the single most important step in terms of developing the counselor's skills.

A skill-based model of counseling

The previous two models of counseling reflected different degrees of complexity. The first model, the behavioral and systems-based model by Byrne, is a global model that takes as its focus programmatic concerns. Thus, this model reflects how a counseling program might be organized. The second model, systematic counseling, narrows the process and highlights the typical stages of interaction between a counselor and counselee.

Background

The third model, a skill-based one, shifts the focus again and narrows it to the specific skills and behaviors that counselors need to display in actual counseling sessions. Rather than focusing on one particular skill model, the model that is presented here is a composite that incorporates contributions from several sources. Proponents of skill models include Carkhuff and Anthony,[4] Egan,[5] Kagan,[6] and Ivey and Authier.[7] Extensive research underlies all these models. The use of skill models has become an important element in counselor training. Theoretical concepts and professional identifications have come alive through the examination of concrete practical applications that evolve from studying these reality-based models. The basic research that underlies these models uncovered actual behaviors counselors normally exhibited in counseling sessions. There is a strong emphasis on displaying specific behaviors as explicitly as possible. This approach is often referred to as microtraining; it removes much of the mystery about the nature and goals of counseling. In order for these skill models to achieve their full value, they must be experienced as live models and buttressed by continual practice and feedback. What is discussed here is adequate only as an introduction to the use of skill models.

Theory

The models generally can be broken down into at least two general skill areas. The first area can be classified as attending skills. These skills permit the counselor to learn what is on the counselee's mind. From these skills the counselor is able to develop a picture of what it is like to be the counselee and what he or she is confronting. A crucial aspect of these skills is that this understanding is perceived by the counselee as evidence that the counselor is caring and skillful enough to really want to know about the counselee. Therefore, relevant attending skills include both listening and responding behaviors.

Role of communication

The second general skill area can be classified as facilitating or influencing skills. These skills permit the counselor to help counselees move in positive directions, thereby learning what is necessary to overcome the obstacles that brought them to counseling.

The skills embodied in the skill models all involve communication. Obviously, counselors and counselees speak to one another, thus,

---

4. Robert R. Carkhuff and William A. Anthony, *The Skills of Helping* (Amherst, Mass.: Human Resource Development Press, 1979).

5. G. Egan, *The Skilled Helper* (Monterey, Calif.: Brooks/Cole, 1975).

6. Norman Kagan, "Interpersonal Process Recall: A Method of Influencing Human Interaction," mimeographed (East Lansing, Michigan, 1976).

7. Allen E. Ivey and Jerry Authier, *Microcounseling: Innovations in Interviewing, Counseling, Psychotherapy, and Psychoeducation,* 2d ed. (Springfield, Ill.: Charles C. Thomas, 1978).

listening skills and responding skills are absolutely necessary for counselors, as noted earlier. But communication can be present even in the absence of words. Gestures, expressions, voice tones, and other similar subtle gestures can provide a wealth of information that is often overlooked in everyday conversation. Counselors must develop observation skills in order to be sensitive to how counselees communicate in this manner. This is often referred to as listening with a "third ear." This kind of listening can reveal feelings that are camouflaged by language. It must also be recognized that counselors communicate in this subtle fashion. Counselors must be careful about what their own actions and gestures are communicating. Boredom, impatience, anxiety—all natural emotions—are nonetheless counterproductive in a counseling session. Counselors must learn to be sensitive to their own feelings and the way these are communicated to counselees.

Attending skills

Attending skills begin even before a counselee enters the counselor's office. A counselor can communicate care and respect by being as familiar as possible with the counselee's case and by being prepared and organized so that when the counselee does enter, counseling can begin with the counselor's full and immediate attention. Throughout counseling, the counselor will want to demonstrate psychological and physical listening. Listening is demonstrated physically by maintaining appropriate eye contact with the counselee. Of course, staring at the counselee will heighten discomfort, but a steady gaze that most often focuses on the counselee's face in a natural way is desired. Avoiding eye contact arouses the counselee's suspicions and sensitivity. Counseling invariably raises the level of one's self-consciousness, thus eye contact must be attentive and comfort producing. The eyes should be able to shift to pick up facial gestures and body movements that convey additional information.

The counselor also demonstrates physical listening by exhibiting facial expressions and body movements that provide assurance in a relaxed way. The counselor should sit facing the counselee, preferably without any physical barriers between them. Fidgeting with pencils, rings, or other objects should be avoided. Sitting quietly and leaning toward the counselee to a slight degree is preferred. Unnecessary movement should be kept to a minimum. Looking too relaxed, by sinking back into the chair, for example, may convey a lack of concern and should be avoided, especially early in the counseling relationship. Attention to physical listening will show that the counselor respects the counselee and wants to devote full energy to enhancing the counseling process.

Value of psychological listening

Psychological listening goes beyond establishing the proper atmosphere for communication and centers on the nature of the communication itself. Psychological listening focuses on the messages being communicated. These messages include content, or the spoken word, and affect, or the feeling that underlies what is being spoken. Affect is communicated in many ways that are nonverbal or associated with *how* something was said, rather than with *what* was said. Often, affect and content are not harmonious. A counselee may discuss a parent in a rather passive way while clenching a fist and knocking it on the arm of the chair. In this instance, a counselor would try to understand the significance of these physical gestures to see if they did not communicate a deeper feeling about the parent.

There are many ways a counselor can demonstrate psychological listening. Restating what the counselee has said indicates that the counselor was listening. Word-for-word parroting, however, should be avoided. Restatements attempt to summarize the content of what the counselee was speaking about concretely so that it becomes clearer both for the counselor and counselee. For example, the counselor might say to the fist-clenching counselee, "You indicate that your mother plans your day for you, and begins by laying out your clothes for you." Restatements should not include reference to feelings.

Reflection, however, is a form of psychological listening that goes slightly beyond a concrete restatement to include a suggestion about the feelings that are associated with what was being described. This is usually stated somewhat tentatively to avoid the appearance of giving an interpretation that might convey that the counselee should experience a certain feeling about what has been described. This tentativeness also leaves the way open for the counselee to clarify whether the feeling suggested in the reflection actually exists. To continue the preceding example, the counselor might say to the fist-clenching counselee, "Although you describe how your mother plans for you in a rather neutral way, it seems from your fist clenching that you may feel quite upset about it."

Value of empathy

Attempts to restate and reflect, particularly when aspects of content and affect are woven together, are often referred to as empathy. When a counselor demonstrates empathy, it is a signal to the counselee that the counselor understands. Thus, empathy also stimulates further counselee disclosure and self-searching. Without appropriate levels of empathy on the part of the counselor, only a strongly motivated counselee would want to continue in counseling.

Turock described another empathic skill called additive empathy.[8] This skill attempts to help the counselee understand his or her behavior and feelings in a broader context than what was immediately discussed in counseling. It is an attempt to find a theme that underlies and unites the seemingly discrete areas of the counselee's life. The counselee may describe various incidents or relationships that seem unrelated, but the counselor should strive to see if these seemingly diverse problems are interrelated in the framework of one theme. If so, the counselee's understanding of his or her concerns can be greatly advanced. To continue the example, after some discussion of other relationships, the counselor might suggest, "It seems that for some reason when you deal with people whom you judge to have authority, you acquiesce to whatever they want in spite of what you personally want, and you build a lot of anger inside as a result."

Attending skills are primarily useful in the early stages of counseling to help stimulate the information flow between counselor and counselee. It is important for the counselor to gain an accurate understanding of the counselee's concerns. The most common method of eliciting information is by asking questions. Since this is so natural, counselors still should keep in mind when and how to use questions within the counseling context. Asking too many questions in a repetitive fashion, as a detective might, would seem as if counseling were an interrogation rather than a two-way communication. Questions should be used to channel the discussion, particularly to help a counselee stay focused on a certain relevant issue. Most often, though, counselees should be given the leeway to lead the discussion. When counselees take this initiative, the communication will flow from them in ways that reveal something about themselves that would be lost if the counselor structured the communication with questions. Questions can be useful, however, when used appropriately. When a counselor needs any specific information such as the counselee's age or work history or any other data often collected during an intake interview, it is most efficient to ask a direct question to pinpoint the exact information desired. Also, direct questions can bring a counselee back to a point that has not been clarified.

Two kinds of questions are used. Direct, or closed, questions anticipate an answer of a certain kind. Open-ended questions avoid any biasing direction from the counselor because no answer is suggested by the question. Open-ended questions usually avoid

8. Art Turock, "*Effective Challenging Through Additive Empathy,*" *Personnel and Guidance Journal* 57 (1978): 144–49.

beginning with "why," require more than a yes or no response, and do not suggest alternatives in the way that either/or questions do. Open-ended questions seek to stimulate further discussion with the counselee. An open-ended question for the fist-clenching counselee might be "What are your feelings when your mother does this to you?"

Facilitating skills

Although attending and facilitating skills are used throughout counseling, attending skills are used mostly to help the counselee define concerns while facilitating skills are used to develop solutions. A simple facilitating skill, often overlooked, is to selectively offer praise for the counselee's efforts to explore his or her concerns, and then to develop ways for dealing with them. Verbal reenforcement can help to maintain a counselee's efforts to be active and self-directing during counseling.

Uses of goal setting

When considering solutions, goal setting is an important skill. A counselor should help the counselee develop an idea of what would be a desirable outcome of counseling. If an outcome can be clearly and realistically developed, this can serve as a motivating factor for developing solutions. Care must be taken to work toward goals that will be sufficiently rewarding and challenging. Idealistic goals will only induce frustration later on. On the other hand, goals that are too simple may not seem worth it or may result in little satisfaction once achieved.

Using information-seeking skills

Often counselees need information that will help them make decisions. Counselors need to judge whether guidance, or information

This counselor serves as a vital resource for the various kinds of information this student needs to make a career choice.

giving, is appropriate or whether the counselor should teach information-seeking skills to the counselee so he or she can get the information on his or her own. Counselors have access to much information such as school schedules, labor-market information, and help-giving sources. If this information is readily at hand, it seems reasonable to offer it to counselees. Care must be taken that any information offered fits the needs of the counselee and is offered without any condition that the counselee is obligated to use the information in a certain way.

At times when information is not available, the counselor should help the counselee explore and develop a strategy for finding the necessary information himself. Information seeking is a valuable skill to learn since it usually is required any time a decision must be made. Information-seeking skills usually include trying to describe the information needed, suggesting likely places where it might be obtained, establishing criteria for judging its adequacy when found, and developing a scheme for recording information. Creativity is an important part of information seeking as it helps to ensure that as many information sources as possible will be checked.

Following the gathering and analyzing of information, decision making is the next step. At the very least, counselees must weigh the goals and strategies they want to pursue. There have been many attempts to construct decision-making models. Typical elements of decision making include stipulating a goal, listing alternatives, weighing the alternatives, selecting an option, implementing it, and finally reviewing the process to see whether the goal has been achieved or whether another strategy must be used. Often, decision making can be the catalyst for uncovering new ways to think and behave.

Related to information seeking and decision making is problem solving. Actually, problem solving includes both of these elements and is the skill area that applies to facilitating in general. It uses an entire range of strategies a counselor can bring to bear on behalf of a counselee. Problem solving is a deliberate process that leads to certain action. The results of this action are then measured against the desired counseling goal, and if needed, additional problem solving is initiated.

Using confrontation

The final counseling skill to be discussed here is one that must be used with great care. This is confrontation. It is presented here in the context of facilitating skills because the need for confrontation becomes most apparent when a counselee's behaviors seem to be discrepant with his or her spoken intentions. This happens most clearly when a counselee voices an intention to pursue a certain strategy and then avoids doing so repeatedly. Usually, excuses are offered that seem reasonable enough, but when taken together, they indicate that the counselee's motivation may be suspect.

When confronting this situation, the counselor must gradually point out the problem, attempting to remove excuses as viable explanations for why an intention was not fulfilled. The counselee typically will not admit that there is any deliberate scheming behind this avoidance. Often, fear underlies this lack of direction and inability to achieve fulfillment. Although the fear must be challenged, it must be done sensitively so the counselee will be assured of the counselor's support and intention to continue with counseling. When confronting, the use of questions might be appropriate to avoid sounding accusatory. Asking "Even though you were committed to going on that interview, I wonder how it happened that you overslept both times?" is more facilitative than saying "I guess you really don't want to work because if you did you would have made it to those interviews!"

Counseling skills, as outlined here, are the essence of what counseling is all about. Without basic communication on verbal and nonverbal levels, no progress would occur in counseling even if all other program elements and resources were developed to their optimum. These skills are the basic building blocks of counseling that counselors must learn and continually develop throughout their careers.

Summary

The three models described in this chapter are indicative of the varying approaches that can be taken to counseling. The purpose of describing these models in such detail is to show that such models exist and to point out their value for guiding the counseling profession. No one model should be accepted in totality, and other models may work as well as these. What is important, however, is that some model be used to structure and guide a counseling program and how a counselor goes about counseling.

Questions

1. Why are models important? In what ways are they of value to counselors-in-training?

2. Do models have to be in use to be effective? Give reasons for your answer.

3. What is the behavioral and systems-based counseling model?

4. What is the systematic counseling model?

5. What is the skills-oriented model? Compare and contrast the three models.

6. Describe the type of staff required in the behavioral and systems-based model.

7. What is the role of the counselor in the systematic counseling model?

8. What is the role of the counselee in the systematic model?

9. Why is it important to define the counseling relationship in terms of time?

10. What follow-up is provided in the systematic counseling model? In the skills-based model?

Projects

1. Invite someone who uses the systematic counseling model to speak to the class about the advantages and disadvantages of this model.

2. Do research on other theoretical models to see how they are similar to or different from the models described in this chapter.

3. Find out how referrals are made in various settings. Report on the advantages and disadvantages of each method.

4. Organize a panel discussion about the weaknesses and strengths of the three models described in the chapter.

The context of counseling 2

4 Role and function of counselors

Counselors often are involved in educational or career counseling in nonschool settings, such as this prison program for career education.

4

Introduction

Recognition of the need for graduate level training in counseling began during the 1950s. Two legislative landmarks provided the funding base for expanding the number of training programs and enabled counselor-trainees to obtain on-the-job experience during schooling. First, the Vocational Rehabilitation Bill was signed into law by President Dwight D. Eisenhower on August 3, 1954. This law led to the establishment of federally supported training programs, including student support, to supply much needed professionals for state and federal vocational rehabilitation programs. Second, the National Defense Education Act of 1958, which was renewed through 1968, spurred the expansion of counselor training programs that supplied counselors to the schools. Counselors also have been trained as community mental-health counselors through the National Institute on Mental Health, as community college counselors through the Educational Professionals Development Act, and as urban counselors through the minority division of the National Institute on Mental Health.

The maze of counseling and guidance personnel in such diverse areas as education, rehabilitation, community agencies, and public health has caused considerable confusion regarding the role of counselors. And in fact, counselors can be found in many varying roles and positions. In addition, there are many ways to specialize within the counseling profession. Professional associations, more than any other source, have taken on the task of clarifying the roles and services that counselors can provide. Various groups have now issued statements defining the roles and functions of elementary and secondary school counselors, as well as rehabilitation counselors and mental health counselors.

Key terms

role
function
role conflict
role expectations
elementary school counselor
middle school counselor
high school counselor
community counselor
rehabilitation counselor

Definitions: roles and functions

It is sometimes difficult to distinguish between the meanings of terms such as *role* and *function.* Basically, the term *role* is used here to refer to the types of outcomes a person in a work setting is expected to accomplish. In general, counselors may be expected to help people solve problems. That is their role. Function, on the other hand, is used to describe the various activities that counselors engage in to fulfill their roles. Some of these functions are defined by the counselor's employer. Such things as record keeping and providing testing might fall in this category. Other practices are under the control of the counselor. These often include the choice of counseling strategies or the decision about which tests are most appropriate to use.

Determinants of a counselor's role and sources of role conflict

To gain a better understanding of the counselor's role, it is useful to recognize that the concept implied by the term *role* is a fluid one. It is rarely as static as written job descriptions imply, for example.

Graen has suggested that roles are determined by three kinds of factors.[1] The first of these is technology. The limits of what one can do are fixed by available expertise, methodology, and equipment. The second determinant is a host of organizational elements, such as a contract or job description, work rules, coworkers, and supervisors. The third determinant is the person fulfilling the role. Personal expectations and values, prior work experience, and the level of education are some of the factors in this class.

When all of these factors and elements are considered, it is apparent that a role is something that is constantly evolving. As any of the determinants change, and it is obvious that many of them do, the role also changes. And the persons in these roles have to recognize that a role is rarely mastered in a permanent sense. Rather, role accomplishment and, therefore, work adjustment, is an ongoing process. Some persons will be comforted to recognize that one of the three role determinants is the personal factor. This means that a counselor can legitimately seek to modify unacceptable portions of a counseling role. Complete control is probably not attainable, however, and continued adjustment and compromise is probably the norm. It seems reasonable that any person fulfilling a role should make some effort to compromise within the constraints of the system rather than to expect and battle constantly only for ideal situations for role fulfillment.

Transitory nature of roles

Given that roles are in continuous transition, it is likely that discrepancies will occur between the persons fulfilling the role, or role incumbents, and those who interact with them. Sources of problems can occur when the role incumbent reacts to the expectations and demands of others. Likewise, authority figures may perceive problems when they observe what they feel are discrepant behaviors between what the role incumbent does and what they feel is required to perform a job satisfactorily. Both expectations and behaviors can lead the parties involved to dissatisfaction with the way the

1. George Graen, "Role-Making Processes within Complex Organizations," in *Handbook of Industrial and Organizational Psychology*, ed. M. D. Dunnette (Chicago: Rand McNally, 1976): 1201–1245.

role is performed. It may be useful to review some of these problem areas as they pertain to counselors.

A counselor, as a person, has many roles to fulfill. Being a counselor is just one of them. Each role, such as being a parent, an employee, and possibly also a supervisor, contains different expectations and makes varying demands. All roles overlap. Any one role can begin to interfere with the fulfillment of another role. Because of this, priorities must be set in terms of fulfilling any of the roles required of a person.

In setting these priorities, decisions based on values are required. For example, one role requirement, such as making counseling services available in the evening to accommodate certain counselees, may interfere with another highly valued role requirement, spending evenings with one's family. Such decisions can be a cause of personal distress for counselors.

Role fulfillment presents other problems. Even the functions required within a counselor's role can cause conflict. Role conflict occurs when discrepancies exist between what one does and what one is expected to do. Some of these functions seem more legitimate than others. For example, record keeping is often felt to hinder or detract from time spent counseling. A counselor resents the time required to do paperwork and opts for shortcuts that may result in poor performance of this function. This may make someone else's role more difficult, such as the administrative aide who must develop summary accounts of records for reporting purposes. For example, counselors need to become cognizant of the relationship between their roles and functions and those of other persons. In another example, a counselor's educational preparation may not highlight the fact that part of the role of a counselor involves daily contact with people who are experiencing much distress. On a day-in and day-out basis, this may result in frustration and fatigue that can be a source of conflict. Role expectations may be too idealistic at the outset of a career or at the beginning of a new job and may have to be changed to resolve the conflict.

Even though a counselor may have a fairly detailed job description, all the expectations of employers and supervisors cannot be communicated formally. Unfortunately, additional communication from these sources is most likely to occur after one has erred, which can in itself be an unpleasant interaction that results in conflict.

Also, coworkers may establish requirements of their own that may or may not be in harmony with that of the organization. When discrepancies exist, one person might be punished by the work group for trying to fulfill the employer's expectations without allowing for the modifications demanded by the work group. For example, a counselor sensitive to the needs of counselees to have evening time available may offer to come in after hours. Other counselors may resent such a precedent, particularly if administrators attempt to make it policy for all counselors.

Even the freedom under which many counselors work can produce conflict, especially for those who are young and inexperienced. In addition, interpretations of professional counseling processes are by no means universal. What one counselor sees as a legitimate counseling technique or behavior may seem unprofessional to another counselor or to a supervisor. When such a situation occurs between counselors or supervisors, the situation can be delicate. Examples of such conflict occur when counselors of different theoretical persuasion work in the same organization. When behavioral counseling first began, many counselors viewed it as mechanistic and insensitive to individual needs and differences. Counselors using behavioral techniques had to defend themselves repeatedly from those who felt deeply about the lack of "humanness" they perceived in the approach.

Since counselors are more likely than many other workers to experience situations that lead to role conflict, simply because most of their work involves human contact, it is essential for them to understand that such events also may occur due to changes within the components of the counseling system. The changes may result from changes in the legitimate demands made upon the system. For example, legislative changes can quickly rearrange a counseling organization's mission if it is supported by public funds.

Resolving role conflicts

A counselor may have many options when role conflict occurs. Resignation, acquiescence, and compromise are obvious possible responses. Since counselors have partial control over their own role definition, negotiation and compromise is often the most viable alternative. In this way, counselors demonstrate not only adaptability, but they also maintain some measure of influence over the impact counseling has on counselees and other constituent groups.

Role conflict, however, remains a difficult issue for counselors. A recent reading of the literature related to this issue draws attention to the ambiguities that exist in the ethical codes of the counseling profession, as well as in the literature.[2] This ambiguity particularly exists where efforts are made to outline the responsibilities of counselors to counselees and to society. And, of course, these responsibilities

2. Marvin E. McMillian, "Conflicting Loyalties: A Literature Review," *Personnel and Guidance Journal* 58 (1979): 17–100.

overlap and further add to the conflict. A recent survey of counselors from different professional organizations confirmed the problem of role conflict for counselors.[3]

Counseling as a profession

The field of counseling and guidance is a professional occupation. A profession is an occupation that requires training in the liberal arts or the sciences and advanced study in a particular area. In general, a profession may be sociologically defined as having three features:

Defining a profession

1. The profession determines its own training standards. Professional associations in an area such as counseling specify core requirements that must be included in each counselor training program. In some cases, these training programs are reviewed for accreditation based on their compliance to the standards.
2. The profession is recognized legally via licensure and certification. Several organizations are already in the process of licensing and certifying various counseling specialties. Professional associations have supported licensure efforts, and in some cases, national certification already exists. For example, the Commission on Rehabilitation Counselor Certification certifies rehabilitation counselors.
3. The profession is likely to be a terminal occupation. Occupations other than professions are more likely to experience more frequent personnel shifts than the professions do. Professional competence assumes a commitment to a specified body of knowledge that has held professionals to performing tasks generally within the range of this competence. Usually, this implies a theoretical base for the body of knowledge which results in the acquisition of unique skill.[4] These factors tend to stabilize the flow of persons in and out of the profession.

There is no clear dividing line between an occupation and a profession, but rather, there is a continuum of variables that determine

3. Marvin E. McMillian and Bruce Shertzer, "APGA Members Measured Client and Organizational Commitments and Professional Orientation," *Personnel and Guidance Journal* 57 (1978): 31–34.

4. William J. Goode, "The Professions: Reports and Opinion-Encroachment, Charlatanism, and the Emerging Professions: Psychology, Sociology, and Medicine," *American Sociological Review* 25.

status. One cannot ask whether an occupation is a profession, but one can—and should—ask how far an occupation has moved in the direction of increased or decreased professionalization. It seems clear that the field of guidance and counseling has moved steadily in the direction of increased professionalization.

Realistic expectations in various work settings

The following sections provide a typical picture of the role expectations of counselors in several educational settings. Also included is a brief description of how counselors function in other community agencies.

Elementary school counselor

The past decade has seen a rapid, although somewhat erratic, increase in the number of elementary school counselors. Although no data exist to prove the exact number of practicing elementary school counselors, other evidence supports indications of the increase. Costar and Hecker[5] found that the expenditure for salaries of guidance personnel continuously rose each year between 1964 and 1974. In 1964, expenditures amounted to $11.5 million. By 1974, that figure had increased to over $41 million. In 1975, about 6 percent of guidance salaries was earned by elementary counselors, and this figure represented a 5 percent increase over the past ten years.

Future funding

In addition, federal funding ensured that more counselors would work on the elementary school level. Under the National Defense Education Act, federal funds were allotted for the training of elementary school counselors, although at the present time, no federal funding supports their training. Until 1973, federal funds were also available for the hiring of elementary school counselors. Federal funding supported approximately 57 percent of the 6,041 elementary school counselors working in 1970, according to Van Hoose and Kurtz.[6]

A joint committee report from the Association of Counselor Educators and Supervisors and the American School Counselors Association (1967) presented a statement defining the role of guid-

5. James W. Costar and Stanley E. Hecker, "First the Good News: School Guidance Personnel Salaries in Michigan, 1964–1974," *Michigan Personnel and Guidance Journal* 6 (Spring 1975): 27–54.

6. William Van Hoose and Sister Marie Kurtz, "Status of Guidance in the Elementary School: 1968–69," *Personnel and Guidance Journal* 48 (January 1970): 381–384.

ance and elementary school counselors.[7] Guidance is viewed as a continuous process of determining and providing for the developmental needs of all students. It is important not so much that the guidance staff actually provide all services necessary to the development of students as that they assume responsibility for the fact that such services are provided. At the same time, the use of the term *elementary school counselor* designates a counselor who works as a member of the professional staff of an elementary school. This counselor is concerned with and accepts a responsibility for working with students, teachers, and parents. The primary concern of the counselor, though, should be the developmental needs of all students.

Educational background

The educational background of the elementary school counselor should contain an educational orientation that includes multidisciplinary studies in such areas as anthropology, economics, education, philosophy, psychology, and sociology. In addition, the counselor should be knowledgeable in the area of child growth and development.

When counseling children of any age, the counselor needs special awareness and knowledge regarding the psychosocial and cognitive development of the child. Several educators have attempted to describe the various stages of a child's development. Piaget, for example, has concerned himself with cognitive development,[8] while Havighurst and others have primarily attempted to describe the tasks involved in psychosocial development. The list that follows shows the steps for psychosocial development, as outlined by Havighurst.[9] He emphasizes that the ages at which individual children will perform these tasks vary greatly; of more importance is the order in which they are performed.

Elementary Age (Age 6–11)

1. Learning the physical skill necessary for ordinary games.
2. Building wholesome attitudes toward oneself as a growing organism.
3. Learning to get along with age mates.
4. Learning an appropriate masculine or feminine social role.

---

7. ACES–ASCA Joint Committee Report, "The Elementary School Counselor," *Personnel and Guidance Journal* 44 (February 1966): 658–661.

8. Jean Piaget, *The Origins of Intelligence in Children,* trans. Margaret Cook (New York: International Universities Press, 1952).

9. Robert J. Havighurst, *Human Development and Education* (New York: McKay, 1953), p. 5.

The school counselor needs a strong background in child growth and development because the counseling of children is limited by each child's cognitive development.

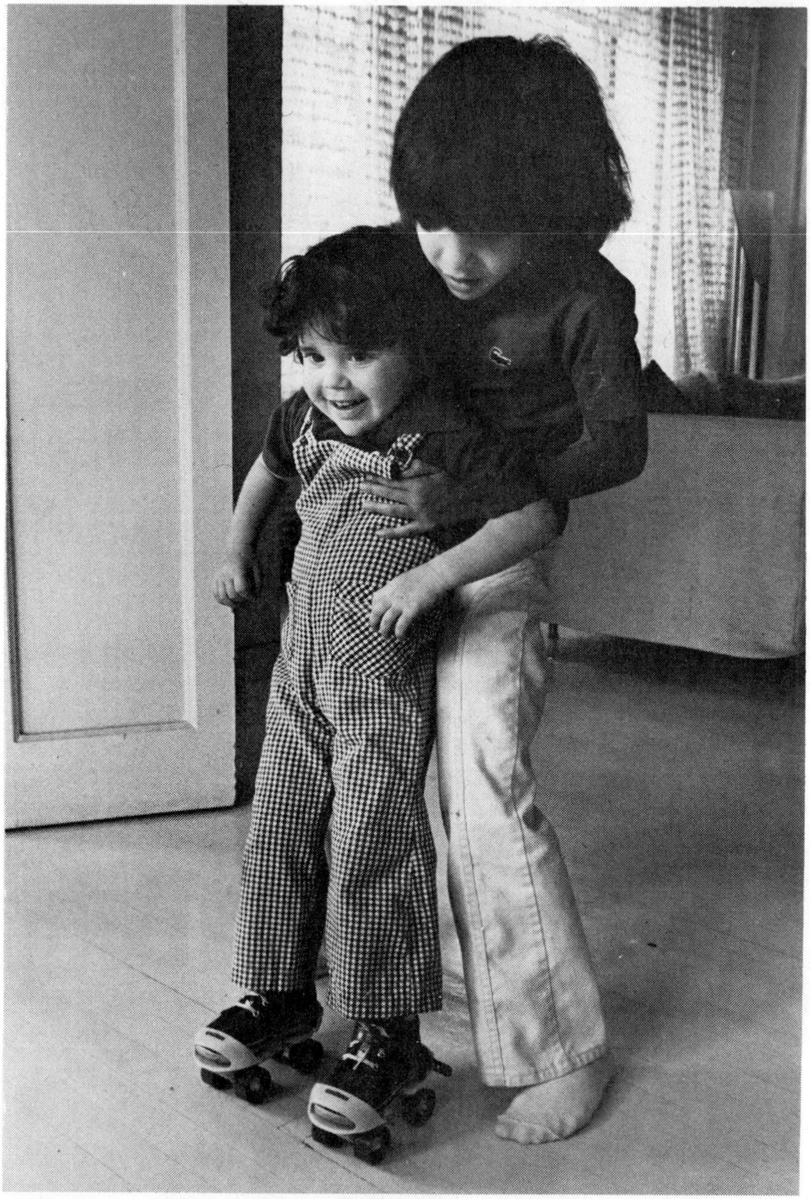

5. Developing fundamental skills in reading, writing, and calculating.
6. Developing concepts necessary for everyday living.
7. Developing conscience, morality, and a scale of values.
8. Achieving personal independence.
9. Developing attitudes toward social groups and institutions.

Areas of responsibility for the school program

A comprehensive elementary school guidance program should include four functional areas in order to provide the needed services for students to grow and develop physically, intellectually, and emotionally.

First, individual and group counseling is provided. It has been recommended that the counselor spend approximately 75 percent of the time working with students in a counseling relationship. Unfortunately, Trotzer and Kassera learned that no more than about 33 percent of the counselor's time is spent in actual counseling of any kind.[10]

Consultation, coordination, and clerical responsibilities

Second, consultation with students, teachers, and parents should be provided. The consultation role tends to focus on the impact of the primary learning environments on the student. Consultation may be provided to students in order to facilitate environmental change conducive to further growth, to teachers in order to design environments that will maximize the potential for student learning, and to parents in order to reduce conflict in the home involving the student.

Third, coordination of the resources within the school and community is another major role of the elementary school counselor. The counselor should function as a liaison between these two major elements, coordinating activities among the various groups who are willing and capable of contributing to the guidance program.

Fourth, clerical functions are a necessary although frequently disliked aspect of the elementary school counselor's job. Trotzer and Kassera (1971) also reported that counselors spend about 20 percent of their time performing clerical functions. This would appear to be an important function based on the amount of time consumed, yet this is time when actual counseling does not get done. Guidance is a relatively new development on the elementary school level. The rationale for moving guidance to the elementary schools after a long period of focus only in secondary and post-secondary education is based on the idea of early detection and prevention of problems. The earlier a problem behavior is identified in children, the more quickly counseling can be provided to resolve the problem. Problems are less likely to fester and worsen if counseling is provided at this early stage.

The functions of the guidance counselor

Although these four functions explicitly define the objectives of most elementary school guidance programs, they do not present the en-

10. James P. Trotzer and Wayne J. Kassera, "Do Counselors Do What They Are Taught?" *The School Counselor* 18 (May 1971): 335–341.

tire picture. There is still much controversy over which of these functions will dominate, and the amount of time that should—or can—be allotted to each function. In fact, the role of the elementary school counselor is still so loosely defined that one result has been that counselors have frequently been expected to perform in many other areas such as change-agent consultant, researcher, trainer of teachers, and psychometrist.

Boy has argued that the most important function of elementary school counselors is to counsel individuals, the very role that is decreased when counselors take on the other above-named tasks. Boy points out that only the elementary counselor is concerned with students' individual emotional health; all other personnel focus their concern on entire groups of students or on those aspects of a student's well-being other than his or her emotional health.[11]

Expanded counseling functions at elementary school level

The longer counselors take to establish a clearly defined identity, the more pressure they will receive to take on new roles. As new roles emerge, there is a tendency for educators to jump on the bandwagon and insist that counselors take on the new roles, resulting in a fractionized image of counselors.[12]

Today, the elementary counselor engages in at least five functions in most settings. They coincide to some extent with the functional areas of most programs. First and foremost, the elementary counselor is engaged in individual and group counseling and guidance activities. The counselor receives referrals from teachers regarding individuals who are having difficulty in school. Some referrals have discipline problems; others have difficulty understanding concepts necessary to educational advancement; and some have difficulties resulting from the home or peer environment. The counselor must decide, in consultation with teachers and parents, the appropriate action to be taken.

In addition to providing individual counseling sessions, the counselor works with the teachers and parents to resolve the student's difficulties. Various strategies may be tried, and strategies may even be varied depending upon whether the counselor is working with teachers or parents. The student, even at a very young age, is encouraged also to play an integral role in planning ways to resolve his or her problems.

To do this, the counselor must be knowledgeable in counseling theories and practices; the appropriate uses of tests and other pro-

11. Angelo V. Boy, "The Elementary School Counselor's Role Dilemma," *The School Counselor* 19 (January 1972): 167–172.

12. H. Maragakes, "A New Image for Counselors(?)," *The School Counselor* 22 (January 1975): 190–193.

fessionals; and information and community resources if effective planning is to be done. As in other areas, there is probably no one theory or counseling technique that works in all situations. Knowing which techniques to use and when separates the professional from the technician.

A second function performed by elementary counselors is that of consultation. Consultation is performed with teachers, parents, community agencies, and others. Sometimes the consultation involves the design of learning environments; sometimes it involves control of student behavior; and at other times it involves changes in the home to effect better living conditions. Recently, consultation is also done in the area of career education. One strategy being used to deliver career education in elementary schools in Michigan is called infusion. Infusion occurs when teachers take existing subject matter objectives and integrate them with career development concepts and objectives. Career development concepts include self-awareness and assessment, career awareness and exploration, decision making and planning, and goal attainment or career placement.

The third function of the counselor is the personal adjustment of students. A lack of personal adjustment at any point in life gives rise to concerns, and frequently, to the need for psychological services. In the elementary school, students are especially vulnerable to the difficulties of spending considerable time with 20 to 30 fellow students. They often need to learn how to share and to cooperate and also how to work independently under the direction of the teacher. When such problems arise, a counselor can spend time listening to the teacher's and the student's perceptions of the situation and then try to develop a strategy that will reduce the problems. Another aspect of the personal-adjustment component is that of gathering the necessary information to serve as a data base for selecting alternative educational experiences, if necessary. This type of assistance is often used as a career-education component, too.

A fourth function is that of public relations. It is critical that the school maintain good relations with the community and parents. Speaking to service clubs and other civic organizations can do much to inform the community of the services available to and being utilized by students. Whenever it becomes necessary for the school to cultivate its relationship with the community, it is helpful to have an ongoing relationship upon which to draw. The principal usually serves as the primary public relations person, but the counselor is a close second. In fact, the elementary counselor also can be an important guide for parents regarding the general development of children. Providing information on normal developmental expectations to parents and responding to views about their children are examples of building a relationship with parents.

Administration, coordination, and planning are also viewed as functions of the elementary counselor, particularly since counselors frequently serve more than one school. Administrative functions frequently include some duties normally assigned to an assistant principal, such as the running of test programs.

Finally, counselors need to know how and where to refer students who may be in need of services which the elementary counselor cannot provide. It is important that counselors be cognizant of the community resources that may be needed by some students, such as community mental health programs, child-guidance clinics, and local social service programs for those in need of medical, nutritional, or basic living services.

All in all, the functions of the elementary counselor are varied and vast. It is the elementary counselor who becomes the major service link between the community, the school, and the individual child.

Middle school or junior high school counselor

The middle school counselor must continue the thrust that was begun by the elementary school counselor. Attention is still focused on the child's early socialization and personal adjustment. Furthermore, the middle school counselor must help the student cope with the impact of physiological and social-group changes that tend to highlight these years. The following tasks have been outlined by Havighurst as age-appropriate for the development of middle school children:[13]

Adolescence (Age 12–18)

1. Achieving new and more mature relations with agemates of both sexes.
2. Achieving a masculine or feminine social role.
3. Accepting one's physique and using one's body effectively.
4. Achieving emotional independence of parents and other adults.
5. Achieving assurance of economic independence.
6. Selecting and preparing for an occupation.
7. Preparing for marriage and family life.
8. Developing intellectual skills and concepts necessary for civic competence.

13. Havighurst. *Human Development*.

9. Desiring and achieving socially responsible behavior.
10. Acquiring a set of values and an ethical system as a guide to behavior.

Functions of the middle school counselor

The counselor in a middle or junior high school usually has four major functions. These include individual and group counseling, consultation on career development, public relations, and administration. In addition, the guidance worker often functions as a referral source and link to other service providers.

The guidance counselor in the middle school or junior high school is necessarily involved in seeing students either on a one-to-one basis or in small groups. The problems that are commonly seen at this age level include:

Middle school counseling problems

1. Peer group problems. Children complain of not having friends and wanting some or feeling pressure from friends to do things about which the student feels uncomfortable.
2. Puberty. Major physiological changes are the norm in children in middle school years. If little or no sex education has occurred in the home or school, the student will be concerned and possibly confused about these changes.
3. Substance abuse. Another issue that frequently confronts middle school children deals with the concern over drug use.
4. Selecting elective courses. Finally, a concern may exist with respect to choosing coursework. Middle school is usually the first time students are given the option to select some courses on their own.

Occasionally, students merely want to talk with someone in order to gain a better perspective on what they are doing and what lies ahead in their futures. Students may need help in integrating certain aspects of their lives. In such instances, the counselor becomes a sounding board. A major role of the counselor in these cases is that of active listener.

The role of consultant on career education has become an increasingly important one as greater attempts have been made to integrate career education into the entire educational curriculum. In this type of counseling, the counselor must shift from the role of dealing with problems that are already present to educating the student to cope with decisions and problems that will arise in the future. Career-education programs are usually planned to help the student learn about the range of choices open to him or her, guide him or her toward information about various careers, and assist the student in making career-related choices at various stages in his or her education. Part of any career-education program involves helping students to choose courses that will be of possible use to them in their future careers or in further education.

The first task of public relations involves making students and parents aware of what is done and what can be done through guidance and counseling. Counselors have often underplayed the services that they can provide. Parents, teachers, administrators, the community, and even students are not knowledgeable about the counseling tools that exist to help them.

The function of administration or coordination is similar to the role played by the elementary school counselor. Time is spent in staff meetings, committee meetings, and in the ever-present and often-increasing paperwork that is required of counselors. Paperwork, in particular, is a frequently maligned task, yet it is often critical to the ongoing delivery of guidance services.

High school counselor

Functions of the high school counselor

The secondary counselor is the "grandperson" of the counseling and guidance profession. The original focus of vocational guidance, and later, of educational guidance, was directed at the secondary school. With the advent of what are considered to be the more "humanistic" components of counseling, emphasis for the secondary counselor has shifted more toward psychotherapy and personal-social counseling. The secondary school counselor specializes in providing counseling to individuals and groups; consultation with parents, administrators, and teachers; career-education services; public relations; administration duties; and referral to other more appropriate specialists. Alternately, these tasks have been described as environmental engineer (Matheny);[14] as human-relations consultants (Pancrazio);[15] as the teacher of psychological growth (Sprinthall);[16] as a contingency manager (Toews);[17] and as an institutional agent (Warnath).[18]

14. Kenneth Matheny, "Counselors as Environmental Engineers," *Personnel and Guidance Journal* 49 (February 1971): 439–444.

15. James J. Pancrazio, "The School Counselor as a Human Relations Consultant," *The School Counselor* 19 (November 1971): 81–87.

16. Norman A. Sprinthall, "A Curriculum for Secondary Schools: Counselors as Teachers for Psychological Growth." *The School Counselor* 20 (May 1973): 361–369.

17. Jay M. Toews, "The Counselor as a Contingency Manager," *Personnel and Guidance Journal* 48 (October 1969): 127–134.

18. Charles F. Warnath, "The School Counselor as Institutional Agent," *The School Counselor* 20 (January 1973): 202–208.

Counseling as primary function

The counseling function of the secondary school counselor is considered the most important professional function. Therefore, considerable time in counselor training programs is spent learning how to counsel individuals. In the past, the tendency existed to consult the counselor only if a severe problem existed for which the student and teacher had no apparent solution. Today, there is a shift to the view that the counselor is available to students who have simple questions, who need directions on where to find certain information or facilities, and who might simply need help in making decisions about classes to take and careers to consider. The counselor, however, remains ready to help with the more severe problems which a student may face.

Counseling services are usually either individual or group. One-to-one counseling has dominated, although within the last decade, considerable emphasis has been placed on increasing the efficiency and realism of counseling through the use of group counseling. (This increasing emphasis has been reflected by the addition of a division of the American Personnel and Guidance Association called the American Association of Specialists in Group Work.) One difficulty with the use of groups, however, is that there are few opportunities in a typical school day to schedule a group of individuals to meet together for counseling.

A closely related function is that of personal adjustment and educational alternative consultation. Counselors in secondary schools often serve as consultants on such issues as drug education and sex education. They may work with school faculty, parents, and the community, as well as the students on these issues.

The continuing concern over career education and guidance among students and parents has been confirmed in several studies.[19] Counselors are being encouraged to play a more active role in this area. Their functions may range from providing occupational information and vocational testing, to conducting job-seeking groups, to planning curriculum activities of a career-guidance nature. This may well be an area where counselors can boost their credibility with school administrators, parents, and the general public.

As was true of counseling at other levels, public relations cannot be neglected at this level. Counseling-oriented programs within schools need to be described to members of the faculty as well as to the community. Involvement in civic clubs, presentations to commu-

19. Richard Gardner, Casimer Heilmen, James Engelkes, "An Evolution of the Career Exploration Programs in Bay Areas and Wayne Intermediate Schools" (East Lansing: Michigan State University, 1976).

nity groups, appearances on radio or television, and coverage in the local press can do much to make the public aware of what is available in this area.

Finally, administration is again a necessary role of the secondary counselor. At this level, administration often involves the scheduling of student classes, arranging for career days, working with advisory committees, and the paperwork that accompanies counseling activities. Another dimension of administration is the establishment and monitoring of a counseling and guidance program within a school.

Finally, when necessary, the counselor should keep in mind the fact that problems will occur that the counselor does not feel comfortable or competent to handle. At such times, other professionals who may more appropriately handle such concerns should be made available. Counselors need to be ready to make referrals to a diverse group of such professionals.

Counselors in other educational settings

Counselors also can be found in vocational-technical schools, community colleges, the armed forces, colleges and universities, as well as a host of other educationally oriented institutions. Counselees in such places differ from public-education students in that they are often older; usually more aware of their strengths and weaknesses; more aware of the world around them; and in some cases, more focused in their need to continue their education.

Multi-role functions of counselors

The role and functions of the counselor in other educational settings focuses on the educational, vocational, and personal and social needs of the students. The student may still need assistance in selecting appropriate courses to complete an educational program, clarifying an appropriate course of study or major area of concentration, clarifying appropriate career goals; and in peer group or sexual relations. In addition, considerable time may be spent on orientating new students to these new environments and on familiarizing them with the available resources. A major area of student concern in the other educational settings is the adjustment period associated with leaving home. Usually, the student is away from home for the first time and must adjust to either a new set of living rules or new freedom and to group living. Concerns related to group living frequently require the assistance of a counselor.

Although considerable individual counseling occurs in these settings, there is also more group counseling. For example, relaxation training, career decision making, job hunting, and other similar programs are frequently conducted in groups rather than in individual counseling.

The training of counselors for most of these settings is quite similar to the training of K–12 counselors. The exception is at major university counseling centers, where a doctorate in counseling psychology frequently is needed to work as a counselor.

In general, counseling services in other educational settings share a problem with K–12 counseling services in that they frequently are not visible enough to the population that most needs them. The counselor has a role to play in promulgating information about the activities of the counseling center in hopes of making more potential counselees aware of the resources available to them.

Counselors in these settings should make selective use of referral resources within the educational or general community. When it appears as though a counselor has insufficient skill or time to work with a counselee, then referral to another counselor should be carefully planned and conducted.

Counselors in community agencies

Since the early 1960s when the Kennedy Administration highlighted the need for more and better services to the mentally retarded, there has been an overwhelming increase in the establishment of service-delivery programs to deal with the problems of these individuals.

In general, counseling has expanded to serve the community at large in the past 15 years. Positions have opened for community mental-health counselors, family service-agency counselors, job-service counselors, business and industrial counselors, marriage counselors, employment-training counselors, pastoral counselors, correctional counselors, counselors for the aging, and alcohol and substance-abuse counselors. Job requirements vary from a B.A. for many positions to an M.A. in others. Many persons only specialize in counseling on the graduate level.

The general duties of counselors in these settings include individual and group counseling and guidance, diagnostic appraisal of the client's past and current conditions, liaison work with other community agencies, record keeping, administration and supervision, and referral.

Expanding need for community counselors

The numerous government-funded programs in this area have been a boon to counseling in noneducational settings. Although some programs exist only for a short time, they are usually replaced by other, similar programs.

More information regarding community counseling programs can be obtained by writing to the appropriate professional association. For information about community mental-health counselors, write the American Mental Health Association, 2 Skyline Place, Suite 400, 5203 Leesburg Pike, Falls Church, Virginia 22041. For information about correctional counseling, write the National Council on Crime and Delinquency, 44 E. Twenty-third Street, New York, New York 10010. For information about marriage and family counseling, write the American Association of Marriage Counselors, 3603 Lemmon Avenue, Dallas, Texas 75219.

Rehabilitation counselors

Rehabilitation counselors are a group of counselors that specialize in providing services to physically and mentally handicapped adults. The services are directed toward returning the handicapped individual to employment upon completion of a rehabilitation program. Services include diagnostic services, evaluation, job training, physical restoration, placement preparation, and personal counseling.

Varied functions of rehabilitation counselors

Many rehabilitation counselors are employed in the joint state and federal vocational rehabilitation programs, which are a free public service. Other employment options include work in hospitals, vocational-evaluation centers, sheltered workshops, community mental-health clinics, state job services, and on employment security commissions.

Graduate rehabilitation-counselor training programs were established initially in 1954 at 10 universities. Currently, there are approximately 85 such training programs in the United States. The training programs place a strong emphasis on counseling and knowledge about disabilities. Often, an internship is part of a master's degree program.

On the job, the rehabilitation counselor is largely responsible for locating and developing referral sources; determining client eligibility for services; collecting, collating, analyzing data; developing individual rehabilitation programs; and career counseling, placement, and post-employment assistance.

Recent research indicates that state rehabilitation agency counselors divide their time roughly into thirds: one-third of their time is spent in counseling and guidance; one-third in planning, recording, and placement; and one-third in professional growth, public relations, reporting, resource development, travel, and supervisory administrative duties.[20]

The referral function is especially important in this type of counseling as a variety of community resources are drawn on to provide help to the handicapped.

Of the existing counseling specialties, rehabilitation counseling has a voluntary program that serves as a certifying body. The Commission on Rehabilitation Counselor Certification was established in 1973 to certify professional rehabilitation counselors. To date, they have certified approximately 10,000 rehabilitation counselors.[21] The American Mental Health Counselors Association also certifies in the mental health counseling area.

Summary

Even though counselors are found in many different kinds of settings, their functions are generally similar. In most instances, the professional counselor assumes responsibility for individual and group counseling, consultations with individuals regarding career education, public relations related to the institution and to the counseling program itself, record keeping, and some administration, although the latter varies in degree with the position. Each specialty, of course, has different ways of approaching each of these areas of responsibility.

Because of the lack of definition in past years of counseling as a profession, many counselors have often assumed other job-related roles, which in many cases have interfered with the major counseling functions. In recent years, though, organizations have begun to define and set standards for the various specialties, and this has resulted in stricter role modeling in counseling.

Regardless of the official organizational definitions of counseling or even written job descriptions, counseling remains very much a humanistic profession, one in which each counselor more or less defines each individual job on a somewhat personal basis.

20. John Muthard and Paul Salomone, "The Roles and Functions of the Rehabilitation Counselor," *Rehabilitation Counseling Bulletin* 13 (October 1969).

21. Roger Livingston, "History of Certification for Rehabilitation Counselors," *Journal of Applied Rehabilitation Counseling* 10 (Fall 1979): 111–18.

Questions

1. What is the difference between a role and a function?
2. What three factors contribute to the role of the counselor?
3. Describe the sources of role conflict in the counseling profession.
4. What are some ways of resolving role conflict? How much control does an individual counselor have over the resolution of role conflict?
5. In what ways is the need to set priorities a conflict for a counselor?
6. How is a profession defined? In what ways does the counseling profession meet the standards set forth in the book for a profession?
7. Describe situations other than educational settings where counselors work.
8. How do counselees in school settings compare with counselees in other institutional settings?
9. What role does record keeping play in the world of the counselor? What are its benefits? What are its drawbacks?

Projects

1. Observe or accompany a public school counselor for one day to learn how his or her time is arranged, what tasks are routinely performed, which areas of the work are most enjoyable, and which ones are not particularly enjoyable.
2. Observe or accompany a vocational counselor in an educational setting for one day to learn how time is arranged, what tasks are routinely performed, and which areas of the work are enjoyable or not particularly enjoyable.
3. Collect as many forms as possible from counselors in two similar settings in different school systems. Compare and contrast the forms for content, ease in filling them out, and the time required to complete them.
4. Invite a recent graduate who has been working as a counselor for no more than two years to discuss his or her expectations of counseling prior to beginning work and after experiencing the realities of the job.

5 Organizational context of counseling

Counselors within an agency frequently meet to discuss individual cases and to work out counseling-management problems.

5 Organizational context of counseling

Introduction

All work is done in some kind of organizational context, and counseling is no exception. The organizational context of counseling is unique, however, because of the special factors that are inherent in the profession of counseling. Counselors inevitably bring their personal identities and philosophies with them as they perform in their professional roles; counseling is too personal an occupation for anyone to do otherwise. Because of the highly interpersonal nature of the work, counselors also must expect a higher level of human interaction and socially coded behavior in their work settings. The very basis of counseling depends on the formation of close, supporting relationships among counselor and counselee as well as among the counseling staff.

In addition, counselors also expect certain satisfactions from their work that set them apart from other professional workers. Part of the job is the satisfaction that comes from helping a person through a particularly difficult period of his or her life, helping someone solve a career crisis, or helping someone to learn a new set of interpersonal skills. Despite these rewards, counselors also anticipate receiving the more traditional rewards of a profession such as a salary commensurate with one's skills, safe and attractive working conditions, and a benefits program, among other things.

In addition to the rewards, counselors share with others in the helping professions a hazard of the business: burnout.[1] This phenomenon, which was mentioned in an earlier chapter, is a growing problem.

All these factors come into play when the organizational context of counseling is discussed. The organizational structures of counseling must cope with the problems that are presented by these expectations and work situations. In this chapter, you will explore aspects of organizational structures that form the context for counseling. You will learn how the structures attempt to adapt to the counselors, and what counselors can do to adapt to the structures. The more counselors know and understand about the structures they work within, the more they will be able to ensure that counseling occurs in a suitable environment. To enhance an understanding of the organizational content of counseling, this chapter contains an overview of systems theory, which has come to dominate the organizational environment in recent years. By understanding how systems work in

Key terms

systems theory
components
inputs
outputs
feedback
internal contacts
external contacts
systems constraints
systems boundaries
systems functions
management-information system
management
system management

1. Charles C. Warnath and John L. Shelton, "The Ultimate Disappointment: The Burned-Out Counselor," *Personnel and Guidance Journal* 55 (1976): 172–75.

general—and how the systems they encounter specifically work—counselors will be better able to adapt to the demands of their work place.

An overview of systems theory

Systems theory has become increasingly popular since World War II. It was during the war that the value of thinking about the interrelatedness of institutions and events became apparent. The Allies needed to mobilize quickly and with a minimum of error at a time when they were unprepared to do so. Inefficiencies were high. Upon investigation, experts soon realized that a process was most effective when it could be successfully linked to a preceding process that had sufficiently prepared the way for the accomplishment of the new process. Even if a process was adequately organized and fueled with appropriate resources, it would still be hindered by a preceding process that had had problems. Each process, in turn, was dependent on other processes. The recognition of a vast array of functioning interdependencies led to the formalization of what is called systems theory.

Recognizing interdependences in systems

Applications of systems theory are practically unlimited. Systems models are used to describe the relatedness and interdependence of the various parts of the human body, many types of business and social organizations, and, as was noted in Chapter 3, a systems model of the counseling process has been developed.[2]

A system can be defined as a set of components that are interrelated by a series of inputs, functions, and outputs. Inputs refer to the people and resources that are available to a system. Functions are tasks and activities people perform using the resources. Outputs refer to the products or accomplishments that result. The interrelatedness of these three components leads to a flow of information, or feedback, throughout the system. Any one system is composed of components, or subsystems, and is itself a component of a larger system, or suprasystem. Counseling is no exception.

Since a system may have many internal and external contacts, there are likely to be many points at which linkages may break down or become inefficient. When information and resources cannot be used efficiently, the system becomes constrained. It is useful to highlight some of the more common systems constraints counselors encounter.

2. Norman R. Stewart, Bob B. Winborn, Richard G. Johnson, Herbert M. Burks, and James R. Engelkes, *Systematic Counseling* (Englewood Cliffs, N.J.: Prentice-Hall, 1978).

Systems constraints on counselors

The limits of boundaries

Berrien, in an excellent overview of systems theory,[3] highlights the problem of systems boundaries. He points out that boundaries are not clear-cut; that is, systems and components may overlap and may be related to various other systems that can cause feedback, or the flow of information back to its originator, to be confusing. The feedback may be conflicting; it may obscure other important information; or it may be irrelevant. For example, the external contacts of counseling systems—funding sources, other professions, the media, the clientele, local neighborhoods, referral sources, and legislators, among others—may have important and sometimes conflicting opinions of any counseling system. The system needs to be aware of these influences. On the other hand, the counseling system should be engaged actively in making sure these external agents have appropriate information with which to form opinions. The ideal situation would be that all external agents have an equally informed and supportive view of a counseling system. This is difficult to achieve. For example, counseling systems that seek to provide residential service to delinquents, prisoners, or retarded people often receive public resistance. Counseling programs for various disadvantaged groups continually expect to justify their existence to the public. Even school counselors have found their existence in jeopardy when school boards are experiencing fiscal problems.

External contacts act as constraints

Warnath's description of the experience of psychologists in Oregon as they achieved licensure is an excellent illustration of how information is interpreted by various bodies and of how the legislative system has an impact on the helping professions.[4] The lesson learned in Oregon by psychologists is particularly instructive for the counseling profession at this time, since there are many efforts underway to provide counseling with the legal sanction of licensure. Although licensure was achieved, it may not be attributable to the ostensible purpose it was purported to serve. Warnath stated:

> *Licensing has little to do with the ideals of counseling or with "helping" as an altruistic enterprise. This is not to say that counselors are wrong in privately believing that a licensing bill will help the public by improving services. Rather, the licensing bill is judged by those who will pass or defeat it*

3. F. Kenneth Berrien, "A General Systems Approach to Organizations," in *Handbook of Industrial and Organizational Psychology*, ed. M.D. Dunnette (Chicago: Rand McNally, 1976), 41–62.

4. Charles F. Warnath, "Licensing: Learning the Game of Politics and Compromise," *Personnel and Guidance Journal* 57 (1978): 50–54.

on its political-economic implications and not simply on the good intentions of the group supporting it.[5]

In other words, counseling systems must carefully establish feedback channels, then monitor the appropriate ones, and finally, be flexible to the additional feedback they provide. There does not seem to be a readily prescribed way of doing this. Much work within the systems theory framework is devoted to this.

Berrien's overview provides some general guidelines. He uses the concept of exchanges to describe the feedback among systems. Exchanges basically refer to the interaction of systems and the information, or impression, each system acquires about the others. These exchanges determine boundaries, which he likens to clouds that seem like firm objects until one is confronted with foggy obscurity upon encountering them.

An exchange occurs when a system receives inputs from other systems. An organization that provides counseling must sort through these inputs to determine what is relevant. This will not be possible unless a counseling organization has set goals for itself delineating the obvious outputs it wants to produce.

The limits of goals

Since counseling systems have many external linkages to account for, it is difficult to come up with goals that satisfy all parties. Many programs attempt to resolve this problem by setting extremely broad goals that have a noble ring to them and thereby cause the program to be widely attractive. For example, programs serving people with various disabilities may purport to rehabilitate these people to gainful employment. School guidance programs may seek to help youngsters enter the mainstream of society. Programs counseling the terminally ill may attempt to provide them with the means of dying with dignity. Most external agents would have a difficult time criticizing such ideals as these publicly. As goals that provide concrete direction for services, however, these statements fall short. Therefore, any program needs to state goals that are useful to people within and without the system and that give everyone a clear sense of the purposes of the system.

Influence of external constraints on goals

These goals should be formed in large part as a response to the needs of the typical clientele the organization serves. Their common needs are a form of input from which goals can be derived. However, a difficult situation can occur because existing goals can color the staff members' perceptions of their clientele's needs. Relevant

5. Warnath, "Licensing," p. 51.

input is sorted by using organizational goals, which may make it difficult to recognize how needs change. This suggests that goals cannot be static, but must always be changing. As feedback is received from the external environment, the system needs to evaluate the information by regarding its relevance to the goals and whether the counseling outputs are actually achieving their stated purposes. It is crucial for counseling organizations and couselors to recognize the complex interdependencies they have with other systems. Mechanisms must be established within organizations and with the external community that will permit an up-to-date and continual flow of information. Additionally, counseling organizations and counselors must have clear yet flexible purposes that are linked to the needs of the people they serve. This requires an understanding not only of clientele but also of other supporting constituencies such as a school board.

Conflicting needs and goal setting

This illustrates the important concept of conflicting needs. For example, it is relatively easy to get in touch with the needs of a counseling system's target population; that is, school counselors continually have access to students. However, the school board also has needs, which often are grounded in law. These social needs may have little in common with those of students, but nevertheless, they are still responsibilities of the school system, and hence, of school counselors, too. Teachers, parents, the local community, as well as the local labor market all make legitimate demands to which the school counseling system must be sensitive. The linkages required to maintain contacts with these groups are not as clear-cut as with students. The necessary relationships may even be threatening. In particular, the school board, parents, and local employers may be at odds with each other.

The importance of change

Even if these linkages are well formed, they cannot be permitted the luxury of remaining static. Boundaries will change; new exchanges will occur; and old ones may become unnecessary. The relevance of any system depends on its sensitivity to the changes that occur in its internal and external environments. Not only is sensitivity required, but adaptability is also needed. Unless a system puts its new knowledge to work in developing appropriate internal changes, it will become irrelevant. This underscores the need for counselors continually to recognize how they might be required to change their ideas and their ways of doing things. They have to be sensitive to the needs of other systems and components, such as the legitimate requirements of their organization's management. In other words, compromises will most often be in order. Ideals should not be forsaken, but often, they can best be approached via a workable compromise. Recognizing the often conflicting interdependencies suggested by systems theory helps counselors understand that many events are controlled by factors beyond their control or accountability. This may be unfortunate, and it does not mean that change efforts should be minimized. On the other hand, a psychological acceptance that things will not always be as one wants them to be may offset some of the frustrations that result from less than optimal circumstances. For example, rehabilitation counselors will have to recognize that society may not be ready and able to accommodate people with certain disabilities with gainful employment. Although counselors should be encouraged to work for change, until it comes, reasonably lowered expectations are legitimate. This awareness will also help counselors set realistic goals for themselves and suggest the exchanges that can best be initiated to accomplish these goals. This, too, should help to increase personal satisfaction for counselors.

Using inputs to create outputs

Another aspect of systems that, if left unrecognized, may also lead to constraints is the obligation of systems to do something with inputs to create outputs. The processes undertaken to convert inputs to outputs are called system functions. In counseling, functions are services designed to achieve outputs, which can include meeting the needs of counselees and fulfilling goals of support groups. When this is the case, a counseling program can expect support. Some outputs may be undesirable from the perspective of the external environment, and opposition may result. Strong, continuous opposition may force a program to shut down. For example, counselors involved with agencies providing counseling about abortions have met with various degrees of public support and opposition. In addition, outputs may be irrelevant to the external environment. The program may be ignored, but over time, this lack of support will stifle it.

Role of systems functions

Basically, for counselors and counseling programs to be successful, services will have to result in useful outputs. This requires an understanding and acknowledgment of all the constituencies of a system. Clientele are rarely the sole constituents. Most counseling programs are supported by public funds, thus, society-at-large is a constituent. The community is often a constituent. In school counseling, the parents are a constituent. Federal and state regulatory agencies often are overseers of counseling programs. These various political constituencies are real, and they make demands that must be addressed in a way similar to those of individual counselees. Services as well as goals must reflect a concern for the needs of this array of external agents. These services must harmonize the needs of individual counselees with the needs of the larger social arena that counselors and counselees interact in. Although counselors are ethically and legally required to prevent their counselees from pursuing the fulfillment of needs through unlawful means, and these limits are easily defined by law, potential violations of social mores and political protocol within the counseling context are not as clear-cut. Counselors will have to consider the potentially short- and long-range outcomes of such violations. For example, should a drug abuser or someone with a history of epilepsy or mental disturbance reveal such information to prospective employers? Many situational considerations will affect how this question is best answered.

The constraint of funding sources

Other constraints affect counseling services. One of these is the funding support of counseling programs. Most programs are dependent in one way or another on public support. When conditions of relative scarcity occur, both competition and evaluation are increased, and less efficient programs are often terminated. To avoid this, counseling programs need to have adequate accountability mechanisms that will provide current, ongoing data on system performance. A management-information system based on the functional interdependence of the counseling program's components could provide knowledge regarding the state of the program's services, as well as the adaptations that may produce the most desired outcomes and thereby help to avoid funding cuts. In times of close scrutiny, such systems have an edge over less efficient programs and programs with no management-information system. School systems currently provide an example of how budgetary and other factors beyond the control of schools are creating constraints for the successful functioning of services—particularly counseling. The last decade has been an uncertain economic time. The energy crisis, as well as inflation and recession, have severely curtailed the ability of school districts to raise funds for programs. In order to manage, cutbacks in services have occurred. Counseling has, at times, been viewed as a nonessential service. Thus, counselors have often been released or reassigned to classrooms, forcing them to forego counseling activities. In the face of this regrettable but real situation, counselors must provide concrete evidence that they are responsive to the needs of students, parents, and faculty. They need to muster the external support of parents and other interest groups so that the appropriate evidence and pressure is brought to bear on school administrators to maintain the counseling service. Coun-

Economics and social demands affect funding

selors need to be aware of the needs of their various constituent groups and capable of initiating suitable action when necessary. Even the act of maintaining this awareness has been faced with constraints recently. Over the past decade, values have changed considerably. People have become more demanding of what they define as their rights. Social institutions have been blamed for maintaining the status quo, thus perpetuating discrimination. Schools have been no exception. Counselors have been accused of supporting existing social mores and institutions and for encouraging people to adapt to them in the face of a tendency on the part of others to push for institutions to adapt to the cultural diversity that abounds in the population-at-large. Thus, counselors are being called upon to shift gears and become social and institutional change agents as well as personal help givers. Counselors have to demonstrate new capabilities in order to gain support from many constituent groups these days. Economics and social demands are two major constraints, but not the only two, that school-based counselors must overcome. The role of the school counselor is becoming more complex all the time. It must if counselors are to maintain their support.

The constraint of referrals

Funds are not the only resources often in short supply. Referrals, too, are a form of resource. Without counselees, there would be no counseling program. Many counseling programs have been forced to compete with other programs for a short supply of potential referrals. The program that first anticipates an impending short supply may be able to establish the firm support of referral agencies so that the flow of counselees is maintained. In Chapter 12 some ways of maintaining referral contacts and relationships are suggested. Ultimately, though, referral agents respond to how appropriate a program's services are and to what the program accomplishes.

Meeting the needs of counselees

Interdependencies among social service agencies

Another system constraint is that rarely can any one counseling program meet all the needs of its counselees. Other community resources will have to be tapped. Understanding that community service agencies form a suprasystem can lead to the proper linkages that are needed to expedite services. Interdependencies are most likely to be acknowledged as worthwhile as long as overlap and duplication are minimized. Again, in Chapter 12 suggestions are made regarding how these links can be forged. It is unfortunate that so many community agencies, even when they have similar goals, seem to be mired in competition rather than in mutual support.

Cooperating programs especially need to develop and allow an informal information network to operate.[6] Even when agencies have agreed to cooperate, too much reliance on formal channels of information can result in additional constraint. Often, formal procedures restrict the flow of information, as when, for example, so much extra paperwork is required to facilitate an exchange of information that employees prefer to forego the exchange entirely. If appropriate information channels can be maintained within and among related systems, uncertainty can be reduced and better decisions made. Berrien suggests that a properly functioning system will provide an environment that creates suitable levels of satisfaction for those performing system functions.[7] This happens when the roles people fulfill meet their needs. A system can meet the needs of individuals within the system only when it fulfills the requirements of its constituencies and receives adequate support.

Linking the components within a system

Baldridge has developed a framework that links the various levels of an organization, or system.[8] He believes it is important to acknowledge that organizations exist in a political environment and that the different levels of an organization can be managed better if understood in their context. He calls his view the political systems perspective. Using a scheme developed previously by Udy,[9] Baldridge describes five components of an organizational system. Transposing these components to fit counseling-related structure, the five levels include:

Political systems perspective

1. The technology and methods of a program—that is, the services a counseling program offers.
2. The individuals involved in the organization, including staff and counselees. Primary importance is centered on the attitudes and morale of these individuals.
3. Staff interactions and communication networks, which more often than not are informal structures.

6. Mark Granovetter, "The Strength of Weak Ties," *American Journal of Sociology* 78 (1973): 1360–1380.

7. Berrien, "A General Systems Approach," p. 51.

8. J. Victor Baldridge, "Organizational Change: The Human Relations Perspective Versus the Political Systems Perspective," *Educational Researcher* 1 (1972): 4–15.

9. S. H. Udy, "The Comparative Analysis of Organizations," in *The Handbook of Organizations*, ed. James G. March (Chicago: Rand McNally, 1965).

4. The formal administrative structure.
5. The relationship between the organization and its environment.

The key to this political systems view of organizations is information. Each level of the system develops its own information pool. Information must flow freely up and down and throughout the system. Any change taking place in one part of the system must be evaluated carefully in terms of how the change will affect other levels. The level developed around the external linkages of the system is crucial as it keeps the organization reality-oriented. Each level of the system affects the inputs of the system, its operations or functions, and finally, its outputs or achievements. Figure 5–1 illustrates how each level of an organization interacts with these typical system components. Many more relationships could be inserted into the figure, but for purposes of simplicity, they are omitted. In addition, probably each counseling program would have its own unique set of relationships. The purpose of the illustration is to show that individuals within each level of a counseling organization have certain capabilities and knowledge that the total system needs in order to carry out all its responsibilities. Much of Figure 5–1 focuses on the skills and knowledge needed by the counselor.

Management: its roles and functions

An important part of the organizational context is the management or administration that directs the institutions offering or supporting counseling services. Counselors need to understand the role and functions of management because managers exert a great deal of influence on the role and functions of counselors. As counselors understand the purposes of management and the typical approaches managers use, they become better able to form more legitimate responses to the demands made upon them by management. An appreciation of the manager's responsibility should serve to temper the harsh criticism frequently directed at him or her.

Three basic tasks of management

Peter F. Drucker in his book *Management* has outlined three basic tasks of management in any organization.[10] The first task is to see that the organization accomplishes the purposes for which it exists. The second task is to maintain necessary levels of productivity for the organization as a whole and for employees. The accomplishment of this task must recognize that employees have goals of their

10. Peter F. Drucker, *Management* (New York: Harper and Row, 1974).

	Inputs	Operations	Outputs
Counselees	Determine which services are needed.	Determine which services to pursue.	Achieve individual goals.
Individual Counselors	Provide skills and experience.	Determine which services to pursue.	Achieved goals and new services result from services.
Counselor Networks	Specify resources needed.	Collaborate to provide effective services	Provide data to document outcomes.
Administration	Acquire basic resources Reflect goals of program through services. and help determine outcomes and new programs.	Set service objectives.	Evaluate outcomes.
External Members of System	Provide essential resources	Monitor services for ethical, moral and professional concerns.	Evaluate suitability of program goals.

Figure 5–1 The relationship between organization levels and system components in counseling programs

own that will be different from the organization's goals. These individual goals may have little to do with the actual work, but they may be dependent on work. Such a goal might include participation in valued leisure pursuits using the income received for working. Managers must recognize that the productivity of individuals may well be mediated by the extent to which their individual goals outside work are accomplished. The linkage between individual goals, individual productivity, and organizational goals is an important one for managers to cultivate. The third managerial task, as seen by Drucker, is that managers must attend to the social responsibilities and the impacts of an organization.

These three tasks of management become more meaningful when they are viewed in the context of systems. They are highly interrelated and must be attended to constantly with an awareness of the reciprocal effects that one task will have on another. It is easy for most people, including managers, to fail to appreciate the interconnectedness of managing systems even though an action in one area will affect the system's entire performance. This ripple effect should not go unrecognized.

Internal and external demands on managerial goals

The goals of an organization may change as a result of both internal and external demands. For example, increased costs, coupled with restricted or static income, may cause a program to reduce or redirect services. Legislative changes can impose an entirely new mission on a program requiring an overhaul of previously effective services. Managers are responsible for being sensitive to the need for change and for initiating mechanisms within the organization to respond to and cope with these demands. As goals change, so should the functions of the system, which, in turn, lead to new outputs. Management must attempt to foresee the type and extent of outputs to ensure that they will not become socially offensive. Employees of organizations also are affected every time goals change, mostly because their functions change. Also, the way that external support groups within the social environment of an organization view its outputs could have a direct effect on how well the organization will be funded, thus affecting its ability to reward its employees. If employees perceive inequities in terms of rewards for their productivity that will hinder the attainment of their own goals, they will, in most instances, limit their productivity or redirect it to more rewarding channels.

Managers monitor shifting goals

Counselors versus management

As employees of an organization, counselors also have to recognize the difficult role administrators of programs have. Counselors must not fail to see that they have responsibility for how well the counseling system works, however, just as administrators do. Administrators will affect counselors, but counselors also must not fail to influence administrators actively. Acquiescence, or even passive resistance, are rarely legitimate counselor responses to management. Management decisions occur in varying degrees of certainty. Counselors can help to reduce the uncertainty facing managers by relating their own needs and insights as individuals and as components of a counseling system to the administration. Counselors must also recognize, though, that other demands may be placed on the system that will cause managers to take actions that may not seem to be the most desirable from the counselors' point of view. Such decisions should be accompanied by a rationale that defines the decision. Counselors can then choose to react by making clear to the administration what the likely impacts of such actions will be for

The need for compromise

counselors and counselees. This, in turn, will form the basis of new information upon which the administration can act. For example, counselors in any setting may perceive that it is important to offer services in the evening to accommodate the time counselees have available. Being open extra hours will obviously entail additional expenses in terms of staff time, maintenance, and utility costs. Management will tend to view the suggestion for evening hours negatively, and counselors should expect this. A likely compromise might be a trial period of evening hours, which might result in increased referrals. If the increase is large enough to overcome increased costs to a reasonable degree, then evening hours might become a standard feature of the program. If the hoped-for referrals do not materialize, then counselors might recognize that evening hours were not as greatly needed as they anticipated.

This process should again highlight the give-and-take nature of being a counselor, or a member of any organization, for that matter. If the process is pursued in good faith, the needs of individuals should be served at the same time that the organization's interests are being served. If an individual's view cannot be reconciled with that of the organization, this will also be recognized at an early point and may even lead to a separation before either the individual or the organization has invested too heavily. What is most essential is the maintenance of open communication channels through which honest and current information can be passed. All system members are responsible for this.

Public versus private organizations

Drucker presents another interesting hypothesis that is relevant to counseling organizations. Although he maintains that managements in all organizations are basically confronted with the same tasks, service-oriented, or public, organizations are different from goods-producing, or private, organizations.[11] The difference stems from the fact that service institutions, many of which have counseling embedded as a function, are financed through public funds rather than by the exchange of goods or services. The result is a different accountability process. A business organization is accountable to the marketplace. Does the public buy what the business produces? That is its measure of success, its accountability, so to speak. The business is linked directly to its consumers. A publicly sponsored service organization, on the other hand, is accountable in a much less direct way to those who use its services. For one thing, the

Role of accountability in service organizations

11. Drucker, *Management*, Chapter 12.

people who make funding decisions are usually not the consumers. In such situations accountability is more likely to become political and is not always entirely economically based. As has been pointed out, the political constituencies of a service organization can be many. Drucker disagrees that service organizations ought to be run as a business. His point here is that business and service organizations are held accountable in different ways, and because of this, cannot be run in the same way. Managers of service organizations may have to be less concerned about fiscal efficiency and keeping budgets and more concerned about the political climate in which the organization is embedded than the manager of a business organization is. This additional requirement complicates the role of a service organization administrator. Those who work in service organizations need to be more sensitive to these complexities and recognize that their own actions can also affect the political standing of a program. Regarding this issue, Drucker makes an important distinction between effectiveness and efficiency: Effectiveness refers to doing the right things, and efficiency refers to doing things right.[12] For counselors and their administrators in service-oriented organizations, determining what are the right things to do and then how to recognize when they are done correctly are problems still awaiting solutions.

An overview of human-service organizations

Levels within the organization

There is much more to a counseling organization than administrators and counselors. Organizations have other roles and functions. The Social Welfare Research Institute issued a report in which it was suggested that human-service organizations have three basic structural levels.[13] These are the policy level, the management level, and the operations level. These levels are somewhat different from the human-service organization levels outlined by Baldridge and are more static and structural. These levels basically reflect the personnel hierarchy of organizations, whereas Baldridge's scheme reflects the fluid nature of organizations and interrelations of all levels. It is important to recognize that both structures may exist side-by-side,

Organization of personnel hierarchy

12. Drucker, *Management*, Chapter 4.

13. Social Welfare Research Institute, *A Conceptual Framework for the Description and Analysis of Human Service Delivery Systems* (Denver, Col.: University of Denver, 1972).

although Baldridge's levels may reflect reality more completely than the formal structure of the Institute report.

The Institute report, however, is an excellent way of obtaining an overview of human-service organizations. The policy level typically consists of a board of governors or directors and top executive staff. Broad policy statements and boundaries are developed at this level, which also sets the general direction for the program. The members of this group must be aware of what is occurring within and without the system. Information channels must be developed to all relevant constituencies and maintained to keep the information current if this level of staff is to make knowledgeable decisions.

The second level is the management level. Members of this level are usually midlevel executives who are not members of policy-setting boards. These managers are responsible for the everyday functions of the organization. They allocate the resources that the policy level part of the structure provides for them, and they determine the specific directions an organization will take, based on the broad policy guidelines developed at the policy level. This management group specifies which tasks the organization will pursue.

The third level is the operations, or service, level. This is typically the largest group of personnel within the organization. Counselors are classified within this group as are support staff such as clerical, paraprofessional, and custodial personnel. It is this group that actually carries out the tasks of the organization on a day-to-day basis.

Collaboration within the levels

All structural levels are responsible for collaborating to carry out several functions; each level has certain tasks to attend to. In order for any organization to be effective and efficient, all levels must do their part to see that the following functions are performed:[14]

1. Problem identification
2. Policy formulation and goal setting
3. Planning
4. Program operation
5. Evaluation

The collaborative role of counselors

Counselors can contribute to the performance of these objectives. To aid in problem identification, counselors can contribute data they receive about counselee concerns. Similar information can also be obtained from referral sources.

14. Social Welfare Research Institute, *A Conceptual Framework*.

During this initial interview, this marriage counselor will explain the services available through her agency and evaluate the needs of the potential clients.

In terms of policy formulation and goal setting, counselors are responsible for helping to make the organization's goals and objectives operational. For example, how well counselors perform their tasks influences how the public judges the success of a program. Being a service provider is a powerful and highly responsible position within the overall organization. All levels of the structure have to recognize this and support counselors as they try to implement goals and objectives.

Competition versus cooperation

Counselors also have an important responsibility for the planning function. They are often the first link in the information chain to many constituent groups. The contact that counselors have with counselees is one source of input that can provide direction for planning. Probably of equal importance are the networks that counselors maintain with peer professionals in other organizations. Often, service programs are competitive even though their humanitarian aims may be similar. Competition can be healthy, but only when there are adequate resources to compete for. Usually, this is not the case in the public-service sector. Instead, survival of programs may depend heavily on cooperative planning to ensure that all resources are used without duplication and unnecessary overlap.[15] Joint sharing of information, knowledge, and resources among counselors and professionals of other organizations can provide program policy makers with credible information that will make cooperative planning a viable activity. This cooperation must occur at all levels of organizational structure, but it is particularly important at the service level, where cooperation has its most real impact. It is at this point that counselees will receive the benefit of any cooperative activity.

The function of program operation is obviously a responsibility of counselors. Other structural levels provide the support for counselors actually to carry out services. Providing services is the basic reason that a program exists. If counselors do not fulfill their obligations, the program is probably not worth maintaining.

Counselors should also recognize the responsibility they have for the evaluation function. Their professional existence may depend on what information program evaluations reveal about the utility of services. Counselors are in an excellent position to indicate what should be evaluated, what constraints should be considered, and what actually transpires during service delivery. No other professional is in a better position to stipulate the parameters of what should legitimately be evaluated regarding a counseling program. Of course, counselors have their own biases. These should be checked by including other parties who do not have a vested interest in the services being evaluated. If counselors do not participate in the evaluation function, however, it is possible that their interests—and those of their counselees—will be overlooked. Chapter 13 explores the evaluative function in much more detail, highlighting the responsibilities counselors legitimately can assume.

The performance of these functions by persons on all levels of an organization depends on a clear recognition of which tasks need to be done and who has responsibility for doing them. Understanding the structure and functions of an organization within the conceptual framework of systems theory permits each member of the organization to see how individual roles and functions can blend. Again, it is important to recognize the need for close collaboration, compromise, and mutual support. Since control must be filtered through all levels of the program in order to perform system functions properly, all groups must recognize that certain decisions or events may not be the most desired from their particular point of view. Yet, when con-

15. Joseph A. Olmstead, "Organizational Factors in the Performance of Social Welfare and Rehabilitation Workers," in Working Papers no. 1, *National Study of Social Welfare and Rehabilitation Workers, Work, and Organizational Contexts,* (Washington, D.C.: Dept. of Health, Education, and Welfare, Social and Rehabilitation Services, 1971), p. 120.

sidering how all levels must meet their obligations and receive their monetary as well as psychological rewards, total satisfaction for any one level is unrealistic and inappropriate. When considering obligations and rewards, equitable distributions among all levels must be sought. The achievement of equitable distributions is probably best accomplished by a joint participation of all groups in planning for the performance of all program functions.

The value of system maintenance

In order for a program to perform its functions in this way, careful system maintenance must be preserved. System maintenance is primarily a function of the management level. System maintenance is analagous to lubricating a machine to keep it running. Managers can attend to system maintenance via the following tasks:

Management responsibility for system maintenance

1. The formulation of objectives and rules for the organization
2. The development of core personnel
3. The formulation of ground rules for working
4. The development of an effective communication system
5. The provision of a high level of motivation
6. The setting of standards of performance

Counselors should expect and support these kinds of activities as they are performed by their managers and supervisors. If a well-functioning system can be maintained, then individuals from all levels of the program will benefit, and ultimately, services to counselees can be highly effective.

The systems view of organizations, as described here, is a highly rational model. The actual structure and functions of organizations often do not have such clear-cut boundaries. Systems theory acknowledges this, but to promote understanding of the model, the uncertainty of boundaries of necessity is understated. In reality, structures, functions, and boundaries of systems will always be in a state of flux. Adaptations will constantly be required if an organization is to maintain its viability.

Need for flexibility

Patton has cautioned against the tendency to adhere too rigidly to the perceived mission of a program, as well as the need to be wary about too forcefully pursuing program goals and objectives.[16] Although statements of purpose, goals, and objectives are desirable and provide a sense of mission, they can be misdirected or even become nonessential as time and events change. Therefore, for a variety of tasks, such as considering program purposes, evolving

16. Michael Q. Patton, *Utilization-Focused Evaluation* (Beverly Hills, Calif.: Sage, 1978).

3 Theories and process

6 The counseling relationship

A counselor needs to listen to the client, his posture and facial expression communicating his genuine concern.

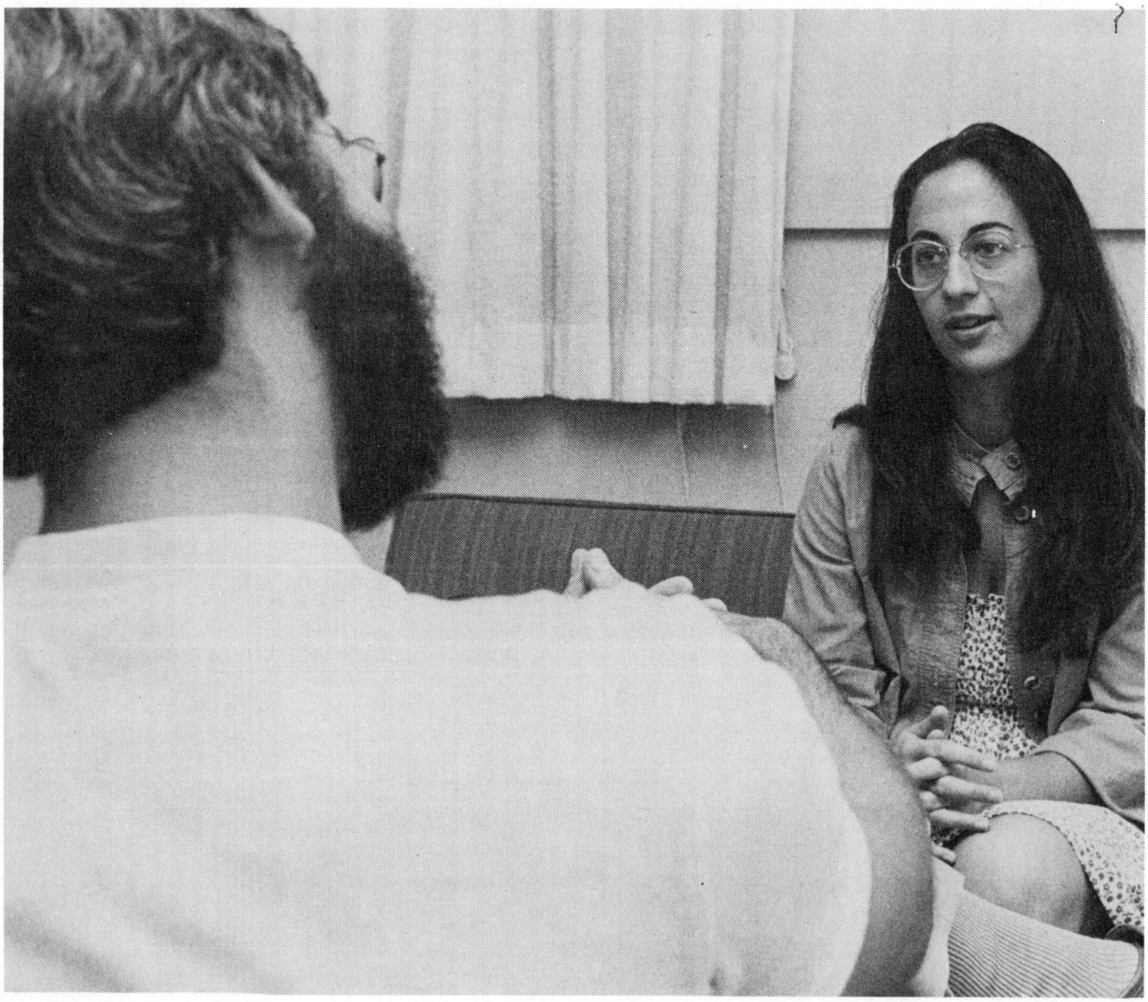

6

Introduction

The counseling relationship is most easily defined as an outgrowth of the interaction between a counselor and a counselee. This does not tell anything, however, about the purpose of this relationship, nor does it indicate how this relationship differs from other relationships between two persons. It is important to consider just what is meant by the counseling relationship. It is difficult, however, to arrive at a consensus concerning its meaning. Probably, if ten counselors were asked to define the counseling relationship, ten seemingly adequate, yet quite different definitions would be offered. Many of the answers would be based on theory or philosophy related to the counseling profession. Yet, individual counselors, because of theoretical and philosophical attitudes, have differing ideas about the development and purpose of the counseling relationship.

Someone observing such a situation might become confused and consider counselors as being somewhat less than professional. After all, if counseling is a profession, shouldn't those who intend to use counseling services have a right to expect some consistent definition of those services? It is important, however, to recognize that counselors—as those in other professions—need to express their professional opinions individually. This, at times, may be confusing to the counselees. We may, then, look to a different aspect of the profession for clarification; that is, the basic shared experience of counselors. They enter the profession because they want to be of social service. On the other hand, it is probably true, at least in most instances, that counselees come to counselors out of some need, either their own or that of someone else. Looked at in this way, some clarification of the counseling relationship can be found in the view that it is a help-giving profession.

Key terms

counseling relationship
communication process
case-study method
counselor attributes
congruence
unconditional positive regard
genuineness
nonpossessive warmth
accurate empathic understanding
skill components
responding skills
initiating skills
additive empathy
personalizing skills
implementation skills

Help-giving role

Intending to help and actually helping may be two different things, though. This possibility has contributed greatly to the confusion surrounding the counseling relationship. Different counselors tend to view the processes and techniques of helping in varying ways. As important as theory is in providing guidance and a framework from which counselors can work, strict adherence to it can lead to very distinct notions concerning how to go about helping. Current efforts toward accountability in counseling can be applauded for the way they demonstrate the link between what the counselee wanted or needed and the services that were provided. Accountability, in part, carries with it the implication that the counseling relationship is one in which help or service is provided as a mutual endeavor. Counselors, then, do not decide what service is to be given or how it is to be given without full agreement and participation from the counselee. This, too, is a fine attitude to have, but the same difficulty exists here as existed in the attempt to use theory to define counseling. Defining counseling as a process carried out with the full participation of counselees in decision making is one thing; carrying this out in practice is an entirely different matter depending on the viewpoints of counselors. And this hardly defines the counseling process, anyway.

Such difficulties in arriving at a consistent definition of counseling seem problematical. It seems that counselors cannot agree on anything. Currently, however, researchers are attempting to apply empirical research methods to reach a better understanding of the counseling relationship. Such study is undertaken with the view that the counseling relationship is a communication process between a counselor and one or more counselees. This helps to clarify the counseling relationship as an interaction between or among people in which information is exchanged with the intention of providing assistance to at least one of the participants. An additional wrinkle has been added recently. Certain types of communication traditionally thought of as possible only when human interaction occurs are now being accomplished by computer and other forms of technology.[1] Technology greatly expands the potential of counseling when used as an aid in gaining and using information.

Several researchers in recent years have begun to delve into the nature of the counseling relationship. The remainder of this chapter explores some of their theories and ideas about this form of communication and its very special meanings.

Carl Rogers and the counseling relationship

The field of counseling as we know it today is a relatively new one. Its history can be traced back only 70 or 80 years. When Carl Rogers began his work during the 1930s, very little was known about the counseling relationship. The writings of Freud and the psychoanalysts who followed in his footsteps were the only materials widely available at that time, and most of what was presumed about the counseling relationship was influenced by Freud's description of the role of the counselor. Freud believed that the counselor should remain a neutral person, even to the extent that the counselee would not always face the counselor during therapeutic sessions. Freud

1. Jack R. Rayman and Joann Harris-Bowlsby. "Discover: A Model for a Systematic Career Guidance Program." *Vocational Guidance Quarterly* 26 (1) (1977) : 3–12.

felt that in order for the counselee to communicate essential concerns, which were often unconscious, the effect of the personality of the counselor had to be removed. If this happened, the counselee also could transfer to the counselor the identity of the person with whom he had experienced major conflict, thereby exposing the counselee's problem to them both. This process was called transference; Freud and other psychoanalysts thought this needed to occur if the counseling relationship were to be successful.

Rogerians versus Freudian counseling

Rogers became uncomfortable with this view of the counseling relationship. He thought Freud's view of humanity was essentially mechanistic and pessimistic, mostly because it grew from a medical model (Freud was a physician), and a "cure" was typically difficult and lengthy to achieve. Rogers saw human nature differently. He was convinced that people were much more capable of overcoming their difficulties if the right conditions existed for them to do so. Rogers began to search for those conditions.

Up until this time, little scientific research had been directed at the counseling relationship itself. The little that was known about it derived from the use of the case-study method, again, a technique of Freud. Independent, nonbiased persons could not observe the process, since such an intrusion would interfere with the transference and ruin the relationship. There was no easy way until very recently to record the activity of counseling in an unobtrusive way. Today audio and videotape recording technology provides much useful information that was not available when Rogers began his explorations. Rogers basically began with the same case-study approach as Freud did, except he started from a very different point.

Rogers came to believe that people had natural inclinations to grow and develop in positive ways, not only for themselves but also in prosocial directions. Society, however, by imposing value judgments on people, inhibited this individuality from being expressed. People learned to assimilate social values and to block the emergence of their own feelings. Rogers saw this as the basis of concern in the counseling relationship. How could counselees become more self-directed so they could experience their full development?

Through his personal observation, Rogers thought possibly that certain counselor attributes were primarily responsible for the change and growth that occurred in counselees. While he was forming his notions (when he was a university professor), the technology that enabled the counseling interview to be recorded was being developed. Rogers was also willing to expose his counseling activity to outside scrutiny. Because of this, he was a major force in originating empirical research related to the counseling relationship.

Unlike psychoanalysis, the nondirective therapy of Carl Rogers gives the counselee a large measure of control in the counseling process.

Rogers felt that the counseling relationship was crucial. He also felt that if positive change were to occur, it had to be demonstrated first in the process of counseling, before the counselee would change in the outside world. This notion coincided with some of Freud's ideas. The difference was that Rogers attempted a more scientific approach than Freud had been able to. Rogers and his researchers began to look for ways to observe and measure the counselor attributes and their effects on counselees. This was no easy task. To understand the degree of difficulty associated with this task, it must be recognized that the field of counseling has not yet developed any precise ways of observing and measuring the variables that surrounded the counseling process.

Rogers first developed a productive research team. By the early 1960s, their research led them to conclude that the most influential factors in counseling indeed were certain counselor attributes. If counselors sufficiently exhibited certain qualities during the counseling relationship, it could be expected that counselees would feel free to experience their true selves without fear of negative social evaluation.

Counselor attributes in Rogerian theory

Basically, four attributes were believed necessary to ensure a successful counseling process.[2] The first of these was called coun-

2. Carl R. Rogers, "The Necessary and Sufficient Conditions of Therapeutic Personality Change," *Journal of Consulting Psychology* 21 (1957) : 95–103.

selor congruence. Rogers felt that this was probably the most important condition. Congruence refers to the counselor's genuineness or sincerity. Rogers learned that counselees needed to know that the feelings of the person who was reacting to them were ones of real concern. Counselees would then be able to see that they could accept another person's feelings about themselves and make a deliberate choice as to whether or not they would accept and integrate the other person's feelings. Counselees would begin to lose their fear of external evaluation.

The second condition was empathy, which referred to a process whereby a counselor attempted to understand the feelings of counselees. Not only was it necessary to identify feelings, but the counselor had to comprehend the significance of these feelings to the counselees. The counselor had to recognize the external and internal situation of counselees, who are often so caught up in their feelings that they lose the ability to grasp the meaning of their experience. Counselors, while understanding counselees' feelings, also need to avoid overinvolvement so they can help counselees see the significance of their emotional experience. Empathy was an attempt on the counselors' part to link counselees' emotional and cognitive processes to ensure proper integration and personality development.

The third condition was unconditional positive regard. The counselor possessing this attribute would accept, without qualification or judgment, the total being of counselees. This would be exhibited by a warm openness. Such a counselor attitude would not be dependent on anything the counselees might do or say, positive or negative. This quality was preferably present, even to the extent that the counselor would refrain from giving counselees interpretations of their feelings. Anything resembling judgment was to be removed from the counseling situation.

The fourth condition was the quality of the counselor's communication of these previous conditions. These attributes had no meaning until they could be perceived by counselees, and perception was dependent upon the quality of the communication. Rogers felt that, given the exhibition of these counselor qualities through open communication, counselees could begin to take a chance on integrating previously unacceptable experiences that had been disruptive and hurtful. If counselees could do this within the counseling relationship, then counseling would be successful. Once this growth process began in counseling, it could be expected to continue, since by nature, people were forward-moving.

Rogers' early research did seem to distinguish various levels of these conditions as offered by counselors, and that higher levels were related to a degree of positive change within the counseling process. This seemed to occur across a wide sample of counselees, including college students and chronic mental patients.[3]

Optimism in Rogerian theory

Rogers' approach to the counseling relationship reflected his optimistic view of human nature. The counselor attributes that he identified as necessary and sufficient in the counseling relationship were soon considered applicable to any kind of helping relationship regardless of the status of the participants. This meant that teachers, parents, job supervisors, or anyone in a person-to-person relationship might engender these conditions and trigger the natural growth process in a counselee.[4] Since these ideas were reinforced by Rogers' apparent scientific findings, they were readily received by many other professionals. Thus, Rogers' contributions were great. He not only introduced an empirical approach to the study of the counseling relationship, but he contributed to the recognition of counseling as a field that could have applications to much of society.

Other research on the counseling relationship

Rogers formalized his notions of the essential conditions in the early 1960s. Since then other researchers have continued to look for the optimum elements comprising the counseling relationship. Although Rogers generated much support within the counseling profession, certain difficulties arose to indicate that he had not completely unraveled all there was to know about the counseling relationship. Rogers believed that counselor attributes were basically qualities that were naturally obtained by counselors through their own personal growth processes. They were not thought of as skills that could be learned in the same way that other skills might be. This notion almost put these attributes beyond the realm of further scientific study, once they had been identified, because these basic attributes could not really by systematically varied for scientific study. This tended to deprofessionalize the role of counselor and risked jeopardizing the counseling relationship itself. Since the essential conditions were not considered teachable, and since anyone in a helping relationship could obtain the qualities through natural growth processes, there was little left to examine or share. But

3. Carl R. Rogers and Rosalind Dymond, ed. *Psychotherapy and Personality Change* (Chicago: University of Chicago Press, 1954).

4. Carl R. Rogers, *Client-Centered Therapy* (Boston: Houghton Mifflin, 1951).

Counselors' values and positive growth

gradually, other questions were raised. If counselors believed that the natural growth process for their counselees was a positive one, and if counselees were to become increasingly more in tune with their essentially good true-selves, how could some counselees choose self-destructive acts, even to the extreme of suicide? Could this be viewed as a positive outcome? Could counselors refuse to make any judgments about such behavior? Could counselors refuse to intervene, thereby preserving respect for counselees' self-directedness irrespective of possible self-injury or injury to society? What if counselees had educational or vocational concerns that only reflected a lack of information? Should counselors refrain from providing any direction, allowing these counselees to "grow" toward finding the right information? Would counselees become impatient with counselors in these instances? It was obvious that more study of the counseling relationship was needed.

Truax's and Carkhuff's research

Two researchers originally on Rogers' team became prominent in the continued research of the counseling relationship. These men were Charles B. Truax and Robert R. Carkhuff. They continued to research the essential conditions needed by a counselor. Truax and Mitchell summarized the results of this research in 1971.[5] They stated that counselors were indeed the major determiners of the quality of the counseling process through the conditions they established within the relationship. This notion is the same as Rogers' thus far; however, differences began to develop. Additional research indicated that just as counselors could help counselees grow through counseling, counselees could also be damaged and could actually regress through counseling. Such a finding increased the professional responsibility of all counselors. It had been acknowledged previously that in some instances counselees did not improve, yet few counselors admitted or recognized that some counselees actually could be hurt. That there was a risk factor in counseling was an uncomfortable notion to accept.

Risk factors in counseling

Another new finding, mainly through the research efforts of Carkhuff, indicated that although counselors were most responsible for the direction of the counseling relationship, counselees also could contribute conditions that affected counseling. Certain counselee conditions, such as a willingness to disclose personal information,

5. Charles B. Truax and Kevin M. Mitchell, "Research on Certain Therapist Interpersonal Skills in Relation to Process and Outcome," in *Handbook of Psychotherapy and Behavior Change*, ed. A. E. Bergin and S. L. Garfield (New York: Wiley, 1971), pp. 299–344.

had an impact on the behavior of counselors. This notion also added a degree of new responsibility for counselors. Now they had to monitor closely how they were being controlled by the counselee. They had to take steps to maintain their professional role within the relationship.

Extending the meanings of Rogerian terms

Truax also relabeled Rogers' earlier conditions in a way that indicated slight changes in perspective. Congruence was referred to as genuineness, since it seemed the essential ingredient was an honest posture. Unconditional positive regard became nonpossessive warmth. This change reflected the obvious difficulty counselors had in accepting all the ideas and behaviors of some counselees, yet despite this, counselors could still show a genuine caring attitude and acceptance of the counselee as a person. Finally, empathy was referred to as accurate empathic understanding, which reflected that this condition was dependent on the quality of communication in the counseling relationship. If this condition were dependent on communication, then a subtle, but important, idea might apply. Communication is a process that is observable and open to scientific inquiry. It should be possible to isolate elements of communication in counseling, vary them, and find out how they affect counseling. This was a very specific but important extension of Rogers' idea of communication. The possibility of manipulating communicative elements suggests that they are discrete entities that might be possessed to varying degrees. If appropriate levels of these degrees can be determined, there should be no reason that counselors could not learn these communication elements to further the amount of empathic understanding in their counseling. Thus, this one condition at least became not so much a counselor attribute acquired through a natural growth process, but a skill learned from a deliberate training process. The success of viewing and isolating one skill component of the counseling relationship had great significance for the field of counseling. This will be explored more fully at a later point.

Truax noted other knowledge that had been gleaned by research. Genuineness seemed to be the condition that came first in the relationship. He also indicated that at least two of the conditions, in any combination, had to be present in the counseling relationship before progress could be expected.

Carkhuff made major attempts to extend the concept of skills in the counseling relationship.[6] He presented a rationale from his own

6. Robert R. Carkhuff and Bernard G. Berenson, *Teaching as Treatment: An Introduction to Counseling and Psychotherapy* (Amherst, Mass.: Human Resource Development Press, 1976).

and related research findings that described the important components of counselor behavior in the counseling process.

Carkhuff began with the conditions first described by Rogers. Carkhuff preferred to view them as skill components, however, rather than as counselor attributes. In so doing, he greatly changed the complexity and uniformity of their arrangement in the counseling relationship. He identified skill areas, each containing a composite of interrelated subskills. The first of these areas were the attending skills. Carkhuff included both physical and psychological attending.

The attending skills

In physical attending, counselors arrange themselves and their physical surroundings in a way so that distractions are at a minimum during the counseling interaction. The counselor sits or stands facing the counselee, with good posture, possibly leaning toward the counselee to minimize the aspect of distance in the relationship. The counselor pays strict attention to the counselee and does not doodle or fiddle with objects while he or she talks or thinks. This is meant to convey respect for the counselee.

Psychological attending shows the counselee that the counselor has indeed been paying attention. Here, empathy begins to be important as the counselor attempts to reflect back to the counselee the content and feeling tone of the counselee's expressions. Reflecting, summarizing, and allowing the counselee time to discuss and explore without interruption indicates that the counselor is listening and attempting to understand. The counselor resists distractions and maintains good eye-contact with the counselee. Again, respect, empathy, and nonjudgmental acceptance are evident during the counselor's attempt to attend in the counseling relationship.

The responding skills

The next general area of skills that Carkhuff identifies are the responding skills. Included here are the counselor's attempts to be an especially good observer of all the actions, expressions, and feelings of the counselee. The counselor has to learn to respond to very subtle counselee communication—communication that in most everyday instances would go unnoticed. The counselor needs to pay particular attention to all the outward behaviors of the counselee such as hand gestures, facial expressions, posture, and other often overlooked behaviors that can communicate more than the words of the counselee. The counselor needs to observe what kind of relationship exists between what a counselee says and what he or she does. The counselor needs to understand the counselee through observation. Understanding, in itself however, is not worth much un-

Need for accurate empathy

less it can be communicated to the counselee by the way the counselor responds. The chief skill in responding is accurate empathy. Given that the counselor understands the relationship between the verbal content of what the counselee has said and the feelings that have been expressed by his or her actions, the counselor must reflect these back to the counselee as fully as possible. If a counselor cannot show a counselee an understanding of what has been said and shown, there is a good chance the counselee will perceive this as incompetence or lack of care and respect. He or she may choose either to leave counseling or cease to make a serious effort. In this sense, any lack of being able to communicate an accurate understanding of the counselee's situation can be damaging as well as unhelpful. This is some indication of the responsibility counselors must feel as they attempt to provide service.

The initiating and personalizing skills

Role of additive empathy

The next skill areas are referred to as initiating skills and personalizing skills. Initiating skills begin the strategy phase within the counseling relationship. The counselor attempts to initiate the counselee into the learning process. Especially essential at this time is the skill referred to as additive empathy. The counselor attempts to understand the counselee's situation to an even greater extent than the counselee does. It is at this point that the counselor recognizes subtle but recurrent themes that seem to pervade even what are seemingly unrelated concerns and events in the life of the counselee. If the counselor is capable of communicating this new awareness to the counselee in a nonthreatening way, the counselee also can come to new levels of awareness and make conscious efforts to deal with the underlying theme. It is also important that the counselor help the counselee continue this deeper level of self-exploration, which can lead to increased understanding. This is the process of personalizing. If a counselor can teach this way of thinking and exploring, then the counselee has a good chance of becoming free of the need for a counselor's special help. The ultimate strategy of the counseling relationship is to teach this learning process so that the relationship is no longer necessary as the catalyst to the counselee's growth. Once a counselee has formed a clear image or model that overlays many concerns, the counselor then needs to help the counselee learn how to develop a model showing what kind of person the counselee would like to become. The skill involved in doing this is the ability to develop goals. Again, the counselee needs to learn how to set goals in order to gain independence from the counseling relationship.

In some instances, counselees fail to explore their hidden levels of awareness, or they actively avoid what they find there. Also, they may superficially ascribe to a goal but offer many excuses for not being able to pursue the goal. At this point, when all attempts to get the counselee to act by using empathy fail, counselors may choose to confront the counselee with the apparent lack of progress. This is a difficult counseling skill and Carkhuff recommends that counselors use it as a last resort when empathy fails. Confrontations that are too strong can give the counselee an excuse to quit counseling. It must be done gently, never forcing the counselee into an either–or position: Counselees must be allowed the room to make decisions and not feel they are being forced in one direction or another. If confrontation is necessary, the counselor should do it questioningly and in an open-ended way.

The implementation skills

The final skill area identified refers to that part of the counseling relationship that specifically deals with the implementation of the learning process toward the goal of the counselee. In essence, if the counselee can attain the more advanced ways of exploring and communicating, then the prerequisite skills have been taught successfully by the counselor. What remains to be done is to teach specific skills in decision making and problem solving that will lead the counselee to the attainment of the goal specified during counseling. And, as with other skills passed on to the counselee by the counselor, it is hoped that the problem-solving and decision-making skills will free the counselee from dependence on the counseling relationship.

Carkhuff has developed training programs to teach these skills; his writings describe them in detail.[7] These have evolved over time to include not only additional types of skills, but also to emphasize a competency-based rather than a conceptual learning process. Training that focuses on specific behavioral elements seems to provide trainees with more effective discrimination and communication skills than training that emphasizes a conceptual approach.[8]

---

7. Robert R. Carkhuff, *Helping and Human Relations*, 2 vols. (New York: Holt, Rinehart & Winston, 1969). Robert R. Carkhuff, *The Development of Human Resources* (New York: Holt, Rinehart, 1971). Carkhuff and Berenson, *Teaching as Treatment*. Robert R. Carkhuff and William A. Anthony, *The Skills of Helping* (Amherst, Mass.: Human Resource Development Press, 1979).

8. Robert W. Cash and Clara K. Vellema, "Conceptual Versus Competency Approach in Human Relations Training Programs," *Personnel and Guidance Journal* 58 (1979): 91–94.

Many others have developed related yet distinct research and training approaches that weave Truax's, Rogers', and Carkhuff's thread into a complex tapestry. Recent research suggests that with verbal skills alone, there exists a wide diversity of potential types of communication with which a counselor should have facility.[9] Among them are the ability to encourage, provide information and guidance, ask questions, interpret, self-disclose, and use silence judiciously. Other skill inventories also have been researched and eventually packaged into training programs. These have been generally well received[10] and, taken together, they provide a good beginning point for clarifying important elements of the counseling relationship.

The counseling relationship as a learning process

The evaluation of strategies

Although most counselors acknowledge the necessity for having skills in interpersonal relations, such skills are not limited to counselors, nor can a counselor be identified as a professional purely on the basis of having certain skills in interpersonal relationships. Furthermore, the skills themselves are not the only necessary and sufficient conditions to produce change. Krumboltz and Thoresen[11] acknowledged the probable necessity of establishing these skills in the counseling relationship in order to create a climate conducive to change; however, they point out that counselees desire changes in many different directions, and it is too simplistic to expect that one basic strategy can cope with the complexities of a person in today's world. Originally proposed by Paul,[12] Bergin also voiced this same concern when he wrote: "What treatment, by whom, is most effective for this individual with that specific problem, and under which set of circumstances?"[13]

9. Clara E. Hill, "Development of a Counselor Verbal Response Category System," *Journal of Counseling Psychology* 25 (1978) : 461–68.

10. Lawrence M. Brammer and Douglas Allmon, "Training Packages," *Personnel and Guidance Journal* 55 (1977) : 612–18.

11. John D. Krumboltz and Carl E. Thoresen, ed. *Behavioral Counseling: Cases and Techniques* (New York: Holt, Rinehart, 1969). John D. Krumboltz and Carl E. Thoresen, ed. *Counseling Methods* (New York: Holt, Rinehart, 1976).

12. G. L. Paul, "Strategy of Outcome Research in Psychotherapy," *Journal of Consulting Psychology* 31 (1967) : 109–18.

13. Allen E. Bergin, "The Evaluation of Therapeutic Outcomes," in *Handbook of Psychotherapy and Behavior Change*, ed. A. E. Bergin and S. L. Garfield (New York: Wiley, 1971), pp. 217–70.

Empiricism and counseling outcomes

Notice the attitude that lies within this fundamental question. It is one of empiricism, more or less a "first show me, and then I'll accept it" pose. The question also acknowledges the diversity of individual differences and events. It is concerned with the application of the scientific process to the study of counseling. By faithfully and carefully applying this process to what happens in the counseling relationship, it can be expected that knowledge will accumulate indicating how to make the relationship more effective. Also implicit in this question is the important value that all decisions occurring in the counseling relationship will be made from as much empirical evidence as possible rather than on value judgments, particularly those of the counselor. As humans interact, it is obvious that there is no way that values can be excluded entirely. If counseling is to achieve professional status, however, counselors are going to have to demonstrate that what they do is based on more than just what they believe. Society has supported counseling in the past without asking too many questions. It is all too apparent that this is no longer the case. Currently, the field of counseling is being burdened with the demand for accountability. It will be unfortunate if the field of counseling reacts only to an external threat rather than to a self-motivated, internal desire also to become accountable in the immediate confines of the counseling relationship.

The role of behavior modification

The early exponents of this scientific approach to defining the counseling relationship were often associated with the theory of behavior modification. This theory attempts to uncover the basic process of learning and performing that underlies all human experience and endeavor. This learning process can then be applied to any counseling concern. Many counselors, however, believed that early formulations of this approach seemed to be too mechanistic. Opponents of behavior modification thought that this theory suggested that counselors only be concerned with outward, observable kinds of behavior. Behavior modification seemed to threaten the humanistic concern that counselors felt was necessary when counselees revealed their most private feelings and thoughts in the counseling relationship. Another criticism is that thoughts, feelings, and personal concerns are difficult to observe and deal with scientifically as the behaviorists were suggesting. In short, since this behavioral approach did not seem to permit counselors to deal with the very personal concerns of their counselees, it was rejected by many. In fact, for a while, any attempts at studying the counseling relationship systematically using a scientific approach were often associated with the behavioral approach and disregarded as being too simplistic and mechanistic to be of significance to the counseling relationship. Counselor attributes were still viewed as more important than any application of technique.

Combining behavior modification and humanistic concerns

Fortunately, as the emotional reactions on both sides of this issue have given way to cooler perspectives, a rapprochement has been proposed that encompasses not only the humanistic concern for the total being of the counselee, but the equally valuable concern that the counselee be given the most effective service based on the best available scientifically derived evidence. The exponents of this new accord are Thoresen and Mahoney[14] and Craighead, Kazdin, and Mahoney.[15] The conditions proposed by Rogers are not discarded by those who apply behavior modification techniques.

Certain assumptions lie behind this expanded view of the counseling relationship. First, it appears that counselee change is the overriding goal that encompasses many, if not all, of the intended outcomes of the counseling relationship. Particularly if it is permanent, change is the chief indicator that learning has occurred. Second, in order to work toward learning or change, one must accept that learning occurs lawfully; that it is not governed by chance. How people learn and change, then, is subject to observation, prediction, and control. If it were not, then applying the learning process in counseling would be nothing more than capriciousness.

Although not everything is known about how people learn, the learning process can be outlined in rather general terms. Care must be taken, however, that counselors individualize the process. They must not assume that the same specific elements of one successful application of the process can be generalized to all situations. Failure to individualize is contrary to the empirical value system of those who have proposed this view of counseling as learning.

The process begins with a mutual agreement between counselor and counselee that some type of change is needed. The need, as it currently exists, must be carefully assessed. It is then important to establish mutually what the desired outcome of the counseling relationship will be. The outcome must be expressed in terms that are objective so that they can be observed and measured. Once the outcome is clearly in mind, the counselor and counselee can de-

14. Carl E. Thoresen and Michael J. Mahoney, *Behavioral Self-Control* (New York: Holt, Rinehart, 1974).

15. W. Edward Craighead, Alan E. Kazdin, and Michael J. Mahoney, *Behavior Modification* (Boston: Houghton Mifflin, 1976).

velop the strategies that will make the learning process successful. The success of any strategy is dependent on a careful assessment of the counselee in regard to the expressed outcome. The counselor also needs to evaluate how the counselee has best learned in the past.

Specific strategy techniques can be derived from many sources. The scientific learning-process approach asks only that the selection of techniques be based on empirical evidence that supports the viability of the technique. If there are several possibilities, then the one that is easiest or most simple should be the technique of choice. It is important to point out that no one theory of counseling is proposed as having a monopoly on best describing how people learn. No assumptions should be made that the learning process differs for a person's outward, observable behaviors and the person's internal thoughts, feelings, and hopes. Even private experiences can be viewed as behaviors, and the same process can apply even though the techniques may differ. The elements of the process may change; the process remains the same.

Summary

The concept of the counseling relationship is a growing and developing one. Research surrounding the many variables linked to this relationship continues today. Although the future shape of the counseling relationship will be dependent on the course of this research, certain basic ideas have and probably will continue to remain constant. This seems reasonable since many of these basics have already been with us for quite some time.

The work of Carl Rogers has contributed much to current notions of the counseling relationship. Counselors have learned that basic to the concept of respect for the counselee is the necessity of providing a climate in which the counselee is free to participate in the decision-making and goal-setting process. Rogers also championed the potential of counselees to grow and assume more responsibility for themselves.

Rogers' theories are being refined today by counselors and researchers who are developing strategies to enhance the self-management capabilities of counselees. Among the prominent researchers are Truax and Carkhuff, who have expanded and further developed Rogers' theories. Carkhuff has made a major effort to develop new categories with broader definitions. These include attending, responding, initiating and personalizing, and implementation skills. Krumboltz and Thoresen, as well as Paul and Bergin, have established the necessity to use skills to ensure the success of the counseling relationship, but they have also done research that shows that a variety of strategies beyond these skills are also necessary. Important researchers who have used behavioral modification to define the counseling relationship include Thoresen and Mahoney, and Craighead, Kazdin, and Mahoney.

Questions

1. Describe the role of the counselor in Rogers' theory.

2. What four attributes did Rogers feel were essential in a successful counseling relationship?

3. Describe the value of nonjudgmental behavior from a counselor.

4. What do you see as the ethical problems related to confidentiality and the occasional need to intervene on a client's or society's behalf?

5. What were the basic premises of the Truax and Carkhuff research? How did they change Rogers' research?

6. What are the attending skills?

7. What are the responding skills?

8. What are the initiating and personalizing skills?

9. What are the implementation skills?

10. Can a counselor work well by adopting one theory and using all its skills to the exclusion of other skills and theories? Give reasons for your answer.

11. What factors should a counselor take into account when planning a counseling strategy?

Projects

1. Invite a counselor to discuss the factors that prompt a change in strategy or techniques.

2. Interview a counselor to obtain his or her views of values in counseling. Find out how these values may have changed since the counselor began working.

3. View a film of a counseling session to see the ways that the counselor demonstrates or fails to demonstrate the traits described by Rogers.

7 Cognitive counseling approaches

Behavioral counseling helps individuals to erase phobias, such as the fear of flying, by involving them in a real situation.

Introduction

The importance of theory

Before discussing specific theories, it is important to understand the ties between individual counselors and the theories they espouse. Theory is perhaps more important in the helping professions than in other professions because it has such a direct relationship with the actions that are subsequently taken by counselors and other, similar workers.

Counselors do not approach their everyday activities without having some philosophical or conceptual frameworks that help them organize their work. When they have been carefully developed and integrated, such guiding principles are often referred to as theories. There have been some noteworthy efforts to formulate theories that provide the field of counseling with a purpose and set of procedures for accomplishing its goals. Counselors, after studying these theories, often integrate all of one theory or parts of many into a framework that directs them in the decisions they make and in the methods of counseling they use. The preferences of counselors prompt them to choose these theoretical notions in unique ways. Because, like all people, counselors are different from one another, theories are rarely, if ever, adopted in a pure form. Although ascribing to the same basic theory, individual counselors may not resemble one another much in how they actually perform their counseling duties. This is not necessarily a bad thing. Although theory-builders have attempted to construct complete models of human nature and the ways that people change, they have not reached the point of having studied and understood all of the many variables that affect people. If this is the goal, it is doubtful that these theories will ever be complete. Although one has to assume that human nature is predictable in order to attempt theory-building at all, as time passes, many new ideas develop. What was understood and controlled yesterday can become distorted and unpredictable tomorrow. It is important, therefore, that counselors never be satisfied with theories, even their preferred ones. They must realize that the only constant thing about theory is the need for revision and updating.

Key terms

action-oriented theory
insight-oriented theory
cognition
trait-and-factor approach
rational-emotive approach
belief system
behavioral approach
respondent learning
operant learning
unconditioned stimulus
conditioned stimulus
extinction
circular reasoning
reenforcer

The nature of theories

Incompleteness of theories

Since theories are so incomplete and in constant need of review, counselors often question the value of developing, studying, and using them. Such criticism, although it appropriately points out the problem, overlooks the tendency of people to order and control their lives. Theories are merely extensions of every individual's efforts to order and control. Theories can be viewed as composites of many people's experiences. Even persons who deny any theoretical allegiance still try to organize their ideas and activities in some systematic way. Since theories are genuine attempts directed toward counselors to help them become more effective, it seems presumptuous for any one counselor to minimize the need to examine carefully the theories that have been developed.

The evaluation of theories

Given that theories are legitimate for the field of counseling, there remains the problem of evaluating them. In part, this is due to the nature of theory. They are usually made up of many principles, which, when combined, attempt to explain how people become what they are. Theories can best be evaluated by looking at the discrete parts and then viewing how well they fit together. Counseling theories attempt to describe what people are like, how they became that way, and how they can change. It should be possible to analyze theoretical principles into such component parts. One criterion then, for evaluating theory, is to assess its completeness.

Theories attempt to explain reality. Each person experiences reality as it is for him or her. This means that each counselor has personal experience with which to evaluate the merits of theory. A counselor should ask this question of any theory. "Does this theory adequately describe my experience?"

Since theories should include principles that suggest ways that people can control change in their lives, tests or experiments should be suggested that can provide evidence as to whether the predicted change has actually occurred. This process is often achieved as hypothesis testing, and it can be implemented by formal research procedures. Any theory should be able to suggest experiments that can be tested in an observable way. Data of such a formal nature need to be collected and presented as evidence for the validity of the parts of the theory. Even though rigorous scientific methods are applied in the accumulation of such data, it must be remembered that proof can never be finally obtained for any theory, in part or whole, related to counseling. This is the nature of theories related to human behavior. Theoretical notions exist as probabilities and not as facts.

Theories should also be evaluated by how well they simplify the knowledge available about people. Life is complicated enough without the presence of unnecessary data. Therefore, those principles and theories that simplify—without becoming simplistic—are to be preferred to those that contain extraneous material.

A final criterion, important but often overlooked in the evaluation of counseling theory, is the clarity with which the ultimate outcome of counseling is presented by the theory. As was indicated in the discussion of the counseling relationship, counselors differ widely in how they view counseling and in what they hope to accomplish. If a theory does not clarify the purpose of counseling, it is severely limited. Any serious theoretical work must contribute to the effort to define just what counseling is and what people can expect to gain from it.

Classification of theories

There have been many attempts to classify theories according to overriding principles that describe types of counseling. An early classification dealt with the level of counselor control recommended by each theory. Theories were compared on the basis of whether they advised counselors to be directive or nondirective in their counseling activity. It is now recognized that all counselors, regardless of theoretical orientation, use controls, some less obviously than others perhaps, but there seems to be no possible way for a counselor to be nondirective.

Another classification attempts to sort theories according to how people learn to change. Do people learn by first understanding what motivates their current behavior? Or do they learn to change by practicing new behaviors under the guidance of a counselor regardless of their past and current behaviors and motivations? Those counselors who recommended behavioral practice whether or not it was accompanied at first by understanding were referred to as action-oriented, and those who thought that understanding must come before a behavior change were classified as insight-oriented.[1] This still seems to be a useful classification.

A third system reflects the relative emphasis that a theory places on cognitive and affective processes. Some theories place a lot of emphasis on the role of cognition, that is, the process of rational thinking, in the growth and development of persons as opposed to the role of the affective domain, i.e., the often unconscious and sometimes conscious emotions.

Shifting nature of theories

This method will be discussed primarily in this book. This chapter mostly describes cognitive theory, which closely parallels action-oriented theory. Chapter 8 focuses on the theories that are affective and insight-oriented. Regardless of the classification system used, theoretical concepts exist on a continuum rather than as separate categories. These theoretical classifications are by no means meant

1. Bufard Stefflre and Kenneth B. Matheny, *The Function of Counseling Theory* (Boston: Houghton Mifflin, 1968) p. 23.

to be interpreted as either-or propositions. In this book, an attempt will be made to place each theory along a continuum. To force any theory into categories is a simplistic approach to the theory and to reality of counseling. The theories that have been selected are ones that have a history of influence in counseling, as well as having been researched. They also are currently used in the field of counseling. They provide a perspective on where counseling has been, where the mainstream is, and what areas are likely to be developed in the future.

Trait-and-factor approach

Background

The person most often associated with the trait-and-factor theoretical approach is E.G. Williamson. Williamson began his work at the University of Minnesota and remained there throughout his working career. The trait-and-factor approach also is referred to as the Minnesota approach.

Williamson traced the trait-and-factor approach back to the late nineteenth and early twentieth centuries when psychologists first began to recognize and classify individual differences by systematic study. The basic approach, which was developed then and continues to be fundamental today, is the attempt to measure behavior in terms of characteristics, or traits, and use the measures for comparisons to group averages. Most typical of such measurement is the collection of data in a highly structured format, such as a written examination or other structured activity that lends itself well to standardized observation and interpretation. Aptitudes, interests, and personality characteristics are frequently assessed by such examinations.

The theory

Underlying this approach is the idea that what a person does and the traits that a person exhibits reflect the characteristics of that person according to a basic structure common to all people. People differ from one another only by matter of degree, that is, by having more or less than the next person of some characteristic. Therefore, the development of measurement approaches and statistical methods is a central element of the trait-and-factor theory. Without data collection and analysis, the theory could not be advanced.

Williamson has acknowledged that most counselors use the measurement methods of the theory without an explicit knowledge of the theory itself.[2] Counselors tend to abstract the measurement-and-analysis portions without integrating the information they find in the way that the theory suggests. It is important, however, to understand the methodology of the theory in its proper context in order to evaluate its use for counseling fairly.

Williamson began by measuring traits that were related to educational and vocational endeavors. He was concerned only with applying this theoretical process to the educational system. Even today, the trait-and-factor theory as it has developed in the counseling profession is most often used in this way. It cannot be taken to task for not being applicable to a wide variety of counseling situations, since the main body of writing and research that has evolved from the theory has been in the vocational-educational context.

Importance of measurements to trait-and-factor approach

Williamson and other contributors to this approach concentrated on measuring individual attributes and comparing these measures to the average score of a large group of people with the same attributes. This comparison could help the counselor and counselee make decisions based on the relative standing of the counselee to this group. For example, a counselee confronted by career decisions might wish to consider only those occupations in which his or her interests and skills fell at least in the average range of workers in those occupations. This method of decision making, given accuracy of measurement, should enable the counselor and counselee to choose careers in which the person has a high probability of success. The ability to develop accurate predictions is an important aspect of this theory.

Central to making successful predictions and subsequent good decisions is a reliable and valid way of gathering measurements over a wide range of attributes of people engaged in many kinds of educational and vocational pursuits. Williamson indicated his confidence in such an approach by stating that certain of these measurements "had been perfected"[3] and it would not be long before many more would be equally as effective. Traits studied and measured were various kinds of educational and vocational skill clusters, or aptitudes, educational and vocational interests, and various personality characteristics. Comparison groups of successful and unsuccessful people in various kinds of educational and vocational

2. Edmund G. Williamson, "Trait-Factor Theory and Individual Differences," in *Theories of Counseling,* 2d ed., ed. Bufard Stefflre and W. Harold Grant (New York McGraw-Hill, 1972).

3. Williamson, "Trait-Factor Theory and Individual Differences," p. 140.

pursuits were identified. By using these comparison groups, individual differences could be identified and used in counseling to make decisions.

Certain characteristics, particularly values, were judged to be more difficult to measure because they were less observable. This, however, was and is only a passing concern for trait-and-factor theorists as they anticipate the development of more sophisticated and refined measurement tools. The theorists believe that there is no point on the scale of human attributes that cannot eventually be measured.

The advantages of this potential data pool to counseling are obvious. Once the appropriate measurement tools become available, much of the risk taking can be removed from counseling. Decisions can be made with much greater confidence than ever before in the eventual outcome.

Influence of external and social criteria

Not quite as obvious an implication for counseling is the fact that in many instances any decision-making event depends upon external or social criteria, which also have the force of acting as averages over large groups of people. This means that for any individual, a successful outcome occurs only insofar as the person adjusts to, or accommodates, certain established social standards. Williamson has stated many times that values are important variables in the counseling process.[4] Value decisions also depend upon the measures that are available for describing the prevailing desires of the American people. Williamson has recognized that our society cherishes certain individual rights, which remain constant regardless of any shifts occurring in social standards. One of the important contributions counselors can make is to help counselees find a way to balance the demands made upon them by society with their own individual rights. Such a balance can help individuals find their way into the positive mainstream of society, where they are likely to receive the greatest personal reward for themselves.

By virtue of where they choose to work, counselors in the educational setting are expected to subscribe to the dominant social ethic that supports public education.[5] Counselors in other settings also subscribe to the idea that they are proponents of the social ethic that supports their employment. Any institutional setting is established to achieve a certain purpose desired by its founders or perpetuators. School settings are established and maintained to integrate people

4. Edmund G. Williamson, "Value Orientation in Counseling," *Personnel and Guidance Journal* 37 (1958): 520–28. Edmund G. Williamson, "Value Options and the Counseling Relationship," *Personnel and Guidance Journal* 44 (1966): 617–23.

5. Williamson, "Trait-Factor Theory and Individual Differences," p. 164.

into society for the mutual benefit of all. Given the methodology of the trait-and-factor approach, individual benefit can only be determined in relation to the dominant social ethic.

Trait-and-factor methodology

Williamson outlined a counseling process that uses trait-and-factor theory and methodology as follows:[6]

1. Analysis, which is the collection of data
2. Synthesis, which is the organization of data
3. Diagnosis, which is the identification of needs
4. Prognosis, which is the identification of resources
5. Counseling, which is the development and implementation of strategy
6. Follow-up, which is the ascertaining of the degree of success

Consider the following case, which illustrates this process. John was an 18-year-old high school senior when he came to the school counselor on his own initiative. Other than having a few brief conversations related to class scheduling, he had not spent time with the counselor. He indicated he did not yet know what he wanted to do after he graduated, other than to get some type of job. While John took several tests that measured personality and vocational orientations, the counselor reviewed his file and found that John had always done average work, had rarely participated in class or school activities, had been somewhat of a loner, but had not been a behavior problem. Little information was available about his family.

After John finished the testing, the counselor spoke with John about any personal ambitions he might have other than to get a job. He also asked about John's family. He learned that John was the fourth and last child. None of his brothers or sister had gone to college. His two brothers had joined the local bricklayer's union, to which his father also belonged. Work was not steady enough due to a slowdown in the construction trade for John to consider this option.

The counselor next attempted to synthesize the data. He concluded that John had rarely been challenged, whether at home or at school, to consider either his future or any potential he might have. His family was hard-working, but had little aspiration beyond working in the manual trades. Steadiness of work was important to them; it meant security to this lower-middle-class family. The family had assumed that John would follow in his father's footsteps as his brothers had. In school, John always did adequate work but neither the quality of his work nor his behavior brought him to the attention of the faculty. He was doing well enough so that his lack of direc-

6. Edmund G. Williamson, *How to Counsel Students* (New York: McGraw-Hill, 1939).

tion was not perceived by himself, his family, or his teachers. John's testing indicated he was not an anxious person, was rather passive, and somewhat unrealistic. He indicated interest in few areas except for construction work. One area of interest was accounting. A check of his records indicated John had some good performance potential in math. The counselor then diagnosed John's counseling needs as a lack of world-of-work knowledge, indifference to his own abilities, and a subsequent lack of planning and decision-making abilities.

The counselor suspected that John's prognosis would be a favorable one, that he would be able to learn about the world of work and his potential role in it. He believed John could eventually make appropriate decisions that would lead to a rewarding career. With this goal in mind, the counselor met with John for counseling. He shared his analysis of information and the conclusions with John. His response was favorable but not enthusiastic. He expressed a willingness to develop a strategy with the counselor that would achieve his career aspirations. Included in the strategy were aptitude testing in business and math accounting skills, exploration of jobs related to the field of accounting, instruction in job-seeking skills, and visits to firms with accounting jobs. During a follow-up phone call in the summer after John graduated, the counselor found out that John had been accepted into a business-preparation course of study at the local junior college and had obtained a summer job in the produce department in a supermarket. John hoped to continue this job part-time while he went to college.

Trait-and-factor theory in educational context

Within the educational context, the emphasis of this process is on learning. In school counseling, this means that counselors deal with counselees for specific purposes, and the content of counseling is determined by each individual encounter. It is important that counselees learn to deal with the specific problems that have brought them to counseling, but it is even more important for counselees to learn a process that they can use in many other situations. Counselors are obligated to help their counselees learn new problem-solving techniques. Problem solving can be greatly enhanced by using the following process:[7]

1. Development of a pool of information in as many areas of life as possible
2. Interpretation of this information in relation to criterion-group comparisons
3. Generation of alternatives and their most likely consequences depending upon the particular characteristics of the individual identified in Steps 1 and 2

7. Williamson, "Trait-Factor Theory and Individual Differences."

4. Implementation of decision making based on the alternatives of Step 3

The foundation of this process is the development of reliable and valid information that is based on a rigorous measurement period. Knowledge of essential individual attributes including skills, interests, values, intellect, and emotions, is essential to decision making. Some of these characteristics, such as values and emotions, are not as easily quantified as others are. Fears are often topics central to counseling, but like all emotions, are difficult to measure against comparisons. The counseling profession has not yet developed the capability to measure them quantitatively. This is the challenge still facing the trait-and-factor theorists.

Related research

The trait-and-factor approach has long been associated with empirical research. Much of the research, though, is conducted by people more closely aligned with psychology than with counseling. Counselors such as E. G. Williamson have borrowed research more than they have developed their own.

The research associated with the trait-and-factor approach normally uses correlational and factor-analysis research models. Such research attempts to relate aspects of individuals or events to one another. Much has been done investigating the various traits associated with personality and intelligence. At one time, intelligence was thought to consist of a single underlying trait, which influenced all the cognitive processes of which people were capable. Guilford, however, has documented that the search for just one trait has never been successful. He provides evidence that a great variety of traits exist, each contributing something unique to the intellectual capability of a person.[8]

The same type of search is fruitful in the area of personality. Research continues to reveal somewhat stable traits that relate to various aspects of personality. Cultural and environmental differences also have some influence, and it is not clear how much of a role heredity contributes to the structure of traits. This piecemeal approach to research and the arguments that surround the findings suggest that trait-and-factor theory is certainly not complete.[9]

8. Joy P. Guilford, *The Nature of Human Intelligence* (New York: McGraw-Hill, 1967).

9. Leona E. Tyler, "Human Abilities," in *Annual Review of Psychology*, Vol. 23, ed. D. H. Mussen and M. R. Rosenzweig (Palo Alto, Calif.: Annual Reviews, Inc., 1972). J. L. Horn, "Human Abilities: A Review of Research and Theory in the Early 1970s," in *Annual Review of Psychology:* Vol. 27,ed. M. R. Rosenzweig and L. W. Porter (Palo Alto, Calif.: Annual Reviews, Inc., 1976).

To many theorists, the variety of human traits suggests that one can speak only of individual differences. They feel it makes little or no sense to measure individuals against groups on one or even several traits because individuals are comprised of so many traits that nothing extensively comparable can be found between any two people. All the characteristics of individuals have not yet been identified, let alone how these characteristics might interact.

Other theorists, however, cannot readily accept the notion of such extreme diversity among people when there is so great a social need to find and develop commonalities. The finding of such commonalities in everyday experience tends to reinforce the popular notion that people are not as diverse as trait-factor research suggests and that there are possibly only a few general factors that really become important.

The vocational area of human experience is one area that has been studied extensively by counselors. Much of the background for this has come from personnel psychology, which first developed tests to measure the correspondence between people and their work environment. Counseling applications of this approach have taken similar directions.[10] Basically, ability and personality characteristics both have been defined in the same terminology, which helps to describe work environments. Such supposed traits as interests, values, and needs have been researched. Once correspondence has been established between vocationally oriented traits and work environments, predictions can be made regarding how well any person will match a work environment. Instruments have been devised to measure work-related human traits and work-environment characteristics. Research and theory development in the vocational area continues to be fruitful.

The rational-emotive approach

Background

Albert Ellis was the founder and remains the leading proponent of rational-emotive counseling. Ellis was originally trained as a psychoanalyst, but as he practiced counseling, he began to develop a different approach that by the late 1950s and the early 1960s had emerged into a theory and method called rational-emotive counseling.

10. John L. Holland, *Making Vocational Choices: A Theory of Careers* (Englewood Cliffs, N.J.: Prentice-Hall, 1973). Lloyd H. Lofquist and Rene V. Dawis. *Adjustment to Work* (New York: Appleton-Century-Crofts, 1969).

Ellis is the author of many books that explain his theories as well as ways to implement the principles of his approach in many practical, everyday situations appropriate to laymen; other books are geared more to professionals who wish to use his therapy in counseling. His books include *The Art and Science of Love*,[11] *A New Guide to Rational Living*,[12] and *The Intelligent Woman's Guide to Man-Hunting*.[13] Of more direct interest to counselors are his books *Reason and Emotion in Psychotherapy*[14] and *Humanistic Psychotherapy: The Rational-Emotive Approach*.[15]

Ellis believes that the most outstanding characteristic of humans is their ability to think. He encourages people to consider how they think—to manage their thought processes.[16] As the wide-ranging writings of Ellis indicate, he believes that if people could apply their rationality in a managed way, there would be no area of life that would not be improved.

In a sense, Ellis is eclectic. He has extensively documented the many psychological and philosophical systems that have contributed to the development of the rational-emotive approach.[17] He draws on such diverse systems as the Stoic philosophers, psychoanalysis, Alfred Adler's individual psychology, and behaviorally oriented researchers such as Pavlov and Wolpe. One wonders if all these conflicting and competing systems could actually have merged to become the rational-emotive approach, or whether Ellis is looking backward and finding support for his theory wherever he can. Such conjectures are not so important, however, when considering the impact that rational-emotive theory has had on counseling practice.

The theory

Negativism and rationalism in rational-emotive theory

Rational-emotive theory begins with the assumption that people are genetically predisposed to behave in negative or self-destructive ways.[18] Such tendencies continue to be reinforced by society. Ellis

11. Albert Ellis, *The Art and Science of Love* (New York: Lyle Stuart, 1960).

12. Albert Ellis and Robert A. Harper, *A New Guide to Rational Living* (No. Hollywood, Calif.: Wilshire Book Company, 1976).

13. Albert Ellis, *The Intelligent Woman's Guide to Man-Hunting (New York: Lyle Stuart, 1965).*

14. Albert Ellis, *Reason and Emotion in Psychotherapy* (New York: Lyle Stuart, 1962).

15. Albert Ellis, *Humanistic Psychotherapy: The Rational-Emotive Approach* (New York: Julian Press, 1973).

16. Ellis, *Humanistic Psychotherapy*, p. 4.

17. Ellis, *Reason and Emotion in Psychotherapy*, Chapter 2.

18. Ellis, *Humanistic Psychotherapy*, p. 88.

cites the propensity of humans for evil and destruction as evidence for this assumption. People, however, have a unique quality that provides them with the capability of overcoming their self-destructive inclinations; this is their ability to think and, especially, to reason. Ellis contends that people can become more human by enhancing their cognitive, or rational thinking, processes.

He makes the additional assumption that these cognitive processes influence all other aspects of experience, namely, behavior and emotion. He describes how this occurs:

A is an Activating experience, which is influenced by B or a person's Belief system to create C, which is a Consequence.[19]

The consequence can take two forms, depending on the appropriateness of the belief system used to interpret the activating experience. If a rational process occurs at point B and a person makes a realistic appraisal of the activating experience, then the consequent action will be appropriate. If, however, the person at point B applies an irrational belief system, the consequent action will be inappropriate and will most likely be self-defeating. Rational belief systems are identifiable by the fact that they are observable and verifiable, while irrational ones are subjective and not verifiable by scientific processes.

Belief systems

Ellis listed irrational beliefs that he feels are at the basis of inappropriate belief systems. Although these can occur in any combination, the basic concepts remain as stated here:

1. The idea that it is a dire necessity for an adult to be loved or approved by virtually every significant person in his community.

2. The idea that one should be thoroughly competent, adequate, and achieving in all possible respects if one is to consider oneself worth while.

3. The idea that human unhappiness is externally caused and that people have little or no ability to control their sorrows and disturbances.

4. The idea that one's past history is an all-important determinant of one's present behavior and that because something once strongly affected one's life, it should indefinitely have a similar effect.

5. The idea that there is invariably a right, precise and perfect solution to human problems and that it is catastrophic if this perfect solution is not found.

6. The idea that if something is or may be dangerous or fearsome, one should be terribly concerned about it and should keep dwelling on the possibility of its occurring.

7. The idea that certain people are bad, wicked, or villainous, and that they should be severely blamed and punished for their villainy.

19. Ellis, *Humanistic Psychotherapy,* Chapter 1.

Albert Ellis, the developer of rational-emotive therapy, believed that persons need to discard inappropriate beliefs before they could grow into maturity.

8. The idea that it is awful and catastrophic when things are not the way one would very much like them to be.

9. The idea that it is easier to avoid than to face certain life difficulties and self-responsibilities.

10. The idea that one should become quite upset over other people's problems and disturbances.

11. The idea that one should be dependent on others and need someone stronger than oneself on whom to rely.[20]

It is the role of the counselor to intervene in a counselee's A–B–C process to help the counselee discover and remove irrational beliefs and replace them with rational ones. This is basically done by thoroughly analyzing each of the A–B–C components and getting the counselee to move on to D, which is the point at which the counselee *D*isputes the irrational beliefs. This sets the stage for the E phase of counseling, which refers to the *E*ffects to be expected from

20. Ellis, *Humanistic Psychotherapy,* pp. 152–53, 242–43.

a successful completion of D. Effects generally affect two areas of an individual's life. First will be a new, rational way of thinking. This, in turn, will lead to a new way of behaving, which presumably will be more congruent with any activating event.

Argument and persuasion as counseling techniques

To facilitate this process, Ellis uses many different counseling approaches and techniques. One that stands out most distinctly from what is usually recommended for counseling is his emphasis on the use of strong argument and persuasion. He forcefully challenges counselees to see how they are using irrational thoughts to produce self-defeating feelings and behaviors. He mainly wants people to accept themselves as they are without constantly evaluating themselves on the basis of day-to-day behaviors. His arguments use a quasiscientific approach that is logical and based on some sort of evidence. He tries to teach counselees the use of inductive and deductive reasoning so they have a factual way of understanding and reacting to what happens to them.

Here is an example that illustrates the rational-emotive counseling process: A young woman had managed a career for some time prior to her marriage. She had enjoyed working and had also appreciated the leisure opportunities she pursued as a result of her income. She also looked forward to becoming a mother and managing a home, something that had been a dream of hers since she was a child. She had three children. They were all young and needed a lot of personal attention. They often fought with each other, thus requiring her to discipline them. She did not want to be a stern mother, yet she found that she had little patience and often was too stern. Time pressures also prevented her getting many leisure opportunities, and the family income also further limited her pursuit of previous interests. She rarely saw friends that she made during her working years and when she did, she realized that she now had little in common with them. She met other neighborhood mothers, but resented the narrow range of family and neighborhood concerns that formed the basis of these relationships. Although she appreciated her husband's efforts to love and amuse her, she felt that she needed more. All of this made her feel guilty, especially when she contrasted her actual efforts at being a mother to her dreams of what she had expected motherhood to be. The frustration and guilt she experienced colored much of her interactions with her family and friends.

Her counselor, following rational-emotive theory, looked for irrational beliefs that intervened between this woman's effort at being a mother, which was the Activating experience, and the Consequences, which were her feelings of inadequacy, frustration, and guilt. Her expectations about motherhood and the role of a husband were probably unrealistically high. Her expectations of her own abilities to maintain control of her children and her own feelings were too high. Her estimates of her own leisure needs were too low. As this young woman revealed these and other beliefs or expectations, the counselor challenged them and pointed out that adhering to them rigidly would only ensure failure. The counselor showed her that no one would be successful operating under such severe criteria. This led to the Disputing stage of the process and finally to the Effects stage. The woman modified her dreams about motherhood to a more realistic level. The fact that she lost patience became more tolerable. She learned to be less punishing of herself and recognized also that children did misbehave and were incapable of much self-management. She found other mothers with similar concerns so that she recognized that she was not the only one with these inadequacies. She arranged special leisure opportunities for herself, leaving her husband to manage the family. It is important to notice that these Effects existed within her thought processes as well as in her behaviors.

Ellis also recommends homework assignments. Once counselees can adequately and accurately assess the reality of their experience, they can begin responding with self-enhancing behaviors. Logical thought processes release counselees from their self-defeating patterns. Often, however, the counselor will need to encourage counselees to perform these behaviors because they appear to be risky. Hence, homework assignments are given to counselees between counseling sessions, and these are then "checked" by the counselor.

Needless to say, the counselor using rational-emotive counseling is a very active counselor. Ellis believes that the role of counselor is more like that of a teacher, and that change does not depend on the quality of the relationship, but rather, on the quality of instruction.[21] Ellis does not feel that the counseling relationship is a realistic interpersonal encounter that can be generalized to other interpersonal relationships. He often recommends that counselees participate in group experiences so they can try out their new thought processes and behaviors in a situation that approximates everyday interaction.

Ellis also feels that counseling must focus on the here-and-now with particular attention paid to ongoing thought processes. Reflections on the past are not considered important except to note how past occurences may contribute to illogical ways of thinking. Current thinking can change without one's knowing how the thoughts originated.[22]

21. Ellis, *Humanistic Psychotherapy,* pp. 152–53.

22. Ellis, *Humanistic Psychotherapy,* pp. 159–61.

Outcomes of rational-emotive counseling

Ellis has described the intended outcome of counseling.[23] He feels counseling must seek to minimize the anxiety and hostility of counselees and provide them with a method of maintaining appropriate levels of each of these. It is important to point out that Ellis does not deny the existence of "bad feelings" or hurt. He does not feel that all anxieties and hostilities can be erased. Rather, he points out that emotional upset even may be desirable if it is based on a realistic appraisal of events, and if it stimulates a person to take appropriate corrective action. He thus distinguishes between fear and anxiety. Fear can be described as an appropriate reaction a person may have toward a given stressful situation. Anxiety is an inappropriate reaction, because it stems from self-evaluative thoughts that assume the stressful situation will become hurtful or that nothing can be done about the situation. Similarly, Ellis distinguishes between annoyance and hostility. People cannot expect to avoid or talk themselves out of annoyance. Certain events dictate that such feelings may be entirely legitimate. Hostility, however, seems to be a reaction based on an inappropriate self-evaluation in which a person feels hopeless to do anything about the pressures other people create. Such helplessness leads to inaction and continuing difficulty. Ellis believes that the counseling goals of individuals can typically be classified under the general goals of minimizing anxiety and hostility. His method of rational-emotive counseling teaches counselees how to assess reality rationally without the interference of self-evaluation. Such rational thinking is intended to maintain minimal levels of inappropriate anxiety and hostility. Remember that Ellis places much stress on change occurring in a counselee's thought processes. Ultimately, change must also occur in how the counselee behaves.

Ellis notes that counselees who will most benefit from rational-emotive counseling will have certain intellective abilities.[24] Highly confused people or those with limited intellectual abilities are not expected to respond well.

Counseling as educative interaction

Basically, Ellis recommends that the counselor engage in a highly educative interaction with the counselee. The counselor is actively urged to challenge the thought processes, especially the evaluative self-thoughts, of the counselee whenever these cognitions are assumed to be causing negative emotions and, subsequently, self-defeating behaviors. Although more attention is paid by Ellis to cognitive processes, he is also concerned about behavioral outcomes.

23. Ellis, *Humanistic Psychotherapy,* Chapter 10.

24. Albert Ellis, "Rational-Emotive Psychotherapy," in *Current Psychotherapies,* ed. Raymond Corsini (Itasca, Ill.: Peacock, 1973), p. 191.

Related research

Ellis originally evolved the rational-emotive approach from his own clinical experience. He incorporated in the theory and process those concepts that seemed to work best for him and his counselees. Little empirical research was done in the early formulation of the theory. Ellis had documented how the work of previous theoreticians such as Adler and Freud contributed to rational-emotive theory and also how the research of behavioral theoreticians supported his ideas. He also tried to incorporate within actual counseling a reliance on observable evidence to refute irrational beliefs or to support new, rational ones. This led him to publish an outcome study comparing the counseling approaches he used as he progressed from a psychoanalytic counselor to one using rational-emotive theory.[25] From this analysis, Ellis felt that his counselees improved to a greater extent in a shorter period of time when he used rational-emotive counseling than when he used anything else. Regardless of how objective Ellis might have been when he did this analysis, such a study is hardly sufficient for validating his theory or his counseling process, and Ellis has done little empirical research of a controlled quality since his initial research statement in 1957.

Other researchers have attempted to investigate the concepts of rational-emotive theory and the effects of the rational-emotive counseling process. Ellis' notion that cognitions or self-verbalizations can affect emotions have been supported by independent researchers.[26] Also, Ellis' theoretical concepts have been reevaluated in the light of current work done with cognitively-oriented behavior modification techniques.[27] Although these studies provide support for the theoretical base of rational-emotive counseling, this evidence also suggests that other, more parsimonious explanations are available to indicate how cognitions affect emotions and behavior. The practical applications derived from these reformulations might also be simpler and more effective. These applications will be considered in the behavioral-approach section of this chapter.

---

25. Albert Ellis, "Outcome of Employing Three Techniques of Psychotherapy," *Journal of Clinical Psychology* 13 (1957): 344–50.

26. Emmett C. Velton, "A Laboratory Task for the Induction of Mood States," *Behavior Research and Therapy* 6 (1968): 473–82. D. C. Rimm and S. B. Lituak, "Self-Verbalization and Emotional Arousal," *Journal of Abnormal Psychology* 74 (1969): 181–87. S. Schacter and J. E. Singer, "Cognitive, Social and Physiological Determinants of Emotional States," *Psychological Review* 69 (1962): 379–99.

27. Donald Meichenbaum and Roy Cameron, "The Clinical Potential of Modifying What Clients Say to Themselves," in *Self-Control: Power to the Person,* ed. Michael Mahoney and Carl Thoresen (Monterey, Calif.: Brooks/Cole, 1974): 263–90.

Relatively few studies are available that attempt to measure the comparative effects of rational-emotive counseling and some of these newer approaches derived from the modification of cognitive processes. Some comparative work has been done comparing rational-emotive counseling to more traditional counseling approaches such as client-centered counseling and systematic desensitization where rational-emotive counseling has been shown to be more effective in changing cognitions and behaviors.[28] In a review of this empirical literature, Elson[29] has proposed that perhaps rational-emotive counseling is effective because it uses, in part, the principles of cognitive-change processes as developed by behavior-modification researchers. If this is the case, rational argument as proposed by Ellis is a rather indirect way of helping people change their cognitions. More direct conditioning approaches might be more effective and even less time-consuming.

The behavioral approach

Background

Behavioral counseling is deeply rooted in the experimental tradition of psychology. Several major contributing concepts have contributed to this approach, each sharing a concern and intent to develop an understanding of how people learn. Behavioral counseling is often referred to as the learning-theory approach. For descriptive purposes, such an association may be acceptable; however, the practical applications to counseling of behavioralism that are derived from learning theory are not necessarily synonymous. Furthermore, the theoretical developments of learning theory have far outstripped the practical counseling applications that are currently in use. Behavioral counselors are continuing to make use of laboratory research findings and the increasing acceptance of behavioral counseling indicates that the gap between theory and practice may continue to narrow in the future.

Contributors to behavioral approach

One of the concepts of American behavioral counseling began first with the work of John Watson, a psychologist who emphasized

28. A. Di Loreto, *Comparative Psychotherapy* (Chicago: Aldine, 1971). Wayne R. Maes and Robert A. Hermann, *The Comparison of Three Approaches to the Reduction of Test Anxiety in High School Students* (Washington, D.C.: Department of Health, Education, and Welfare, 1970).

29. Steven E. Elson, "Cognitive Behavior Modification: An Evaluation of the Effects of Language Techniques Upon Emotional Arousal," Ph. D. dis., Michigan State University, 1975.

that psychological researchers legitimately could study only observable behavior. Psychology, from Watson's point of view, could be considered scientific only if what it studied could be measured. B. F. Skinner, still a prominent psychologist today, advanced Watson's original perspective regarding the study of behavior. Skinner's early research work with animals helped him clarify a theory of learning that he feels is generalizable to all higher-order organisms, including humans. Skinner's theory is often referred to as operant or instrumental learning.

I. P. Pavlov, a Russian physiologist, in the early twentieth century also used experimental techniques to measure certain behaviors, most notably those of dogs. This theory is referred to as classical or respondent learning. This led to the second major concept of behavioral counseling, which is currently used by some counselors to account for the acquisition of human emotions. This is known as respondent learning.

Others have continued to develop learning-theory applications to counseling and have greatly expanded the types of complex human actions that can be made accessible to scientific study. People who have contributed specifically to counseling applications of learning theories are Albert Bandura with his social-modeling procedures; Michael Mahoney and Carl Thoresen with their self-management techniques; John Krumboltz and Carl Thoresen with their emphasis on the use of reinforcement; Joseph Wolpe with his technique of systematic desensitization; and Donald Meichenbaum with his application of behavioral principles to the restructuring of thinking processes.

The theory

In spite of the scientific emphasis on observable events that undergirds the behavioral approach, there is no concensus among behavioral researchers regarding theory. Some theorists and researchers are much stricter regarding their definitions of observable and measurable events than are others. Modern technology has made it possible to measure human physiological processes, and thus, to reveal to the psychologically oriented researcher much more of the formerly forbidden "internal" events of human experience than ever before. Some view these internal events as the emotions of love, anger, or sadness, among others. Others have liberalized the measurement procedures and now accept a person's own account of internal processes as a valid and observable measurement. Such subjectivism was not tolerated a few short years ago, and many researchers still doubt whether measurement based on introspection can supply valid knowledge of how people behave.

Controversy over measurement of emotions

Regardless of these problems, a basic review of operant and respondent learning is presented here. Most counseling applications can best be understood by examining these two formulations of learning theory.

Respondent learning. Respondent learning, or classical conditioning, evolved from the work of Ivan Pavlov. His research showed that dogs began to salivate to the sound of a tuning fork when the sound had preceded the actual presentation of food on several successive occasions.

The process description that accounts for how Pavlov's dogs began salivating to the sound of a tuning fork is described as:

$$\text{CS} \rightarrow \text{UCS} \longrightarrow \text{R}$$

The R denotes a response, or observable behavior, in the case of Pavlov's dogs, salivation. The arrow indicates a time sequence signifying that a UCS, or unconditioned stimulus, precedes the response. An unconditioned stimulus is defined as an event that elicits a response. They occur together without fail and with what seems to be no prior learning. The response occurs with the same strength each time that the unconditioned stimulus occurs in the same form. This pattern of response is referred to as a reflex. The reflex comprises the presentation of food and the immediate salivation response. Such a reflex seems to occur automatically and is often referred to as automatic or involuntary behavior. What causes the response is unclear. Possibly, higher-order organisms are born with such reflexes. However, for most learning theorists, such conjecturing is not important.

The CS refers to the conditioned stimulus. It is a stimulus that by its presentation alone would not elicit any one consistent response; that is, it is a neutral stimulus. It becomes a conditioned stimulus when it is paired in close sequence with an unconditioned stimulus. After a number of trials, the neutral stimulus, or conditioned stimulus, will begin to elicit the same or a very similar response as the unconditioned stimulus. Note that during learning the conditioned stimulus typically precedes the unconditioned stimulus. Any previously neutral stimulus, when paired often enough with an unconditioned stimulus can become a conditioned stimulus and acquire a response-eliciting capability. The sound of the tuning fork immediately preceding the food presentation eventually became a conditioned stimulus that could on its own account elicit salivation in the dogs. Extinction or elimination of this response will occur, however, unless the unconditioned stimulus is occasionally paired with the conditioned stimulus. Without this occasional pairing, the conditioned stimulus will become neutral again.

Extinction

Behaviorism and emotional responses

This description of respondent learning, or respondent conditioning, as it is sometimes called, focuses on external, observable responses. It is also possible to use this framework to describe how emotional feelings develop within a person. For example, people become sexually aroused by many different persons, objects, or situations. Sexual arousal is typically considered a reflexive response. Since there is such a diversity of preferences, ranging from those that are socially acceptable to those that are taboo, it would appear that individuals experience unique learning histories that determine the various conditioned stimuli that lead to their sexual arousal. The notion that "gentlemen prefer blonds" is a popular way of acknowledging these differences. Yet it is not quite as simple as that. Even though there may be typical ways of responding to certain socially accepted stimuli in their proper context, there remain many examples of sexual perversions that have persisted even in the face of severe social punishment. Respondent learning would suggest that sexual arousal to socially inappropriate conditioned stimuli resulted from unintentional (or intentional) pairings of these stimuli with unconditioned sexual arousal stimuli. With such powerful responses, perhaps only one or a few pairings produce the response to the conditioned stimulus. It is now believed that these pairings of conditioned and unconditioned stimuli can be made through imagination. Actual physical and temporal proximity may not be necessary to perpetrate the pairings and the strength of the conditioned stimulus. Treatments of sexual perversions would properly attend to pairing appropriate acceptable stimuli to unconditioned sexual arousal stimuli, such as tactile stimulation, so that sexual responses would occur in the presence of these more appropriate stimuli. According to respondent learning, punishing the sexual response would not really address the problem, which exists in the pairings of conditioned and unconditioned stimuli.

An example of the creation of a feeling of fear would be an incident in which a child is stung by a bee while playing. The sting is the unconditioned stimulus and yelling in pain is the response. Just prior to being stung, the child may have noticed a plane flying overhead, which may become a conditioned stimulus, thereby eliciting a fear-and-avoidance response from the child whenever a plane is noticed. Such a fear may continue and become a fear of flying in later life. Many phobias, as these fears are called, can be explained in this way. Typically, nonthreatening objects can become terrifying because of chance pairings with painful unconditioned stimuli.

Conditioned stimuli, once they acquire eliciting properties, can serve in the same way as the original unconditioned stimulus and generate new conditioned responses to other previously neutral stimuli. This process is referred to as higher-order conditioning. As the process of conditioning continues while a person grows up, it is often impossible to unravel how the chain has developed and what the "first cause" might have been. Strange and rather bizarre reactions can occur to what are neutral stimuli for most other people. However, conditioning history makes these fearful, avoidance behaviors, although bizarre and disruptive of a person's life, a part of a person's behaviors that occurs almost automatically.

Trap of circular reasoning

Since such an observable phenomenon as salivation appeared to be a learned behavioral change, the learning mechanism needed to be found. Respondent learning theory, as is true of most learning theories, attempts to describe how learning occurs rather than to explain what causes learning to occur. Learning theories try to describe the process of learning. This is done deliberately to avoid the trap of circular reasoning.

Circular reasoning begins when an explanatory concept is deduced from certain evidence and is presented as the cause of the existence of the evidence. The circle is completed when the evidence is then given as proof that the explanatory concept exists. One item is deduced from the other without having to go beyond the "circle" for actual validating evidence. Such circularity occurs often in counseling. It is an easy trap to fall into, particularly when dealing with emotions. For example, depression is described clinically, as well as popularly, as a psychological condition analogous to measles as a medical condition. Typical treatments have been developed for this psychological condition. Depression now exists as a phenomenon by itself, regardless of any symptoms that a depressed person may display. Originally, general malaise, apathy, and insomnia were among the symptoms and the evidence that led some persons to deduce that such a thing as depression existed. Now depression in individuals is confirmed by this same type of evidence. The evidence, which, in this case, means the symptoms, is used to point to the existence of depression while the symptoms are said to exist because of depression. Rather than developing counseling strategies to deal with the various symptoms, which may or may not be related, the typical approach is to treat depression in standard ways. Many other internal states, often referred to as drives or motivators, are common elements in psychological theorizing used to explain how people behave as they do. It is the intent of the learning theorists to avoid circular reasoning and conjectured causal internal states that cannot be verified.

Counselors can use this learning paradigm, or explanation for how learning occurs, to form methods that can be used to recondition responses or extinguish responses. It is important to note that new learning or reconditioning can occur without having to understand or know how such behavior originally began. It is not necessary to have the original unconditioned stimulus at hand. To extinguish a response, it is imperative that the unconditioned stimulus actually be absent at the beginning of the process. Someone who has a fear of planes does not have to uncover childhood events to begin changing the fearful behavior. Thoughts, pictures, actual planes, and eventually flying could all be paired with an unconditioned stimulus that elicits approach behaviors and pleasant feelings until the fearful stimuli associated with planes become reconditioned and begin to elicit the same approach behaviors and pleasant feelings.

The Skinnerian approach

Operant learning. While respondent learning describes the formation of what seem to be automatic behaviors and emotions, operant learning, or operant conditioning, describes how purposeful behavior is developed. The word *operant* refers to the process of operating or acting upon something. Operant learning is often called instrumental learning to reflect the same concept. B. F. Skinner is most closely associated with the development of operant learning theory. His research and writing has had major impact on the fields of counseling and psychology, particularly since the publication of his book *Science and Human Behavior* in 1953.[30]

Skinner uses the term *operant* to indicate that the process he describes is one that shows how organisms operate on or influence their environment and how the environment influences the behavior of the organisms. It reflects a reciprocal and continuous process. The major elements of the process can be diagrammed as follows:

$$R \rightarrow C$$

The R refers to a response, or behavior that is emitted by an organism. Note that no UCS or CS elicits the response in the operant paradigm. The arrow again indicates a time sequence, in that the C, or consequence, follows the emitted response. The consequence, however, is said to control the response, and for purposes of illustrating control, the diagram could be:

$$R \leftarrow C$$

Control in this context refers to the capability of the consequence to influence the likelihood of the recurrence of the emitted response. If a consequence increases the frequency of a behavior, it is a reenforcer. If the consequence decreases the frequency of a behavior, it is a punisher. There are two types of reenforcers. The most obvious

30. B. F. Skinner, *Science and Human Behavior* (New York: Macmillan, 1953).

Use of reenforcers

type is a consequence that delivers something positive to the organism and is referred to as positive reenforcement. For people, tangible objects, desired activities, and social praise all serve as positive reenforcers. It must be remembered that a reenforcer functions as such because it increases the frequency of a behavior, not because it seems like a desirable thing or event. What seems desirable to one person may be a punisher to another and may actually decrease a particular behavior. A second type of reenforcer is negative. This term is often confused with punishment. A negative reenforcer is best viewed as a consequence that signals the removal of an unpleasant situation, threat, or fear. Any behavior whose consequence is the removal of such unpleasant, or punishing circumstances will be negatively reenforced and its occurence can be expected again when similar unpleasant situations arise.

An example of positive reenforcement is the use of praise when a habitually late person finally arrives at work on time. If the person arrives at work on time for the next several days, the effectiveness of praise as a positive reenforcer for that person may be inferred. If praise is ineffective, the threat of loss of pay if tardiness continues may be instituted. If the person now begins arriving regularly, then the threat of pay loss is reduced. This is an example of negative reenforcement. If the person arrives late again, and the threat is actually applied and pay loss occurs, then this is an example of punishment. All three might have to be used in combination before an effective behavior change, or learning, occurs. The crucial idea in using reenforcers and punishers is that they are highly individualized, and their effectiveness can be ascertained only after they have been given a sufficient trial. Reenforcers are defined as reenforcers only if they increase behavior, and punishers are defined as punishers only when they decrease behavior.

Extinction in operant learning

Extinction is also an element of operant learning theory. Extinction will occur when a reenforcer is prevented from being applied. Once a behavior receives no reenforcement for a long enough period of time, the behavior should cease.

Also affecting the occurrence of behavior is the rate, or schedule, at which reenforcement is given for a behavior. It has been found that it is easier to extinguish behavior that has been reenforced after each occurrence than behavior that has been reenforced on a noncontinuous basis. Such variation of the schedule of reenforcement is important for maintaining any behavior. For a behavior that is particularly important, for example, teaching a retarded child how to cross the street, it might be best to use a reenforcement schedule during the learning exercises that is not continuous. For example, every third or fourth successful crossing should be reenforced.

Counseling applications of the learning-theory approach have ranged from the very simplistic ones, such as using social praise for reenforcing the positive self-statements of counselees to the complex arrangements of complete environments called token economies, which function according to operant procedures. Although the rules of application can be generalized somewhat, these rules are beyond the scope of this brief theory overview. Examples, to be presented shortly, will be sufficient for purposes of this text.

Respondent and operant theories combined

A–B–C of learning. Respondent and operant learning theory paradigms can be combined to form a larger perspective of how behavior is learned. This combination can be easily remembered as the A–B–C of learning. This should not be confused with Ellis' A–B–C theory. The A refers to antecedents that under the respondent framework are those conditioned and unconditioned stimuli that elicit behavior. The B in this instance signifies a behavior. As in operant terms, the C refers to any consequence that follows the behavior.

These A–B–Cs can be combined in endless chains. A consequence for one behavior can become an antecedent for another, and so on. Although the A–B–C framework seems simplistic, it is actually complicated. It is extremely difficult to unravel all the antecedents and consequences that can control any given behavior or series of behaviors.

Related research

Albert Bandura has developed a counseling application of behavior modification that he calls social learning. He has provided ample research evidence of the viability of his approach.[31] Bandura has used models to teach new behaviors. By providing reenforcement to a model that has performed desired behaviors, an observer can experience vicarious learning. Models, both live and on film or videotape, often can act out complex social behaviors and thereby facilitate the learning of new or revised behaviors by someone who performs these behaviors poorly. The cues or antecedents provided by models, as well as the reenforcement they receive, have been demonstrated to increase the learning potential of observers. By using carefully structured modeling procedures, counselors can teach a variety of complex behaviors. Counselors also can learn to serve as models for their counselees during counseling by using

31. Albert Bandura, *Principles of Behavior Modification* (New York: Holt, Rinehart, 1969).

role-playing procedures. Using models that are respected peers of counselees has also been effective.

Michael Mahoney and Carl Thoresen have outlined a counseling approach that focuses on teaching counselees how to change their own behavior by using learning principles from the operant and respondent frameworks. They have also presented some of the early research that supports the viability of this self-management approach.[32] Counselees can use antecedents and reenforcements in ways so as to increase behaviors they desire and decrease those that are unwanted. This procedure is particularly attractive since it provides counselees with a structured and systematic approach that they can use in many instances throughout their lives without having to resort to further counseling.

John Krumboltz and Carl Thoresen have collaborated to cull from behavior-change research those applications that seem especially appropriate for counseling applications.[33] Although they advocate many behavior-change strategies, they call special attention to the use of behavior consequences, particularly positive reenforcement. Krumboltz was one of the initial advocates of applying reenforcement principles in the counseling field[34] and demonstrated the effectiveness of reenforcement in enhancing the career development of counselees.[35] Reenforcement strategies are particularly attractive for counselors since the basic techniques are quite generalizable; yet proper application demands careful attention to individuality.

Joseph Wolpe developed an approach heavily based on respondent learning, which he calls systematic desensitization.[36] This method is geared toward reducing and eliminating fears people have that prevent them from performing desired activities. Systematic desensitization rests on the assumption that anxiety is incompatible with feelings such as relaxation and assertiveness. The major aim of systematic desensitization is to remove the fear and avoid-

32. Michael Mahoney and Carl E. Thoresen, ed., *Self-Control: Power to the Person* (Monterey, Calif.: Brooks/Cole, 1974).

33. John D. Krumboltz and Carl E. Thoresen, ed., *Behavioral Counseling* (New York: Holt, Rinehart, 1969). John D. Krumboltz and Carl E. Thoresen, ed., *Counseling Methods* (New York: Holt, Rinehart, 1976).

34. John D. Krumboltz, "Behavioral Counseling: Rationale and Research," *Personnel and Guidance Journal* 44 (1965): 383–87.

35. John D. Krumboltz and Wade W. Schroeder, "Promoting Career Exploration Through Reenforcement," *Personnel and Guidance Journal* 44 (1965): 19–26.

36. Joseph Wolpe, *Psychotherapy by Reciprocal Inhibition* (Stanford, Calif.: Stanford University Press, 1958).

ance response from a conditioned stimulus and replace this with a relaxed feeling and an approach response. What is of particular use in counseling is that the method can be accomplished merely by having the counselee imagine how gradual fear reduction and approach learning will feel. The counselor and counselee develop a hierarchy of situations that range from the least fearful to the most fearful, and then they practice imagining being relaxed in each situation until no anxiety is felt in even the most fearful imagined situation. Research has shown that this learning by imagination does transfer to real-life situations, but only for the specific situations desensitized during counseling. Generalization to other areas of fear and avoidance does not occur so readily.

Variations of desensitization have developed. Most notable is a procedure in which the counselee practices fear reduction and approach "in vivo," or in real life, rather than by imagination. Such a technique has the potential and advantage of being self-induced, which makes the counselee less dependent on a counselor.

Donald Meichenbaum has used a variety of behavioral approaches, such as modeling, feedback, and positive reenforcement, as well as other behavioral variations to change the covert self-thoughts that he feels, quite similarly to Ellis, mediate overt or observable behavior.[37] Meichenbaum has demonstrated that these techniques seem to work with people labeled as schizophrenic. The implication for counseling is obvious. Meichenbaum has also experimented with developing a generalized problem-solving approach that counselees can use in other situations to modify what they say to themselves and, in turn, what they actually do.

Since applications of behavior modification are uniquely tailored to the individual, the resulting features often become quite varied. Because of this, some general guidelines are presented rather than specific case histories. Prior to initiating behavioral change processes, counselors need to consider these points.

1. Can the behavior that needs to be changed be described?
2. Does the person want to change this behavior? If he or she does not want to change, why not? If not, it must be important and somehow rewarding to continue the undesirable behavior. How is this so?
3. How often does the behavior occur? Be specific, get down to numbers. Does the behavior really need to be changed?

---

37. Meichenbaum Cameron, "The Clinical Potential of Modifying What Clients Say to Themselves," pp. 263–90.

4. When does the behavior that is to be changed occur? What happens just before it occurs, and just as important, what happens just afterward?
5. What is the reenforcer that causes the behavior to occur again and again? Why is this particular reenforcer important to this person?
6. Is this reenforcer legitimate? If so, how can the person get the same thing through the use of more acceptable behavior? If not, will the person accept a different reenforcer that is powerful enough to change behavior?
7. Can a specific program be developed that can be followed by the person so that he or she knows what has to be done to obtain the desired reenforcer? Did the program specify only one goal? Is the program broken down into small enough steps? Is it within the ability of the person? Does the person really want to earn the reenforcer agreed upon? Does whoever administers the reenforcer really want to do so?
8. Is the change program administered consistently? Are reenforcers given only at the proper time, that is, when all the conditions agreed upon are met? Or are other reenforcers given that are unplanned? Are they ever not given even if they are deserved?
9. Does the person fail to change and still receive some kind of reenforcer? Be careful, maybe reactions to his or her failure are more reenforcing than reactions to success. Maybe it pays for the counselee to fail because more attention is given when he or she does.
10. Are there plans built into the process to deal with failure? Remember, the counselee is trying to change behavior that has been learned over a lifetime. The counselor has a few weeks, at best, within that lifetime to influence change. Is the motivation there on the counselor's part to expend the needed time and effort?

The planning guide presented in Figure 7–1 can be used to organize the information gained from answering these questions. Many different applications are possible, and this planning guide cannot substitute for an in-depth knowledge of behavioral-change technology. Counselors have a continuing obligation to remain current with regard to the many procedures available to help counselees deal with their undesired behaviors.

Counselee: ______________________________

Date: ______________________________

Involved Staff: ______________________________

Figure 7–1
Planning Guide for Behavioral-Change Program

Step 1 Description of the behavior the counselee would like to change: ______________________________

a How often does it occur? ______________________________

b When does it usually occur? ______________________________

c Are there certain conditions that usually accompany the behavior? ______________________________

Step 2 Description in specific terms of the behavior the counselee wishes to perform: ______________________________

Step 3 Description of particular reenforcements for this person. List several. Check the one that seems most appropriate. ______________________________

Step 4 Description of any conditions that will be changed in efforts to stimulate the desired behavior: ______________________________

Step 5 Anticipation of possible counselee behavior in response to efforts in establishing a behavioral-change program. Note reactions to each behavior. ______________________________

Step 6 Program implementation. Observe and react according to your reenforcement plan.

Step 7 Evaluation. Is desired behavior occurring?

Step 8 Revision. If necessary, recycle to Step 3.

One widely used procedure, behavior contracts, will be illustrated because it highlights many of the principles that are necessary for sound behavioral-change programs. Behavior contracts are explicit attempts to specify the behavior changes that are desired. The contracts specify the reenforcers and punishers that will apply and who is to administer them. The sample contract in Figure 7–2 describes the behavior-change program developed for the AB family by a mental health counselor. The high-school son Andrew had refused to comply with his parents wishes to do his homework and to do chores around the house. Andrew felt he was being treated like a baby and that he should be freer to direct his own activities and pursue his own goals.

Figure 7–2 Behavioral Contract for AB Family

PRIVILEGES	RESPONSIBILITIES
General As a means of remaining together and preserving some semblance of family tranquility, Mr. and Mrs. AB and Andrew agree that:	
Specific In exchange for the privilege of attending regularly scheduled school activities on weekends,	Andrew agrees to attend school every day, complete his homework assignments, behave acceptably in classes, and not violate any school rules.
In exchange for the privilege of attending special activities, such as hunting, fishing, roller skating, playing hockey, and watching T.V., during the week, or on weekends,	Andrew agrees to work on his studies, under the supervision of a volunteer tutor from 6 to 7 P.M. Monday to Thursday.
In exchange for the privilege of going out with his friends on weekends,	Andrew agrees to obtain the permission of his parents, tell them where he will be, and when he will be home. If there is a change in plans, he will call home and notify his parents. In all cases, he will be home no later than 10 P.M. unless special permission for later hours has been arranged with the parents.
In exchange for the privilege of receiving his weekly allowance or spending money,	Andrew agrees to complete the household jobs ordered by his parents.
In exchange for the privilege of having Andrew comply with his part of the contract,	Mr. and Mrs. AB agree to provide transportation for the privileges he has earned and to refrain from hiding his boots, jacket, etc.

In exchange for the privilege of having Andrew comply with all aspects of this agreement for a period of one month,	Mr. AB agrees to allow Andrew to work part-time at his gas station and to spend or save his earned money in the manner he sees fit.
PREMISES	**BONUSES AND SANCTIONS**
If Andrew does not meet the study requirements for one night,	he will work on his studies two hours the next night.
If Andrew is 1 to 30 minutes late in coming home,	he must come in the same amount of time earlier the next time he is out.
If Andrew is more than 30 minutes late,	he loses the privilege of going out one night on the weekend.
If Andrew fails to complete his chores,	he will not be given his allowance.
If he raises his school grades to a C average by the end of the school year,	Andrew will be able to select a special gift or privilege.

Monitoring
Mr. and Mrs. AB agree to keep written records of Andrew's daily behavior on the forms provided.

Andrew agrees to keep written records of his own behavior and the behavior of his parents on the forms provided.

Signatures

____

____

____

The contract indicates how each of the involved parties, Andrew and his parents, would behave if they were to reenforce one another. These procedures illustrate the strategy phase of counseling. The information necessary to develop such appropriate behavioral-change programs depends on a thorough knowledge of the counselee by the counselor.

Summary

This chapter has explored three major theories based on cognitive learning. These include the trait-and-factor approach, the rational-emotive approach, and the behavioral approach.

Trait-and-factor counseling relies heavily on the cognitive processes for managing information, including its collection and analysis. The information is then used in the decision-making components of counseling. Trait-and-factor techniques are used not only during the counseling process itself, but also to teach the process to counselees, so they will have the knowledge and skills necessary to make them less dependent on counseling. Trait-and-factor counseling is often used in vocational counseling.

Rational-emotive counseling, founded and developed by Ellis, is based on the idea that people can and should be taught how to handle their thought processes to their benefit. Ellis believes people are basically self-destructive, but that they have the skills to overcome their self-destructive tendencies. Ellis believes that most people operate with a set of misbeliefs that lead them into destructive behavior. He sees the role of the counselor as one of challenging those misbeliefs directly to persuade the counselee that certain cognitions or self-verbalizations are creating difficulties in his or her life that repeat themselves unnecessarily. The counselor and counselee work together to replace the destructive behaviors with a set of constructive ones. Of the three cognitive theories discussed in this chapter, rational-emotive counseling encourages the most active role for the counselor.

The behavioral approach attempts to describe what is observable about the learning process rather than creating theories about the ways in which learning may occur. There is no social goal in behavioral counseling; rather, behaviorally-oriented counselors use whatever learning techniques are most effective with their individual counselees. Usually, the goals are very specific, i.e. to change a single behavior or a fairly small range of behaviors. The behavioral approach has received criticism for its emphasis on only working with those behaviors or learning processes that can be directly observed. Current efforts address this concern and seek to change how people think and feel about themselves. Still, a concrete body of theory and practical techniques has emerged from the behavioralists, and the counseling techniques have proven to be effective in many situations.

Questions

1. What are some of the problems related to building theories about human behavior?

2. Describe the difference between a cognitively-oriented theory and an affectively-oriented theory.

3. What is trait-and-factor theory? How is it applied to counseling practice?

4. What kinds of research support the trait-and-factor approach? What problems occur in this kind of research?

5. What is the rational-emotive approach? How is it used in counseling?

6. What is the behavioral approach? How is it used in counseling?

7. What kinds of persons are most likely to benefit from each kind of therapy?

8. Compare and contrast the role of the counselor in each kind of therapy.

Projects

1. Discuss which cognitive approach or combination of approaches would work best with the following counselee problems:
   a. fear of going into large department stores
   b. lack of self-confidence
   c. inability to hold a job
   d. inability to stop smoking cigarettes
   e. inability to decide on a major area of study
   f. indecision over whether or not to get married
   g. feeling that success is something that is not possible

2. Watch a film on one of the approaches described in this chapter. After the film, discuss the strengths and weaknesses of the technique.

3. Write a historical description of the major career-related decisions you have made. Did you use trait-and-factor theory? Describe the ways in which you might have used it if you failed to do so.

4. Read a book written by one of the proponents of the theories discussed in this chapter. Report on how your view of the approach changed as you read the book.

8 Affective counseling approaches

Sigmund Freud, who developed psychoanalysis, wrote many books explaining his theories about the unconscious and its role in human development.

8

Introduction

The subject of this chapter is the theories that emphasize learning, which, if it is to be lasting, must involve the emotions, conscious or unconscious. These emotions influence how people respond to events around them. Overt behavior and conscious thought are considered to be directly affected by the emotional, or affective, state of people. Counselors who have such theoretical leanings prefer to let the feelings of the counselee emerge naturally in order to gauge the effect of the emotions on how the counselee functions.

Of course, all counselors to some degree attend to behaviors, thoughts, and emotions. But just as cognitive-oriented counselors lean heavily on the role of the rational thought processes, so do affective-oriented counselors place most of their emphasis on emotional processes. Four models of affective counseling are presented in the pages that follow. These include psychoanalysis, Gestalt, transactional analysis, and client-centered therapy.

Key terms

affective
psychoanalysis
personality structure
repression
transference
Gestalt psychology
perceptions
unified totality
transactional analysis
structural analysis
crossed transactions
client-centered counseling
personality reorganization
positive growth

Psychoanalytic theory in counseling

Background

Freud as developer of psychoanalysis

The progenitor of the psychoanalytic approach was Sigmund Freud, who began developing this theory in the 1890s and remained an active clinician and writer until his death in 1939. Although other theorists have modified Freud's constructs and techniques, he has remained the chief force in psychoanalytic counseling. Psychoanalysis has paved the way for widespread cultural acceptance of psychological applications to almost every realm of human experience. Freud, however, began with some very narrow concepts, and the far-ranging impact of psychoanalysis in so short a time is a tribute to the appeal of his ideas.

Freud was trained as a medical doctor. His original interest was in the functioning of the brain. The medical model at that time held that every type of disturbance in human functioning had a physiological basis. Thinking and behaving processes that seemed different or abnormal were thought to result from an abnormal brain or nervous system structure. Yet medical researchers looked in vain for malformed structures, even in situations where actual physical symptoms existed, such as a paralyzed hand attached to an otherwise functional arm. Often, no physical reason could account for such phenomena.

Two factors influenced Freud's early thinking. He was exposed to hypnosis, and he became aware of a "talking cure," whereby physical symptoms were eliminated through extensive verbal discussion. Freud was puzzled as to how a mental process such as suggestion could affect physical symptoms. Freud tried to account for such inexplicable events by hypothesizing a nonphysical structure, that is, a personality structure common to everybody, that could influence how a person behaved or thought.

Personality structure in psychoanalysis

Freud attempted to apply the processes of the medical model to the study of how humans thought and behaved. He patterned his methods after the medical research model of his day by describing a personality "structure" and by developing a diagnostic system for resolving "structural" problems. The prevalent medical science of his time is reflected throughout his explanation of basic personality structure. Freud also probably viewed himself more as a researcher than as a clinician. His counseling applications were viewed as therapeutic manipulations from which observations were obtained and inferences drawn about the underlying personality structure.

Other psychoanalytic approaches have evolved from Freud's initial efforts, including some theoretical constructs and emphases that contrast with those of Freud. The same concern, however, with personality structure and dynamics, pervades all of these theories.

The theory

Freud recognized that certain events and behaviors could not be accounted for by physically oriented, medical explanations. He believed that other structures needed to be discovered that were not physiological in nature. Freud first posited that in some way emotions could disrupt normal behavior and bodily processes. Freud then needed to explain how such mental forces as the emotions could create these disturbances in a person's behavior and physiology.

Freud suggested that personality could be structured into three separate but interacting parts. The first part is called the id. The id, Freud said, contains those instincts that are necessary to support life. These instincts are self-serving and, possibly, are indicative of the basically evil nature of humans. The energy needed to activate the id is supplied biologically. The id is seemingly mindless in its self-serving demands and is gradually brought under control by the emerging ego. Essentially, the ego formulates the intellectual processes by which a person consciously controls his or her actions. The ego needs to gain control of the energy that originates in the id, yet it must also continue to supply the id with its instinctual demands. If the ego becomes weakened, the id's instinctual demands will seek to be fulfilled in reckless, ill-considered ways. This problem becomes compounded by the formation of the superego, a third part of personality that is gradually developed by social and cultural demands. Through the superego, society seeks to mold the individual to fit accepted social patterns. Often, though, these social patterns are not in harmony with the self-serving instincts of the id. The superego will then also attempt to divert energy from the ego to suppress the id. The ego must continually control the energy demands of the id and the superego. When either the id or the superego becomes dominant over the others, the result is the abnormal functioning that manifests itself sometimes by physiological symptoms or by strange behavior. These abnormal functionings are generally referred to as neuroses. If the ego loses all control, the subsequent severe loss of functioning is called psychosis.

Personality dynamics in psychoanalysis

This structure is dynamic because it occurs within the individual and receives its energizing support entirely from within the individual. Even though external demands can influence the person through the superego, it can only do so when the ego has been drained of its capability to control matters. Internal weaknesses allow unhealthy structural interactions to occur. Therefore, for change, that is, a cure, to occur, these internal problems must be overcome. This suggests a treatment method that is geared to changing structures within the individual rather than structures in the external environment.

The dynamic force within a person constantly seeks an outlet. The effects of this energy will emerge with or without the support of conscious processes. Even the act of repressing of undesirable emotions and thoughts cannot prevent the unconscious expression of the energy. Any instinctual demands that are prohibited socially, incest, for example, would be repressed by the ego. Yet, since this energy needs to be expended, it may take different forms of expression through leisure and work activity and be released by the person in ways that may not seem to be related at all to the original instinctual desire. Often, the person is not aware of how such expressions and diversions from the original desire actually occur. This gave rise to Freud's claim of the discovery of the unconscious, one of Freud's more important concepts.

It was the goal of counseling, or therapy, as Freud referred to it, to uncover the unconscious repressions and to relate them to the basic structural needs of the person. Although much of this energy was released as emotion, or affect, Freud thought it needed to be brought under the conscious control of the ego and expressed in a way that best met both the internal and external demands made on the person.

Sexual development in psychoanalytic theory

Freud's work with his patients led him to conclude that the basic reason people became neurotic—at the mercy of repressed, unconscious emotion—was due to inhibited sexual development. Freud held that a person's sexual development progressed not only physically, but also emotionally. He introduced the new and highly controversial concept that emotional sexual development proceeded alongside physical development. Freud also thought that sexuality began with infancy. Freud believed that by age five, a child should have progressed through three sexual phases, which he labeled the oral, the anal, and the genital stages. These labels reflect the physical body parts that are thought to provide fulfillment of drives in the young child. Gradually, the child learns to seek satisfaction for these sexual desires from other people. For boys, the mother becomes the object of this satisfaction, and, therefore, the father becomes the child's rival for mother. Freud labeled this rivalry the Oedipus complex, after a Greek myth that describes just such an unconscious rivalry. Freud believed that if this simultaneous attraction and rivalry were not resolved, emotional sexual development would be repressed, and sexual drives would not be adequately met. Such repressed drives might disrupt a person's functioning by attempting to gain release in some other way. Other traumata that interrupt the development of sexual maturity will also lead to repressed drives and other neurotic symptoms. These repressed sexual drives could find many outlets for expression besides sexual ones but Freud found that many of his patients reflected stunted sexual growth. He further believed that most of the retarding traumatic events occurred before the age of five.

The therapeutic processes that Freud developed were geared toward helping people identify their unconscious repressions, thereby gaining cognitive, conscious control over these disabling emotions. Since Freud believed these unconscious processes were interjected into all phases of a person's life, he applied his diagnostic inclinations to such diverse areas as dreams, free-flowing speech, simple mistakes and "accidents," as well as other manifestations of neurotic behavior and thought, all of which eventually pointed to the type of drive that was being repressed. Depending upon the type of object that was sexually desired and then repressed, Freud tried to determine at which stage sexual development had been interrupted and what traumatic event had occurred. If a person could consciously reexperience this traumatic event and allow the ego to control the demands of the id and superego, normal sexual development would begin again, and neurotic behavior would gradually recede.

Therapeutic techniques

The major technique Freud used to uncover such trauma was called

Transference, free association, and Freudian slips

transference. Freud believed that his patients would project their repressed feelings regarding another person onto the counselor if he managed to keep his own personality from interfering too much with the therapeutic process. In an attempt to minimize the personal aspect of the relationship, he seated himself behind the patient, who was expected to recline on a couch. He also thought the therapist should try to maintain his posture as a clinical observer, interjecting only his interpretation of repressed materials. Minimizing the interaction between counselor and counselee in order to enhance transference continues to be used in contemporary psychoanalysis.

A technique that heightened transference was free association, which required the counselee to discuss all the thoughts that coursed through his or her consciousness during a session. Freud found that many repressions near the surface of consciousness provided symbols for the deeper unconscious. Analysis of dream content also held a key to the symbolic vividness of the contents of the unconscious. Freud believed that the ego had less control during sleep, so that unconscious drives could emerge in dreams.

Freud also analyzed misstatements and forgetfulness, which have become popularly known as "Freudian slips," such as substituting the name of one person for another, thereby indicating an unconscious preference. Freud felt that misstatements and forgetfulness, which he called parapraxes, were really the subtle emergence of unconscious, repressed drives.

By using such techniques, Freud could help a person expose, identify, and consciously allow expression of repressed and disruptive material. Once fully expressed, hidden drives would no longer produce neurotic symptoms. A person would need to mobilize the energy of the ego, however, to effect constant exposure and interpretation of repressed emotions. Only the ego would be able to sort rationally all the demands of the id and superego.

The strength of Freud's approach and theory is evidenced by the fact that for most of the first half of the twentieth century, his theory was used extensively and influenced the theory building of many others. Not only in the field of counseling, but in areas of art, literature, and history, his influence was felt.

This is not to say that others did not contribute to the continued development of psychoanalysis. Freud's daughter, Anna Freud, extended the concept of the defense mechanisms used by the ego to control against unconscious drives.[1] Melanie Klein developed

1. Anna Freud, *The Ego and the Mechanism of Defense*, rev. ed. (New York: International Universities Press, 1966).

methods to apply psychoanalysis to the study and treatment of children.[2] Erik Erikson extended the concept of life stages throughout the life span and posited ideas about the tasks people needed to achieve to proceed successfully through all the required stages.[3] Erich Fromm applied psychoanalysis to the study of cultures and human social development.[4]

Other psychoanalytic theorists

There also have been departures from Freud's theoretical and practical applications that have been influential in their own right. Alfred Adler and Carl Jung were both among Freud's closest followers early in the century, but both believed that causes other than sexual trauma contributed to neurotic behavior. Adler developed a system known as individual psychology, which attributed abnormal development to anxiety-ridden attempts to compensate for personal feelings of inferiority.[5] Jung differed from Adler and Freud in that he believed people contained within them more than just a structure, or mold, into which content was poured as a result of life's experiences. Rather, he thought human beings possessed a universal linkage to all humankind, past and present. These linkages, or archetypes, emerged through the unconscious to influence thought and behavior. Jung sought to help people get in touch with their mythical inheritance and to help the archetypes emerge. They represented creative capacities.[6]

Other theorists have become identified as neo-Freudians. Two of the most influential of these have been Karen Horney and Harry Stack Sullivan. Horney identified a series of interpersonal needs that people must resolve. Problem behavior would occur as a result of these needs going unmet. Horney felt the family structure often set the stage for the way a person developed.[7]

Sullivan's ideas also emphasized social needs. His focus on the counselee's present concerns deemphasized the role of the past and encouraged the counselor to become more active in helping a person solve problems and learn new approaches to social situations.[8] All these theoretical systems, however, present anxiety as the

---

2. Melanie Klein, *The Psychoanalysis of Children*, 3rd ed. (London: Hogarth Press, 1959).

3. Erik H. Erikson, *Identity and the Life Cycle* (New York: International Universities Press, 1959).

4. Erich Fromm, *The Sane Society* (New York: Holt, Rinehart, 1955).

5. Alfred Adler, *The Practice and Theory of Individual Psychology*, 2nd ed. rev. (Totowa, N.J.: Littlefield, Adam, 1969).

6. Jolande Jacobi, *The Psychology of C. G. Jung* (New Haven, Conn.: Yale University Press, 1962).

7. Karen Horney, *Neurosis and Human Growth* (New York: Norton, 1950).

8. Harry S. Sullivan, *The Fusion of Psychiatry and Social Science* (New York: Norton, 1964).

major source of concern, particularly when it becomes severe enough to interfere with a person's adjustment. Thus, the dynamic theory of Freud's system has remained constant, even in those systems that recognize the effects of the external environment in a way that Freud did not.

Although many counselors have attempted to use Freudian dynamic concepts in their counseling applications, traditional psychoanalysis has been much too time-consuming and expensive to be applied in most counseling settings such as schools and rehabilitation facilities. Psychoanalysis, which requires intensive therapy over several years, has been much more applicable in private practice situations than anywhere else.

Several people are noted for their attempts to inject psychoanalysis into more typical counseling settings. C. H. Patterson[9] documents the work of E. S. Bordin and F. Alexander as examples. Bordin's significant contribution was to organize counseling around psychoanalytic personality constructs, particularly in the explanation of vocational development. Alexander presented a framework that greatly reduced the time requirement of regular psychoanalysis, which usually requires almost daily contact over several years. He worked with weekly contacts that lasted only a year or more. Alexander also recommended a much greater degree of counselor involvement and activity during the counseling session than traditional psychoanalysts had. King and Bennington[10] also tried to adapt psychoanalytic concepts to typical counseling settings in an effort to shorten the time involvement. They, too, recommended a more active role for the counselor in interpreting to the counselee unconscious repressions. These more recent developments require the counselor to instruct counselees in the interpretation and meaning of symbolic materials.

There are many sources for anyone interested in reading more about psychoanalytic thought. The interested reader is referred to Wyss' *Psychoanalytic Schools*[11] and Brenner's *An Elementary Textbook of Psychoanalysis*[12] for more in-depth overviews. Each of the psychoanalytic theorists previously mentioned have also written widely and are important sources for an in-depth study of the psychoanalytic approach.

---

9. C. H. Patterson, *Theories of Counseling and Psychotherapy* (New York: Harper & Row, 1973).

10. P. T. King and K. F. Bennington, "Counseling and Psychoanalysis," in *Theories of Counseling*, 2nd ed., ed. B. Stefflre and W. H. Grant (New York: McGraw-Hill, 1972).

11. D. Wyss, *Psychoanalytic Schools* (New York: Jason Aronson, 1973).

12. C. Brenner, *An Elementary Textbook of Psychoanalysis* (New York: International Universities Press, 1955).

Related research

Case-study method versus controlled experimentation

It is difficult to summarize all the evidence that exists under the heading of psychoanalytic research. Freud's primary research tool was the case study, a clinical observation method that was patterned after typical medical research of his day. In a case study, the therapist keeps copious notes on the sessions with the counselees and also adds his or her own comments. Freud never attempted any other kind of research, and it is the major research technique of psychoanalysts even today. Controlled experimentation, frequently used by behaviorists and other therapists doing research, is considered unacceptable by psychoanalysts who feel that the techniques involved in measuring behavior would greatly interfere with the therapeutic process. Even the use of tape recorders is often considered too much interference. Nonpsychoanalytic researchers feel that this reluctance to use measurement techniques and other tools available to the therapist is what keeps psychoanalysis from being as scientific as it might be.

Psychoanalytic research is also compounded by the fact that very few people use traditional psychoanalytic techniques. Most psychoanalytically oriented counselors have varied their techniques to fit the time demands of counselees. This is referred to as psychoanalytical psychotherapy in order to distinguish it from psychoanalysis. The applications of these therapists are so varied that it is difficult to generalize from them or even to find commonalities that can be consistently researched. The use of pure psychoanalytic theory, however, has influenced their emphasis on the personality structure of counselees and the reorganization of the personality to better help counselees cope with social and environmental demands.

Evaluation of psychoanalysis

Very little controlled research is available that can be used to evaluate the psychoanalytic approach. In a review of the quantitative research of psychoanalysis available,[13] Luborsky and Spence found very little to comment on much that has significance. One generalization they find is that psychoanalytic techniques work best with those counselees who have a lot of education, are young, and have few emotional problems. Such a finding could also explain why so few counselors who work in publicly funded counseling settings find psychoanalysis useful. Clientele of these agencies rarely reflect these characteristics. Most people who use psychoanalytic techniques are in private practice.

---

13. L. Luborsky and D. T. Spence, "Quantitative Research on Psychoanalytic Therapy," in *Handbook of Psychotherapy and Behavior Change*, ed. Allen E. Bergin and Sol L. Garfield (New York: John Wiley & Sons, 1971).

It does not seem that the impasse over what can be considered adequate research evidence will soon be resolved. Those who favor psychoanalysis feel that their clinical methods are self-validating. Most empirically minded researchers demand more external evidence before they can agree that psychoanalytic approaches have been validated. Since so many psychoanalytic constructs are hypothetical and inferential to begin with, psychoanalytically minded counselors will be hard-pressed to present external evidence.

Gestalt applications to counseling

Background

The most prominent person associated with counseling based on Gestalt principles is Fritz (Frederick) Perls. Perls was trained as a psychoanalyst but came under the influence of Gestalt psychology. The word "Gestalt" is a German word that is practically untranslatable; thus, the German word is widely used. *Gestalt* conveys the meaning that a person, object, or event must be looked at as a whole. A study of the parts would not permit one to understand the whole of something. Gestalt psychology is very much concerned with how a person perceives and understands anything that comprises his or her experience. Gestalt psychology emphasizes the physiological foundations of perceptions, as well as the environmental factors that affect them. This concern with the interaction between the person and the environment continues to influence the theory and application of Gestalt counseling. The person and the environment are considered a unique whole that constantly is changing. It is not considered viable to study the person or the environment as separate parts, abstracted from their interaction.

Perception in Gestalt theory

Perls came to the United States following World War II. He has had a wide ranging impact on counseling in this country. Many counselors think of themselves as belonging to the Gestalt school of counseling, and Gestalt techniques have been incorporated into many other modes of counseling as well. Perls wrote extensively and was an energetic teacher. From his writings, two books, *Gestalt Therapy*[14] and *Gestalt Therapy Verbatim*,[15] are particularly recommended for theoretical detail accompanied by extensive practical material.

14. Fritz Perls, R. Hefferline, and Paul Goodman, *Gestalt Therapy* (New York: Julian Press, 1951).

15. Fritz Perls, *Gestalt Therapy Verbatim* (Lafayette, Calif.: Real People Press, 1969).

Frederick (Fritz) Perls was a leader in the Gestalt therapy movement, which held that a person and his or her environment formed a complete whole and that persons were capable of coping with any situation they might confront.

The theory

Gestalt counseling begins with a basic assumption that people are complete in and of themselves and have the capability of coping with whatever happens to them. Everything that people experience is goal-directed and purposeful. Perls hypothesized that needs would gradually emerge and, if perceived, could be fulfilled. People experience emotional problems because they block their awareness of needs, which then do not become adequately perceived and resolved. In order to meet their needs, persons must aggressively pursue solutions and take responsibility upon themselves for their lives. People must attain independence or they cannot expect to feel fulfilled. Difficulties in gaining awareness often occur because people allow external factors, such as the judgments of others, to interfere with how they value their own needs. In other words, people view their own desires and needs as unworthy, illegitimate, or through guilt-ridden eyes, which forces them to resist perceiving these needs. Unmet needs, if not allowed full expression, will continue to interfere with the perception and fulfillment of a person. Coping ability is stifled, and life becomes increasingly limited. As in psychoanalysis, the internal dynamics of people's emotions can drastically disrupt pursuit of personal fulfillment.

Unified totality and Gestalt theory

Like psychoanalysis, the basic underpinnings of Gestalt theory rest in the biological aspects of human nature. It is at the biological level that the essential interaction between people and their environment becomes most evident. Without the external environment, humans could not exist. Existence is defined by how a person interacts with the external reality that makes up the environment. Perls believed that the emotional and intellectual aspects of human nature, as well as the biological, can only be understood in combination with the external environment. People cannot be defined by specific traits because all aspects of life interact with and depend upon one another. People are not merely biological, social, or emotional beings; each person exists as a unified totality. When people are viewed and treated as other than complete human beings, artificial structures are set up with boundaries that prohibit open and respectful interactions.

Even though it is human nature to interact as a unified whole with the environment so that one's naturally emerging human needs can be met, the external social structure can become too controlling. Individual needs are often stifled for fear that the needs of society would be harmed. Growth and change in individuals can become risky to the society, which has a stake in maintaining the status quo. Social controls are transmitted by parents to children. The children are then expected to become self-regulating and permit only socially safe needs to be fulfilled. In this fashion, individual human growth and development is kept at the lowest common denominator. The price is high, because so many people carry around frustrated needs that limit their capability to experience and enjoy life. Once people try to manage and deliberately control situations, they have thwarted their capability for naturally fulfilling their existence. This concept of Gestalt theory stands in sharp contrast to the learning principles of those who believe people should actively manage their lives for positive behavioral change. This type of control, as judged by Gestaltists, restricts the natural interaction of persons and environment, which, in turn, hinders satisfaction and a sense of fulfillment.

This seems to create a dilemma, if one were to conceptualize individual counseling concerns from a Gestalt perspective. If counselees are not expected to manage their behavior, what can a Gestalt counselor hope to accomplish?

Techniques and goals of Gestalt counseling

Perls recommended that counselors take an active and direct role in guiding their counselees not toward improved management skills but toward total awareness of their existence, which is consistent with Gestalt theory. Existence becomes meaningful only when the needs of the person are allowed to emerge and be fulfilled. Fulfillment depends upon perception of needs. The goal, then, of Gestalt counseling, is to help counselees understand that they seek harmony and fulfillment with the environment around them. Counselees must learn to trust their own personal needs and seek gratification for them without having to control them. Counseling activity must focus on helping counselees become aware of their needs without concerning itself with conscious efforts at control and arbitrary need satisfaction based on socially accepted standards.

Gestalt counselors use the frustrations of counselees to help them become more aware of themselves. Anxiety is viewed as a sign of an unmet need. Accordingly, counselors often focus on it and even increase it so that it can be better understood. This process is sometimes painful to counselees, but Perls recognized this discomfort as the breaking off of rigid, growth-inhibiting attitudes. Attempts at real growth are painful because the consequences are unknown and, therefore, risky.

Gestalt counseling also emphasizes the present as opposed to the past or future. The focus is on what is going on with the counselee at the time of counseling since unmet needs that are being blocked are the most important factors with which one has to deal. Content regarding the past or future is not avoided, but it is placed into the context of the present so the counselee can examine how he or she is currently being affected by it.

Since Gestalt counseling is based on the theoretical premise that people are a unity rather than being composed of discrete parts, a concerted effort is made to bring the total person into the counseling session. One's intellectual material is not denied, but special efforts are made by the Gestalt counselor to help counselees become aware of their emotional and physiological selves as well. Perls and his followers also demonstrate how the interpretation of body language and other nonverbal modes of communication reveal extensive amounts of information about a counselee. How a person sits, what repetitive or spontaneous movements a person makes, and speech factors such as tone and speed, can be used to uncover areas of need that a counselee is suppressing.

Use of role playing in Gestalt counseling

Gestalt counselors also make use of a counselee's fantasies and dreams since unmet needs will emerge through these channels if they have been blocked from consciousness. Often, to capitalize on this, Gestalt therapists set up role-playing situations in order for people to act out these fantasies. Such techniques have been elaborated upon greatly and have become a central element of the encounter-group movement. These techniques were not meant to become gimmicks that people would casually experience. Perls used them only with specific individuals with specific areas of needs. He also individualized his use of such techniques, which increased their meaningfulness for those experiencing them. Gestalt counselors are interested in increasing the impact of the experiences so that they can be perceived more easily and better understood. This highlights the growth pattern projected by Gestalt theory. As experience becomes awareness, people will anticipate and move toward additional experiencing. Growth and development continue. They never stop as long as the person allows an uncontrolled expression of the potential to experience and to perceive.

Gestalt counselors usually recognize that the counselee's interpersonal relationships are the highest plane on which the person and the environment can interact. Much is made, therefore, of the counselee-counselor interaction since it is from such a relationship that knowledge and understanding of the counselee's other relationships can be gained. The counselor does not hold back personal feelings, even those that confront the counselee, since the counselee will grow from experiencing them and doing something about them, if need be. The counselor has to be careful, however, of becoming judgmental. Gestalt counselors want counselees to perceive the reality of how others see them, but not view it as an external evaluation that demands change. The counselor would expect the counselee to make decisions about change based on perceived internal needs. This attitude reflects the faith of the counselor in the capability of the counselee to assume responsibility for growth and action.

Related research

Controlled research has been neglected by Gestalt counselors, basically because of their preoccupation with theoretical concerns. Since Gestalt theory stipulates that reality amounts to the ever-changing perceptions of persons as they interact with others and the environment, there is no such thing as a variable that can be measured and manipulated. The very act of trying to measure something requires it to remain constant for a time. Something that does not change for Gestaltists is something that is not growing. The act of measurement, therefore, is an act that, at least for a time, limits growth and development. All forms of controlled research have the same effect, according to the Gestalt framework.

Some previous work has been done regarding how perceptions emerge for humans, but this research has not been undertaken by counselors who use Gestalt theory. They have borrowed from such research, however, to substantiate their beliefs regarding the interaction between the figure/ground constellation in the environment and the state of the individual doing the perceiving.

Gestaltists also point to natural processes and ecological balances as support for their concepts that organisms seek life-fulfillment on a continuing basis. They contrast these natural phenomena against what they view as the restrictive behavior of many people in our society. They also use the self-reported life changes of people who have experienced Gestalt counseling as proof of the validity of their concepts.

Transactional analysis

Background

Transactional analysis (TA) is a rather recent addition to the stable of counseling theories. Eric Berne was the originator of transactional analysis. He began to publicize his ideas in the 1950s. As was the case with so many other theoreticians, he was trained as a psychoanalyst. It was as a practicing psychiatrist that he gradually began to evolve his concepts of transactional analysis.

Transactional analysis and psychoanalysis

There are many similarities between transactional analysis and psychoanalysis. Both have similar formulations of personality structure, and both are systems that are energized by the interactions of the structural parts. Other similarities become apparent when the theory is presented in greater detail. One clue as to why Berne saw fit to evolve a separate theoretical formulation from psychoanalysis, even though the essential elements remained similar, may be found in the words of Thomas Harris, who wrote *I'm OK—You're OK,* a book that explained transactional analysis to laypersons.

One difficulty with many psychoanalytic words is that they do not have the same meaning for everybody. . . . Vague meanings and complicated theories have inhibited more than helped. . . . The vocabulary of Transactional Analysis is the precision tool of treatment because, in a language that anyone can understand, it identifies things that really are. . . .[16]

This suggests that while transactional analysis may be a derivative of psychoanalysis, it is formulated in such a way as to make it much more comprehensible to counselor and counselee alike. Furthermore, counseling applications differ significantly, and in that sense, transactional analysis does deserve to be viewed as a separate entity.

Transactional analysis and Gestalt

Others have also pointed out the similarities between transactional analysis and Gestalt theory. Possibly, the uniqueness of transactional analysis lies in the blending of psychoanalytic and Gestalt concepts. James and Jongeward have recognized the potential of this combination in their book *Born to Win: Transactional Analysis with Gestalt Experiments*. They formally link the systems together. They wrote:

Transactional analysis gives a person a rational method for analyzing and understanding behavior; gestalt therapy gives a person a useful method for discovering the fragmented parts of his personality, integrating them, and developing a core of self-confidence. Both methods are concerned with discovery and fostering awareness, self-responsibility, and genuineness. Both methods are concerned with what is happening now.[17]

Other aspects of transactional analysis

Other applications of transactional analysis also seem related to behavioral counseling practices, particularly the use of contracting, which is described later.

Berne has written extensively, and many of his books have become best-sellers. His appeal to the layperson is widespread. Among his books are *Games People Play*,[18] and *What Do You Say After You Say Hello?*[19]

Early in the development of transactional analysis, Berne began holding weekly seminars for local counselors and therapists in San Francisco. These sessions were very productive, and others became enthusiastic about transactional analysis and even began

---

16. T. A. Harris, *I'm OK—You're OK* (New York: Harper & Row, 1967): xx

17. M. James and D. Jongeward, *Born to Win: Transactional Analysis with Gestalt Experiments* (Reading, Mass: Addison-Wesley, 1971): ix.

18. E. Berne, *Games People Play* (New York: Grove Press, 1964).

19. E. Berne, *What Do You Say After You Say Hello?* (New York: Grove Press, 1972).

contributing to the body of theory. Berne, however, remained the most important figure in the movement until his death in 1970.

The weekly seminar evolved into the International Transactional Analysis Association, which publishes the *Transactional Analysis Journal*. The association has developed a training and certification procedure to ensure that those who practice transactional analysis use it in a professionally sound manner.

The theory

Transactional analysis is a theoretical framework that states that the affective, often unconscious, part of the personality influences the conscious behavior and feelings of a person. It attempts to help people gain active, rational control over these unconscious processes. Its goal is to integrate the affective and cognitive components of the personality.

Analytic areas in transactional analysis

According to the theory, four basic areas of a person's life need to be analyzed. The first is the basic personality structure, and the analysis of it is called structural analysis. This is the analysis of the inner structure of the personality, the structure that determines what a person is. The similarity between this structure and the id, ego, and superego of psychoanalysis will be apparent shortly. The second area, referred to as transactional analysis, is the study of the communication patterns among persons. Specifically, this analysis focuses on the part of the inner structure that originates the communicated message. The third area concerns itself with how people structure and spend their time. This is called game analysis. Certain behavioral patterns tend to recur often with consistent outcomes. The fourth area concerns itself with the total person. Transactional analysis counselors believe the course of a person's life follows a certain pattern, or life-script, which predicts how the person's life will turn out. This fourth area, therefore, is known as life-script analysis. Each of these analyses are described in more detail.

Structural analysis

Structural analysis examines the interaction among the ego-states of the personality. The first ego-state is referred to as the child. It refers to those occasions when a person, regardless of age, acts and responds as a child would. Therefore, it is emotion-laden. The second ego-state, which is the adult, is emotionless. This state is highly deliberate, rational, and analytical. It tends to be the decision maker for the personality. The third state is the parent. This state contains the values, attitudes, and actions that are acquired from significant others. Value-laden decisions, which emerge from the parent, often may supercede the decisions of the adult. This implies that social values may determine a person's course of action rather than the needs of the individual. This can have positive and negative implications. The similarities between the id and the child, the ego and the adult, and the superego and the parent should now be self-evident.

Each of these ego-states has control of a person at various times. The appropriate one depends upon specific situations. If one state fails to operate when a situation requires it to do so, the one that supercedes it will create problems. The fact that each ego-state has its appropriate time and place is a fundamental difference from psychoanalysis, where the ego is required to maintain the balance between the id and superego. The role of the transactional ego-states has been described as follows:

> *It might be said that the Parent is ideally suited where control is necessary: control of children, of unknown situations, of fears, of unwanted expression, and of the Child. The Adult is suited to situations in which accurate prediction is necessary. The Child is ideally suited where creation is desired: creation of new ideas, procreation, creation of experience, and so on.*[20]

Recent theoretical and clinical developments have added a new dimension to structural analysis. Each of the major ego-states, the parent, adult, and child, are now viewed to have sub-states, which also can be analyzed. Each ego-state is believed to have within it three sub-states that are analogous to the parent, adult, and child. This greatly adds to the complexity of structural analysis.

Ego-state interaction: transactional analysis

How these ego-states interact can be observed and understood, both by self and others, through conscious processes. This conscious observation primarily takes place during the second counseling stage, which focuses on the communication between people. In order for good personal and social adjustment to occur, proper communication is essential. Good communication from person to person must be complementary. These transactions occur when the message from the ego-state of the sender is perceived and responded to by the desired ego-state of the message receiver. The verbal and nonverbal messages people send indicate which ego-state is in control. For example, the adult of one person asks for the time, and the adult of the other responds with the correct information. The child of one person who has just lost a loved one asks for and receives comfort from the adult of another person.

Communication transactions in transactional analysis

20. E. Berne, C. M. Steiner, and J. M. Dusay, "Transactional Analysis," in *Direct Psychotherapy*, vol. 1, ed. R. M. Jurjevich (Coral Gables, Fla.: University of Miami Press, 1973): 377–78.

Crossed transactions indicate poor communication. They occur when the message sender does not receive a response from the ego-state of the receiver to which the message was sent. The adult ego-state asking for the time may receive the response of the parent of the other person in the form of scoldingly chiding the person for not wearing a watch. A grieving child ego-state, looking for comfort, may receive a cold, judgmental parent ego-state response that carries the message that each person must bear up under such situations since death is a natural part of life.

Ulterior transactions are another form of poor communication. These transactions occur on two levels. The social level contains the obvious meaning of the transaction as it occurs between two people. However, there is a psychological level, which contains the real or hidden agenda of the transaction. Two people may mourn the loss of a loved one on the surface, but underneath, they may be communicating a joy that shortly a large inheritance will be theirs. The ego-states that communicate the ulterior messages are in control.

Figure 8–1 illustrates the various types of transactions. Complementary transactions are diagrammed as parallel communications. Messages are delivered to and answered by the desired ego-state. Crossed transactions occur when the response received does not come from the desired ego-state of the communicating partner. Often the returned message is delivered to an ego-state other than the one that sent the message. Ulterior transactions reflect the fact that the real communication between ego-states of persons is not the one that occurs on the obvious, observed level, but rather, is one that occurs on the psychological level. This type of communication usually is reflected in nonverbal messages that supercede the content of spoken messages. The Gestalt influence is evident in this regard.

Game analysis

Game analysis in transactional analysis

Analyses of transaction patterns are called game analyses. According to Berne, the games that people play in their everyday interactions "(1) consist of an orderly series of transactions with a beginning and an end; (2) contain an ulterior motive, that is, contain a psychological level different from the social level; and (3) result in a payoff for both players."[21]

Analysis of games can provide the reasons that people interact with one another in the way they do. People are believed to have a

21. E. Berne, C. M. Steiner, and J. M. Dusay, "Transactional Analysis," p. 380.

Figure 8-1
Different types of communication transactions

Complimentary

Question:
What time is it?

Response:
It's three o'clock.

Crossed

Question:
What time is it?

Response:
Why don't you carry a watch?

Ulterior

Question:
What time is it?

Response:
It's two o'clock.
(We can take a break now; no one is around.)

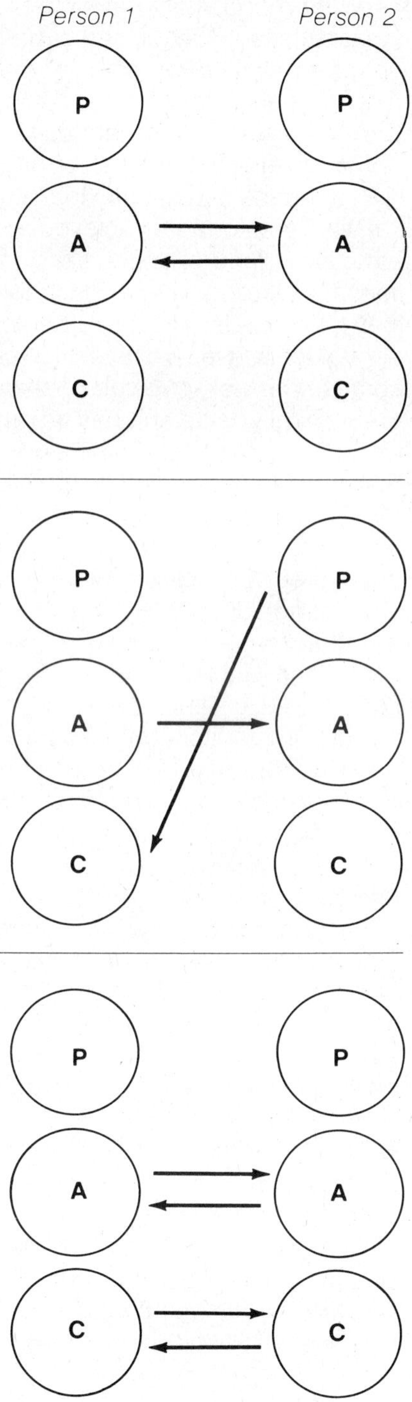

need for recognition that stems from an underlying biological need for stimulation. The playing of games that result in personal recognition is referred to as getting strokes. Strokes can consist either of actual touching or of symbolic touching through the spoken word. Strokes can also be either positive or negative. Some people, in fact, come to believe that harsh strokes are better than no strokes at all.

People also play games that allow them to fulfill their social needs. Familiar, comfortable social positions are maintained by games. Unfortunately, familiar social positions do not necessarily refer to situations that are positive or desirable. A negative but known situation may be more desirable to a person than a new situation in which the person feels insecure, even if it may potentially result in positive outcomes. The risk involved in trying something new may seem too great. Finally, a person has a basic life-view of self and the relationship of self to others. This life-view can take several different forms. Some of these are as follows:

I'm OK; You're OK.
I'm OK; You're not OK.
I'm not OK; You're OK.
I'm not OK; You're not OK.

Confirmation of this life-view can be gained through game playing. Again, the Gestalt influence in game analysis is apparent. Game playing can fulfill personal and social needs and provide a structure for daily interactions with others. Games also illustrate how the internal dynamics of an individual can emerge to dominate the behavior of that person and maintain behavioral patterns that can actually be detrimental to the person.

Life-script analysis

Focus of script analysis

The internal dynamics that give rise to game playing are the focus of script analysis. The life-script is usually determined in childhood and is perpetuated by the child ego-state throughout life. The script is derived in childhood from the response of the parents to the child ego-state. The child's child ego-state attempts to please the parents' parent ego-states and gain strokes from them. Current behavior, through games and transactions, also provide directional evidence related to the life-script. This direction centers on the sense of being OK that is ascribed to self and to others. These scripts often have been illustrated using common fairy tales. A person might be described as Snow White, always waiting for her prince to come along and remove her from a difficult situation Likewise, a person could be a golden-haired prince, always looking for Snow White or Sleeping Beauty.

The counseling process in transactional analysis

The goal of counseling is to help the adult ego-state reevaluate the life-script developed by the child ego-state and to implement a new script actively. How is this goal accomplished? How can the counselee make decisions that will reorient the script so that harmful games are eliminated or replaced by more acceptable ones? Counseling usually begins by instructing the counselee in the theory and terminology of transactional analysis. Since the concepts and terms of transactional analysis are meant for the layperson, a feeling of equality, or partnership, is generated between counselee and counselor. The counselee feels as informed as the counselor, and, therefore, professional distance is minimized. Counseling in groups is preferred to individual counseling because the group allows the potential for recreating a variety of social situations that will generate many transactions and games, thus revealing the basic life-scripts of the group members. The process begins with structural analysis, proceeds to transactional analysis, then game analysis, and finally, script analysis. Each analysis must be carefully done as subsequent analyses depend on the previous ones. The counselor is actively involved in helping counselees interpret the transactions, games, and scripts as they emerge.

Role of change in transactional analysis

When the analysis is complete, the counselee is faced with the decision to change inappropriate life-scripts. The counselor and group offer support to the members confronted with this decision about whether or not to alter a life-script. It is a difficult one to make because a lifetime of learning and behaving has been invested in the old script. To help facilitate this decision making, contracts are often developed between the counselor and counselee. Contracts are statements that specify a plan for change, which the counselee will seek to implement. The contents of a contract are meant to be as specific and descriptive as possible so that the counselee can clearly understand what needs to be done to change inappropriate transactions and games. A contract will be useless unless the counselee has made a firm commitment to change his or her life-script. The counselor and group members will provide the strokes and feedback necessary to help the counselee fulfill the requirements of a contract. Even though the counselor helps develop the contract, the contract itself should really be viewed as a contract among the ego-states of the counselee. Each ego-state of the counselee must want to participate in the contract or it will not work.

The transactional-analysis counseling process should be clearly distinct from that of psychoanalysis. The group situation and the active involvement of the counselor are clearly different. The unconscious direction of the life-script is indicative of the unconscious dynamics of psychoanalysis, but the emphasis on rationally changing the script is much greater from the TA perspective.

Related research

Transactional analysis, as a rather new counseling system which borrowed heavily from the clinical research methods of psychoanalysis and Gestalt counseling, has been subjected to extensive research, mostly using the case-study method. Little experimentally designed research has been undertaken to provide empirical support for its constructs. Much of the research is published in the *Transactional Analysis Journal.* One recent article, which critiqued transactional analysis research, found that it did not meet typical academic research standards.[22] The article cited the lack of experimental rigor as a factor in the weak research and recommended that this type of research be undertaken. According to other journal articles, empirical, quantitative research does appear to be in the offing. Other recent articles indicate that transactional analysis is successful with schizophrenics and children, but the descriptions of treatment were vague, and the outcomes measured generally were not accepted ones.[23] Another study indicated that the basic introductory course, which attempts to teach new counselees the structure and language of transactional analysis, does help to maintain an interest in and knowledge of transactional analysis after three months.[24] Also, another study indicated that persons trained in transactional analysis could make reliable judgments about the ego-state structures of test subjects with only a minimal amount of contact.[25]

Compared to the client-centered, behavioral, or rational-emotive theories, transactional analysis research is empirically limited. Its practitioners subscribe mainly to the clinical case-study approach so prevalent in psychoanalysis and Gestalt counseling. The effort to supplement this with empirical evidence is to be applauded.

---

22. V. J. Bannon, "Standards of Experimental Research," *Transactional Analysis Journal* 6, no. 3 (1964): 318–22.

23. J. Schiff, J. Erb, K. Warner, S. Schiff, D. Kline, and D. Bowman, "Biochemical Evidence of Cure in Schizophrenics," *Transactional Analysis Journal* 7, no. 2 (1977): 184–87. N. Amundson and D. D. Sawatzky, "A Summative Evaluation of the 'Transactional Analysis with Children' Educational Program," *Transactional Analysis Journal* 6, no. 3 (1976): 326–28.

24. P. J. Friday, "A TA 101: Does It Make a Difference?" *Transactional Analysis Journal* 7, no. 2 (1977): 176–77.

25. W. F. Sowder and R. A. Brown, "Experimentation in Transactional Analysis," *Transactional Analysis Journal* 7, no. 3 (1977): 279–84.

Since transactional analysis is still in its early stages of theoretical development, and since it aspires to common-sense simplicity, it will be appropriate at this point to analyze the empirical relationships among the various theoretical constructs of transactional analysis, particularly those of the ego-states. It is unfortunate, however, that even before these major constructs can be validated, structural analysis has become even more complicated by the introduction of the concepts of substates within the major ego-states.

The client-centered counseling approach

Background

Carl Rogers is the person most closely associated with the client-centered approach to counseling. In Chapter 6, his ideas were described as they relate to the development of the counseling relationship. Truax and Carkhuff were also introduced at that time as fellow researchers and developers of Rogers' approach to counseling. It was pointed out that not only had Rogers developed a counseling theory and methodology attractive to many counselors, he also was a major pioneer in introducing a scientific research approach to the study of counseling. Rogers has been, therefore, and remains, very influential in the field of counseling.

Rogers initially had contemplated entering the ministry but was eventually trained as a child-guidance worker within a psychoanalytic framework. He followed the lead of psychoanalytic theorists like Sullivan and Horney by recognizing the influence of social relationships in determining personality and behavior patterns. He began to formulate an approach of his own.

As indicated by his initial attraction to the ministry, Rogers had a philosophical orientation. He came to disagree with the primarily pessimistic Freudian view of the nature of human beings. This philosophical difference dictated to Rogers that a radically different approach to counseling was needed.

Rogers began publicizing his ideas during World War II. His optimistic view of human nature and his positive approach to learning were welcomed by a nation struggling with the trauma of a world in conflict. Rogers initially called his approach nondirective counseling. It was soon apparent, however, that the goal of nondirectiveness was too difficult, if not impossible, to achieve. Rogers then chose to call his approach client-centered counseling, a term that captured an element of his philosophical orientation. Rogers has expanded his initial formulations for individual counseling to include group counseling as well.

The theory

Rogers' philosophical view of human nature is essential to the development of this theory. He believes people are inherently good, endowed with a potential to live full and satisfied lives in harmony with others. Rogers wrote that "the basic nature of the human being, when functioning freely, is constructive and trustworthy. . . . Man's behavior is exquisitely rational, moving with subtle and ordered complexity toward the goals his organism is endeavoring to achieve."[26]

Value of individual growth in Rogerian theory

Rogers views the learning process, therefore, as one that permits the individual to discover the potential within him- or herself and then to choose those external resources that can be used to enhance the fulfillment of personal and social needs. Individual growth, if allowed to emerge from the self, will not be detrimental to the growth of other persons, but rather, people will grow in harmony with one another.[27]

It is obvious, however, that conflict rather than harmony earmarks not only interpersonal and social relationships, but also pervades the expressions of human nature within individuals. People are not at peace with themselves, nor with their fellows. Rogers accounts for this by describing a process that prohibits the natural emergence of the basic personality. This process occurs over time because persons mistakenly permit the evaluations of others and of society to supplant their own judgments regarding what is proper and important for them. Social pressures dictate values and behaviors that may not be congruent with one's inner self. This results in feelings of conflict. When people suppress their own natural inclinations in favor of external values, their own needs and values will still seek to emerge, thus causing emotional states of conflict and confusion. This conflict and confusion pervades the activities and relationships of the individual. General dissatisfaction often is an early result. Persons also build rigid defense systems that block their capacity to assimilate new experiences. Psychological growth is retarded.

Rogers believed that reality is what each individual perceives, regardless of what may appear real to other observers. Each person's reality is, by definition, different from that of anyone else.[28] Rogers' view precludes any categorization of people into diagnostic classes. Counselees must be viewed as individuals. Stereotypes and attempts at classification must be severely limited, as these ac-

26. C. R. Rogers, *On Becoming a Person* (Boston: Houghton Mifflin, 1961) p. 194–95.

27. C. R. Rogers, "Divergent Trends in Methods of Improving Adjustment," *Harvard Educational Review* 18 (1948): 209–19.

28. C. R. Rogers, *Client-Centered Therapy* (Boston: Houghton Mifflin, 1951) p. 484.

tions overlook the unique characteristics of each individual. Counselors must attempt to understand each counselee's phenomenological field. The phenomenological field of each individual depends to a large extent on the view that each person has of his or her inner self vis-à-vis the world. Because of social pressures, the self-concept often becomes distorted. Individual differences are viewed as abnormalities rather than as unique qualities. Individuals begin to perceive themselves according to what they feel are the views of others about themselves and not according to what they are really like. The true self is submerged under these external perceptions. The person attempts to achieve an ideal-self that is formed on the basis of external pressures. Whether these pressures are based on reality or not is irrelevant. They are real as long as they are felt.

The conflicts that occur at this stage are incongruent with the real self, and they stifle true growth and creative experience. The frustration that results often leads people to enter into the counseling relationship.

The counseling process

The process of counseling must begin with the counselor's acceptance of a central hypothesis about what leads people to change. Rogers stated:

I have come to feel that the more fully the individual is understood and accepted, the more he tends to drop the false fronts with which he has been meeting life, and the more he tends to move in a direction which is forward.[29]

This presents Rogers' fundamental view regarding the change process in counseling. Regardless of how good a counselor's technique may be, if there is no strong belief in this basic hypothesis, counseling will not be successful.

Counseling, thus, begins with the counselor's total acceptance of the counselee. The counselor must have an active faith in the positive-growth inclinations of the counselee. The counselor and counselee need to share mutual perceptions. Rogers wrote:

In the therapeutic experience, to see one's own attitudes, confusions, ambivalences, feelings, and perceptions, accurately expressed by another, but stripped of their complications of emotion, is to see oneself objectively, and paves the way for acceptance into the self of all these elements which are now more clearly perceived. Reorganization of the self and more integrated functioning of the self are thus furthered.[30]

29. C. R. Rogers, *On Becoming a Person*, p. 27.

30. C. R. Rogers, *Client-Centered Therapy*, pp. 40–41.

Counselor skills in Rogerian counseling

Although not explicitly stated by Rogers, there are two counselor skills that determine whether or not the counselor will establish the proper counseling climate. The counselor first must be able to listen to what the counselee is communicating. Then he or she must be able to express to the counselee the essence of what the counselor perceives. This communication, furthermore, must be done without any evidence of judgment on the part of the counselor.

As the counselee discloses information, the accepting attitude of the counselor will become apparent. This will enable the counselee to disclose material that is more threatening and that is usually submerged for fear of unfavorable evaluations from others. The counselee will gradually explore and uncover more aspects of the self that were even unknown to him- or herself. This process leads to a more thorough understanding of the self in the absence of external evaluation.

When the counselee and counselor come to perceive previously repressed material, the counselee has an opportunity to gain new personal understandings. Rogers wrote:

> *As these demand elements of experience are brought into awareness, a process which we have come to think of as the reorganization of self is necessitated. This picture of self, which the* [counselee] *has had, must be altered to contain these new perceptions of experience.*[31]

The counseling process gradually permits the counselee to gain a better perspective of what the real self is like, shorn of the burden of fear of external evaluation. The arbitrariness of the ideal-self also becomes apparent, and as counseling proceeds, the real- and the ideal-selves become more congruent. More important, the ideal-self becomes determined not by external pressure, but by the natural expression of internal needs.

The new perceptions of self lead to new behavior, both in and out of the counseling sessions. Rogers wrote: "The realization that one segment of personality organization has been reconstructed, and that new forms of behavior result from it—this it is that builds the [counselee's] confidence in his own ability to make progress in exploring himself."[32]

This process does not occur easily. Rogers often describes the pain and anguish a counselee experiences as personality reorganization occurs.[33] If the counselor can provide security and support, however, the counselee will come to experience positive growth.

31. C. R. Rogers, *Client-Centered Therapy*, p. 77.
32. C. R. Rogers, *Client-Centered Therapy*, p. 83.
33. C. R. Rogers, *Client-Centered Therapy*, p. 193.

This growth is reflected in perceptions of self that are relatively unaffected by external evaluation. The counselee is able to allow the inner self to unfold, which will permit greater contentment and a better adjustment. Concurrent with enhanced self-satisfaction is a renewed acceptance of others. How this comes about is somewhat unclear. Possibly, since external evaluation by others is discounted in favor of self-evaluation, less tension is perceived within relationships with others, making acceptance of others easier. Such inner congruence would also be reflected in consistency of behavior. The counselee can become more goal-directed in all facets of life. These new attributes are the expected outcomes of client-centered or Rogerian counseling. Change must result from the counseling relationship, according to Rogers. The relationship is not a genuine one if change does not become evident during the course of counseling. As the inner self becomes understood, the counselee can evaluate it personally and choose what is acceptable and what needs to be changed. In this way, the counselee can let the inner self emerge, experience new growth and creativity that previously was restricted, and therefore, learn to value the inner self much more. Without the burden of conflict, the counselee can pursue freer personal activities and interpersonal relationships, thus increasing the chances of further satisfaction. For the counselee, the process gradually becomes self-sustaining. As counselee growth emerges, the counselor actively supports and encourages the counselee.

Outcomes of client-centered counseling

Rogers believes that the interpersonal encounter that occurs in the counseling relationship is the most important factor in contributing to the counselee's success.[34] The counselor cultivates this relationship by helping the counselee clarify and integrate the affective and cognitive parts of the self. Often, the pervasiveness of emotional discomfort denied at the conscious level by the counselee is apparent to the counselor in the verbal and behavioral components of the counselee's expression. By reflecting feelings as well as factual material; by empathically helping the counselee to see the relationships between thoughts, actions, and feelings; by accepting the counselee as legitimate and lovable in spite of self-rejecting thoughts and actions, the counselor is able to prepare the counselee for self-acceptance.

Rogers has summarized the process and outcome of client-centered counseling as follows:

In general, the individual sees himself as entering [*counseling*] *in distress, decidedly maladjusted, very unlike the person he wants to be. During*

34. C. R. Rogers, "The Interpersonal Relationship: The Core of Guidance," *Harvard Educational Review* 32, no. 4 (1962): 416–29.

[counseling], he moves significantly in the direction of adjustment and integration, becomes inwardly more comfortable and less tense, sees others as more like himself, and relates more comfortably to them. He understands himself better and is more confident and self-directing. He alters his personal goal in a realistic and more achievable direction.[35]

Emphasis on phenomenological view of counselee

A counselor using the client-centered approach would be most interested in the phenomenological, or self-perceived view, of the counselee. Case histories and accounts of the past are important only insofar as they create an impact upon the present. Diagnostic categorizing and the use of psychometric tests are minimized. The counselor seeks to decrease the impact of external value systems, including that of the counselor, and trusts that the counselee will be able to arrive at the decisions necessary to implement change in the proper directions. As these changes occur, the counselor provides support. Since the relationship that develops is potentially a close one, the counselor needs to be aware of resistance to the termination of counseling. Still, a counselee undergoing important changes should soon be able to perceive the necessity of termination and should not view it as rejection. If this occurs, it is a good indication of the success of counseling.

Related research

As was pointed out in Chapter 6, Rogers was a pioneer in developing a research approach to the study of counseling that went beyond the clinical case-study method. Rogers opened the counseling session to empirical scrutiny. His own research and that of others who follow his theoretical formulations, notably, Charles Truax and Robert Carkhuff, has centered on counselor attributes and skills that relate to changes counselees make during and following counseling.

The role of the counselor in the counseling relationship certainly deserves the attention that client-centered research has accorded it. In addition to studying the overall importance of the counselor, client-centered researchers have focused on the value of specific characteristics of counselees, the counseling setting, specific behavioral change strategies, decision-making and problem-solving strategies, and the impact of community supports. Details of this research are presented in Chapter 6.

In retrospect, Rogers' research methods may seem less than scientific. Many research techniques have been applied to counseling,

35. C. R. Rogers and R. Dymond, ed. *Psychotherapy and Personality Change* (Chicago: University of Chicago Press, 1954) p. 418.

however, that have greatly expanded the scope, and therefore, the complexity of counseling. In this light, Rogers' research must be seen as honest attempts at increasing understanding of his theory.

Summary

Of the affective-oriented counseling approaches, four are discussed in this chapter: psychoanalysis, Gestalt, transactional analysis, and client-centered therapy.

Psychoanalysis, developed by Sigmund Freud, is based on the medical model in terms of its research applications and its clinical applications. Freud constructed a model of personality based on the psychosexual development. The components of the model were the id, ego, and superego; Freud believed that maladjustment occurred whenever the superego or the id took over too much control. These unconscious emotions that stifle the development of the personality structure usually originate at some point during childhood; they continue to interfere with a person's normal functioning into adulthood. Freud felt that repressed sex-related trauma accounted for much of the maladjustment, although modern psychoanalysts have expanded the bases for maladjustment.

Because psychoanalysis is a costly form of therapy in terms of time and money, only a few persons undergo it, but counselors have adopted many of Freud's premises about personality structure and the role of the unconscious in maladjustment. The goal of counseling is to uncover the subconscious processes and to assist the counselee in reasserting the ego as the chief controlling agent of the personality.

Gestalt therapy, developed in large part in the United States by Fritz Perls, consists of the theory that all experience is part of a whole, and that the parts only exist in relationship to one another. Counselees cannot break down their lives into separate components if they are to achieve full understanding of themselves.

The goal of Gestalt counseling is to encourage persons to experience their total selves without fear of judgmental reactions by others. They need to learn to place their own needs in the foreground so they can examine what it is that they truly want from life.

Transactional analysis is a blend of psychoanalysis and Gestalt therapy. It moves through a series of analyses that prompt the counselee to pinpoint his or her unique personality structure and the theme—or life-script—of this personality. The counselee also studies his or her communication and interaction patterns to see how he or she might better relate to others.

Counseling usually takes place in a group, in which the counselor attempts to teach each counselee the steps of the self-analysis until he or she gets to the point of recognizing his or her underlying life theme. Once this theme is determined, the counselee is encouraged to commit him- or herself to change and to relate to others in a healthier way. Counseling then focuses on a support strategy for the counselee who is undertaking change of his or her life-script.

Client-centered counseling, often associated with Rogers, assumes that the counselee knows best and contains the potential for managing his or her own growth and development. It is the least interfering of the approaches. A proper climate must exist for counseling to be effective. It is thought that counselors must show genuineness, nonjudgmental acceptance, and empathic understanding of the counselee for change to occur. The counselor must fully accept and analyze the counselee's views and then encourage the counselee to reorganize on his or her own for better self-realization and self-acceptance and also to be less judgmental of others.

Questions

1. What is psychoanalysis? How are the theories developed in psychoanalysis used by other counselors?

2. What is the Gestalt approach? How is it used in counseling?

3. What is transactional analysis? How is it used in counseling?

4. What is the client-centered approach? How is it used in counseling?

5. What kinds of persons would be most likely to benefit from each approach?

6. Compare and contrast the role of the counselor in each of these approaches.

7. What are some of the basic problems with psychoanalytic research?

8. Compare and contrast the research methods in Gestalt, transactional analysis, and client-centered therapy.

Projects

1. Watch films of Gestalt therapy and client-centered therapy to see how the two methods are similar and different from each other.

2. Read a book by one of the proponents of the approaches discussed in this chapter. Report to the class on the book.

3. Interview a Rogerian-oriented therapist to see what techniques he or she uses to maintain a nonjudgmental approach.

4. Form a panel of counselors to discuss these different approaches and the way in which the role of the counselor varies with each approach. Also check for similarities among the counselors in their approaches.

9 Group approaches in counseling

An obvious advantage of group counseling is the opportunity to interact with and receive the support of peers.

9

Introduction

In previous chapters of this book, the focus most often has been on counseling as it occurs between a counselor and one counselee. Counseling largely has been defined as a private affair between two persons. Yet counseling can and does occur in contexts where more than two people are involved. This chapter highlights the activities of counselors during group counseling. Group approaches will be examined from two perspectives: a social psychology perspective and a counseling theory perspective. These two perspectives can be viewed as contributory streams of thought to the overall knowledge that counselors who work with groups can use.

Key terms

group
social psychology perspective
counseling theory perspective
naturally formed groups
experimental laboratory groups
group guidance
group counseling
group therapy
process groups
growth groups
self-help groups

Social psychology perspective

The social psychology perspective focuses on variables that affect the ways in which groups function. This perspective is concerned with the processes that groups experience during the course of their existence. Naturally formed groups, such as a neighborhood, are often studied. From this research, social psychologists attempt to determine if there are typical sequences of activities that a group must go through to maximize its functioning. In addition, naturally formed groups are studied to determine how groups originate, how group leaders emerge, how characteristics of individual members affect the group's functioning, how leadership style affects group performance, and the many other factors that can influence group behavior. Social psychologists also attempt to understand how groups operate by contriving experimental laboratory groups. Such laboratory studies allow researchers to control and manipulate factors of their choosing, thus getting a more direct understanding of the effects of these factors. Group counselors could learn how to build positive factors into counseling and minimize those that detract from group functioning. Although such direct manipulation and understanding is valuable, laboratory studies must be viewed with caution due to the problem of generalizing from an artificial laboratory situation to naturally occurring groups. Both natural and laboratory research must complement one another. Shaw, in his book *Group Dynamics*,[1] documents much of this research and places the value of both types of research into perspective. Shaw also provides information concerning the current knowledge of how the various factors, singly and in combination, affect group process. Coun-

1. Marvin E. Shaw, *Group Dynamics*, 2nd ed. (New York: McGraw–Hill, 1976).

selors need to extract and consider this information to guide their own interaction and participation with groups. Journals that provide further information of group process from a social psychology perspective include the *Journal of Applied Behavioral Sciences, Journal of Social Psychology*, and the *Journal of Personality and Social Psychology*.

Counseling theory perspective

The second perspective, which is derived from counseling theory, is a more familiar one to counselors. It is a way of looking at groups based on their theoretical foundations. Various counseling theories have spawned applications to groups. Theoretical applications to groups have been derived for rational-emotive, transactional analysis, Gestalt, Rogerian, and behavioral theory. In most instances, these group approaches have at most been variations on counseling as done with individuals. George Gazda, in his book *Basic Approaches to Group Psychotherapy and Group Counseling*[2] compiles a variety of these counseling theory derivations for group applications. Journals that provide articles and research in this area are the *International Journal of Group Psychotherapy, Journal of Counseling Psychology*, the *Personnel and Guidance Journal*, and *The Journal of Specialists in Group Work*.

One problem with these two perspectives is that they rarely converge. Counselors lack methods and models for combining them, even though the potential benefit of such a linkage should be obvious. The empirical insights of social psychology could be blended into the theoretical frameworks, thereby creating a more complete process that would serve to validate, modify, or create new counseling methods and theories. It is hoped that the future will bring further integration than has been the case in the past.

Justification for counseling in groups

Many justifications have been offered for group counseling. Explanations vary from economic to theoretical ones. Let's examine some of the economic reasons.

Economic reasons for group counseling

Many counselors are burdened by heavy caseloads. Individual counseling under such circumstances would be difficult to accomplish, and, if done at all, would probably be reserved for a select

2. George M. Gazda, ed., *Basic Approaches to Group Psychotherapy and Group Counseling*, 2nd ed. (Springfield, Ill.: Charles C. Thomas, 1975).

few. Counselor contact with counselees in a group setting is a means of increasing contact beyond that which can be gained by relying only on individual counseling. Group procedures also free the counselor to engage in other necessary activities that might be neglected if all counseling were individual. For example, those persons who need individual counseling might be better served if their counselor, by using group procedures with others, could devote more individual time to them. Group procedures increase the efficiency of a counseling facility by increasing the number of persons served, increasing the use of the physical plant of the facility, and taking advantage of the obvious economy of presenting learning opportunities to groups rather than to individuals.

Theoretical reasons for group counseling

Probably of more substance are those reasons for group counseling that have a theoretical basis rather than an economical one. People spend most of their time and activities in group interaction. They are born into families. They attend school in classes. They play on teams. They work in units of organizations. Group interaction reflects the reality of everyday life. Many of the problems that people have do not exist in isolation, but in the social context of relationships with other people. Since so many of these concerns involve groups, it only seems logical to attempt to remedy these social concerns in a group setting.[3] Group counseling interaction simulates more closely the majority of interactions people have in everyday life. If a group member can learn to resolve social concerns in the context of a group, then the likelihood that this learning will transfer to everyday group situations is much greater. Since people spend so much time in groups, it only makes sense that group counseling provides a major resource for helping people adjust. Whether or not this rationale is legitimate awaits more extensive research into the overall impact of group counseling on interpersonal relations.

Group counseling as source of supportive environment

Another widely held theory related to the value of group counseling is the idea that the group context provides a substantially more supportive environment than other change processes do. Each group member can provide a measure of care and encouragement that is not available during individual counseling. This assumes, of course, that the group climate is a warm and secure one. To see that this is so is a major responsibility of the counselor.[4]

3. Clarence A. Mahler, "Group Counseling," *Personnel and Guidance Journal* 49, no. 8 (1971): 601–8.

4. Betty D. Meador, "Client-Centered Group Therapy," in *Basic Approaches to Group Psychotherapy and Group Counseling*, 2nd ed. ed., George M. Gazda (Springfield, Ill.: Charles C. Thomas, 1975), 175–95.

Another potential benefit of the group context is the opportunity that it offers for individuals to learn to provide care and support for others in a genuine way. Often, society prohibits persons from expressing serious concern for the well-being of others. In some segments of society, such sensitivity is frowned upon. This attitude can serve to isolate individuals. The group context provides a learning situation in which caring people can find ways of supporting others. This support, in turn, can be expected to reap its own rewards as others begin to reciprocate the same genuineness.[5]

This kind of sharing and support depends heavily upon the skill of the counselor to develop a secure and supportive group environment. This responsibility possibly requires a skill that may not be part of the typical tool kit of those trained to do individual counseling. If this is true, then there is a case for the argument that counselors who do group counseling need special training and supervision beyond what is needed for individual counseling.[6] This has often been a topic for debate. Other issues have been raised concerning group counseling, and a brief review of these issues is presented in the next section.

Another important benefit derived from the group context is the opportunity for counselors to observe how counselees behave in an interpersonal situation. As mentioned, the group context is one in which people find themselves every day of their lives. Personal problems often stem from social interaction, and the counselee often contributes to the problem. Problematic social behavior may emerge in the group context that would never be observed in individual counseling. Such problems can be dealt with very effectively in the group context.

Issues related to counseling groups

Theoretical definitions of groups

One of the major issues confronting proponents of group counseling is definitional in nature. It is the way that various kinds of groups can be distinguished from one another, or even whether distinctions can be made at all. Also of concern is whether these types of groups overlap in function and what this means to a counselor. This problem, admittedly a theoretical one, is nevertheless central to many

5. C. Gratton Kemp, *Foundations of Group Counseling* (New York: McGraw-Hill, 1970), 144–48.

6. George M. Gazda, J. A. Duncan, and P. J. Sisson, "Professional Issues in Group Work," *Personnel and Guidance Journal* 49, no. 8 (1971): 637–43.

other issues related to group counseling, such as the appropriate size and setting of the group, the purpose of a group, and more important, the skills and qualifications required of a counselor. To date, groups are most often classified in one of three categories. These are group guidance, group counseling, and group therapy.[7]

Functions of groups

Group guidance. Group guidance typically is associated with an instructional context. The leader intends to provide a learning experience, such as disseminating information, to achieve a particular purpose, which is usually determined by the leader. The setting is often a classroom. Little interaction is expected from the group members. The process has a predetermined structure from which little deviation is expected.

Group counseling. Group counseling is not as easily described. The purpose of group counseling, if a general view is appropriate at all, is usually one of providing people with an opportunity to learn how to resolve personal problems. These problems are usually confined to a certain life area, such as an inability to make friends, find a job, rear children, or other such concerns that typically beset people as they become exposed to new life-task requirements. Group counseling, then, is often described as a means of helping people cope with the new developmental tasks they face as they mature. The group structure is relatively informal, and individuals may have the same or different purposes for being in the group. The leader does not necessarily structure learning experiences, but does try to provide a climate that encourages mutual problem-solving and support.

Group therapy. Group therapy, in contrast, is usually associated with persons who have problems of a much broader scope. These problems can pervade almost all aspects of the person's life and often are quite disruptive. The problem is not limited to one or two life-tasks. In many instances, counselees may require psychiatric hospitalization or, at least, rather extensive attention of a psychiatric or psychological nature. The purpose of these groups is usually to help the members understand and control the deep-seated and often unconscious causes that contribute to their generalized disturbances. As this overall goal is being accomplished, the groups also help counselees deal with specific crisis situations that must be managed in order to maintain progress on the larger task of gaining insight into one's general behavioral patterns. This can often re-

7. Jonell, H. Kirby, "Group Guidance," *Personnel and Guidance Journal* 49, no. 8 (1971): 593–98. Mahler, "Group Counseling," 601–608. Myron Gordon and Norman Liberman, "Group Psychotherapy: Being and Becoming," *Personnel and Guidance Journal* 49, no. 8 (1971): (611–17).

quire extensive time and financial investments. Because specific individual objectives are difficult to establish and may be varied, the structure of such groups is rather nebulous. Depending on the leadership style of the counselor, many variations, even within the same group, can occur.

Some researchers feel that distinctions between group types cannot be made legitimately because counselors perform all of the roles just described. Counselors can be viewed as instructors, problem solvers, or interventionists in a severe emotional crisis, depending on the situation. These task requirements all relate to dealing with people in a counseling context, and people require various kinds of interventions, depending on their needs and situations. The counselor's involvement with them may be more or less intensive as determined by the circumstances. In short, the helping process remains essentially the same regardless of the problem. Therefore, a truly qualified and sensitive counselor can be efficient as an instructor, problem solver, and crisis interventionist. This view suggests that any counselor should be able to use instructional techniques as in group guidance, problem-solving methods as in group counseling, and crisis-intervention methods and insight development as in group therapy.

Whether or not counselors who work with groups, in fact, have these skills, as well as whether or not they *need* these skills, are problems that await the results of research. There is, as yet, no evidence to prove that different skills are required for group counseling than for individual counseling. At this stage, persons interested in doing group counseling should attempt to get training that applies group counseling to their target population after they have developed individual counseling skills. If research shows that group counseling does require totally different skills from those used in individual counseling, programs of study will undoubtedly be established to accommodate these needs.

Group interaction and goals

The problems of definition have other implications for counseling in groups. One issue relates to the purpose for which a group comes together. Does the leader, or another external authority, impose a purpose, or do the group members evolve their own purpose? If the group is responsible for generating its own purpose, is there one purpose for the entire group, or does each member have a unique purpose? Can there be individual goals *and* common group goals? Another issue resulting from the problem of definition relates to the optimum size of the group. How many people make up a group? When are there too many people involved to render group processes ineffective? Another issue relates to how long counseling groups should last. Should they be ongoing with no definite termina-

Emotions sometimes run high in group counseling, as members of the group confront an individual with highly-charged, interpersonal issues.

tion in mind? Should there be a predetermined cutoff date? Another definition-related issue pertains to the processes established for the group situation. What processes can legitimately be described as helping processes in the group context? Which ones are detrimental? Another troublesome issue relates to the selection of group membership. If there are real differences in the types of counseling groups available to people, whose judgment is to be used to determine which type of group is most suitable for a person? This becomes a value-laden issue. Finding an answer that is satisfactory to most group practitioners is sometimes very difficult.

In an effort to contribute a positive note to what may seem like a bewildering situation, the following definition of counseling in groups is offered: Group counseling occurs when a minimum of three persons come together on a regular basis, usually for a specified period of time, to accomplish either individual and/or group goals that can be specified in measurable terms. When goals have been accomplished, then suitable learning can be inferred to have occurred.

This definition is meant to encompass the many different conceptions of counseling in groups. By broadening the definition of group counseling, there will be less concern with polemics and more emphasis on specifying the skills that are needed for group counselors in various group contexts.

Group leadership styles

Another skills-related issue is the concern with the various kinds of leadership styles of group counselors. In most group contexts, the counselor is perceived as the leader whether or not he or she wants such a role. Given that counselors are the natural leaders within the group counseling context, what styles and behaviors should the counselor assume? Authoritarian styles can facilitate productivity in accomplishing certain kinds of tasks.[8] Such a style could be applied in groups by having counselors assign homework to group members and refuse to allow the group to proceed until all assignments are completed. Usually, though, counselors prefer a style that is democratic in nature. Also, counseling tasks may not be concrete enough to be achieved easily by authoritarian counselors. This question is usually decided by individual counselors rather than by empirical evidence.

Ultimately, all these issues come back to the problem of defining groups. It is still unclear exactly what group counseling is. Perhaps researchers and counselors should stop trying to force group approaches into the arbitrary categories such as therapy groups, counseling groups, or guidance groups. Instead, groups should be described by their overall purpose, by setting, by theoretical orientation, and by group membership. Such a group would have its own personality and goals. A description of such a group might read:

A group of former alcoholics have sought counseling to help them maintain their alcohol-free living patterns. They have requested the help of a private practitioner who prefers to use the theoretical concepts of transactional analysis in the group context.

This description describes some of the important parameters of group counseling. This kind of definition places the context of counseling in groups into a more scientific perspective and reduces much of the speculative discourse that is too often the focus of group-counseling literature.

Facilitating counseling in groups

In spite of these problems, guidelines for group counseling can be recommended. The purpose of group counseling is to facilitate individual development and problem resolution in each group member. The basic unit of interaction is still one person who has a specific concern to be assisted by a counselor or some other person in

8. Shaw, *Group Dynamics*, 272–79.

the group. The possibilities exist for all possible permutations of interaction with a given group size. Conceptually, then, group counseling is the concurrent resolution of several individuals' problems and their subsequent personal development.

Selection of counselees

It may be necessary in some cases to have a preliminary interview to determine a person's purpose for wanting to enter a group. It is extremely difficult to begin a group with a miscellaneous collection of individuals who have nothing at all in common. A preliminary screening interview serves to identify commonalities among potential group members and also informs the individual about the activities and format of the group.

Common factors of group membership

Once the preliminary screening has been performed, the counselor must decide on the nature of the group composition. Common factors that can serve as basis for group membership include sex, age, prior acquaintanceship with other potential group members, background, and personality characteristics. For example, it might be better to have same-sexed groups with preteen children since they are more secure with same-sexed peers and would probably become more actively involved in the group. For most other groups, a mixed-sex group works better since it more closely simulates everyday reality. In some instances, age becomes an important factor. If a group were focused upon career-related experiences, for example, then individuals who were at similar stages in their careers would function better as a group. If the goal of a group is to develop socializing skills, then such personality characteristics as being withdrawn and introverted might be basic factors around which a group would be formed. The inclusion of gregarious extroverts could hinder the development of socializing skills in those who lack them and could cause them to withdraw further.

A group can also be ineffective because a wide range of personal needs exist among its members. Individuals with widely diverse problems—some academic, some vocational, and some personal and social—may lack the desire as well as the experience in dealing with problems so unrelated to their own. It is important, then, to be sure the composition of the group is such that one could readily expect everyone to work well together.

Group procedures in counseling

The role of the counselor

The counselor is the focal point in any group-counseling situation and functions as the primary person in assisting group members in resolving their concerns. The counselor needs to be well versed in principles of learning, the nature of behavior, and the necessary conditions for behavioral change to occur. The counselor also should be warm, empathic, and concerned.

Integrating a counselee into a group

Counselor decisions about groups

Some bases for the decision of the counseling format—group versus individual—relate to the nature of the problem and the frequency of the problem in a counselor's case load. The more individuals a counselor has with similar problems, the greater the tendency to consider a group approach.

As mentioned earlier, the first step is to interview the potential group counselee. During the preliminary interview, the counselor should inform the individual of the purpose, responsibilities, focus, and limits of group counseling. Group counseling should be described to the individual as a relationship in which help can be obtained in dealing with the normal concerns that occur in the course of development as well as immediate assistance in problem solving. Counseling is also a learning experience—a way of developing more effective ways of coping with some of the problem situations that confront people. The counselor should also communicate that counseling provides a secure environment in which to try out new behaviors and receive feedback from others as well as from the counselor.

Counselor and counselee responsibility

Both the counselee and counselor also have responsibilities. The counselor is a professional person who provides assistance by listening to concerns, observing and interacting, and monitoring the interactions of the counselees in the group. The counselor also should assist counselees in specifying concerns and by suggesting courses of action that might be pursued to alleviate problems.

The responsibilities of the counselee include frank discussions of concerns and open participation in the sessions by providing needed information. The tasks assigned to the counselee by the group or counselor must be carried out.

Limiting the counseling relationship

The limits of the counseling relationship must also be presented to the group. The counselor must communicate the voluntary nature of counseling. The types of concerns that are considered appropriate in group counseling are those that are typical of individual counseling, with the exception of severe emotional crises or problems. A time limit should also be set for each group session, and an estimate should be made as to the number of sessions that are thought necessary to resolve the problems within the group.

Another limitation on the counseling relationship is that of confidentiality. In individual counseling, the counselee usually has complete control over the information released from that relationship. In group counseling, more individuals are involved, and thus, the vulnerability of each member is greatly increased. The vulnerability can be considerably reduced if the counselor can explain the limits of confidentiality in the initial meeting of the group, and if need be, reiterate it occasionally throughout the sessions.

Dealing with problems

Once the group knows the structure within which they will function, it is time to attempt to deal with problems.

Each group procedure should be done with each member of the group before proceeding to the next procedure. This keeps the group members on an equal footing and helps to keep everyone working at approximately the same level.

Model building within a counseling group

The first step is to construct a model of each counselee's concerns in the group. Each individual in the group begins by reporting some of the concerns that prompted him or her to join the group. The counselor and other group members actively try to understand the individual's problems. There is little hope for assistance if the problems are not clearly defined and communicated. After each group member has shared concerns, the counselor initiates the process of selecting a concern to work on in the group. The nature of the concern may also have shifted somewhat between the preliminary screening interview and this first group session. It is ultimately the counselee's responsibility and right to select the concern for focus in the group.

The components of the concern must also be identified for more complete understanding on the part of the counselor and the other members of the group. These components usually involve the behavioral, temporal, and situational aspects of the problem. The behavioral component is the actual behavior that is the concern; the temporal component is the time dimension, that is, how long the problem has existed, as well as the times when it becomes a problem; and the situational component is the context in which the problem behavior seems most likely to occur.

When problem behavior has been identified, it is time to search for the causes—those elements that have allowed this behavior to persist. Identification of the reinforcers of a problem behavior provides insight into how the problem was learned. It offers hints regarding the conditions that need to be changed in order to extinguish the behavior.

Model verification within a counseling group

The final function necessary to the construction of a model of the counselee's concerns is to verify the model as it exists in the perceptions of the counselor, the other group members, and even the counselee. Unless mutual and accurate understanding of the counselee's concern exists, it is fruitless to proceed. The counselor or other group members must continually try to restate each other's concerns until they are in agreement regarding the problems that are faced by each member.

When a problem's important dimensions have been identified, the counselor can proceed to urge that a goal be established. Should counselees be reluctant to establish goals, the counselor can discuss the need for goals in counseling. Without them, a counselee has no set direction in which to move during counseling.

Each counselee needs to determine the things that will serve to indicate that sufficient progress had been made, as well as the goal that must be reached before counseling can be terminated. The counselor must also decide if he or she has sufficient skills to handle each counselee's problem. Once a mutual decision on the outcome has been established, the counselor and counselees have a yardstick against which to measure progress. A final phase of goal setting is to determine if the counselee's motivation is sufficient to work toward the goal. If the motivation for performing all the tasks that will be necessary to meet the objective is lacking, the counselor must talk to the counselee about the need for commitment.

The next step is to plan the strategies that seem most appropriate to accomplish the goals. The group-counseling process itself is, in a sense, a strategy, as is individual counseling. Additional strategies must also be determined—desensitization, reenforcement, problem solving, skill building, and information seeking are but a few of the potential choices.

It also helps to choose smaller goals along the way to the major one. Usually, too, within each strategy, there are many intermediate steps that can be selected as intermediate objectives on the way to the ultimate goal. For example, if a counselee's major goal is to be able to make friends, intermediate objectives might be to make three friends—two from school and one from the neighborhood church. Or the strategy could include even smaller components, such as taking the initiative in speaking with a prospective friend, initiating conversation with at least three individuals in a group, or talking about two subjects with three individuals during the next two days. The two subjects might even be preselected, i.e., to give one's name and to select one item from the newspaper to discuss with the other person as a conversational topic. Such intermediate goals make the ultimate goal seem less formidable. After these strategies have been sufficiently outlined for the counselee, he or she can begin to take the required actions. Checks should be made along the way, probably at each session of the group, to see whether or not the tasks have been carried out and to provide support if they have not been and encouragement to go on to other tasks if they have been.

Evaluating strategies

Evaluation of the strategies is a necessary step; it should be provided regularly until the counselee has reached his or her major goal. Comparisons should be made between the performance of the counselee after fulfilling several intermediate goals and the counselee when he or she began counseling. Evaluation should also be used to determine whether or not the counselee has achieved the feelings he or she hoped to through the strategies used. If the final goal has not been achieved, the counselee, with the help of the counselor and the group, needs to determine where he or she wants to go from here or whether the success achieved in intermediate strategies will be sufficient. If the major goal has been reached, then a decision about termination is the next step. Alternately, there may be additional work to be done on another problem. If this is not the case, though, counseling should be terminated.

The termination procedure

When clients have progressed well and continue to make progress, the counselor may inform them that there will be a few more sessions. These sessions may continue on the same time schedule as the preceding schedule or may be spaced at longer intervals until termination is completed.

When this point is reached, the counselor begins by informing the counselees that this is the last session of the group. When resistance arises, as it often does, the counselor may have to take time to manage these feelings before termination can occur. Perhaps counselees have enjoyed working together so much that they find it hard to stop. The counselor should indicate to the counselees that if further problems arise, he or she would be happy to see any one of them again, and that they could certainly see each other again as part of their social interaction.

The final procedure of the termination phase is to review the learning strategies, particularly problem-solving skills, that were used in the group and to discuss ways the counselees can try to use these skills in everyday life. The procedures of defining and selecting a problem, deciding on a goal, selecting a strategy, putting it to work, performing the tasks, and evaluating the performance should be explained to the counselees as a means of reenforcing their ability to handle problems that arise in the future.

Finally, the counselor must evaluate his or her own performance with the group. What things happened that should not have occurred? How can these things be prevented during the next group experience? Evaluation is useful in honing the counselor's skills in preparation for succeeding groups.

Other types of group approaches

Apart from the basic counseling process just described, there are other applications that have been identified as valid group approaches. It is sufficient to describe these groups as they function rather than attempt to force them into arbitrary theoretical categories. The groups that will be discussed in this section are process groups, growth groups, and peer or self-help groups.

Process groups

Process groups are usually convened to help group members experience a structured small-group situation. One purpose is to enable members to transfer what they learn to other group situations. The National Training Laboratory (NTL) has developed the usual format in these groups. NTL groups are also referred to as training groups, or T-groups. These groups grew out of the work of Kurt Lewin, a group-dynamics researcher in the 1930s and 1940s. His goal was to implement planned social change through group dynamics. He also wanted to develop ways to humanize bureaucratic organizations. Since that time, NTL groups have also established the goal of providing a group experience designed to increase the awareness individual group members have of their own feelings, the feelings of others, and the interdependence people in groups have on one another. Group members can learn to respond to their increased sensitivities, and thereby, enhance their own accomplishments as well as those of the group.

Today, most participants in NTL groups are associated with an organization such as a corporation. They usually do not know each other. As individuals, their everyday activity requires interaction with a small group of people, and NTL training is sought so that they can learn to interact more effectively. Although the training is usually done with strangers, there is some feeling that the process will work with naturally formed groups occurring in work settings. The training is usually scheduled over a period of several days. It typically convenes at a relaxing retreat away from the everyday world and concerns of the participants. Four major premises operate in most major NTL groups:

Basic premises of process groups

1. The knowledge gained from the study of group dynamics in a retreat (or laboratory setting) must be transferable to the everyday social interaction of the participants.
2. A feeling of closeness, or cohesion, among group members must occur if the training is to achieve its goals. Cohesion is best achieved when all the members participate freely.
3. Sensitivity to feelings of self and others must be used to increase a small group's productivity.
4. The best way to learn about the small-group process is to experience a structured small-group as it is led through the typical stages of small-group dynamics by an experienced NTL leader.

The training experience. The training process is one that actually appears to have no structure. This is intentional, however, because the lack of structure is meant to allow each participant to act according to his or her natural inclinations. Emphasis is placed on expressing feelings as they occur rather than reflecting on the past. It is important that an NTL leader know how to develop a climate of freedom and security so that the members can let their natural inclinations emerge. Members are encouraged to support one another's efforts at being open and honest. Immediate feedback among members is encouraged, not to be judgmental, but to provide an accurate account of how the behavior of individual group members affects other group members. It is in this context that the essential learning of group process occurs. This spontaneous, open, and nonjudgmental sharing of feelings, and the subsequent support it engenders among members, is the type of behavior that is expected to be transferred to the everyday social interaction of NTL process-group participants. The group leader is expected to model these behaviors for the members during the course of the training.

Shaffer and Galinsky in their book *Models of Group Therapy and Sensitivity Training* describe the NTL group process and other group-process models in detail.[9] Readers interested in exploring the group process further are referred to this excellent source.

9. J. B. P. Shaffer and M. David Galinsky, *Models of Group Therapy and Sensitivity Training* (Englewood Cliffs, N.J.: Prentice-Hall, 1974).

Growth groups

Growth groups are sometimes confused with process groups, largely because both are often referred to as sensitivity groups. It is true that each is concerned with helping people become more aware or sensitive to their own feelings and to those of others. Still, there are differences in purpose and format that make the two groups different.

Growth groups, also referred to as encounter groups, have received extensive publicity, particularly during the early 1970s. This glare of public exposure has done little to inform the public about the true purpose and functioning of such groups.

Differences between process and growth groups

Growth groups evolved from the same origins and at the same time as process groups. In fact, real distinctions did not emerge until the late 1960s. Growth groups are not so concerned with everyday applications as process groups are. Rather, the emphasis is on immediate emotional absorption. The assumption is made that people in today's world are confronted by social conditions that tend to split existence into artificial compartments. This results in dehumanization and in people becoming alienated from themselves, particularly by losing contact with their emotional or spiritual selves. A split within the self naturally prevents any real integration with other people. The social, and sometimes very personal, trauma experienced by many Americans during the Vietnam War provided strong evidence that humans had indeed lost something. The almost mystical and spiritual awareness offered by proponents of growth groups seem to many to be the needed antidote for the perceived ills of society. An attempt is made to structure the group so that members integrate their total beings—their physical and emotional sides—to experience what it is like to be a complete person. The experience is intense and occurs in a brief period of time.

Despite its early mystical beginnings, efforts increasingly have been made to provide a more rational, rather than an emotional, framework in growth groups. This has occurred in the wake of accusations that harm could possibly come to participants who were psychologically unprepared for deep, emotional encounters that occurred in these groups.[10] Also, due to the sudden and rapid rise in the popularity of growth groups, some unskilled opportunists took advantage of the public demand and provided group experiences that showed a greater concern for profit making than for the welfare of participants. Since then, efforts to legitimize the growth-group experience and control quality have occurred.

10. Kurt W. Back, "The Group Can Comfort But It Can't Cure," *Psychology Today* (December 1974): 28–35.

Theory behind growth groups

William Schutz has provided a theoretical framework for the growth-group experience. It is referred to as the Fundamental Interpersonal Relations Orientation (FIRO). He has also written-extensively, describing group exercises that he and others have developed to prepare the proper climate for growth groups. Schutz's views place growth groups into their proper therapeutic context.[11]

Growth groups are usually limited to a small group—fewer than twenty people. The experience is usually extended over a minimum of three to six hours and sometimes is stretched over several days, often over a weekend.

There are many variations on growth groups, but there are certain basics that apply to most groups. One of these is the emphasis on the responsibility of group members for whatever they do and experience in the group. Usually, too, structured exercises are provided by the leader. These blend physical and emotional aspects of experience, although most exercises are active and physical. Intellectualization is not desirable. These exercises are intended to restore a sense of human sensitivity and the kind of expression that is presumed to have been stifled by social pressures. The objective is to restore this balance only within the group itself; efforts are not typically expended in preparing people to maintain their experience outside the group context. Growth groups have been criticized for this. Critics fear that some people will use growth-group experiences as a narcotic to provide emotional highs on a periodic basis while they neglect other aspects of their lives. Lieberman, Yalom, and Miles have attempted to document the long-range effects of growth-group participation.[12] They have uncovered some of these negative outcomes of growth-group involvement—and some positive ones as well, where people truly felt enriched. Since there are so many variations and purposes among the various growth groups, it is dubious that any research can be widely applied.

Self-help groups

Self-help, or peer groups, have a long, varied history. Their development probably began with Alcoholics Anonymous, the group most often cited as the originator of the self-help concept. This group has been the most publicized, and in that sense, is the most successful of the self-help groups. Whether or not Alcoholics

---

11. William C. Shutz, *Joy: Expanding Human Awareness* (New York: Grove Press, 1967).

12. Morton A. Lieberman, Irvin D. Yalom, and Mathew B. Miles, *Encounter Groups: First Facts* (New York: Basic Books, 1973).

Anonymous originated the concept is irrelevant. The fact remains that Alcoholics Anonymous has gained the public's attention and has greatly benefited many persons with alcoholic histories. Many other self-help groups have been started based on the goals and concepts of Alcoholics Anonymous. Recovery, Inc. is a national organization that has established local self-help groups for persons receiving psychiatric care. Weight Watchers provides similar organizational services to overweight persons. Hundreds of thousands of persons participate in such groups throughout the United States. Some of these are affiliated with national organizations, while others are organized locally for a specific purpose for a particular group of people. Again, the variety of self-help groups makes anything but a very general description almost meaningless.

A current trend is for self-help organizations to develop political as well as therapeutic goals. For example, there are organizations of persons who have physical impairments. In addition to their other activities, their groups are active in promoting legislation to remove architectural barriers and job discrimination. As a group process, the activities of most groups are focused on helping people accept and deal with common personal problems.

Jacques and Patterson have presented a comprehensive overview of self-help groups.[13] They distinguish between two types of groups. The first is a group of persons who are peers of one another in that they share a common concern, such as a drinking problem. The second type consists of family and friends of the persons who have the problem. For example, Alcoholics Anonymous has spun off several derivative groups such as Alanon and Alateen for family members of alcoholics. These organizations, primarily developed to help people deal with problems on a personal basis, have expanded their activities to assume a political posture that attempts to change social conditions believed to precipitate the problem of concern. Another benefit of participation in these self-help groups is the social interaction that frequently develops among members. The opportunity to socialize in an accepting environment is often viewed as one of the more attractive features of self-help groups. It is through this social interaction that group members learn to give and accept help. Sharing is an integral part of the self-help group process.

Primary activities of self-help groups

In their article, Jacques and Patterson have listed the primary process activities that are germane to self-help groups. These include the following:[14]

13. Marceline E. Jacques and Kathleen M. Patterson, "The Self-Help Group Model: A Review," *Rehabilitation Counseling Bulletin* 18, no. 1 (1974): 48–57.

14. Jacques and Patterson, "The Self-Help Group Model."

1. Gaining information about the members' mutual problem
2. Learning how to cope with the problem from those who have successfully coped
3. Supporting each other
4. Modeling effective problem-solving strategies for new members
5. Providing supportive feedback to one another
6. Achieving a sense of belonging
7. Helping self by helping others.

The groups expect new members honestly to acknowledge the existence of the problem shared by all group members. All members are expected to be responsible for learning coping behavior and for helping others learn it. The learning principles, which include modeling, feedback, and supportive reenforcement in a peer context, are well established in academic and professional circles. The groups meet on a regular basis, but members are expected to be supportive of others at any time as needed on an individual basis. Alcoholics Anonymous members have someone to call on at any hour of the day they need to. Group membership is dependent on contributions made to other group members and self-improvements. Accomplishments not associated with the group are irrelevant to a person's status within the group. Membership can continue indefinitely.

Opposition to self-help groups

Jacques and Patterson also describe the difficulty helping professionals have had in accepting the viability of self-help groups. Psychiatrists actively opposed Recovery, Inc., and other self-help groups have met with similar professional resistance. The dynamics behind this resistance are unclear. What is more important, however, is the current realization that the self-help principle is a viable source of support. Professionals and self-help groups are learning how to work together so that maximum resources can be brought to bear to help people cope with their problems. In an attempt to integrate professionals into peer groups, Fairweather developed the Lodge Program, which provides a social and vocational environment for formerly hospitalized psychiatric patients.[15] Professionals help Lodge members learn their new roles and encourage them to continue to use professional help on a consultation basis. Otherwise, members are responsible for fending for themselves, using group support. The concept of leaderless groups, that is, groups without counselors, has also been introduced into psychiatric and

15. G. W. Fairweather, D. H. Sanders, H. Maynard, and D. L. Cressler, *Community Life for the Mentally Ill* (Chicago: Aldine, 1969).

psychological treatment practices.[16] In these instances, group members meet without direct professional help, but the structure has been professionally organized, and consultation is available. Most group approaches, however, do have a leader present for their sessions.

It has been noted that professionals have resisted the growth of self-help groups, covertly if not always overtly. In part, members of self-help groups also have resisted seeking professional help. They tend to believe that a person who provides help to another for a particular problem must first have experienced that problem and have dealt with it successfully. Although there is no proof that this is true, persons who enter group counseling from self-help groups may have some of the these feelings, and as a result, must be treated with some sensitivity.

Ethical concerns in group counseling

Counseling in a group context raises another crucial issue beyond those already discussed. Providing helping services to human beings demands the highest degree of ethical practice. Ethical practice must be based, as much as possible, on scientific foundations. Professionals who provide human services need to be able, with a reasonable degree of confidence, to assure their customers that they will receive the help they need. This implies that helpers have the capacity to predict the outcomes that can be achieved as a result of their services. Yet, counseling professionals have not yet achieved this degree of scientific control in individual counseling, much less in group situations where the number and complexity of factors are increased. This does not mean that counseling in groups should not be done; rather, it means that counselors who work with groups need to carefully consider the actions they take in the group context. Counselors have not been left without support in this serious undertaking. Ethical standards related to this and other issues have been developed by various professional associations. For the most part, these standards have addressed the counseling relationship between counselors and counselees in the individual counseling context, but they can often be carried over to the group context. The American Personnel and Guidance Association in its current statement of standards includes the special concerns that group

16. B. Berzon and L. Solomon, "Research Frontier: The Self-Directed Therapeutic Groups—Three Studies," *Journal of Counseling Psychology* 13 (1966): 491–97.

counseling creates in the counseling relationship.[17] All the standards that apply to individual counseling also apply to the group context. Certain qualifications also extend especially to groups. The control that a counselor has over any physical or psychological harm that could happen is diminished in the group interaction, and there is a greater chance of harm caused by someone else in the group. This requires that the counselor carefully screen counselees entering the groups. Personal knowledge of the participants is especially desirable.

During short-term group situations, which usually preclude screening and follow-up, group members need to be made aware of professional help that is readily available after the group terminates.

Ethical standards should be carefully reviewed and should always be part of the working knowledge of every counselor. Appendix A consists of the current Ethical Standards of the American Personnel and Guidance Association. The American Psychological Association also has published ethical standards that are helpful to counselors.[18] Recently, the Association for Specialists in Group Work, a division of APGA, proposed guidelines for the conduct of groups, an important advance in the field.

Ethical standards, although helpful, are not always sufficient for easing all situations. Zimpfer has pointed out several areas that are not adequately addressed by current standards.[19]

Special issues in group counseling

Zimpfer notes that outcomes are difficult to predict, even in individual counseling, but he asserts that the chance of negative outcomes may be greater for group situations. The counselor's ability to control the situation is diluted by the group's participants, each of whom asserts an influence on the outcomes. The standards do not indicate how the counselor is to maintain this balance without negating the voluntary participation of group members. Even if counselors can manage to maintain a supporting atmosphere within the group, as many do, research in group counseling has not been developed to the point where the long-range implications of applied group procedures are adequately understood.

Zimpfer asks that precautions must be taken to have help readily available at any stage during or after group counseling. The stan-

17. American Personnel and Guidance Association, *Ethical Standards* (Washington, D. C., 1972).

18. American Psychological Association, *Ethical Standards for Psychologists* (Washington, D. C., 1972).

19. David Zimpfer, "Needed: Professional Ethics for Working with Groups," *Personnel and Guidance Journal* 50, no. 4, (1971): 280–87.

dards fail to clarify how long this protection should be available after the group terminates.

Zimpfer raises other questions such as how long groups should last and how to mesh individual goals with group goals. Such questions are not easily answered. Research still needs to address these problems, one hopes, with the result of obtaining some standards related to the issue. Although the recently revised APGA standards have begun to acknowledge special considerations for group counseling, Zimpfer's warnings are still very appropriate.

In *Basic Approaches to Group Psychotherapy*, Gazda speaks to many of these same issues.[20] One area that he emphasizes concerns the qualifications of the counselor who uses the group situation. Gazda believes that training in the use of group procedures is necessary, and that the trained counselor should have to present evidence to counselees to verify the extent of training. A group counselor who lacks credentials should be closely supervised by someone who has credentials. Gazda suggests that the group counselor should initiate data-collection activities on process and outcome that will provide evidence to others that he or she has been effective with previous groups. Also, Gazda points out that training should never stop. The professional counselor should seek further education and experience to upgrade the quality of counseling service offered to counselees.

Summary

The chapter opened by discussing group counseling from two different perspectives: counseling theory and social psychology. The economic and theoretical reasons for group counseling were discussed in detail, as were the major issues related to counseling in groups. These included developing new ethical perspectives, leadership styles, and strategies to use within the groups; prescreening members of the group; and terminating the group.

An effort has been made to explore the varied approaches to group counseling, while at the same time engendering in group counselors the need to take special care that no psychological or physical damage is done to counselees.

20. Gazda, *Basic Approaches to Group Psychotherapy and Group Counseling*.

Questions

1. Compare and contrast the counseling theory and social psychology perspectives.
2. What are some of the difficulties in defining and classifying various kinds of groups?
3. Describe some of the reasons to use group counseling instead of individual counseling.
4. Are the same skills required of a group counselor as for an individual counselor? Why or why not?
5. Why is confidentiality more of a concern in a group than in individual counseling?
6. What things should a counselor take into account when interviewing a potential group counselee?
7. Describe the general group-counseling process, including strategies.
8. What are T-groups? How do they function?
9. What are growth groups? How do they function?
10. What are self-help groups? How do they function?

Projects

1. Interview a participant in a self-help group to learn what is gained from membership in this kind of group.
2. Watch a film of a group-counseling session to see what the strengths and weaknesses of this particular group are.
3. Study the standards in Appendix A and report to the class on how they might be revised to encompass the concerns of group counselors in a more definitive way.
4. Observe or participate in several group-counseling sessions. Report to the class on the interaction of counselees and the counselor.

Issues and applications 4

10 Types of problems in counseling

Arnold Lazarus (right), one of the first proponents of relaxation training (shown here) and desensitization techniques, often helps group members prepare to confront their problems.

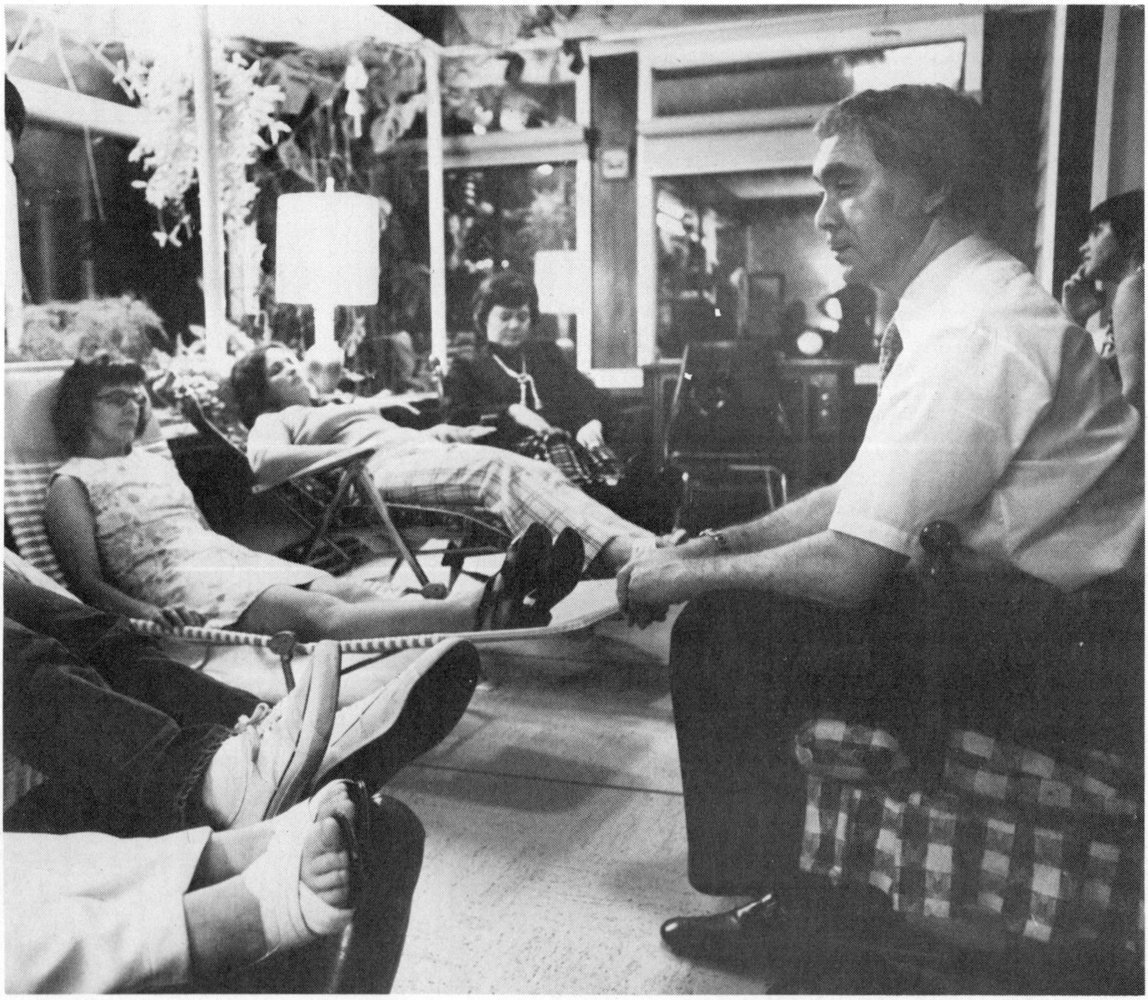

Introduction

The word *counseling* implies that there is some need for assistance to resolve some problem that an individual has been unsuccessful in resolving either alone or with the assistance of others. Occasionally, a person is referred to a counselor for assistance in resolving a problem that one may not recognize as being a problem, but which the referral source feels is worthy of discussion and resolution. This type of problem is frequently found in counseling situations where the client is required to have contact with a counselor based on information submitted to the counselor by a third party. The third party feels as though there are difficulties that the individual is experiencing and wishes the individual to seek assistance in resolving such problems. The nature of these problems frequently is focused on an individual's lack of motivation to seek assistance with regard to the perceived problem. This may stem, in part, from an individual's lack of awareness that certain behaviors, thoughts, attitudes, or feelings present problems in the eyes of another individual. A second type of problem deals with the individual's response to a set of internal or external conditions that he or she is unable to resolve or even respond to.

When one defines problems in these ways, one is faced with the realization that each problem is a highly individual and unique set of conditions. No two individuals facing the same set of conditions will necessarily respond in the same way. Therefore, an individual may be faced with a set of conditions that do not give one the feeling of having a problem, and is in fact not a problem for that person, even though it may be a problem for others or for society.

The purpose of this chapter is to examine the range of problems that confront human beings. The discussion will focus on individual differences and the way that they are used to define the extent and nature of problems, at what point certain conditions can be considered a problem, the classification of problems for purposes of counseling, and the possibilities for resolution of the problems.

Key terms

problem
intelligence
physical characteristics
emotions
spirituality
perception
attitude
appropriate behavior
interpersonal problem
intrapersonal problem
developmental problem
environmental problem
individual counseling

Individual differences and problems

Because every human is unique, every person's problems are unique. The composite of human characteristics, which includes intelligence, physical attributes, emotional makeup, spirituality, perception, behavior, and attitudes, must be taken into consideration by the counselor who seeks to help any person resolve a problem or set of problems. Furthermore, each of these characteristics must be understood in relation to one another and in relation to the individual's problem.

Intelligence has been defined as the ability to learn or understand or deal with new or trying situations, as well as the skilled use of reason. In addition, it is defined as the ability to apply knowledge to manipulate one's environment or to think abstractly as measured by objective criteria such as tests. Considerable controversy has existed in recent years regarding the meaning of intelligence, its definition, and its measurement. One of the major criticisms focuses on the cultural bias ingrained in the measurement of intelligence. Although it may be difficult to rely totally on a measure of intelligence as a predictor for an individual's future success occupationally, socially, or educationally, intelligence is at least one component that contributes to the uniqueness of an individual. Some persons have less difficulty than others in being able to reason through problem situations and come up with solutions that are acceptable. There are considerable differences among persons with regard to each person's ability to learn, understand, or deal with new or trying situations or to use reason in a skilled way. Even if all other characteristics of individuals were equal, the differences based on intelligence would still be enough to account for major differences among individuals.

With the possible exception of identical twins, no two individuals share the same composite of physical characteristics. Individual physical differences include hair color, eye color, skin color, size of body frame, size of trunk, length of legs, size of hands and feet. Some individuals are tall; other individuals are short. Some individuals have unique physical characteristics that are sometimes handicapping conditions. Others appear on the surface to have no handicapping conditions, but may have internal handicapping conditions such as heart disease, malignancies, or diabetes.

A person's physical attributes—or as often, the way a person perceives his or her physical attributes—can either be a source of well-being or a source of problems for that individual.

Emotional reactions and problems

A third component of the composite is a person's realm of emotions or feelings. Emotions may be defined as the affective aspect of consciousness, a state of feeling, and a psychic and physical reaction such as anger or fear subjectively experienced as strong feeling and physiologically involving changes that prepare the body for immediate vigorous action. As a result of prior experiences, individuals tend to respond to different stimuli with a variety of possible emotions. Stimuli that may be obnoxious and aversive to one person are pleasing and approachable by others. Yet, at the same time, each person experiences to some degree a full range of possible emotions from anger and hate to love and warmth. The affective response to situations contributes to the uniqueness of each individual.

How a person reacts emotionally to the world around him or her—for example, some persons respond to everything with anger while others fail to show anger even when it would be appropriate—varies with the individual and has a lot to do with how a person is able to handle problems.

Many persons have a spiritual component to their lives. They believe in God in one form or another, and they may practice or belong to an organized religion. Others reject the existence of a Supreme Being. Regardless of an individual's choices in the matter of spirituality, the ultimate belief or value placed on it, as well as the rejection of the notion of a Supreme Being, affect the individual and his or her interactions with the world. One's feelings about spirituality, in fact, often are the basis for one's value system. They greatly influence how one sees the world and how one relates to others.

Perceptions of problems

Individuals also tend to differ with regard to the perception that they bring to bear in any situation. Perception has been defined as a mental image, a consciousness, a physical sensation interpreted in the light of experience. Due to the individual nature of experience, one again finds that each person tends to perceive or see things differently from others. In certain situations, some individuals tend to look more on the negative components or the negative possibilities of the situation and see nothing but doom, sadness, loneliness, and depression in most of their perceptions. Others tend to see the positive elements that exist in most situations, including the exciting opportunities the challenges, the growing, and the excitement of striving. How one perceives things can either facilitate normal adjustment to life situations or contribute to maladjustment. Although it is difficult to find anyone who is totally negative or totally positive with regard to life experiences, persons do tend to range on a continuum from negative to positive in their perceptions of life and life situations.

Attitudes regarding problems

A final component of individual differences is attitude. Attitude is the mental position with regard to a fact or state, a position assumed for a specific purpose, and an organismic state of readiness to respond in a characteristic way to a stimulus such as an object, concept, or situation. It is a feeling or emotion toward a place or state of being. It would appear as though there is a predeterminedness—one's attitude—to an individual's mental state that facilitates one's response in a characteristic manner when new situations arise.

The characteristics described exist in varying degrees in all human beings; they combine to make each person unique. These differences also form the basis for how individuals respond to intra- or interpersonal stimuli. Overresponse or underresponse in any one area can throw a person off balance and become a source of enmity in one's life.

When a situation becomes a problem

Why do some persons seem to have so many more problems than others do? What makes an individual reach the point where some form of outside help is sought to resolve the problem? The answers to these questions are the same: Persons are so highly individual that each one has a different point at which he or she finds that problems have become too overwhelming to cope with. At this point, an individual either responds by seeking outside help or begins to exhibit behavior of a nature that causes others to worry about him or her enough to recommend help. (This last category includes persons involved in antisocial or criminal behavior.) It is important, too, to remember that problems exist only in the mind of the beholder. What devastates one person may be of little or no consequence to another.

In addition to the personal makeup of a person and the way it incites him or her to seek outside help, there are other dimensions to a problem that lead one to seek outside help. These dimensions are frequency of the problem, its context, intensity, and severity. Each dimension requires closer examination.

Frequency of problems

How often does one need to confront a noxious stimulus before realizing that the situation is producing a problem? If a student were to be sent to the principal's office for disciplinary action every day of the school year, most persons would conclude that the individual student was having some type of problem. How much less frequent could the trips to the principal be and still be viewed as a problem? It may depend on the reasons that the student is sent to the principal's office. These may vary from time to time. It may also depend on the tolerance of the teacher and/or principal on any given occasion that leads him or her to refer the student for discipline or to discipline sometimes when the behavior occurs but not necessarily at other times. The frequency dimension of a problem may result in one's feeling as though there is a problem or in others feeling that an individual has a problem, but rarely is frequency alone enough reason to assume that a problem exists.

Context of problems

Another dimension that helps to define the severity of a problem is the context in which the behavior appears. Behavior that is appropriate in one context may be totally inappropriate in another. For example, one is expected to laugh during a funny speech but not during a serious speech such as a sermon or a eulogy. In large part, the kind of behavior that is expected is determined by a society. Some societies expect chief mourners at the funeral of a loved one to wail and beat on themselves, while in other societies, much greater restraint on one's emotions over the death of a loved one is expected. Sometimes persons fail to learn appropriate behavior; these persons can be taught how to behave in certain situations. If they have been taught how to behave, however, and they persist in misbehavior in certain contexts, then this is one dimension of a problem, one sign of maladjustment. When dealing with misbehaviors based on context, counselors need to recognize that appropriate behavior also varies within a society, depending upon one's cultural or ethnic affiliation, religion, socioeconomic group, and education.

Intensity of problems

Another dimension of a problem is the intensity with which a thought, idea, or behavior is exhibited. Some individuals are naturally more intense than others, and this must be taken into account just as other individual differences are. Others find themselves in life situations where intensity is a normal reaction. This kind of intensity, often generated by a major life change such as a wedding or the death of a loved one, often subsides of its own accord or with only a brief period of counseling. Not to feel intense about these situations would be abnormal. Certain individuals, though, who are not normally intense may have difficulty in accepting new situations or may exhibit unusually intense behavior. So high a level of intensity is not normal. The intensity is often uncomfortable and the reason that one will seek outside help.

Severity of problems

The final definition of a problem is its severity. Severity is difficult to separate from intensity, but in general, severity refers to the depth of a problem or the length of time it lasts. A person might have feeling of intensity about a new job that is more severe than normal and which will eventually interfere with the ability to perform the job. Such a person needs treatment for the severity of the problem. Today, stress is often treated as a symptom of the severity of a problem. Life has become more stressful in recent years, and some persons are far less able to cope with stress than others. When stress becomes a lasting feature of one's life or interferes with one's day-to-day pattern of living, it is severe enough to warrant professional attention.

In light of the dimensions just discussed, a person needs professional help for a problem whenever it becomes too frequent, too intense, too severe, or produces behavior that is out of context with the normal standards of behavior. Any one of these dimensions alone, however, may not be enough to warrant attention. The decision ultimately must be based on the individual's makeup.

Classification of problems

A variety of diagnostic classification systems have been devised to reflect the various types of problems counselors are likely to encounter. The rationale for developing diagnostic classification systems, which may seem to contradict the earlier emphasis on individuality, is to provide the counselor with a framework within which to place individual behaviors. Ideally, any classification system should have nonoverlapping categories so that the categorization can be used as a basis for treatment. A system also needs to be simple enough so that it will be useful in facilitating growth and change on the part of the individual. There should be no need for a counselor to teach an entire "philosophy" in order to prepare the counselee for treatment; simplicity in categorization eliminates this need.

One of the earliest classification systems was developed by E. G. Williamson and J. G. Darley. Their system describes five categories into which problems can be divided: personality, education, vocational, financial, and health. At the time in which Williamson and Darley worked, in the 1930s, these were viewed as reasonable if somewhat overlapping categories for describing common problems.[1]

Psychological classifications of problems

Edward S. Bordin attempted to remove some of the overlap from the Williamson and Darley system and tried to focus more on the basic psychological issues that were inherent in problem classification. He, too, devised five categories into which problems could be classified; these were dependence, lack of information, self-conflict, choice anxiety, and no problem. Bordin emphasized the source of a problem rather than its content.[2]

Harold B. Pipinski modified Bordin's classification system. First he suggested that "lack of assurance" be substituted for the "no problem" category. He further subdivided the self-conflict category into three groups: cultural, interpersonal, and intrapersonal. Finally, Pipinski added a "lack of skill" category.[3]

1. E. G. Williamson and J. G. Darley, *Student Personnel Work* (New York: McGraw-Hill, 1937).

2. Edward S. Bordin, "Diagnosis in Counseling and Psychotherapy," *Educational and Psychological Measurement* 6 (Summer 1946): 169–84.

3. Harold B. Pipinski, "The Selection and Use of Diagnostic Categories in Clinical Counseling," *Applied Psychological Monographs* 15 (February 1948).

Another important classification system is that developed by Robert Callas, who suggested the following breakdown of problem types: vocational, emotional, and educational. While these categories in and of themselves were not new or unusual, or for that matter, even particularly useful, Callas went on to define these three categories as ones that could be used to pinpoint the goal of counseling, or the problem area that would be worked on. Callas developed still another facet to classification, which was based on the cause of a problem. He thought causes could be attributed to lack of information about or understanding of self, lack of information or understanding about the environment, motivational conflict within self, conflict with significant others, and lack of skill.[4]

Another system, developed by the authors of this book, contains yet another two-dimensional method of classifying problems. In this system, problems are first classified based on whether they are intrapersonal or interpersonal. An intrapersonal problem exists within the person him- or herself; an interpersonal problem exists between an individual and another person or persons.

The second classification dimension, which is interrelated to the first set, relates to whether a problem is developmental or environmental in nature. If a problem is developmental, a person experiences difficulties based on what happened or is happening during a particular developmental stage of one's life. For example, problems may be related to adolescence or to mid-life. Or one may reach adulthood without having learned certain necessary coping skills that were normally acquired during adolescence. Alternately, an individual may not have resolved problems appropriately during a certain developmental stage of one's life and may now need to retrench a little and resolve those problems. Environmental problems, on the other hand, are those that an individual experiences due to a current set of conditions or a current complex of stimuli.

Resolution of problems

Once the problems have been identified and classified, the next step is to seek ways of resolving the problems. Many resources are available that can serve as interventions in the problem process

4. Robert Callas, "Diagnostic Classification as a Research Tool," *Journal of Counseling Psychology* 12 (Fall 1965): 238.

Biofeedback is a mechanistic counseling tool that allows one to correlate emotional, or subjective, responses to physiological changes in the body, such as blood pressure, galvanic skin response, and muscle tension. Subjects try to teach themselves to control these reactions on a conscious level.

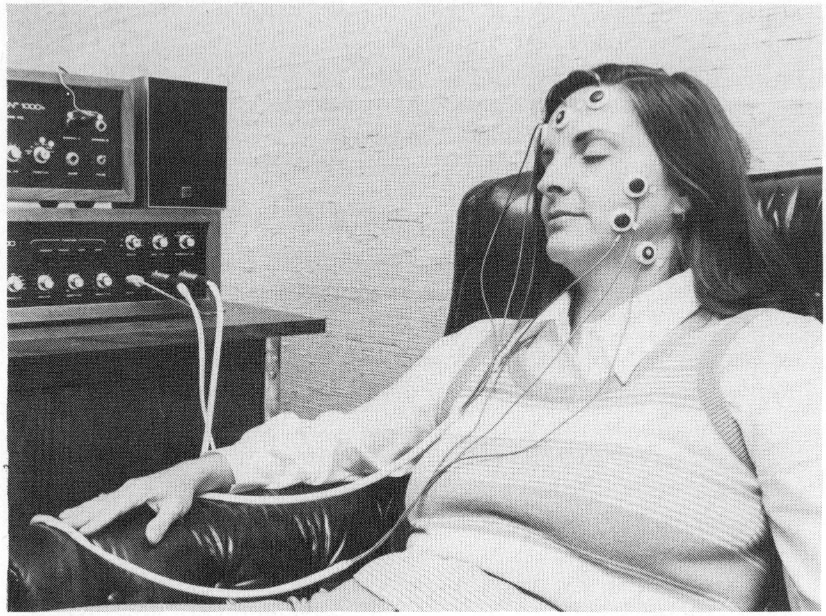

and, one hopes, result in the resolution of the problem. These include individual counseling, group counseling, and a variety of ancillary strategies such as biofeedback, relaxation training, and role playing.

Major strategies

Individual and group counseling

The single most used strategy for problem resolution is individual counseling. In individual counseling, the counselor and the counselee work together on a one-to-one basis to identify and understand the nature of the problem. They then attempt to establish a goal for eradicating the problem or lessening its effects. The counselor next works out ancillary strategies that can be used to resolve these problems.

Group counseling is the other major strategy for resolving problems. It works especially well on problems of an interpersonal nature, because the interaction of the counselee with the group affords the counselor an opportunity to view first-hand the problems that a counselee would only describe second-hand in individual counseling. Group counseling, as noted in Chapter 9, also can be used to resolve other problems such as the economic burden of individual counseling and the lack of time on the counselor's part to treat a person individually.

Ancillary strategies

Although these strategies are numerous and are described in greater detail in other chapters throughout the book, three will be presented here for purposes of fitting them into this classification system.

Biofeedback, relaxation training, and role playing

Biofeedback has been helpful in resolving a variety of specific difficulties ranging from stress to chronic pain problems that are intrapersonal in nature.

Relaxation training, which is closely akin to meditation, works to resolve problems in which counselees feel they need to learn a greater sense of personal control. It is a method of teaching a counselee how to relax and to free the mind from problems temporarily. It may work to relax a counselee so that he or she is better able to discuss problems with a counselor, and it may have the effect of lessening the tension involved in many interpersonal and intrapersonal problems.

A final ancillary strategy is role playing. In role playing, the counselor and counselee or counselees assume the roles of persons that exist within the counselee's life situations. By replaying encounters with these persons, the counselee is able to gain insight into the ways that he reacts and interacts and into possible sources of problems. Needless to say, the counselor also gains a great deal of insight about the counselee from role-playing situations with a counselee. This is primarily useful when interpersonal problems are suspected.

In a sense, these three ancillary strategies represent three related levels of problem strategy and resolution. Ancillary strategies are always intended for use along with individual or group sounseling when they are used as strategies for problem resolution. Other strategies and elaboration of the ones presented here can be found in Krumboltz and Thoresen.[5]

---

5. John D. Krumboltz and Carl E. Thoresen, *Counseling Methods* (New York: Holt, Rinehart and Winston, 1976).

Summary

The focus of this chapter has been on problem identification. The ranges of individual differences such as intelligence, physical characteristics, emotions, spirituality, perception, and attitudes were explored in relation to how they affect problem resolution. The second section dealt with the difficulty of defining and classifying a problem and with the highly variable nature of being able to define it in such a way that it has meaning and can produce helpful responses on the part of a counselor. The third section reviewed several classification systems for counseling problems. The final section of the chapter briefly explored a sample of the resolution strategies available to counselors.

Questions

1. At what point is an attitude or behavior usually considered a problem? How is a problem defined in relation to the person who experiences it?

2. In what way are individual characteristics inherent in the nature of the type of problem any individual has?

3. Explain the difference between the intensity and the severity of a problem.

4. How does context influence the definition of problems?

5. What role does frequency play in the definition of problems?

6. What is the purpose of a classification system for problems?

Projects

1. Watch a minimum of four films on ancillary strategies and keep a running list of the ways in which each one may be used. Use class discussion to further expand the lists.

2. Set up several role-playing situations among class members. Discuss what you were able to learn about the persons from the role playing.

3. Do some library research to uncover other methods of problem classification. Report to the class on the value of these other systems and on how they compare to the ones discussed in this chapter.

11 Issues in counseling

Many persons struggle to confront their problems alone because they are unaware of the counseling programs available to them.

Introduction

Key terms

mid-life crisis
social development
community-corrections program
interpersonal communication
vocational rehabilitation
aging-assistance center
peer counselor
child abuse
spouse abuse
women's shelter
mental retardation

This chapter consists of nine case histories designed to illustrate the types of problems presented in Chapter 10. Case 1 deals with marriage and family problems and their lack of positive communication. It serves as an illustration of interpersonal-environmental problems. Case 2 is concerned with an individual going through a mid-life career crisis. It also illustrates intrapersonal-environmental problems. An interpersonal-development problem is illustrated by Case 3, the history of a high school student who is alone much of the time and has no friends. Case 4 is about a person who is in a community-corrections program and seems unable to adjust to the community. He has an intrapersonal-developmental problem. An interpersonal-intrapersonal-environmental problem is illustrated by Case 5, which is about a traumatic right-arm amputee. An interpersonal-intrapersonal-environmental problem is captured in Case 6, which is about a 71-year-old retiree with adjustment problems. An intrapersonal-environmental-developmental problem is illustrated in Case 7, about a woman who was abused as a child and who currently is a child abuser. An interpersonal-developmental-environmental problem is illustrated in Case 8, about a young father with abusive tendencies tied to his relationship with his father.

The final case concerns an interpersonal-intrapersonal-developmental-environmental problem and is illustrated by a mentally retarded teenager who is sexually active.

The cases begin with the simplest and proceed to the most complex case. The cases are essentially true, but have been disguised to change the identity of the counselees and to illustrate variety in the types of problems that exist. Furthermore, each case is designed to illustrate the variety of settings in which counseling can be conducted.

Marriage problems—a career-oriented wife

Marital counseling

Harry and Jane were married five years ago in a small church wedding ceremony. Harry had just graduated from college, and Jane was working as a legal secretary in a small university community. Harry took a job as a management trainee with a large national retail chain. Two years ago, they had a baby girl. Harry and Jane had often talked about a family, but felt they should wait to do some traveling and save some money. When Jane became pregnant unexpectedly, they had the child anyway, and now they needed to cope with the situation. Jane was angry and bitter; she felt that the about and concluded that the stifling effect of his former job did not allow him the things in life that seemed important to him. Throughout the process of quitting his job, John had remained calm and composed, but now he was angry, resentful, and full of doubt about his decision to quit. He was no longer sure that his new attempts at assertiveness were appropriate.

John's problem can be classified as intrapersonal-environmental. Because John has experienced difficulty with an internal conflict over where he plans to go with his life, his problem would be classified as intrapersonal. John's problem would also be classified as environmental because it was the situations generated by his job-related difficulties that caused him to question himself and limited his ability to assert himself positively. Unresolved developmental issues were not involved to any great extent. Problems such as John's are fairly common. Many individuals stop to reflect on where they have been and evaluate where they would like to go in the future. Occasionally, a mid-life crisis results in major changes in careers, marital status, or in gaining a better perspective of one's life. Agencies such as Community Mental Health, the Job Service, private personnel and placement services, rehabilitation agencies, and other professional employment counseling centers handle cases similar to John's.

The counselor's role

The counselor began by establishing a relationship with John in which John would be comfortable enough to explore his concerns. The counselor brought up the feelings that John had concerning his frustrating search for employment, which also brought up the feelings that had led him to quit his former job. Before long, John was explaining feelings he had about his childhood and significant others of his youth. John became more aware of the controlling influence his father had on his life and became angry at himself for allowing such an influence to continue. The counselor suggested that John focus on whether he wanted to permit this influence to continue. He suggested some ways for John to lessen his father's influence and some methods for asserting himself more. Within six sessions, John's new assertive behavior had led to positive consequences, and at the end of the ninth session, the counselor and John terminated.

Counseling skills needed in intrapersonal-environmental problems

The skills employed by the counselor in assisting John included: (1) facilitating the development of an open and honest relationship, (2) directed explanation of the current problem and its antecedents, (3) clarification of the current problem so that alternate solutions could be found, and (4) support and encouragement to learn and grow. All four of these skills were helpful to John in resolving his problem.

Teenage relationships

Adolescent-adjustment problems

Mary is a 16-year-old girl who is a sophomore in high school. Mary is the younger of two daughters. Her parents divorced five years ago after 13 years of marital harassment and ridicule. Both her parents worked, and Mary spent most of her time alone. Mary's older sister was active in many school activities and spent little time with Mary. Mary was an average student academically but was extremely shy and withdrawn. Mary did not participate in any extracurricular activities. She spent her leisure time stamp collecting, watching television, and reading fiction.

During a routine class-scheduling interview with her high school counselor, Mary began to cry. The counselor asked what seemed to be the problem. Mary related her feelings of loneliness and of not having anyone whom she could relate to. She said that her one good friend had moved to a different city during the fifth grade. Mary recalled crying to herself in her room for several months over this. She related how badly she wanted at least one good friend, but said she was afraid that she would only get hurt again as she had been in fifth grade.

Mary's problem could be classified as interpersonal since it pertained to her difficulties in establishing and maintaining relationships with others. Mary's problem could be classified as developmental. Early in Mary's life, she had begun to experience the hurt and pain associated with broken relationships.

The counselor's role

Her inability to resolve her feelings about those broken relationships at or near the time that they occurred prevented her social development in the area of personal/social relationships.

Mary's problem is found frequently in school, agency, and mental health settings. The need for support, encouragement, and skill building are important underpinnings for individuals like Mary to feel comfortable enough to take a risk and embark on learning new things and growing as a person.

Together, the counselor and Mary explored the feelings Mary had. They began identifying areas of relationships where she felt more and less comfortable. A key factor seemed to be Mary's fear of rejection, which had accumulated from experiences with her parents, sister, and her friend who had moved away. They discussed comfortable risk taking, which resulted in Mary's willingness to say hello to five girls in school during the following week. She progressed to five more the second week, and eventually began expanding her greetings into discussions. Within eight weeks, Mary was feeling better. She had developed two relationships so well that she invited these friends to spend a night at her home. The counselor talked with Mary about how she could continue to make friends on her own. They terminated the counseling relationship after nine interviews.

Counseling skills in interpersonal problems

The counselor used the following skills in working with Mary: (1) developing a supportive and encouraging relationship, (2) identifying the components of the counseling strategy, (3) developing a sequenced learning approach to building relationships, and (4) ongoing monitoring and adjusting of the sequential steps and support for Mary's progress. All four of these skills were helpful in assisting Mary in resolving her problem.

Return from prison

Correctional counseling

Gary was 22 years old and just released to a community-corrections program. He had served two years in prison on a three-year sentence for robbery. Parole could be considered if he responded well to the community-corrections program. His record indicated that he had been in and out of trouble ever since his early teens. He had not finished high school, but had managed to acquire a General Education Diploma while in prison. This achievement had been an important factor in his release to the community. It was hoped that prior to his outright release, Gary would live in a half-way house where he could be supervised while pursuing additional vocational preparation.

Gary's educational records indicated that he had a difficult time adjusting to the demands of a school setting. A consistent pattern emerged from teachers' comments: He was often tardy; he had a short attention span; he was disruptive and had many conflicts with other students. Psychological reports indicated that Gary was in the average range in intelligence. Little else remarkable appeared in the reports except for opinions expressing the likelihood of a hyperactive condition, which contributed to his learning disability. Gary had not achieved a reading level higher than fourth grade.

Socially, in his early school years, Gary was reported to be an active participant with other children in play activities. Throughout his elementary years, however, there were increasing references to fights and other kinds of conflict with his peers. Gary became easily frustrated when things did not go his way. During his adolescent years, Gary spent little time joining the mainstream of school life. Rather, he and several others formed their own gang and enjoyed the reputation of being the local toughs. Gary and this group increasingly engaged in destructive activity, which eventually led to several encounters with the police and Gary's imprisonment.

In prison, Gary was basically a loner. He knew no one there, and he did not mix to any degree. He was not a problem in any way, but several instructors informed the counselor that Gary was sullen and did his work with little enthusiasm.

The counselor contacted Gary prior to his release, but little real communication occurred. Other than to review the details of his release and his new living situation, Gary was not interested in communicating.

After Gary began his residence at the half-way house, the counselor attempted to develop a plan for his rehabilitation. In order for Gary to gain parole, he would have to be active in a program that would result in his being able to support himself. Thus, vocational planning and preparation would be important. Gary again did not exhibit any real interest, and he tried to rely on the counselor for decisions. To Gary's surprise, the counselor refused to prescribe anything for him and pointed out the consequences of not having a plan, one of which would be a return to prison. He also pointed out that he would help Gary plan but only if Gary cooperated. Gary did not seem to know how to respond to this, but his surprise was evident. In prison, Gary was not expected to make decisions. Also, given Gary's background, the counselor suspected that he would like someone to make his decisions for him. He wanted to make it clear to Gary that the role of counselor was that of a resource and not an authority figure against which Gary could rebel. The counselor made the point early on that Gary would have to be responsible for making his own final decisions.

Counselor's role as resource person

The counselor also wanted to inform Gary of all the possibilities open to him at the residential center. Gary's participation in these programs was another prerequisite for his parole. Again, the counselor only indicated the extent of services from which Gary was to choose. These included individual counseling; group counseling; basic education courses from the local adult education program; and job-preparation, which consisted of evaluation programs at a rehabilitation facility and training in local skill-training programs or on-the-job training with local employers. Also, recreational facilities were available to the residents, but these activities had to be "purchased" with points obtained by following the rules of the program.

The residents usually had little money when they first entered the program, but they were expected to obtain work when they were able so that they could leave the program on a self-sufficient basis. Usually, a prerequisite of parole required that this self-sufficiency be accomplished or achievable in the near future, so it was important that Gary recognize the need to take charge of his life in a positive way in order to achieve parole early and have a good chance to remain in society.

Since this was a need that many of the residents had, the program staff struggled with how much structure would be necessary without doing too much for the residents. It was agreed that concrete future educational or vocational plans would have to be forthcoming from the residents within the first three weeks of their stay, or a resident would have to be returned to prison. This rule was strictly enforced. Another requirement was that the residents had to participate in at least six hours of programming a day. This was usually easy to do since the amount of scheduled programs was more than adequate for keeping someone busy for twelve hours. The residents were allowed to come or go on their own to these programs, but they had to return signed vouchers documenting their participation. Two unexplained absences or an outright escape attempt would result in an immediate return to prison. It was important that new residents understand the importance of these rules and learn to exercise their freedom within these structures.

Gary continued to meet with the counselor on a daily basis. Gradually, communication became easier between them. Gary also participated in a group that included former residents who had made a successful transition via this program. These seemed to be mainly discussion groups, and Gary noted that he felt there was a lot of "preaching" going on.

After his first week, Gary had made little progress in forming a plan, but otherwise seemed to fit in. The counselor noticed that Gary became quite fidgety when he was not doing something active. He had a lot of time on his hands during this first week since he did not have enough points to keep himself occupied in the recreation room. Although he rarely entertained himself by watching television or reading, he also did not mix with other residents even when participating in leisure activities with them. He basically appeared anxious and uncertain.

The counselor suggested that Gary visit a psychologist for evaluation to see if they could gain more information to work with. Gary agreed, and the evaluation was done in the next week. The psychologist's report stated that Gary had suitable potential, but that there was evidence of a learning disability that could be discerned in hyperactive behavior such as his inability to remain occupied with the same task for any length of time. The counselor felt this was consistent with his own observations and with Gary's records. The psychologist suggested that Gary might benefit from learning how to relax and from channeling his energy into an active lifestyle. Vocational testing indicated that Gary was interested in outdoor and mechanical work and that he liked to see the accomplishments of his work.

The counselor reviewed these findings with Gary and offered to help him learn relaxation. Each counseling session began with relaxation exercises. Gary was skeptical but managed to practice the exercises during counseling. He was not sure he would do them on his own. After these were finished, Gary seemed more attentive to counseling, and his participation improved.

The psychological evaluation also helped Gary consider his vocational plans. He concurred with the direction the evaluation suggested but could not help to refine it. The counselor suggested that a work evaluation would be helpful in gaining more information. Gary was scheduled to visit the evaluation unit at the rehabilitation center the next week. The counselor met with him each morning before he left to run through the relaxation exercises. Gary seemed to welcome these now and thought he might try them on his own.

At the evaluation unit, Gary did fairly well. He participated in all the exercises, but he rarely interacted with the evaluators or with others in the program. The information obtained suggested that Gary had good manual skills, good mechanical comprehension, and good strength and coordination. His mechanical skills, however, were undeveloped. The evaluators also felt his lack of communication would hinder the proper development of supervisor and co-worker relationships.

The community-corrections program helped to develop a relationship between Gary and a local gas station owner who had provided on-the-job training to previous residents. This training consisted of working the pumps, light mechanical work such as oil and lubrication jobs and tire changing, and the opportunity to assist and learn from the garage mechanic. The counselor felt that this would be a good opportunity for Gary to be exposed to employment and to acquire some of the personal communication skills so essential to being a satisfactory worker. Gary would also receive wages.

The owner agreed to try Gary for a week; he would be willing to extend the time if the relationship was working out for everybody concerned. Gary agreed. In discussing the offer with the counselor later, Gary indicated his surprise that someone would want him to come to work. The counselor felt this was a good sign and helped Gary explore how this was different from what he was used to.

The next week Gary practiced relaxing with the counselor each morning before going to work and participated each day at the gas station. The counselor visited the station several times, and the owner indicated Gary was learning well but was very quiet and acted suspicious. The owner felt that Gary would have to loosen up a bit more before he would be comfortable with Gary servicing customers at the pump. There would be enough work for him in the garage in the meantime.

Development of interpersonal-communication skills

The counselor discussed this with Gary and wanted to know if he wanted to change this. Although he seemed bothered, he said he didn't care much. The counselor pointed out this discrepancy and wondered if Gary could explain it. The counselor knew that Gary had had little interpersonal communication with other people in his life except for his gang during his adolescent years.

The counselor suggested that Gary try group counseling and spending more time with other residents at the half-way house. The counselor also said that Gary might consider enrolling in a mechanics-training course. These contacts would give Gary the opportunity to interact with other people. The counselor also suggested that he and Gary try role playing different ways of approaching and communicating with people, particularly with those persons at the gas station. The counselor said he hoped that Gary would soon be able to work the pumps. He discussed this with the owner and offered to spend the afternoon with Gary and help him work on this. The owner agreed. This program schedule continued for the next month. Gary attended class in the evening three nights a week, a group meeting one weeknight and on Saturday, saw the counselor each morning prior to going to work to practice relaxing, and tried to schedule other time for recreation both inside and outside the half-way house. With his income from the gas station, he could afford more leisure activities.

As progress was being made in this area, the counselor asked Gary if longer range plans could be considered. Gary seemed pleased with the prospect of becoming a mechanic. The counselor knew he would need more formal training and suggested that Gary consider a CETA opportunity, a two-year program consisting of class instruction, shop experience, and employment for 20 hours a week. He would earn a full-time salary during training. If he participated, Gary could initially stay at the half-way house but also could soon expect parole and outright release to the community. Thus, he would have to begin working on suitable housing alternatives. The counselor hoped he might meet others in his training program who would consider a roommate arrangement. The counselor would continue to work with Gary throughout this period. Gary agreed with this plan when he saw it could help him become a mechanic and obtain his parole.

The counselor's role

Counseling skills in correctional counseling

The counselor had been able to recognize Gary's developmental deficit and his resulting lack of appropriate intrapersonal maturity. He attempted to work around the deficit by providing a stimulating environment that required Gary to shift attention from one constructive activity to another. Using environmental supports is an important counselor skill illustrated by this case. Along with this, the counselor helped Gary focus on how to properly interpret social interaction and respond to it with the expected degree of maturity. The counselor attempted to be with Gary in as many of his day-to-day activities as possible and did not rely solely on one-to-one office discussions. Another important element was the practice Gary gained by making his own decisions. This was crucial to his intrapersonal development. Thus, this case shows that the counselor used skills of developing and facilitating a good relationship with Gary. Other skills included reviewing and analyzing case records, role playing, observation, modeling appropriate behaviors, and seeking community resource information.

Adjustment to disability

Becky was a 27-year-old housewife who had been married for eight years. Her husband worked for an excavating company, and they had two children, ages six and two. Their marriage had been typical until Becky was in a severe auto accident, as a result of which her right arm, her arm of preference, had to be amputated. Although she suffered other injuries, none of these resulted in permanent damage.

Becky had relished her role as a housewife and mother. She had done little else since graduating from high school. For a year prior to her marriage, Becky had worked as a salesperson in a department store, but that was the extent of her work experience outside her home.

Her physical recovery, considering the extent of her injuries, was excellent. Her mother-in-law was able to care for her family during this period of recovery. Becky was grateful to have this help. It comforted her to know that her family was in good hands so that she could concentrate on her recovery. She normally had somewhat distant relations with her mother-in-law, but as long as their contacts were infrequent, she was able to enjoy her mother-in-law's company. Her own parents had retired and moved to a southern climate due to her mother's ill health.

After Becky returned home, her mother-in-law, who was widowed, continued to do most of the chores and cared for the family. There was little discussion regarding how long this arrangement would last. Her husband and mother-in-law seemed to be quite content with the situation. Neither indicated that Becky should soon think about resuming her role as housewife independently of her mother-in-law's help.

Although Becky's recovery was proceeding well, and she received special therapy to learn how to handle life's daily tasks with her prosthesis and remaining arm, her attitude did not reflect her progress. Her physician noted this and commented to her about her depressed state. With little prompting, Becky poured out her tearful feelings of not being needed and feeling useless. She felt she was now a burden rather than a caretaker of her family. She recognized how helpful her mother-in-law had been and could not understand why she should have feelings of anger toward her. The physician recognized this reaction as a rather typical one for a person who has experienced a traumatic loss resulting in a permanent physical disability. The fear that results from loss of functioning that threatens one's fulfillment of a previously desired role often leads to anger, which soon becomes tempered by guilt since one often receives a great deal of support after such an injury. The conflicting nature of these emotions often leads the individual to suppress them, which results in a depressed state. Becky seemed to be following this pattern. The physician decided that Becky might be a good candidate for vocational rehabilitation and suggested to her that she look into it. Becky was unfamiliar with vocational rehabilitation so the physician explained his view of it. He felt that vocational rehabilitation helped individuals with disabilities find a suitable job or situation that made good use of a person's remaining abilities or retrained them in a new skill that would lead to increased independence. Becky didn't see how this applied to her since she was a housewife and not employed, but the physician wasn't sure if this mattered. He said he would be happy to make a referral, and Becky agreed. After several weeks, Becky received a letter inviting her to come in to the local vocational rehabilitation office. Her emotional state had not improved, and her husband did not really encourage her to go. He did not see how she could qualify or benefit from the program. Her

Vocational rehabilitation counseling

physician encouraged her to follow through, nevertheless, and Becky kept the appointment.

The counselor spent about an hour reviewing the vocational rehabilitation process with her, explaining that she could become a client and receive services even if she wanted to remain a housewife. She explained to Becky that they would need to get her medical file from the physician to certify her eligibility for services. Becky signed a release for her physician to send her records. The physician complied, and within two weeks, Becky made her second visit. The counselor discussed Becky's future plans, but Becky related that she had thought little of her future other than in her role as a housewife. The counselor discussed the value of having more information at hand to plan for the future while also assuring Becky that being a housewife was a worthy goal. She suggested that Becky visit a psychologist for a vocational assessment and attend a work evaluation at a local rehabilitation facility to learn more about herself. Becky again was hesitant, but she was intrigued by the possibility of doing something on her own. The cost would be borne by the agency.

Work-evaluation report

The work evaluation was completed in three weeks, and two weeks later, the reports were in. The counselor began the interview by asking Becky how things were going. Becky was distressed by her relative lack of purpose but noted that at least on a rational level, she could not complain about how well the situation was working out for her family. The counselor recognized Becky's needs to be fulfilled as a person who cares for others and indicated that much of the evaluation pointed out Becky's desire to be of service to others. They then discussed the ways Becky could help her family and the different kinds of occupations that involve being of service to others. The evaluation uncovered the fact that Becky had mastered many skills with her prosthesis and could do many tasks as long as they did not require a great deal of lifting or fine dexterity. These reports also indicated that Becky would have little difficulty assuming the role of an independent housewife. Becky seemed relieved at this, but indicated that her mother-in-law, as well as the rest of her family, had adjusted so well that she didn't think they would want to change. Also, sharing the costs of the household with her mother-in-law was proving to have its benefits. Becky also felt she would hurt her mother-in-law's feelings if she said she didn't need her anymore. The counselor asked Becky what the ideal situation would be. Becky responded that she felt she would like to have her mother-in-law live close by so she could still feel like a helper, but Becky wanted to run the household by herself. She also felt that extra income would make it easier for her husband to support her. The counselor suggested that part-time work for Becky might be a way to accomplish this ideal and also suggested that Becky could learn to be more assertive in gaining control of her role with her family again. Becky seemed willing to explore this possibility, and another interview was scheduled.

Prior to this interview, the counselor reviewed the part-time possibilities that were available for Becky's interests and skills. Several possibilities appeared, including light housekeeping for convalescing or otherwise incapacitated people, a job as a day-care center aide or as a dietician aide in a school or hospital. Training was not needed for any of these except for a certificate for the housekeeping job. All of these appealed to Becky, but she especially liked the idea of working among children. The counselor offered to help Becky come up with a job search strategy if Becky felt she could convince her family to accept her wishes to assume control of her role within the family. Becky felt unsure of this point, so the counselor offered to work with her on this. The counselor and Becky then developed an individualized written rehabilitation plan that outlined the type of counseling Becky would receive and the job-seeking skills she would develop.

Strategy for rehabilitation

For the next four weeks, Becky and the counselor met once a week to think through the details and strategy needed to accomplish her plans. Becky role played situations in which she discussed with her husband her own desires and the means to fulfill them, as well as the way this would accommodate her family's needs, including those of her mother-in-law. Becky felt that her husband would be particularly sensitive to her feelings about his mother. She also wanted to be sure she did not sound ungrateful to her mother-in-law in wanting her to move out of the house. She was unsure if her husband would see her point of view about work very readily.

After a time, Becky felt she had a good argument to offer, one that had benefits for all concerned. Her initial discussion with her husband went fairly well, especially since she pointed out she could add to the family's income and would still need her mother-in-law's help on a day-to-day basis to care for the youngest child while Becky was working. Becky enlisted her husband's support in discussing her plan with her mother-in-law. They indicated their gratefulness but pointed out how important it was for Becky to manage the house again. They also pointed out that they would need her to help quite often, but that since she was getting older, they felt it would be in her best interests not to be burdened full-time with the chores generated by a young family. Her mother-in-law seemed saddened by this but acknowledged that she did often feel tired and could use fewer full-time responsibilities. She also indicated that she would appreciate a vacation soon, and Becky promptly offered to help pay for a special vacation after she got a job. Her husband seemed surprised at this, but did not comment.

Next Becky had to find a job so she could make all this happen. She was quite eager for this and made plans with the counselor to pursue this as soon as possible. There were no immediate openings, so the counselor enrolled Becky in a special class where Becky could learn job-seeking skills. The counselor also contacted local schools and hospitals for part-time positions. Becky attended the class daily and uncovered several leads of her own. After practicing filling out applications and interviews, Becky developed a resume and visited several potential employers. She found no immediate openings, but one personnel officer had a colleague at a community college who had mentioned the need for help in a student snack shop. He offered to call and see if this was still open. A time slot was open in the mornings during the week and Becky was asked to interview. This turned out to be a successful interview, and Becky was asked to start the next week.

The counselor stayed in touch with Becky for the next six months, and things progressed well. Becky demonstrated that she could handle the job and her household responsibilities with ease. Her husband was pleased. Her mother-in-law had moved out, but came daily to care for the baby and help with some household tasks. Over Christmas break, when the snack shop was closed, Becky would be able to stay at home, so her mother-in-law could be free to go on her vacation. Becky was putting money aside to buy her mother-in-law new vacation clothes and to help pay some of her travel expenses. Becky indicated she was very pleased with the help she received from the counselor. She saw the counselor as the major reason that she was motivated to take control of her life again.

The counselor's role

Emotional reactions to physical disability

The counselor recognized that Becky's reaction to her disability was emotional as well as physical. Not only physical restoration but emotional healing was needed. Becky felt that she had lost her purpose in life. Her interpersonal relationships had necessarily been disrupted for a time due to the injury and recovery period, but she felt as though she had lost more than her arm. This interruption of her interpersonal responsibilities had caused her to doubt herself, thus causing intrapersonal problems as well. The counselor helped her regain control of her life again by helping her to get in touch with her own feelings and desires again. Once this was accomplished, she helped Becky plan how to take charge of the environment around her and, thus, take control also of her interpersonal responsibilities again. The counselor was very supportive of Becky, acknowledging her needs and helping her to plan for them accordingly. She facilitated the use of many services that could provide Becky with the time and information that she needed in order to take stock of herself. She helped Becky regain control of her life and gradually resume her responsibilities as wife, mother, and daugher-in-law. She provided occupational information to Becky and the resources for Becky to get her own job, a very important confidence builder. She maintained contact with Becky for some time after her plans were essentially implemented to make sure that Becky had reached her goal of independence again.

Issues in aging

Jacob was 71 years old when he was brought to the attention of the aging-assistance center by his son, who had heard of the services offered on the radio. This program provided a variety of services to those of the local population who were 55 years and older. Recreational facilities were available, along with leisure-time pursuits. Educational and hobby activities were offered. A cafeteria service and a mobile food service were also part of the program. There was a volunteer coordinating bureau and a placement counselor to help those who wanted to find part or full time paid employment. There also was a referral service for medical care and other health-related problems. A central part of the services of the assistance program was counseling. The counselors served as the coordinators of all these services and for other community resources as needed. The counselors attempted to develop individualized services for each person and to involve the families of the counselees in the counseling process. The assistance center promoted a philosophy of helping older people stay involved with their families if this could be done in a positive and constructive way for all concerned.

Jacob was a plumber who went into business for himself after the Depression. He had worked long, hard hours and had earned a decent living. His poverty during the Depression and his long hours at work had precluded much socializing. Jacob had stayed to himself, living in a boarding house. He had maintained few social contacts, and marriage had seemed remote to him. However, just after World War II, Jacob had become romantically involved with a waitress who worked at a diner he had frequented. She was 11 years younger than Jacob.

After their marriage, Jacob's routine had not changed much. He still spent many hours working and running the business, which had become quite large. Four other plumbers were employed by Jacob at this time. The son, Tom, had come along within a year after the couple had married. Jacob's wife was not pleased with the relative lack of attention from her husband but she had thoroughly enjoyed her new son and had sought out other women in the neighborhood for companionship. She frequently had joined church groups and clubs and had become an avid reader. Tom also had received little attention from his father but he was included often in his mother's pastimes. She had read stories to him that whetted his curiosity to learn and explore. He became an eager student, and his hobbies had reflected his desire to learn more.

Each family member soon had become used to the routine of the others. Jacob's main concern had been his business. Family life had not been strained but Jacob had not been central to the emotional needs of his wife or son.

Life-adjustment problems

A difficult period arose, however, when Tom had finished high school. He wanted to go to college and had the ability to do so. Jacob had secretly hoped his son would join him in the business but Tom had shown little interest. By now, the business was quite large and included a plumbing supply house as well as field crews. The family income was more than adequate, although little display of wealth could be discerned in the family's activities except for what Tom's mother spent on his education and other learning pursuits. Jacob felt that the lure of an assured and lucrative income would accomplish his goal of bringing Tom into the business. Tom, however, went off to college.

After college, Tom had become a management trainee at a large corporation in another state. After six years, he and his family, which included a wife and two young daughters, moved to Tom's hometown, where he accepted a job. His father again offered Tom a partnership in the business, which was as successful as ever, but Tom said no. Jacob, at that time, was in his late 60s. His response had been to sell the entire business immediately. Jacob and his wife would have no further concern about money for the business had enabled Jacob to amass a large savings, and the sale brought in another large sum. Tom had expected that his parents would have ample opportunity to enjoy their retirement. He had felt that his mother's relative young age and energy would be a good influence on Jacob and would permit the two of them to have a fulfilled retirement.

For Tom's mother, little actually changed. She continued to pursue her busy lifestyle. She was involved in many community activities and had wide-ranging interests and hobbies. Jacob, on the other hand, had never cultivated any interest other than in his business. When that was no longer available, he had little to do. This was not an apparent problem at first. Tom's mother seemed to carry on as before. Soon, though, Tom's mother told him that Jacob was becoming openly angry at her and was voicing much displeasure about Tom. On the day prior to Tom's coming to the assistance center, Jacob had struck his wife, who had run from the house and down to Tom's house. She had been very frightened. Tom had visited his father later that evening, but he, too, had been met with hostility. There had been no possibility for discussion. Late in the evening, Tom's mother had returned home and had been able to talk with Jacob. He had begun to weep openly, expressing his remorse, not so much for having become hostile at his wife and Tom but for having sold his business. His wife perceived his feelings of uselessness and also recognized his loneliness. She also recognized his disappointment at Tom's refusal to enter the business, which she conveyed to Tom. Jacob had held these feelings inside for many years, but his empty life had caused these feelings to rush to the surface. Surprisingly, both Tom and his mother had felt a great deal of guilt over neglecting Jacob.

Jacob's problem was brought on by his aging, as well as by his rather circumscribed social development. Jacob's lack of social development had interfered with his interpersonal relations, even within his family, for the major part of his life. When he retired, he no longer had the self-satisfaction of managing his business and earning a good living for his family. He had nothing to turn to, and his family had long since learned to live without him. This feeling of uselessness was more than he could tolerate. His intrapersonal struggle became a severe interpersonal problem, which endangered his ability to live with his family.

The counselor's role

The counselor assured Tom that this was not an unusual situation, particularly for people who had lived through the Depression with few familial or other social supports. Many of these individuals seemed to have spent much of their subsequent lives pursuing financial security, often to the neglect of other interests and family life. The counselor commended Tom and his mother for having compassion for Jacob, since in many cases, older individuals such as Jacob are scorned by their families for their earlier failures at being a father or husband. Tom's feelings of guilt surfaced again, and the counselor tried to help Tom see how he and his mother might attempt some new things to help Jacob find a role for himself, especially since his health was still good.

Counseling strategy

The counselor thought it might be best if one of the retired volunteers who served as a counseling paraprofessional would visit Jacob and invite him to the assistance center. Several who had been active businessmen had formed a volunteer group to help local businesses, particularly nonprofit ones, with business problems. The counselor asked this group if any of them knew Jacob. One of them was a retired contractor who had bought supplies from Jacob and knew him slightly.

This man visited Jacob to inform him of the volunteer retired businessman's club and the assistance center. He invited Jacob to come down and visit the facility to see if he might want to participate. Jacob's wife encouraged Jacob to look into it. He agreed and accompanied the man to the center the next day. Jacob toured the facility and had coffee with the other retired businessmen in the lounge. After this meeting, Jacob and his acquaintance, who was trained as a peer counselor, went to a private office where the peer counselor gave Jacob more information and questioned him about his retirement. Jacob related some dissatisfaction with his life, but did not describe his behavior of a few days previously. The peer counselor asked if Jacob would like to bring his wife back for a visit to meet with a counselor who could explain how they could use the center as a couple. Jacob agreed to do this.

At the first session with the counselor, Jacob and his wife reviewed their retirement years. It quickly became apparent that Jacob was frustrated with having nothing to do, no real needs to attend to. His wife, on the other hand, recounted her busy schedule. Their differences became quite apparent. The counselor suggested that the center might provide the means for them to find something to do together of a social nature and also provide Jacob with new pursuits of his own. Jacob mentioned his interest in the retired businessmen's group, which the counselor thought was a good beginning.

Later that week, the peer counselor dropped by to invite Jacob and his wife to a party at the center. They accepted. At the party, one of the retired businessmen discussed a problem he had run into with a local rehabilitation workshop for handicapped people. Jacob was brought into the conversation and showed an interest. He was asked if he would like to help on the problem. He agreed to do so.

Tom remained in contact with the counselor at the center for several months. The counselor and peer counselor introduced Jacob to more of the center's programs. He was actively engaged with the retired businessmen. Tom's mother also became more involved, not just for Jacob's sake, but because she was naturally attracted to what the center had to offer. Tom recounted to the counselor that his father had not repeated the outburst and that he seemed much more communicative with Tom and his mother. Tom took an active, and also a natural interest, in what the retired businessmen were doing. Tom was happy that he and his father had something to share, and he was pleased with the assistance the center had offered his family.

The counselor recognized that much strength existed in the family and in Jacob. The center provided counseling skill training to paraprofessionals who were also senior citizens. The counselor recognized the value of using one of these individuals who was also an acquaintance of Jacob to bring Jacob and his wife into the center. The counselor, recognizing that each member of the family had to have a reason for being in touch with one another, made every effort to show concern for Tom and his mother as well as for Jacob. By staying in touch with Tom, the counselor provided Tom with the encouragement he needed to stay in communication with his father. Soon this too was happening in a natural way. The case of Jacob illustrates how a counselor can use peer counseling and natural social supports, particularly families, to provide a needed array of services.

Child abuse

Parent-child crisis

Rita is a 34-year-old mother of two children who has been married twice. She divorced her second husband two years ago. Rita grew up in an upper-middle-class family along with two younger siblings. Her father was an insurance salesman, and her mother was a housewife. Rita recalled having been severely physically abused on several occasions between the ages of 6 and 14 for no reason apparent to her. She felt that the beatings administered by her father were severe overreactions to the situation. Her younger siblings had never been as severely beaten as she was, although they, too, were the victims of stern discipline.

Rita got pregnant at age 17 while she was a junior in high school. She married the child's father. She felt relieved to leave the stultifying atmosphere at home. Soon after the baby was born, though, Rita began to feel overwhelmed with the responsibilities of motherhood. She likened her feeling to that of living at home when her father was about to beat her. She felt now that her father beat her when he was overwhelmed with responsibilities at work and at home. One day,

Rita beat her own child. When she had finished, she felt remorseful, guilty, and also somehow relieved. Upon seeing the child, her husband became extremely concerned about what had happened. Over the next three years, Rita continued to beat her child. She continued to have feelings of being overwhelmed with life and the responsibilities she had assumed so suddenly. Her child would trigger being beaten and abused by Rita when he persisted questioning her about life and when he got into fights with the neighbor's children. After several attempts to resolve the problem with her husband, they finally divorced. Her husband was awarded custody of the child. Rita felt that losing custody of her child was harsh and unfair punishment.

Two years later, Rita married again and a similar sequence began. She became pregnant. After the child was born, she began experiencing the same feelings of being overwhelmed, and, again, she resorted to beating her young child. Her second husband divorced her and was awarded custody of this child, too.

Rita became concerned with the way she had handled her life to this point and referred herself for counseling. Rita learned that the beating or abusive response was natural for her, and thus, she assumed the same position in raising her own children.

Rita's problem could be classified as intrapersonal in that her problems stemmed mainly from her inability to understand and control her emotions. The problem would be classified further as environmental because it was ongoing in the context of her daily life with her children. Finally, the problem would be specified as developmental because it was one that had developed early in her life. Rita had no satisfying alternate means of coping with feelings that had occurred at an earlier developmental stage.

The counselor's role

Problems such as Rita's are often found in protective child services agencies, probate courts, departments of social services, private counseling, or community mental health centers.

The counselor began by obtaining an extensive life history on Rita from as far back as she could remember. Her early feelings of being overwhelmed were identified. The counselor helped Rita to see that her response to the home atmosphere while she was growing up made it difficult for her to accept responsibility and cope with it as an adult. She also had not learned to be a loving parent. Her father's methods of dealing with his feelings by beating her appeared to her as an effective though hateful way of dealing with the demands of children.

Counseling skills in child abuse

The counselor skills involved in the case of Rita included: (1) developing a facilitative relationship, (2) obtaining pertinent case history or life history information, (3) learning attentive coping mechanisms such as relaxation to handle the problem. All of these skills seemed essential to help Rita resolve her problem.

Spouse abuse

Jack was 24 years old when he and his family were brought to the attention of the family services center in their local community. His wife, Mary, had gone with their two-year-old son to the police station. She was in such poor shape that police officers took her to the emergency room of a local hospital for treatment of facial lacerations and bruises. During questioning, Mary admitted that her husband had beaten her. She said she feared for her two-year-old son's safety since the argument that had led to her beating was prompted by his crying, which her husband had found excessive. She explained that her son had been ill with a cold, and she suspected that he had developed an infection. Jack, however, insisted that the son was spoiled and only needed a spanking. When Mary attempted to prevent this, Jack struck her. She fell. He left the room, but returned soon in a rage to strike her again. He finally ran from the house, after which Mary grabbed her son and drove to the police station.

Unusually explosive and angry reactions to everyday events are often a sign that counseling is needed.

The police brought Mary and the boy to a women's shelter operated by the family services center. Later that evening, Jack was arrested and detained for questioning.

Crisis-intervention counseling for family problems

The next morning, Mary was visited by a counselor. The counselor inquired into her condition as well as the baby's and indicated that a physician would visit shortly. She then sat with Mary for a time, who was still quite distraught. She was guilt-ridden because she had gone to the police. She felt responsible for Jack's arrest, a common reaction in this situation. The counselor empathized with these feelings, and showed regret that this had happened to Mary. The counselor acknowledged that Mary wanted her family to stay together and offered to help bring Jack and Mary to an understanding of what had gone wrong. She assured Mary she would visit Jack immediately.

When Jack saw the counselor, he was in no mood to discuss the previous night's events. He was angry and resented the intrusion of the counselor and the family services center into his family life. He wanted his family back. The counselor indicated she wanted this for Jack, too, but it would only happen if he cooperated. Jack would not discuss anything further.

The counselor went back to Mary, who now felt physically better, but was anxious to leave the shelter. The counselor spent a few minutes reviewing the legal concerns involved, but Mary wanted to go home and not pursue pressing charges. The counselor gave her card to Mary and asked if it would be all right if she called now and then to see how things were going. Mary said this would be fine.

A day later, the counselor called Mary to see how things were. At first, Mary seemed hesitant to talk, but then began sobbing. It took her several minutes to gain enough control to continue the conversation. She related that Jack, incensed over the incident, had blamed her, although he had promised he would not hit her again. Mary said this had happened in the past, and that she really didn't think this promise would be kept. The counselor said she would be willing to come to Mary's house to talk, and Mary agreed to see her the next morning. She said Jack would not be home then.

The next morning, Mary gave the counselor a brief review of her married life. She had been married for four years, and she and Jack had known each other for five years. Although Jack had displayed an occasional temper before they married, he had never physically abused her except for one pushing incident, which at the time, had seemed like an isolated event. After the baby came, Jack seemed to be irritated quite easily, and had punished the child for excessive crying, spilling food, and other routine childish behaviors that were beyond the child's control. On several occasions, Jack had punched her in the arm, but the recent violent display was a new level of anger that had deeply frightened Mary. The counselor wondered if Jack were under unique strain from work or some other situation, but Mary could think of none. Mary could offer no obvious explanation for Jack's behavior. She recounted that Jack was pleased at being a father and did not understand what significance the baby played in Jack's resorting to physical abuse. Mary now felt violence could happen again.

The counselor wondered about Jack's life prior to the time he met Mary, but she knew very little. Jack had not lived in the area, nor did he have family or friends close by. Jack had worked for a large out-of-state construction firm that had contracted a job in the area; he had been transferred to work at the construction site. Mary was a secretary for a local consulting engineer who worked on the project, and she and Jack had met at a Christmas party. Jack said his parents were both dead and that he had no brothers or sisters. After he proposed to her, he got a job with a local construction firm where he was now a foreman. He did well at work.

The counselor's role

The counselor assured Mary that she would be willing to help and described the counseling offered at the center. The counselor said that the center tried to help families who had experienced similar difficult situations to find ways to cope without resorting to rage. She assured Mary that the marriage could probably work out. She also suggested that Jack's behavior, although frightening, could be changed. She assured Mary that she probably had done nothing unusual to set off such a rage. Such problems often were related to events of childhood that had created scars that reopened during adulthood. These reopened scars often coincide with a major change in a person's life, and the birth of their baby could have opened old wounds. The counselor encouraged Mary to join a group of other wives who were facing or had faced similar difficulties. She thought Mary might get some ideas regarding how to deal with Jack's behavior.

Self-help group support for wife

Over the next two weeks, Mary attended these group meetings. Other wives shared their trials and successes with her. It became obvious to Mary that Jack's problem was not uncommon, and also that he would have to try to work through these problems and want to change. She felt she could not cope on her own. The counselor and others in the group helped Mary plan a strategy for getting Jack involved in counseling. Mary thought she should recount her own experience at the center and the help she had received. She also wanted to confront Jack with the depth of her fear for herself and their son and tell him that she could not continue indefinitely with this threat hanging over her. The counselor felt that if Jack agreed to come for counseling, he should see another counselor instead of her since Jack had a negative encounter with her at the police station. A back-up strategy included an opportunity to have Jack meet one of the men who shared his problem of abusing loved ones, but who had been successful at changing as a result of counseling.

That evening, Mary discussed this with Jack. He tried to brush off the incident and accused her of overreacting. Mary stood firm, however, and said she could not live in fear, that she needed some reassurance that Jack would be able to channel his anger. She felt she deserved at least to understand who might be creating this problem, since she could not see how she or the baby were the cause. Jack must have sensed Mary's urgency for he began to listen to her. She recounted her experience at the center, including the advice that Jack meet with a counselor or one of the men who had received counseling. Jack indicated he would meet with a counselor but only to show everyone that there was no problem. An appointment was scheduled, but Jack missed it, saying he had to work overtime. Mary promptly rescheduled it for a Saturday, and Jack went.

During the first meeting Jack appeared aloof and did not communicate much. The counselor suggested that Jack attend a group meeting the next week as well as a follow-up meeting with the counselor. Jack said he saw no real purpose in this and wasn't sure he could come. Mary insisted that Jack attend. Jack did so.

Group and individual counseling for husband

At the group meeting, other husbands and fathers related their own experiences. Many described their own frustrations, their feelings of being unsuccessful fathers and husbands. They also indicated that their counseling experiences were helping them understand the sources of their frustrations. Some indicated they were not so afraid of themselves anymore, as if they had sympathy for whatever produced their rage. Jack was quiet throughout all this, but contemplated the session all week. Mary noticed this, but did not press him for explanations. On Saturday, at the individual counseling session, Jack expressed his amazement that these men seemed to have the same feelings as he did. He wanted to know more about them. The counselor suggested that Jack return to the next group meeting and attempt to share backgrounds with them. The counselor also went over some illustrations of situations that had generated some of the frustrations of these men. These illustrations typically recounted childhood or adolescent episodes of rejection, fear, loneliness, and often physical abuse from a loved one. Often, these men had strong urges to be excellent fathers. They tried to give their children material things they never had. Somehow, their hopes never materialized, difficult circumstances for these men to handle.

Jack eventually began to discuss his own youth. His mother had died when he was a boy. He was an only child. His father took him to a sitter's house during the day when he was small. After he went to school, he stayed at the sitter's house until his father picked him up. He did not remember much of his preteen years. He recounted few joys or sorrows. When he no longer needed sitters, he was pretty much on his own. His father did not remarry, although increasingly, his father stayed out later and later. On several occasions, his father vanished for a day or two at a time. These absences were never explained. When Jack was fifteen, his father was in a car accident. He was severely injured, but he survived. The doctor explained to Jack that his father had been drinking. He wanted to know if Jack knew how much his father drank, but Jack had no idea that he drank at all. Jack was taken in by some people in the neighborhood. A few weeks later, a psychiatrist told Jack that his father was an alcoholic who needed to receive extensive treatment. Jack's father was in a mental institution for two years. He was released, and he committed suicide within a week. Jack's father had refused to see him after the accident and during his entire hospitalization. As soon as Jack graduated from high school, he got a job with the construction firm, which sent him to jobs in various places throughout the country. After relating this history, Jack broke down and cried. He said it was the first time he had cried since his father's accident.

Jack continued in counseling, eventually participating in family counseling as well as in group and individual counseling. He came to recognize his own feelings of rejection and his fear of it. He wanted to be the father he never had but needed, yet felt threatened that his son would disrupt his relationship with Mary, which he valued highly. All of these ambivalent feelings were mixed with his feeling of grief over his own childhood and his father's death. He felt as if he were to blame for his father's problems, and he felt guilty that he never realized that his father was an alcoholic. The counseling focused on helping Jack uncover these feelings and sort out what he could and could not be accountable for. He and Mary tried to set reasonable expectations for themselves as parents. They tried to agree on the kind of handling that they both felt was best for their son. This was done for as many situations as possible so that their reactions to their son's behavior could be planned rather than spontaneous. Jack learned to recognize when his frustrations were getting the best of him. He practiced relaxation therapy.

Mary also attempted to learn the warning signals so they could sit down and discuss things as a way of relieving the pressure. Special effort was made to plan for times when Jack could be with his son and free of other obligations so that he could gain a sense of accomplishment for himself as a father. Jack remained in counseling for over six months. He felt that sharing his experience and his growth was important for other fathers to learn about.

The counseling Jack and his family received helped him grow up emotionally. It helped Jack to put his past into perspective and helped him resolve the grief and guilt he felt over his relationship with his father. Once Jack gained more control over his emotions, the counseling helped him set proper expectations for himself. At this point, the key feature was helping Jack structure the environment of his home in such a way that Jack could be the father and husband he so very much wanted to be.

Counseling skills involved in this case include establishing and maintaining a good relationship, using support groups and individuals, and supporting and encouraging change and growth.

Mental retardation

Lorraine was a girl of 15 who was obese and who looked younger than her age. In fact, her appearance would lead one to suspect that she had not yet reached puberty. When she was six, a diagnosis of mental retardation had been made. IQ testing placed Lorraine in the mildly retarded range. She was put in special education classes and had performed well within that special setting. Lorraine had always been a quiet, gentle girl, compliant and responsive to teachers and her parents. Lorraine's family was highly religious. She was the baby of her family, and had been born when her parents were quite advanced in years. They were now approaching 60. Since Lorraine had been a gentle child, she was always easy for her parents to care for. Five other brothers and sisters ranged from 5 to 15 years older than Lorraine. They viewed her as the baby, and despite her advancing years, continued to expect babyish behavior from her.

After her fifteenth birthday, however, marked behavior changes appeared that were greatly disturbing to her parents. It was quite shocking to them to discover from Lorraine's teachers that she had quite recently and rather openly been involved in sexual encounters with several boys in her special education classes. Her parents initially responded severely with strong warnings about the consequences of what they saw as her immoral behavior. Lorraine was openly distraught over her parents' strong rebukes. She had rarely been punished before. In spite of her parents' verbal threats and even spankings, Lorraine continued her sexual activity. Lorraine became tense. She was afraid to do things on her own and wanted to stay close to her parents, not even wanting to be out of their sight when she was at home. She was willing to go to school and performed quite well. She also continued her occasional sexual activity.

The counselor's role

Role of consultation in family counseling

Her activities were noted by her teachers who informed the school counselor of Lorraine's behavior. The counselor met with Lorraine. Lorraine discussed the situation with the counselor, but seemed rather unconcerned about her behavior. She was ignorant of the potential consequences of her sexual activity. The counselor thought it would be in Lorraine's best interests to initiate discussions with her parents. They agreed hesitatingly to see the counselor.

The reason for hesitation was soon apparent, since it was difficult for the counselor to maintain the focus of the conversation on Lorraine's sexual behavior. The parents found it difficult even to discuss this subject. The counselor thought it best to back off a bit from discussing Lorraine directly and instead reviewed the natural sexual development that all youth, regardless of intellectual capability, experienced. Lorraine could be expected to be no different. The counselor asked if the parents were concerned about their daughter's sexuality, and if so, would they care to have the counselor help them deal with Lorraine's sexual development? The parents seemed willing to pursue this so the counselor began by reviewing Lorraine's developmental history. This included, in particular, Lorraine's social development. The picture that emerged was that she had lived a very sheltered life. She rarely played with friends, and spent most of her time with family members. She never left her parents except to visit married older brothers and sisters. She liked to play with her nieces and nephews, all of whom were much younger than she. No one had ever discussed her sexuality with her, nor had anyone explained the physiological changes that she would experience. She looked and acted too childlike for anyone to see the necessity to do so. It was at this point that the parents recounted how upset they were to learn of her sexual activities and that they did not know how to handle it since their punishments were ineffective. The parents became willing to discuss the problem and potential solutions with the counselor at the conclusion of this first meeting.

The counselor also discussed Lorraine's behavior with her teachers, after receiving consent to do so from her parents. Because similar situations had occurred with several other special education students, the teacher and counselors thought it might be best to address Lorraine's situation in the context of the special education program. A plan was developed to teach students many kinds of social roles, as well as to supply information about sexuality. This plan was presented to all parents. The counselor suggested the importance of parents participating in this effort, not only to plan it but also to support the plans at home. At this time, the parents also voiced concerns about the impending graduation of their children and what might happen to them after that. The counselor suggested that a committee be formed of teachers and parents to coordinate school and home activities.

The plan that finally evolved included class instruction devoted to proper social behavior in a variety of situations, including dating, job-seeking, and the handling of certain financial transactions. The parents were helped to prepare a proper climate at home, along with the appropriate added instruction, that would enable them to interact with their children concerning the physiological, emotional, and behavioral implications of their developing sexuality. Discussions regarding birth control were included. Efforts were made to reenforce this learning at school. School activities were designed to provide students with a forum to practice new skills, as well as to meet their needs for social interaction with their peers. An effort was made to help them participate in typical school activities, and other teachers were encouraged to consider any ways that these students could participate in the routine social events of the school.

The parents became particularly involved in developing a program to inform the students of the various occupational roles the community offered. A local rehabilitation workshop was contacted, which agreed to furnish work exposure and other services to students on a part-time basis during the school year and summers.

Lorraine herself participated in counseling to help her integrate her new experiences. She had difficulties accepting herself with the equanimity that she had displayed previously. She had lost a great deal of confidence in herself as a result of the punishment she received from her parents. She had been unable to link the punishment with her sexual conduct since the sexual contact had been gratifying to her. She had enjoyed the sexual attention she received. Her parents maintained contact with the counselor and made a good effort to participate in the plan to address the students' social needs and the parents' concerns for the vocational future of their children.

Lorraine participated in the school effort to teach the students proper dating behavior. While this instruction was going on, the counselor met with her to help her deal with her parents' feelings of shock and anger. Soon she was able to identify what situations were permitted by her parents and which ones were not. In this way, she was able to predict what she would be punished for. Her parents came to a session to discuss with her what they actually could not agree with and what they could. The counselor served as facilitator and reported to them that Lorraine was aware of many of the problem areas. Both Lorraine and her parents were pleased that their values were beginning to harmonize. Following this session, the counselor met with her parents without Lorraine to help them plan ways they could respond to her in a more adult fashion. The counselor urged them to ask Lorraine about her plans and to discuss with her how they felt about them. They were encouraged to help Lorraine consider the consequences of her choices. The parents also requested help regarding how to punish her, if necessary. They felt that physical punishment was not appropriate, but did not know of alternatives as to how they could convey the depth of their concern when Lorraine engaged in sexual activity. The counselor urged them to be open to Lorraine about what they wanted her to do. They would listen to Lorraine's point of view as well. The counselor agreed to help mediate the discussion if everyone thought this was all right. The counselor suggested that they review how the older children had been dealt with when they were Lorraine's age. Immediately, the idea of grounding surfaced. The parents, however, did not see how this would work since Lorraine rarely went anywhere without family members accompanying her. Lorraine seemed to take offense at this, stating that she was old enough to be grounded. She evidently liked to be compared to her older brothers and sisters. The counselor pointed out that various school events were coming up and that Lorraine and the other special education students were making plans to participate. Her parents felt that she could go. Lorraine said she was ready to be grounded if issues could not be resolved. The counselor again suggested that the parents carefully review the conditions with Lorraine until they were sure she understood.

A month later, the counselor was pleased to find that Lorraine had attended two school functions and one church event. One of these had been a date. She had not been grounded for any misbehavior. Her parents felt more comfortable in their relationship with Lorraine, particularly in their ability to discuss things with her. They were especially pleased that she was making more of the important decisions about what was proper and what was not. Her teachers reported that she was participating in all the learning activities and had been overheard telling a boy she would not do "that" with him anymore, presumably referring to sexual activity.

This was a very complicated situation. Lorraine's slow intellectual development naturally affected her social development. She did not know how to respond properly to her new sexuality, which created potential interpersonal problems with her peers and certainly with her parents. Neither the school nor the family had provided the proper environment for Lorraine's social development. Any attempt at discipline further complicated matters because Lorraine did not associate her punishment with her sexual behavior. She suffered intrapersonal distress, which resulted in a reversion to infantile dependence on her parents.

Counselor skills/resources needed in counseling mentally retarded

The counselor used a wide variety of services and skills to address Lorraine's problems and the concern of her parents and teachers. Consultation with parents and teachers was most important. This was coupled with individual counseling and support for Lorraine. A major result was a deliberate restructuring of the school and home environments so that these would attend more closely to the social needs of Lorraine and the other students. The counselor also used community resources, namely, the rehabilitation center and selected employers, to begin addressing the vocational needs of the students.

Summary

In this chapter, many of the more common issues and concerns counselors encounter today have been examined through the use of case histories. An attempt has been made to show how counselors can effectively use their knowledge and skills to help people with their problems. The case histories have also emphasized the variety of services that can be used to facilitate helping others. It is important for counselors to know what services they can offer and in what ways they can be offered, as well as when it is appropriate to offer them.

For purposes of discussion, these cases were all resolved positively. Prospective counselors need to recognize, however, that not every counseling case is so easily or neatly resolved as the ones in this chapter. These cases were based on actual persons and facts, though, and as such, are highly representative of the types of situations the average counselor encounters daily.

Questions

1. What are some advantages of learning from the case history method? What are some of the disadvantages of using this method?

2. Based on these case histories, what are some times when an entire family or couple should be drawn into counseling rather than just giving individual counseling to the person who presents for treatment?

3. In what ways are intrapersonal problems different from interpersonal ones?

4. How may a person be affected later in life by developmental problems?

5. How do developmental problems influence one's interpersonal and intrapersonal life and relationships?

6. Describe some of the services offered by counselors in these case histories. Discuss the importance and need for each.

Projects

1. Write up examples of problems. Distribute them to members of the class, making sure that no person gets the case he or she has written. Each person should then prepare a written report discussing the strategy and services that might be used to counsel the person in the case. Discuss the reports with the class.

2. Visit several community centers in your community to see what services they offer and to whom they are offered. Class members should meet to compare notes on what they have learned in an attempt to determine whether or not services to the overall community are adequate or inadequate.

3. After careful investigation, prepare a written report on an area of mental-health services that is inadequate in your community. Submit it to the proper authorities.

Administration of counseling services 5

12 Coordination and administration of counseling programs

Follow-up, often done by telephone, is a reassuring stage of the termination process in which the counselor maintains casual contact with the counselee.

12 Coordination and administration of counseling programs

Introduction

The focal point of this chapter is the type of administration counselors can and should expect from their employing organizations. But in counseling, as perhaps in no other profession, the atmosphere and work conditions are as much a function of the role of the workers and their interactions with management as with management itself. Even though a counselor may have no designated administrative responsibilities, the counselor as an employee acts as an agent of a program and must effectively and efficiently administer its processes and make use of the resources provided by it. A program's administration is only a tool to help counselors deliver quality service. Counselors must interact with the administration, and, therefore, they must assume partial responsibility for what the program accomplishes or fails to accomplish. A program can even impede service delivery by careless policies and procedures. Counselors have a responsibility to act as change agents when such problems appear. The counselor's ultimate loyalty remains with the counselees of the program.

The counselor is not alone, however, in being an organization watchdog. Each counseling setting should have an advisory committee with well-defined responsibilities that will seek to maintain the integrity of the program. A description of the composition and role of advisory committees is included in this chapter.

This chapter also contains suggestions on ways that counselors can use their skills and abilities to better the organizations they work for. Entire books have been written about the management and organization of programs that provide counseling services. This chapter can, at best, only present highlights of several such programs. For greater detail, the reader is referred to the Calia and Wall book *Pupil Personnel Administration*,[1] which focuses primarily on a school setting, and to the Cull and Hardy book *Administrative Techniques of Rehabilitation Facility Operations*,[2] which provides some insight into rehabilitation-facility management.

The purpose of proper coordination and administration is to provide the resources, facilities, processes, and feedback to ensure quality counseling services. The elimination of unnecessary red tape and delays is both the organization's and the individual counselor's concern.

Key terms

coordination of services
external coordination
internal coordination
formal channels of communication
informal channels of communication
interagency linkages
personnel policy
holistic approach
administration of services
advisory committee
educational placement
vocational placement
follow-up services
consultant

---

1. Vincent F. Calia and Bartholomew D. Wall, eds., *Pupil Personnel Administration* (Springfield, Ill: Charles C. Thomas, 1968).

2. John G. Cull and Richard E. Hardy, eds., *Administrative Techniques of Rehabilitation Facility Operations* (Springfield, Ill.: Charles C. Thomas, 1974).

The need for organization

There are many reasons that organization is important for counseling. It is important because it affects the quality of counseling services and the subsequent effect of these services on counselees. Any organizational structure or policy, therefore, must have a relationship to the delivery of quality counseling services. The major goal of any counseling system is to meet the needs of its counselees. This must always be kept foremost in the minds of administrators and counselors alike.

Both management and counselors have four major areas of responsibility that largely determine the successful running of a program. These are the coordination of services, the administration of services, public relations, and fiscal responsibility. There are many creative ways counselors and their employing organizations or agencies can contribute to quality service delivery in these four areas.

Coordination of services

This is the largest and most important area. In order to provide boundaries for this rather large area, it will be broken down into external and internal coordination activities. External coordination refers to those activities that counselors and counseling programs can do in cooperation with other systems, such as the cooperation that can occur between a rehabilitation agency and a high-school guidance office. Internal coordination consists of those activities that result from the interactions of counselors within their own programs, such as the counselor's maintenance of counselee records as required by the program administrators.

Formal and informal channels of communication

There are two other boundary distinctions. These are the formal and informal channels of coordination. Formal channels are rather specific agreements between two counseling systems or counselors and administrators to cooperate in specified ways, or to follow the established procedures of communication. For example, one program might agree with another in referring its clients for a certain service at a reduced fee. Informal channels refer to those agreements that exist among individuals who work for different programs or within the same program and who have found ways to work conveniently and casually with each other. For example, a counselor from each of the cooperating programs just mentioned could find ways to streamline referral procedures, thus minimizing red tape between the programs. These channels are often spoken rather than written. These personally developed relationships may be the more powerful means of service coordination, since they are

	Formal	Informal
External	A rehabilitation agency and a high school guidance office agree to identify high school students who may be eligible for rehabilitation services.	A counselor maintains contacts with local businessmen by means of membership in a local tennis club.
Internal	A community counseling agency requires that counselors complete a form each time a counselee receives counseling.	A group of counselors in a high school agree to rotate hours in order to provide walk-in service two nights a week.

Figure 12–1
Channels for service coordination: examples

usually founded upon the friendship of professionals interested in facilitating personal achievement within their area of service. Figure 12–1 contains an example of each possible kind of coordination activity.

Cooperative formal efforts. Numerous agreements have been developed among counseling programs to benefit the counselees of the programs. Mostly, these agreements serve to facilitate the referral of the counselees from one system to another. For example, state vocational rehabilitation agencies have entered into cooperative agreements with high-school guidance offices, where either the high school counselors or the rehabilitation counselors do initial screening of high school students to determine their eligibility for rehabilitation services. This cooperation allows eligible rehabilitation counselees to receive services at the earliest possible time.

Another area where counseling programs have cooperated well is the delivery of services to mutual counselees. Again, state rehabilitation agencies provide ready examples. Formal agreements have been developed between rehabilitation agencies and state job-service commissions to offer job-placement services to counselees eligible for service in both programs. The Veterans Administration also has entered into similar agreements with state rehabilitation agencies.

Recent efforts have been made to develop umbrella organizations in which various service agencies cooperate to streamline their services to overlapping counselees.[3] This type of arrangement has the

3. J. K. Benson and J. T. Kunce, "Coordinating Human Services: A Case Study of an Interagency Network," *Social and Rehabilitation Record* 1, no. 7 (1974): 28–33.

potential of eliminating duplication and time delays as counselees move through the multiple-service system. Of course, as systems get larger, there is a greater chance of impersonalization and bureaucratization occurring. As with most things, the advantages and disadvantages of formal, external agreements must be carefully investigated. These agreements, sometimes referred to as interagency linkages, usually are described in writing, along with the policies and procedures that will facilitate the cooperative effort between the programs.

Role of personal relationships in coordination

The second type of coordination is the external, informal agreement. These agreements, which usually occur between the personnel of counseling programs, in no way formally bind systems to cooperate with one another. Rather, these agreements evolve from the personal relationships developed among counselors as a result of their concern for mutual counselees, recurrent contact through referrals or service requests, and by fellowship in professional associations. Such agreements are rarely written, but are maintained by close contact and frequent communication. The bonds of these friendships are often stronger than any formal agreements. Informal relationships serve to improve services to counselees, and they also provide counselors with rewarding relationships. These types of informal agreements can and should occur with almost no limitations. Occasionally, they supercede formal ties. For example, informal relationships often develop with counselors of other programs to speed the referral of counselees even though formal procedures are available. Providing fast interagency service for counselees has always been a problem. The formal procedures take time that can be saved through the use of informal channels. These friendships do not require that formal guidelines be circumvented, for that would be unethical, but rather, they operate alongside the more formal channels. Close personal and professional relationships among counselors assure that efficient, fast referrals will be available. This type of informal relationship does not have to occur only among counseling professionals, but can also occur among counselors and clergy, psychologists, medical workers, and attorneys. Educational and vocational counselors should develop relationships with admissions officers, business persons, and prospective employers, for example. Direct placement may be one outcome of these relationships, but the information and resources available from these persons also can be used to improve the variety and quality of services. Through these contacts, counselors can keep abreast of local educational, training, and employment opportunities.

The third type of coordination activity is formal and internal. Every system that employs counselors has policies and procedures that govern all aspects of program operation. Some of these formalities exist because of the legal requirements of state and federal laws. Every school, rehabilitation agency or facility, and community agency is required to maintain some records to document the extent and effectiveness of its services. Counselors are responsible for providing much of the required, relevant information for these records. This may mean that clerical and paperwork activities are a necessary part of a counselor's job. Although sometimes viewed as unpleasant, clerical duties and paperwork provide a valuable service by helping the counselor organize services. And without such backup, services to counselees would not be permitted by legal authorities. An organized, up-to-date counselor with efficient clerical support can usually maintain the required record keeping with a minimum amount of intrusion into the time spent on actual service delivery. A well-organized counseling program should provide the necessary clerical support to accomplish this. Also, record keeping should be kept to the basic minimum requirements. Any paperwork required of counselors must be justified, and counselors should not be expected to perform unnecessary tasks.

Role of formal organizational framework

Any program employing counselors will also have a formal organizational framework through which decisions that affect the entire organization will be made. If possible, this framework should be made available to counselors, preferably in the form of an organizational chart that illustrates formal lines of authority. Counselors need to know which decisions they can make in their own right and which type of decisions are routinely made by persons with higher or lower levels of authority. Counselors should expect some latitude in decision making in matters related to their own counselees. The degree of latitude varies, however, from program to program, and counselors should carefully review policies and procedures regarding this early in their employment. An administration has the responsibility for carefully and completely orienting a new counselor to the formal requirements of a program.

Changes also must be announced to all counselors as they occur, and routine procedures must be established for this purpose. Counselors, of course, should be willing to contribute to policy and decision making, and any responsible administration will actively seek their input and use it.

Counselors must also remember that they are professionals and act accordingly on those occasions when their views cannot be adopted by administrators. Policies and procedures are often compromises to accommodate external or budgetary constraints. Counselors also must remember that they work with other professionals such as teachers, parole agents, or rehabilitation workshop supervisors. These professionals will have their own emphases and own way of providing services. When cooperation between two or more professions is required within a program, compromises are to be expected and should be graciously accepted.

Job benefits for counselors

Another formal set of system guidelines that is required is personnel policy. Each counselor, as an employee, needs to know the benefits and responsibilities that exist as a function of employment. Sanders has highlighted some aspects of a good personnel program.[4] Among them he includes promotion or transfer opportunities to jobs suited to skills of employees; fair performance-appraisal procedures; salaries that are competitive within the local labor market; further education and training opportunities; reasonable working hours; clean and safe working conditions; insurance sufficient to meet adequate medical, disability, and retirement needs; holidays and sick days; and grievance procedures. Unless counselors feel that their employers are concerned enough to provide for their personal needs, they are not going to be readily disposed to meet the needs of others.

The final area of consideration in coordination is informal, internal coordination. Like informal, external coordination, informal, internal coordination attempts to facilitate the functioning of formal program processes. Within any counseling program, every staff member performs a different role. Even when formal specifications are available to help the various people work together, real teamwork will not be achieved until co-workers develop close, comfortable working relationships with one another. These informal relationships clarify which of the various personnel have special capabilities and how these skills can best be used. For example, a counselor who has an exceptional knowledge of the local employment scene may be the best person to counsel persons who have employment concerns, while a counselor experienced in counseling families could handle a majority of the cases with family concerns.

Teamwork can also be used to share and spread out some of the least desirable counseling tasks. The intake of new counselees, which involves a lot of paperwork, may be routinely shifted from counselor to counselor so that only one is responsible for it at any given time. Some programs rotate both intake and orientation activities among the staff. Teamwork, when handled this way, is a way to maximize efficiency.

Holisitic approach

There is yet another reason for developing a well-coordinated team. Many are of the philosophy that one profession, or one per-

4. Bert C. Sanders, "Personnel Administration in Rehabilitation Facilities," Cull and Hardy, eds., in *Administrative Techniques of Rehabilitation Facility Operations*.

son, cannot possibly provide all the comprehensive services needed by people. Services can be delivered adequately only by applying an approach that includes multiple disciplines to meet the needs of the whole person. This has been called the holistic approach. Shontz described the holistic approach by noting that the counselee is a functioning member of the team who must be kept well informed, given a chance to provide input to the team, and allowed to make the decisions about courses of action that will be taken regarding him or her. Of course, professionals must supply the leadership and information necessary so that the counselee can make the best available decision. Shontz highlights one problem with the holistic team approach that will confront anyone who attempts to use this model. This is the decision as to who will be the team leader. Shontz resolves the issue by suggesting that as each new counselee joins the team and specific concerns arise requiring some hard decisions, the professional who has emerged as the most adept team member at dealing with a particular concern should assume team leadership for that decision. The leadership would shift when another issue arises. Shontz refers to the leadership role as one of coordinating all the necessary services that need to be delivered to meet the needs of the counselees. In order for this holistic team approach to work, the various professionals involved must have developed well-coordinated working relationships. These relationships must be of a sufficient personal nature to overcome any potential professional rivalries.[5]

The coordination of services is important. Without suitable external and internal relationships of both an informal and formal nature, no service delivery can be made. The channels of delivery must be developed and maintained by close working relationships among various service providers. This groundwork must exist before any counselee can enter the service delivery system.

Administration of services

Proper coordination of services relies heavily on the administration of services. Counselors are responsible for performing many administrative tasks. Carkhuff and Berenson have summarized research that describes the activities of guidance counselors. Besides seeing counselees, counselors do clerical work, consult with parents, teachers, and administrators, visit colleges and employers, and at-

5. Franklin C. Shontz, *The Psychological Aspects of Physical Illness and Disability* (New York: Macmillan, 1975).

Variety of administrative tasks

tend various meetings.[6] Muthard and Salamone report similar research regarding rehabilitation counselors. They found that besides counseling, rehabilitation counselors spent much time in clerical work and case recording, job-placement activities, travel within the community, and public relations work.[7] It is apparent that counselors, regardless of setting, have many administrative tasks to perform.

Time administration

One of a counselor's primary administration tasks, in fact, is efficient time management. It is important to accept that no one task is more important than another. Interviewing counselees is certainly another primary task, but sometimes a counselor may be doing more for a counselee by visiting a parent or employer or by coordinating psychological or medical services than by counseling directly. Since there is no easy way to set priorities on time management, counselors must be able to set priorities based on counselee time needs. Counselors must be organized enough to give counselees individualized service when they need it.

Counselors also need constantly to regulate shifting demands on their time. For example, a counselor should not assume that the only vehicle available for meeting a counselee's needs is individual counseling on a weekly or biweekly basis. Once needs have been identified, counseling may be needed only on a periodic basis. The counselee might fare better in a group at that point. The counselor must be able to coordinate the necessary services and accept their accompanying demands on his or her time. Time priorities must be set for each individual counselee and reviewed regularly.

In addition to worrying about and managing the time needs of individual clients, a counselor has to be aware of limiting his or her case load to a manageable number.

Need for flexibility

Counselors must have flexible enough office hours so that they can accommodate an occasional unscheduled, urgent appointment. One way to do this is to set aside certain times when the appointment calendar is kept clear so that unscheduled counseling can occur. At times, evening hours can be substituted for regular hours so that counselees who may not have an adequate opportunity for counseling during regular hours will still find the counselor accessible.

---

6. Robert R. Carkhuff and Bernard G. Berenson, *Teaching as Treatment* (Amherst, Mass.: Human Resource Development Press, 1976), Chapter 10.

7. John E. Muthard and Paul R. Salamone, "The Roles and Functions of Rehabilitation Counselors," *Rehabilitation Counseling Bulletin* 13, no. 1-Sp, (1969): 81–168.

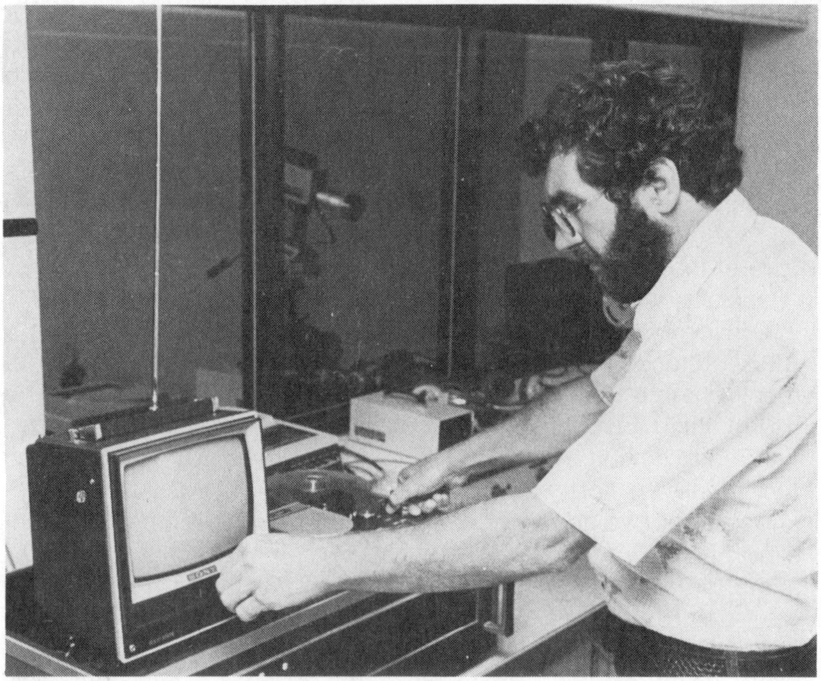

A counselor should set up all measurement tools, such as a tape recorder, prior to the client's arrival so the entire session can be devoted to the counseling process.

Record keeping

This is one of the more important administrative tasks to which counselors must attend. Record keeping must above all facilitate counseling. It should never be allowed to become an end in itself or a task that is done entirely by rote to satisfy the requirements of the agency. On the other hand, record keeping must never get in the way of delivering services to counselees. When services are forgone to maintain records, then either a counselor has become misguided about his or her primary function or the record system needs revision to make it easier to use.

Content of records

The nature and content of records is also an important consideration in record keeping. Records should primarily consist of past, present, and future events. Speculative thoughts regarding the reasons for a counselee's problems and unfounded diagnoses of a counselee's difficulties should not be a part of the record. Factual material that can be verified is most desired, and only material that has direct bearing on a particular case should be included. The counselor should also remember that records are not recognized as confidential under the law, and that a court can subpeona both the records and the counselor for testimony. In most states, counselors do not enjoy protected confidentiality, such as physicians do, for example. This is another reason that record keeping should be kept at a minimum. If a counselor needs to keep ongoing notes of a more subjective nature, these should not be a part of the regular file, nor should they be kept in a formal way, since a court can also subpeona subjective notes—if their existence becomes known. Subjective impressions can be helpful, but they should be discarded when they are no longer needed. Preferably, the counselee should approve of the accuracy of the record's contents.

Basically, records should contain the information used to identify the service needs of counselees, including verification of the accuracy of professional judgment, such as a psychologist's report, documenting the needs. Also, service plans and objectives should be spelled out in advance. As services are completed, the data should be noted to enable a comparison of actual events with the intended plan. Finally, a note regarding termination is needed, which describes what has actually been accomplished as a result of counseling.

Federal law requires that people have access to records kept about them by federally supported programs. For example, state rehabilitation agencies are required to develop individualized service plans for each counselee, which the counselee then signs. This is also the case for mainstreamed students in the public education system. Such a plan is a required part of the counselee's record and illustrates one way that plans developed in counseling can be used directly as a part of the record without further counselor involvement. Integrating record keeping with direct service delivery illustrates one way that record keeping can be organized efficiently. Having the counselee participate in developing the record also aids efficiency, indicates that the record is accessible to the counselee as required by law, and ensures that counselors will not insert unjustified labels to describe the concerns and problems of counselees.[8] Improper labeling can be damaging to a person's opportunities for the future, particularly if the records are passed on to other agencies or employers. If the emphasis is placed on factual data and all labels are avoided, there should be no problem with record keeping and compliance with the law.

There are record-keeping administrative tasks other than maintaining individual records. If records pertinent to counseling can be obtained elsewhere, they should be. The counselor should have an efficient system for obtaining a counselee's written release for the

8. Louise M. Riscalla, "Records—A Legal Responsibility," *Journal of Rehabilitation*, 40, no. 1 (1974): 12–14.

records and for requesting the records. In part, this is because a counselee should not be required to undergo information-collecting procedures such as social, psychological, or medical work-ups if these have been developed recently elsewhere, but also because duplication of record keeping wastes time and money.

Finally, a counselor must ensure that any request for records about a counselee from another agency will be used by that agency in a professional manner. No records should ever be forwarded without obtaining the written permission of the counselee each time a release is requested.

Records of resources

Another important facet of record keeping is to maintain accurate records of available resources for counselors' use. All the counselors from one program could pool knowledge of community resources, and listings and contact information for volunteer services, medical services, employers, local training and educational opportunities, and civic groups should be centrally stored. All counselors need easy access to this information at all times.

If done well, record keeping can help a counselor plan how services are to be delivered. It can help a counselor and counselee set priorities and make sure that counseling is progressing as planned. This ensures efficient use of time and resources.

Arrangement of physical surroundings

Administrative organization can also help a counselor prepare the physical surroundings so that a suitable psychological climate is available for counseling. Figure 12–2 contains suggestions for office arrangements and procedures that will allow a counselee to feel comfortable and facilitate recognition that the counselor intends to give his or her undivided attention.

The physical surroundings in which counseling is to occur, however luxurious or meager, should reflect the counselor's concern for the counselee. Generally, the room should be uncluttered to minimize distractions. Precautions should be taken to guarantee against interruptions. Tape recorders or testing instruments should be readied ahead of time so that they can be integrated into counseling with a minimum of fuss or distraction.

There are times, however, when counseling may occur so unexpectedly that time does not permit this type of preparation. A counselor must be willing to deal with counselee concerns whenever and wherever they occur. A counselor would communicate a lack of concern if counseling were delayed until preparations could be made or a desk could be cleaned off.

Figure 12–2
Establishing a climate for counseling

Preparation of physical surroundings

Seating arrangements
1 Comfortable chairs; preferably with arms
2 Seats facing each other approximately 3 to 5 feet apart
3 Tables or desk should not separate the participants

Remove all unnecessary clutter; straighten out desk

Make arrangements to avoid interruption
1 Use "do not disturb" signs
2 Help your colleagues understand the need for no disturbance
3 Arrange for secretary to screen calls

Lighting: natural lighting is preferable; avoid harsh light but provide adequate light

"Tools of the trade" you expect to use during counseling should be readily accessible to avoid fumbling and delay (tape recorders, tests, etc.)

Establishing agenda for interview

Review case information

Establish current level of progress

Set goals for the interview

Another important factor to consider is physical accessibility. It is now illegal for schools, agencies, and businesses that use federal funds to have architectural barriers that prohibit people with physical impairments from using their facilities. Counselors should make sure their offices are accessible to all persons with or without impairments.

Public relations and fiscal responsibility

Although this may seem like a strange combination, a counselor's organizational concern for public relations and fiscal responsibility actually go hand in hand. The financial soundness of a counseling system often depends on how well a program is promoted to the general public. Some professionals maintain that this turns counselors into politicians who must worry more about how to pull strings and make deals in order to keep the funds flowing than about services. Indeed, if counselors had to resort to this kind of activity to keep counseling going, it probably would not be worth the effort.

Counselors should, however, be able to make a strong case for counseling on the basis of how successful counselees are in resolving the problems that brought them to counseling. That is the kind of public relations that is important and necessary.

Role of social mandates

Most counseling programs are supported in one way or another by public funds. School guidance offices, rehabilitation and community agencies, and correctional facilities all derive support from tax dollars. Accompanying this support are social mandates issued to each of these systems to accomplish certain tasks. Schools are mandated to educate students and prepare them for participation in a society. Rehabilitation agencies are expected to help people who have disabilities prepare to participate as fully as possible in the economic mainstream of society. Correctional agencies are expected to help ex-offenders participate legally within our society. Mental health agencies are expected to provide support, feedback, and consultation to individuals so that they can function within society. To the extent that counseling systems can document that they are fulfilling their social mandates, and as long as society desires such services, funding can be expected to continue. Such documentation frequently involves informing the public about the program.

The process of documenting program accomplishments for purposes of continued support is also called accountability. Formal program-evaluation procedures increasingly are required for such documentation. Merely having laudable objectives is no longer sufficient, and evidence of the fulfillment of these objectives is now expected. Chapter 13 describes the ways counselors can contribute to and benefit from program evaluation. It is sufficient for now to recognize the need for careful administration of accountability procedures. Counselors should be prepared to help with data collection, analysis, and reporting.

Accountability also must be part of each encounter a counselor has with a counselee. The administrative and counseling procedures presented here are designed to permit a counselor to provide service to every counselee that can withstand even the most rigorous demands for accountability and program evaluation. To the extent that counselors implement counseling that is accountable, they can be assured that they are fostering public support and the fiscal integrity of the counseling programs of which they are members. Providing efficient and quality counseling services to counselees is the most important public relations a counselor can undertake.

There are other ways, however, that counselors can contribute to good relations with the community. Public speaking, although not a skill possessed by everyone, is one excellent way counselors can inform the public about the purposes and values of counseling. Many volunteer and civic groups would contribute financially and materially to social service programs if they fully understood them. Counselors who possess public speaking skills should be willing to meet with such groups. Public speaking can also serve to inform the general public about the purposes of counseling in general. The public may be misinformed about those who use counseling services. Often persons who seek counseling are viewed as unbalanced emotionally, crazy, or incapable of managing their lives. This stereotype has prevented many who might benefit from counseling from pursuing it. Counselors should be ready to try to erase this stereotype whenever they have the opportunity to do so.

Since public speaking is not possible for everyone, counselors who are uncomfortable with it are encouraged to use their counseling skills to listen and discuss the values of counseling services informally. Individual contacts can achieve the same purpose as public speaking.

Counselors as community leaders

One final promotion activity all counselors can participate in is to recognize that, as helping professionals, they are viewed by the community as moral leaders. The conduct of counselors is closely watched. Local standards of behavior are especially applicable to counselors. How counselors are accepted, and by association, the acceptance of the profession of counseling itself, depends to a large degree on the kind of evaluation a community makes of counselors' behavior. Whether this community judgment is legitimate or not, or even fair, counselors still cannot avoid it. They need to be cognizant of the fact that how they conduct themselves in public could affect their capacity to provide quality counseling in the community in which they live.

The establishment of an advisory committee

Advisory, or steering committees, are relatively new to the field of counseling. They can be compared to the board of directors of a corporation, except the advisory committee does not actually have the power to make or implement policy. Rather, as the name implies, advisory committees advise. They provide guidance to counseling program administrators. Unless program administrators decide to formalize the advice in the form of policy, there is nothing binding about advisory committee recommendations.

Is there then any real need for advisory committees? Or are they just publicity gimmicks that have little real impact? In some instances they are, but it is worth the effort to consider how advisory committees can be meaningfully integrated into the overall activities of a counseling program. The first is to ensure that a service program is sensitive to the needs of those it serves. The second is to help the program gain credibility from its target audience, support group, or both.

The composition of the advisory committee

Each group or faction of the counseling program staff and the potential consumers of the counseling program should be represented on the advisory committee. An advisory committee should be well balanced between staff, consumers, and third parties. A useful third-party addition to an advisory committee is one or two counselor educators from a nearby college or university. Other professionals, such as an attorney, might also serve ably on an advisory committee.

Appropriate members of advisory committees

In schools, the important consumers of guidance services are students, parents, and teachers. Each of these needs to be represented. As students mature, it is assumed that their needs will change and, therefore, it is wise to include several levels of their representative groups on the committee. In a high school, it may be the youngest and oldest grades. A recent graduate may also be an appropriate member. The staff representatives will most likely consist of at least one counselor, one counselor administrator, a teacher, and a school administrator, a principal, or assistant principal or whoever oversees the counseling program. Third parties, such as counselor educators or attorneys, if available, would complete the committee.

In a rehabilitation setting, consumer representatives may come from several sources. Usually, one counselee from each counselor's case load should serve. Many rehabilitation counselees belong to self-help groups composed of people with similar disabilities, and representatives could be drawn from these groups. Suitable members also should be drawn from the ranks of counselees who have completed the rehabilitation or counseling process. Members of the community who live near the facility should be included, particularly if they are prominent in neighborhood activities. Prospective and actual employers are suitable choices. The staff should be represented by at least one counselor and administrator or supervisor. Since rehabilitation programs typically use medical and psychological consultants, some of these also should be represented. Finally, support staff such as clerical and paraprofessional personnel should round out committee membership.

The functioning of the advisory committee

The advisory committee, like any other committee, requires officers. Usually, these are limited to a president and a secretary. Office holders perform the organizational chores that are necessary to ensure that the committee functions on a regular basis. Without designating who will perform these duties, there is a good chance that they will be forgone or only haphazardly done, which could seriously weaken the effectiveness of a committee.

The role of the advisory committee

The advisory committee serves as a monitor or watchdog of the counseling program's activities. For this reason, it is so important to have an adequate representation of consumers, since they will be aware of the impact the counseling program has. It is the role of the advisory committee to ask relevant questions regarding program operation and outcome. If the questions can be answered, well and good, because that indicates the program is responsive and current. If the questions cannot be answered, then discussion must center on how to provide answers and information.

The advisory committee can advise about program problems and can serve as a guide for an empirical assessment of the situation after all the ramifications of a problem and its possible solutions have been explored. This airing-out period produces important discussion and works against making hasty decisions.

Advisory role most important

Finally, the advisory committee suggests new policies and program procedures. The added wealth of knowledge and experience available from the advisory committee may enable a program to be responsive and innovative as never before. A vigorous advisory committee, if fully used by a counseling program's administration and staff, can more than make up for the time that administrators and staff must give to it. In terms of time, probably bi-monthly meeting of the entire committee would be appropriate. If subcommittees arise, such as one for public relations, these, too, would require regular meetings.

The impact of the advisory committee

An important by-product of a viable advisory committee is the credibility that can be expected to accrue from assigning the role of advisor to the consumers of services. If consumers learn that they will be listened to and that real effort will be expended on their behalf, then the impact of the counseling program will become much more positive. This has obvious advantages for the public relations program that is so necessary to generate ongoing support in the community.

The advisory committee is to be used to provide program review and analysis, and the extent that the committee's suggestions are implemented is an indication of the impact of the committee. A committee has no formal means of implementing new policies and procedures, so in order for a committee to have an impact on service delivery and program evaluation, its suggestions must be concrete and within the capability of the counseling program to carry out. A committee's impact can be expected to be measurable only if the committee can offer suggestions that are reasonable, considering the staff and funding resources available.

Another important impact the committee may have is to allow the representatives of the various groups to use the committee as a clearinghouse for grievances. If candid discussion is a facet of the committee's functioning, then the chances for a reasonable settlement of grievances are excellent. Without the opportunity for full expression, even minor grievances from the staff and consumers can become a cancer and seriously weaken the services of the program. Third-party committee members such as university faculty can be especially useful as arbitrators when such grievances arise.

In these and other ways, advisory committees can help to maintain the harmony needed to keep a program functioning well. The specific suggestions and recommendations offered by the committee can be used to keep the program up-to-date and responsive to its consumers and the community. Future program directions can be evolved as the committee is used as a springboard for new and creative ideas.

The administration of selected counseling services

Thus far, this chapter has highlighted the general responsibilities counselors have for coordination and administration. Counselors, however, are responsible for the conduct of services in more specific ways. How they administrate their own tasks and responsibilities is an important facet of their work. This section describes how counselors can administrate effectively certain important counseling components. Particular emphasis will be given to developing and using community resources. Increasingly, counselors have a functional responsibility to make sure that community resources are appropriately integrated into counseling plans. Two prominent counselee concerns, vocational and educational placement, will be addressed as a means of illustrating the potential use of community resources. A special look also will be taken at how counselors might go about administrating the counselee follow-up and consultation services.

Using community resources

Providing comprehensive services can be a difficult function for counselors. All available resources need to be harnessed to lighten the load any one counselor has to bear. Fortunately, in many communities, there are ready and willing resources. Unfortunately, little has been done to explore the skills that are needed on the part of counselors to bring about an efficient use of such resources. This section contains some suggestions that counselors from any counseling setting should be able to initiate.

Importance of informal communication networks

One of the principle problems preventing adequate use of community resources has been the overreliance on formal interagency agreements. Although these agreements may be necessary, additional, informal understandings that facilitate the functioning of the formal mechanism are equally important. These informal understandings must be developed between the persons of cooperating organizations who are actually involved in providing services. Too often, the formal agreements contrived on an administrative level have little resemblance to the everyday reality of service delivery. In a sense, a counselor can develop a series of these informal contacts to facilitate every step of the counseling process. Referrals can be generated from persons who have direct access to the counseling target population. Even follow-up can be enhanced in a similar manner. In this way, the counselor builds an informal communication network of persons who are interested in basically the same thing: Seeing that needed services are provided to a certain group of people to achieve certain desirable outcomes.

How does a counselor build such networks? First, a counselor should carefully review the case loads that are served by his or her program. Careful attention should be paid to the referral sources and concerns of the target population. General patterns will soon emerge. Contacts should be made with the referral sources who frequently send counselees to the initiating counselor's agency. Individuals should be identified within these referral sources who can serve as a direct contact. The counselor and the referral contact can discuss how best to facilitate the referral process to match the needs of counselees and the specialties of the professionals within each organization. The procedural demands of each agency can be accommodated in many creative ways to streamline the flow of services to counselees. For example, a referral form could be developed that contains all necessary information for screening. Such a form could eliminate the time and cost it sometimes takes to gather these data from different sources.

In terms of providing services, a case load inspection could also indicate what kind of services are most frequently offered and where. As with referral sources, service-delivery contacts can be cultivated on a personal basis so that there is an easing of formal requirements. Personal relationships and understandings among the service providers of cooperating agencies can go far toward establishing timely and appropriate services to benefit the mutual counselees of the cooperating parties. Also, new resources can be uncovered if a counselor continues to update a list of sources. When a new source is uncovered, it can be contacted via the formal network that a community normally has established. There are many ways to tap into this formal network. Many communities have published directories of local social-service providers. The Yellow Pages can be informative. Local departments of health or a mayor's office also can provide important information regarding social-service agencies. Informally, other counselors can be asked to share their contacts, particularly if a promise is given in return, to share any new resources. Also, as new contacts are made, a counselor can ask to be included in information sharing with the public or other professionals.

Counselees can even be taught how to develop the informal networks that facilitate the formal mechanisms of service delivery. Better yet, a counselee should be able to experiment with this new skill by tapping into the informal networks of the counselor and using it him- or herself. In this way, a counselee may be able to share some of the coordinating burden of the counselor. This not only provides the counselee with some guided experience in getting and using information, but it also frees the counselor for pursuing other necessary tasks.

Having counselees use informal information networks has special implications for job search and placement development. Since the strength of using friends and acquaintances to develop job leads has been recognized, each counselee should be helped to prepare a list of persons who might have the potential to uncover job openings and possibly even facilitate the hiring process. Care must be taken that counselees use their networks profitably. They must be able to express their vocational needs to their contacts in a way that clarifies how the contact can help them. When people understand how they can help someone, and what their help will mean, they can be expected to participate and contribute enthusiastically. Vague solicitations do not earn much reward. The counselor should also ask personal contacts to tap into the network on behalf of the counselee. This can provide a great extension of networks and increase the chances of developing suitable job offers. It also will help the counselee develop further information about local labor markets and thereby, further facilitate planning for the job search.

Educational placement

Value of educational placement to counselees

Counselors will probably deal more often with counselees who are trying to develop the appropriate skills and knowledge to choose an occupation than with counselees who are ready to proceed immediately with vocational placement. In most instances, counselees are not even sure what their occupational goal is, but they do know they should acquire some education and training. Unfortunately, unless this education and training is directed, at least toward a general occupational area and level, much of it may become useless. Few persons can pursue education merely for the sake of acquiring knowledge. Although this aspect of learning is valuable and should not be ignored, constraints on personal and social resources invariably dictate that education must have a greater utilitarian purpose. When education and training pursuits are integrated into a person's plan for career development, then a greater personal and social return can be expected. It is important that a counselor and counselee carefully plan for the appropriate educational activities. This planning is predicated on establishing a suitable career goal based on the capabilities and aspiration of the counselee. Once education and training pursuits have been linked to a career goal, then the rest of the career development process falls more easily into place.

Educational placement refers to the event of choosing an educational or training opportunity that will provide enough productive skills and knowledge to enable a counselee to enter the career of his or her choice. In order to make such decisions, information sources need to be tapped. Too often, advanced education and training are pursued without the person's having a clear-cut idea of what will be gained. Recently, for example, some have seriously questioned whether advanced education can provide the return of investment that people assume it does.[9] For persons pursuing certain professions, college may be a necessity, but for many others, other forms of education and training may be more valuable in the long run. When gathering information for occupational preparation, it is necessary that many different kinds of experiences and opportunities be investigated.

High school and liberal arts colleges are geared toward providing students with the general skills they need to pursue a variety of career options. For many occupations, a high school diploma or its equivalent is enough of a base from which to launch further educational or vocational training. When a student has not obtained a high school diploma, programs must be structured to help him or her

9. Caroline Bird, *The Case Against College* (New York: McKay, 1974).

obtain the equivalent skills; usually, this is done by enrolling the person in a General Education Diploma program. For most careers today, some skills training or further education is needed in order to specialize.

Choosing a specialty requires knowledge of the conditions of the labor market, not only as it stands for the present but as it will develop during the next ten or twenty years. If a person wants to enter a field that is already overcrowded, he or she must be made aware of this, and must attempt to hone his or her educational skills so finely that he or she will be able to find suitable work. Others who have a less definite idea of the career they want to pursue might do well to look for and train to enter one of the less crowded vocations where workers are needed. Career education programs must be set up to disseminate this kind of information. A program must also help a student take into account all the many factors that enter into a vocational decision.

Impact of career education on the schools

Recently, career education has had a great impact on the curricula of schools. Many schools are now more inclined to teach a blend of general and specific skills, as opposed to the unstructured, general programs that became the fashion in the 1960s when many kinds of jobs were plentiful. Technological and craft occupational training are almost as widely available in high schools today as are college-preparation courses. High schools are also making wider use of the work-study and employer co-op programs, which were traditionally only used as part of special education programs to prepare the less able student for careers. These programs are being extended to give all students a chance to gain work experience before making any final decisions. Schools are also trying to promote part-time summer employment for the same reasons.

Colleges, too, are offering more career-oriented training. Many community colleges are providing skills-oriented programs, such as bookkeeping and accounting instruction. This type of preparation should be attractive to prospective employers since they will not have to bear the costs of training new employees in the specialized skills needed to the degree that they had to do in the past. Almost all specialized training was previously received on-the-job, and in a tight job market, this is not readily available to persons entering the work place Apprenticeship programs coordinated by labor unions are also examples of this new kind of specialized preparation. This training, however, requires a substantial amount of investment on the part of the employer.

What value will this emphasis on career have? In fact, the pendulum may be swinging too far in this direction. A concern voiced by some persons is that students are required to select career goals long before they are mature enough to do so. This is a legitimate reason for caution. But perhaps the maturity of students is questioned because they have never before been given the opportunity to learn how to respond responsibly to career concerns at such an early age. As career education makes an impact on an entire curriculum, from kindergarten through grade twelve, students can be expected to be more aware of how to make mature career decisions. They do not necessarily need to make them any earlier than in the past.

The field of counseling has important contributions to make at the high school level to students' career planning. Not only can counselors aid individual students in the development of career-preparation activities, but they also can serve as consultants to teachers and administrators in their attempts to develop comprehensive career-related services and programs in the school and community.

Vocational placement

Vocational placement, in terms of an individual counselee, refers to when he or she accepts a job offer. For counselors, there are many related tasks that lead to this decision. A recent trend is that of teaching counselees how to conduct their own job searches. This involves helping them set up suitable job goals on the basis of up-to-date local labor market information, teaching counselees job-application and resume-writing skills, providing instruction and practice for interviews, and helping them learn how to make contacts that will uncover job leads. All of these activities require a great deal of coordinating on the part of the counselor.

Value of informal contacts in vocational placement

The concept of developing informal relationships with community resources is particularly applicable for counselors who attempt this kind of program. For counselors who deal with counselees having vocational concerns, this approach can be facilitated by recognizing that employers also can benefit from the services the counselor can offer. Employers need a labor supply and a source of applicants who have the support of a counselor behind them. Once counselors perceive that they can be resources for employers, the way is opened for mutually rewarding relationships. When counselors fail to recognize this, they tend to feel that employers are either difficult to work with or that they have nothing to offer them. Employers, in turn, may have not had an opportunity to deal with counselors before and may view them and their clients with suspicion until a relationship is established.

One way to approach employers is to use an existing relationship with a mutual contact. The contact can provide necessary background information about the employer and help arrange a meeting. Finding this contact is usually easier than one might think. Within a counselor's wide range of acquaintances, there are several possibilities.[10] Getting some information about employers before working with them is important for many reasons. First, the information provides valuable local labor market information that is up-to-date and useful for helping counselees select job goals. Most labor-market information is culled from a variety of resources and is usually too general to be of specific help in a local community. Also, by the time such information is published, it is likely to be out-of-date. Preliminary information also can be used to screen the employer's potential as a resource for the counselor. Perhaps working conditions are not good, advancement is poor, or the jobs are too technical for the counselees the counselor works with. This information also can be used to determine what kinds of employees are needed, what problems the employer may be having recruiting appropriate applicants, the nature of the employers' business, and the hiring criteria the employer uses. This type of knowledge is useful not only for counselees but also for helping the counselor determine the needs of the employer so that any approach can be meaningful. Having this information prior to an actual contact with the employer permits the counselor to initiate the contact from a position of strength. This knowledge will be impressive to an employer and facilitate trust in the counselor.

When making the actual contact with the employer, or the person who does the hiring, the counselor might consider using the contact person to help open the door. This might not always be possible, or appropriate, but it should always be considered. The contact's positive relationship with the employer will provide some credibility to the counselor. Without this, the counselor might do well to request a personal interview. Personal and direct requests are much harder to refuse than are impersonal solicitations by mail.

Supportive services for employers

After a relationship has been established, the counselor should review the features of the counseling program to see how it can aid the prospective employer. The most obvious benefit is the availability of a prescreened applicant pool that will provide good candidates for the employer's work force. Along with this, counselors usually offer to maintain supportive services to aid the counselee's adjustment to the new job. The applicant pool and support service are important services that employers are likely to value. The counselor should be prepared to help the employer identify other

10. Mark S. Granovetter, "The Strength of Weak Ties," *American Journal of Sociology*, 78 (1973): 1360–1380.

needs that they might address together. It is at this point that the counselor's knowledge of the employer's business will be most valuable. If the counselor demonstrates awareness and knowledge of the employer's business concerns, the employer cannot help but be more interested in seeing what potential the counseling program actually has. For example, employers may have current employees who are experiencing personal or interpersonal difficulties that are minimizing their productivity. The counselor might be able to suggest ways these problem employees could receive counseling services before their difficulties become more disruptive to them and their employer.

Once employers recognize the benefits a counselor has to offer, they will be more likely to provide labor market information and participate in other aspects of job skills training for counselees. Samples of application blanks and preferred formats of resumes can be obtained for counselee's use. Employers can even be used to measure the reality of simulated job interviews. Employers may also be willing candidates for advisory committees. Most important, employers who become actively involved in the counseling program and who begin hiring counselees are likely to become information contacts for other employers. Other new employers will be readily inclined to accept the credibility of the counselor when the recommendation is made by a fellow employer.

Follow-up services

There is much confusion regarding follow-up services, yet they are a necessary part of educational or vocational placement. Follow-up services must be distinguished from program outcome evaluation, which is also frequently referred to as follow-up, but is used in another context. This second type of follow-up attempts to assess the impact, or effectiveness, of a variety of counseling services after they have been completed. Contact is usually made by mail survey or interview, either in person or by telephone. Service delivery may be extended anew to a counselee if a need is uncovered, but this is not the primary purpose of this type of follow-up. Program outcome evaluation is discussed in greater detail in Chapter 13.

Service delivery follow-up in vocational and educational programs has been described as follow-along,[11] which seems to be a more accurate description of what this service is. Follow-up, or follow-along, when used in this sense, is a service provided by the coun-

11. Donald E. Shrey, "Post Employment Services for the Severely Disabled," *Rehabilitation Counseling Bulletin* 19 (1976): 563–71.

selor to help a counselee assess the progress being made and to determine if new counseling strategies need to be devised to facilitate the counselee's development.

Value of follow-up to counselees

Follow-up contact should be routinely built into the counseling process. Particularly when counseling is focused on career-development activities such as educational or vocational placement, an ongoing follow-up plan is necessary. The long-range success of the placement is measured by how well the counselee works out after his or her placement. It is to this goal that follow-up activity is directed. Placement, although seemingly a difficult enough accomplishment, is only the beginning of a long-term adjustment process. Many counselees, regardless of the setting, will have had limited experience in educational or vocational pursuits from which to draw on to guide their adjustment process. Educational settings may provide supportive resources for students, but they are limited in their ability to simulate actual employment. Rarely will employers tolerate a new worker with long-term adjustment problems, and most employers do not provide any supportive resources for this problem.

If a counselor wants to maintain personal contact with a counselee after placement, a schedule should be set up for maintaining regular contact until the counselee has achieved a reasonable adjustment. Such monitoring may require only an occasional telephone contact, and personal visits may not be necessary. Care must be taken during follow-up not to interfere with normal work or learning activities. If counseling is required, the times should be selected to minimize disruption of the counselee's work. Evening or weekend hours could be used so as not to remove the employee from what may be a touchy work setting.

Termination of formal follow-up

After six months or so, if the counselee seems to have mastered the work or learning environment, formal follow-up could be terminated. Throughout the follow-up period, the counselee should be assured that the counselor is available should a serious difficulty arise that needs immediate attention. Care must be taken, however, that such crises do not become an everyday occurrence. Some counselees will revert to this dependent behavior once they realize that regular counselor contact will have to be forgone for work or school activities. This probably will not be a common occurrence, but it does occur. A gradual weaning procedure helps to avoid this.

If problems occur after placement, counseling can resume as before. If the counselee is not able to demonstrate problem-solving ability, and adjustment becomes difficult, this might be evidence that the counselee has a severe problem-solving skill deficit. Special attention should be directed at teaching the counselee general coping strategies, as well as addressing the specific areas causing trouble.

The counselor must also keep in mind, however, that adjustment problems may not always be a direct result of a counselee's lack of skill or interpersonal problems. Environmental situations create difficulties to which a counselee cannot or should not adjust. For example, job conditions may be quite different from what the counselee was told prior to placement. Discrimination and prejudice could be directed toward the counselee. Skill requirements might exceed the abilities of the counselee to so great an extent that remedial training or on-the-job training cannot overcome the deficit. In such instances, it may be to the counselee's advantage to leave the placement and begin a new search for a job that will not present environmental difficulties.

In other instances, however, it may be possible for the counselor to influence environmental change so that the counselee can perform better. For example, employers can be consulted in situations where job conditions interfere with employee satisfaction. For counselees who have physical impairments, architectural barrier removal and task modification that might benefit other work personnel could be effected. Prejudicial attitudes may also be changed if the counselor can intervene in a positive way so that people are given exposure to situations that permit them to develop more accepting attitudes.

There also may be problems in other areas of a counselee's life that make adjustment to work difficult. Excessive social activities, improper rest and diet, poor financial management, lack of transportation, and a host of other factors can and do jeopardize a suitable adjustment. A counselor must be sensitive to such possibilities and carefully lead the counselee through a thorough assessment so that all potential problem areas are exposed. When such problems become apparent, then counseling strategies can be applied to them.

If job placement has resulted in a counselee moving so far away that follow-up is difficult or impossible, then a counselor might help a counselee identify new resources to use in follow-up. Long-distance contact may be appropriate, but if additional services are needed, local resources should be identified and available.

Unfortunately, too little attention is paid to follow-up. Case-load-management problems due to large case loads or lack of resources often make such follow-up difficult. Still, every effort should be expended to develop the means to make follow-up activity a routinely offered counseling service.

The role of consulting

Consulting is a special service through which counselors are able to influence people on a broader basis than they can in individual or even group counseling. In recent years, an awareness has developed that it is sometimes institutions and organizations that need to change rather than individuals. This is particularly true in post-World War II society in which larger and vastly more complicated organizations and institutions play an increasingly important role in the lives of everyone. From this awareness has grown a special concern for finding ways to help individuals exist more cooperatively within organizations and institutions. The concern has directed itself toward changing the organizations and institutions, where possible, or at minimum, explaining the needs of individuals to the organizational and institutional management. This task is called consulting.

Consultant as change agent

A consultant is a counselor who is an expert in planning change processes for organizations and institutions. These changes enable organizations and institutions to improve their policies and procedures and to meet the needs of their consumers and employees more adequately.

The systematic consultant-accountability process model

The model for consulting that is described in the pages that follow was developed at Michigan State University. It is patterned after the systematic counseling approach model discussed in Chapter 3. The principal contributors to the model are Dolore Rockers, Roger Livingston, David Vandergoot, and James Engelkes.

No attempt will be made to define the consultation process beyond the brief description just given of its role. Since the development of the consultation process for counselors is a very recent phenomenon, a description of the process is sufficient for the purpose of this book. This model is developed for the use of counselors in school and social-service agency settings. It is an accountability model and, as such, it requires the consultant to apply a process that is responsive to the needs of those being consulted. One means of doing this is for the consultant to acquaint the consultees with the consultation change process prior to its actual implementation. To accommodate this objective, the model will be described in detail from the beginning of the process to its termination. Figure 12–3 illustrates the model.

Subsystem 1.0. The Consultant. The counselor who assumes the consultant role can either be a part of the program seeking to

Figure 12–3 Consultant accountability process model

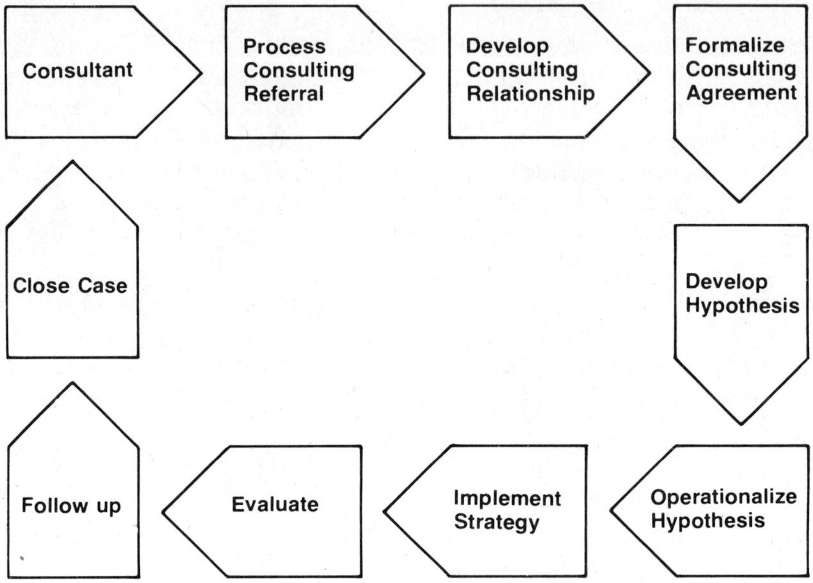

change or a person outside the program who has been especially requested to implement the change process. The first type of consultant is often referred to as an in-house consultant.

Skills of consultant

Special skills are needed by the consultant, but counselor training seems ideally suited for the consulting process. Skills include listening, clarifying, problem identification and solving, decision making, and functional analysis, all skills that are central to counseling. Even though the goal in consulting involves organizational change, this can only be accomplished by relating to people.

Subsystem 2.0. Process Consulting Referral. The consultation process is initiated with a referral. This model most typically will be used by counselors who are in-house consultants as opposed to those who are external to a program. This model will point to how counselors can become effective agents of change within their own setting. Therefore, the person or group requesting service will most likely have had previous contact with the counselor/consultant. Referrals for consultation service will not be readily forthcoming unless the counselor/consultant has effectively and ethically fulfilled all previous functions required by the organization. Assuming that this is the case, the counselor/consultant is in a good position to expedite the referral process. As an in-house consultant, the counselor may already have enough information to make a decision regarding the appropriateness of the referral request. An outside consultant might have to spend a great deal of time with the referral source before such a decision could be made. If the request for consultation cannot be fulfilled because the counselor lacks the time, skills, or has other limitations, suggestion can be made regarding where to obtain alternative services.

In a school system, a counselor/consultant can expect referrals from teachers about classroom management, from administrators about maintaining staff morale, and from parents about child-management concerns. Student groups might also request services. Agency counselors can expect similar requests from staff, administrators, and agency clients.

Subsystem 3.0. Develop Consulting Relationship. As a consulting relationship progresses, it should become increasingly more specific and defined. This requires that the consultant have an overview of where the process is leading. The consultant must also be aware of personal limitations that can impede certain parts of the process. Therefore, in the first formal meeting with the consultee, the consultant should present this overview and honestly describe any potential limitations. The overall goal of this subsystem is to clarify the purpose of consultation and the responsibilities and limitations of the process. This ensures that all parties involved are operating under the same set of expectations. It is a preventive measure against future misunderstandings.

Dual purposes of consulting

When developing the relationship, the consultant should describe the process as a system with distinct components, as it is presented here. Generally, consulting can be viewed as a problem-solving process. Its purpose is twofold. It is not only concerned with problem identification and solution, but it also attempts to teach the consultee the skills and resources that are needed that will enable him or her to deal with future problems independently. Because consultation is a human endeavor, however, weaknesses within the system will appear. These must be acknowledged to whatever extent possible. Following this, the consultant must explain the responsibilities of all those concerned. As the consultant demonstrates openness and honesty, so must the consultee also be willing to disclose any and all information relevant to the consulting task. Consultation is a joint effort. Cooperation will be required for successful consultation.

Subsystem 4.0. Formalize Consulting Agreement. Once the informal discussion of the consulting relationship has been outlined, the relationship should be formalized between the consultation parties for the specific situation before them. This requires a formal, written agreement.

This subsystem begins with a discussion of the concerns of the consultee that prompted the consultation request. This will cover only subjective impressions and will be exploratory in nature. Formal data gathering will occur later. Upon completion of this superficial, broad examination of the problem situation, the formal agreement can be drawn up. Included in this contract will be an estimate of the time and resources the consultant will give the consultee while working on selected areas of concern. Estimates of costs to be covered by the consultee should be included. The consultee will also provide permission and establish the ground rules under which the consultant will interact with the program of the consultee. Systematic review and revision procedures should be built into this agreement.

In this fashion, the consulting relationship becomes formalized. Even though new aspects will arise, it is to the advantage of all parties to formalize the relationship in mutually agreed upon terms by an administrative agreement before the consulting process begins.

Subsystem 5.0. Develop Hypotheses. After the areas of concern have been specified by the administrative agreement, an analysis of all available data is begun. Typically, the consultant gathers data during the referral process and also when the consultee reviews the concerns that prompted consultation. All other potentially relevant organizational data should be scrutinized. From these data, the consultant will generate hypotheses concerning problem causes and potential solutions. These will be shared later with the consultee. These hypotheses are important because subsequent events will be determined by them. It is important to specify not only hypotheses about the causes of the problem, but also to set forth positive hypotheses about what the organization could be like once the problems are removed. Stating hypotheses in a positive way has several advantages. It will become apparent that many specific things can be done to resolve the problems. Strategy procedures begin to emerge immediately. As this occurs, the consultee will see the potential for success and will exert renewed energy and motivation toward problem solution. Care must be taken, however, to refrain from implementing any strategy, regardless of how obvious it may seem, until the next part of the process is completed.

Subsystem 6.0. Operationalize Hypotheses. Once hypotheses have been developed and verified by the consultee, strategy planning can begin. This is done by seeking strategies for the hypotheses that express solutions, or the outcomes that the consultee desires. This subsystem consists of establishing goals, operationally defining objectives, collecting baseline data, planning strategy tasks, and finalizing a strategy agreement.

Goal establishment

Goal establishment consists of synthesizing the various hypotheses into a general statement that describes the final desired outcome. This and all consultation process activities are done mutually with the consultee and others designated by the consultee to work with the consultant. Next, operationally defined objectives are developed. Operational objectives specify the tasks and behaviors that are needed to accomplish the goal, as well as the circumstances under which they are to be done. There could be several objectives or only one. This really does not matter as long as the objectives contain the final goal. An important component of operational definitions are the criteria that will be used to assess whether an objective has been accomplished. The means by which the successful achievement of the criteria are to be measured must be included. Developing measurable criteria is a necessary step toward achieving the accountability this consultation model provides.

If adequate specific and measurable criteria are not developed, the next step, which is the collection of baseline data, ends up being a futile gesture. The criteria determine what data are to be collected and in what fashion.

Data collection

Data collection does several things. First, it permits an immediate comparison between what is desired and what is the current situation. Sometimes data collection uncovers the fact that a problem does not really exist and that the consultee needs only to change perceptions. More often than not, the data does serve to distinguish the real from the ideal. Data also provide the basis for the eventual comparison of the outcome of the consultation process with the original problematic situation. This procedure is basic to the accountability of this model. Data collection is the basic building tool of strategy development. The extensiveness of the strategy that will be needed to resolve the problem becomes apparent from this realistic collection and assessment of data.

Baseline data can be developed in various ways. Interviews and surveys of program personnel can be done. Standardized or specially developed instruments can be used. Records can be reviewed, and observations of program activity can be done. The services of the consultee organization can be analyzed, and consumers of the organization's services can be contacted to determine quality of services. There is no limit to the means by which data can be gathered. As long as the data relate to the objectives derived from the goal and hypotheses previously formulated, the measurement process can take many shapes and forms.

The development of strategy tasks is the next phase of operationalizing the hypotheses. Strategy tasks must be stated very concretely. Whatever activity is to be performed, to what degree, when, and by whom are typical components necessary to the specification of tasks. The tasks need to be stated with as much detail and completeness as possible. When the development of strategy tasks is finished, a detailed checklist should be made for use as a guide during the step-by-step implementation of the tasks.

When all strategy tasks are drawn up, those persons involved in the consultation should again enter into a formal, written agreement that specifies who is responsible for the implementation of each task of the strategy. This also permits giving credit to the appropriate person or persons at a later time when the task has been successfully completed. Any opportunity for providing reenforcement should not be missed.

Subsystem 7.0. Implement Strategy. The next step is to implement the strategies. Before strategy tasks can be initiated, however, one procedure has to be given special consideration. In many instances, certain persons or groups may belong to an organization that requested consultation services but who were not part of the prior consultation process. These people may actually be the target population for the change that is desired. For example, a rehabilitation agency supervisor may be required to implement new administrative procedures for the staff to follow. Consultation may be requested to plan for this and, although some of the staff may participate in the process, all staff must be prepared for the impending change. It is in the interest of promoting good learning strategy to inform these people about the change and the reasons for the change at this stage. It is necessary to ensure their cooperation to do this. They should be given an opportunity to review the change strategy and to offer suggestions for plan modification. In this way, the plan can be improved, and all persons can have a chance to participate in plan development. People seem to respond more favorably to planned change when they have been given the opportunity to invest in its development. This procedure is a highly important accountability feature.

Once the target population has been informed adequately and their cooperation has been secured, the strategy tasks can be performed. At this point, it is helpful to have a checklist and time chart available to guide the smooth application of tasks. This permits the consultant to evaluate the ongoing progress of the strategy and provides a clear-cut decision point as to whether all the tasks have been completed. Upon completion, evaluation can begin.

Subsystem 8.0. Evaluate. Evaluation begins with the collection of another set of data. This data should parallel those facts that were collected previously. The same methods should be used to collect these data as were used to collect the baseline data. This will permit a comparison between pre- and post-strategy data, which will, in turn, indicate how successful the change was.

Comparison of pre- and post-strategy data

To facilitate a complete evaluation of the strategy, two additional comparisons must be made. The outcome data should also be compared to the criteria set forth in the objectives. If the criteria are met or exceeded, then a check needs to be made to see if the consultation goal has been reached. If the objectives were originally derived properly, there should be no problem. If the goal has been met, a decision must be made regarding whether any further consultation is needed. Several possibilities exist. The current strategy can be maintained to ensure even better results, or it may be modified somewhat. An entirely new consultation process might be initiated for work on other problems. It could also be evident that no further consultation is necessary, and the relationship can be terminated. Termination at this point refers to the cessation of active consultant involvement. The process is not yet over, however, and the subsystems that follow must still be attended to.

If the strategy has not been successful, the process must be reviewed. This review should begin with a check of the hypotheses to see if they were appropriately formed. If they were, each subsequent procedure must be checked to see if oversights occurred. As problems are found, corrections must be made, and each succeeding step must be redone until the strategy is finally successful.

Subsystem 9.0. Plan Time-Span Follow-Up. After a decision is made to terminate the consultation relationship, it is the consultant's responsibility to arrange for follow-up activities. These activities are referred to as a time-span follow-up plan because follow-up should be done as a series of events over a specified period of time that is usually no shorter than six months. If the results are still being maintained or improved upon after six months, the consultant can be reasonably sure that the achieved change will become permanent. Included in the plan should also be a description of the type of information that will be needed to verify the continued maintenance of the desired change. The time-span follow-up plan should also consist of a written agreement. Follow-up is an activity that is easy to forgo, but without it, accountability is diminished. A written agreement which specifies the type and timing of follow-up activities, and the responsibilities of those concerned, helps to ensure that follow-up will be done.

Subsystem 10.0. Synthesize Follow-up Data. Once adequate follow-up data becomes available, the consultant should synthesize this data and provide a ready means for the consultant to help the consultee recognize the problem-solving strategies available for future problem situations. At this point, no further dependence on the consultant should be needed. At this point, a report and review of the process can be completed.

Subsystem 11.0. Close Case. In closing a case, the consultant does not simply close the file and throw it away. Rather, the consultant should carefully review in detail the specifics of the case. The hindsight so readily available at this point can be used to improve one's foresight in the next consultation opportunity.

A review of the history of consultation in counseling suggests that it has been a part of counseling services for quite some time.[12] Only recently, though, have models such as this one been developed to provide a perspective on the consultation process. Better understanding of the total consultation effort can only lead to more effective use of it. Other models can be found in Kurpius and Brubaker[13] and in two special issues of the *Personnel and Guidance Journal*.[14]

Summary

In this chapter, both program and personal administrative strategies that are available to counselors have been illustrated. Counselors can interact effectively with their program's administration constantly to upgrade the quality of services to their counselees. Administrative functions, often viewed skeptically as an avenue for bureaucratic misuse, can often be efficiently blended with service delivery. This ensures that the program-maintenance functions of the administration and the service-delivery functions of counselors will be adequately met. When this occurs, the counseling program should be in a good position to document its effectiveness. Suitable evidence of accountability is necessary to maintain program credibility and support. Therefore, counselors cannot ignore the administrative requirements of their jobs, even if they are not assigned specific administrative duties.

12. William M. Kahnweiler, "The School Counselor as Consultant: A Historical Review," *Personnel and Guidance Journal* 57 (1979): 374–80.

13. DeWayne J. Kurpius and J. Craig Brubaker, *Psychoeducational Consultation* (Bloomington, Ind.: Indiana University, 1976).

14. "Consultation I", *Personnel and Guidance Journal* 56 (February 1978). "Consultation II", *Personnel and Guidance Journal* 56 (March 1978).

Counselors are responsible for a variety of services related to individual counseling. These services require a high degree of coordination. The services described in detail in this chapter include the use of community resources, educational and vocational placement, follow-up, and consultation. A proper blending of these services can greatly enhance the effectiveness of counseling services. The use of formal and informal information networks was highlighted throughout the chapter.

Questions

1. What is the purpose of administrative and coordination activities?

2. What role do counselors play in administration and coordination activities?

3. What are the purposes of record keeping? How can efficient record keeping be ensured?

4. What are some of the issues that face counselors as they plan how to use their time?

5. Why are public relations important? What is the counselor's role in public relations?

6. How important are the physical surroundings in which counseling occurs? What can be done to physical surroundings to facilitate the counseling relationship?

7. Describe the role of the advisory committee. What kinds of persons should sit on an advisory committee?

8. What is consulting? Why has it become increasingly important in recent decades?

9. What is the role of follow-up services? Describe ways that follow-up can be effectively managed.

10. Describe the relationship between formal and informal and internal and external channels of service coordination.

Projects

1. Interview several counselors to learn what informal channels of service coordination they use. Find out how they integrate these with formal channels.

2. Read one of the books mentioned in the introduction or a similar book on coordination and administration and report on it to the class.

3. Invite a consultant who has worked for a service agency to speak to the class on how he or she builds relationships with counselors.

13 Research and program evaluation in counseling

Questionnaires, an important research tool, sometimes require careful attending skills on the part of the interviewer.

Introduction

This last chapter focuses on two activities that counselors may not closely identify with, but which nonetheless have a great deal of influence on the counseling profession. Research and program evaluation are processes that are often performed by other people, such as university faculty or consultants hired by administrators, to provide certain information, often of a statistical variety. Counselors often rather arbitrarily decide that research and program evaluation are of little value to them, mostly due to an underlying philosophy that any activity not directly geared to specific counselee needs is a luxury. For many dedicated counselors who understand the value of relationships developed during counseling, the essence of counseling cannot be reduced to cold quantities of statistics. Therefore, the research and evaluation aspects of counseling appear not only worthless, but may actually be viewed on occasion as harmful. The counseling relationship cannot be expected to develop under the curious gaze of the disinterested researcher or evaluator. Such scrutiny may also be interpreted as a violation of the confidential trust necessary to lend credibility to counseling.

These and other quite similar misgivings are often heard by counseling researchers when they approach field counselors seeking cooperation in implementing counseling research. Evaluators, too, are mistrusted, particularly so when they are called in by program administrators to evaluate a program. The very word "evaluation" suggests that a judgment is going to be made regarding the goodness (or badness) of a counseling program. A counselor with a personal investment in his or her work cannot help but resist these activities on some level.

There is even a germ of truth to counselors' notions about research and evaluation. Research and evaluation require a high level of skill and understanding to be done well. Poorly or inadequately done research and evaluation are of little value, and they do occasionally cause harm under certain circumstances. As activities, they are neutral; however, as activities performed and carried out by persons, they can work for good or ill.

Many counselor training programs offer at most one course, at the master's level, on research and evaluation techniques. Unfortunately, a lot of ignorance results from this small amount of knowledge. In this chapter, you will be introduced to research and evaluation as an ongoing and necessary activity that has value to counselors in their daily work. Counselors will learn the ways that they can put research and evaluation to work to do a better job of counseling. This chapter contains a detailed description of a

Key terms

research
theories
program evaluation
basic research
applied research
laboratory research
field research
survey research
ex post facto research
experimental research
statistics
evaluation design

program-evaluation process and suggests ways that counselors can participate in research and program evaluation activities.

The neutral nature of research

Research has been an accepted and valued part of western civilization for many centuries. The scientific method has been revered as a means for expanding human knowledge and expectations. It would not be possible to imagine the world without the impact of research. The standard of living, health, modes of transportation, even the aging process have been changed by research.

Defining research

Some persons see these technological developments not as progress, but as calamity. The Industrial Revolution and its byproducts of environmental pollution and unruly urbanization have often been blamed on research. Even materialism and the rather inevitable changes in values have been viewed as the result of scientific progress. As people view these events as side effects of progress, which is engendered by research, it is no wonder that counselors, who form part of the first line of defense against these seeming enemies of humanity, have become skeptical about the role of research and its ties to progress. That a link exists between technological development and these side effects is highly debatable. And one must be able to place research in its proper perspective. Kerlinger has done this well. In exploring what science and research are, he has written that "the basic aim of science is not the betterment of mankind, it is theory."[1] Scientific research is intended to develop new knowledge. Most persons can accept that self-knowledge and knowledge about the world are important. How people use that knowledge can be helpful or harmful, though.

Technology, on the other hand, is the application of knowledge. As such, it is not research. Technological development is dependent on the persons who implement it, and depending upon the circumstances, it, too, can be either valuable or abusive. It is not appropriate, however, to ascribe the unwanted side effects of technological development to research. Rather, the blame for the faulty use of research should be directed toward those who participate in the implementation of technology, including counselors.

Since counselors are basically involved in an educational enterprise, it is reasonable to expect that they value the aim of science and research, which is the development of knowledge. On a day-

1. Fred N. Kerlinger, *Foundation of Behavioral Research*, 2d ed. (New York: Holt, Rinehart, 1973), p. 9.

to-day basis, counselors attempt to develop new knowledge about counselees, which can then be used in a beneficial way. Viewed in this light, the goals of researchers and field counselors are compatible and can even reenforce each other.

The value of research to counselors

Research is the gathering of facts and seemingly unrelated bits of information and their eventual shaping into some manageable, understandable form. These forms are called theories. Theories are attempts to make sense out of seemingly unrelated bits of data. They are descriptions of how things might work. Theories develop out of research, and then more research is needed to confirm the validity, or truth, of theories.

Role of research in theory building

In their daily work, counselors are hit with a barrage of facts, usually coming from counselees. Sometimes counselors are able to identify a common thread from among the many facts that they collect from counselees. But since their primary task is to help individual counselees, more often than not, the common threads, or theories, are identified and defined by researchers, who then place this set of information at the disposal of counselors.

Counseling theories and systems are valuable guidelines for showing counselors how they relate to counselees and how they can go about organizing counseling technology to achieve desirable results. From this explanation, it should be evident that research counselors and field counselors have similar interests and can contribute to each others' efforts with mutual benefits.

Another value of research for counseling is related to its aim of expanding and organizing knowledge. One basic goal of research is to predict future behavior and behavior outcomes from a particular set of circumstances. As forecasting becomes more accurate, a degree of control may be developed over current circumstances that will permit the creation of a particular set of conditions conducive to a desired future accomplishment.

As people learn more about themselves and their environment, they are able to gain greater control of their lives. Such growth can only increase individual freedom.[2] Knowledge gained from research contributes to the ability of counselors and counselees to gain this freedom and control over their lives. In this way, the aims of counseling are furthered by research.

2. W. E. Craighead, A. E. Kazdin, and M. J. Mahoney, *Behavior Modification* (Boston: Houghton Mifflin, 1976), Chapter 10.

The value of program evaluation

In a sense, program evaluation takes research a step further. It documents how well a program meets its objectives and goals. It analyzes the processes of a program to see how it might be improved. Basically, program evaluation is of value to counselors in much the same way that research is. It helps to provide counselors with an overview that they are often unable to detect as they fulfill their responsibilities to individual counselees. It also helps to expand knowledge, in this case, about the functioning of counseling programs, in a way that can help counselors perform their tasks better than they might without the knowledge.

Program evaluation also has an additional value beyond that of research. This is that program evaluation, as an information-gathering process, is an essential part of a management system. It is necessary for the efficient administration of counseling programs. Ongoing, carefully planned program evaluation is an important component in a management system. As such, its most important function is to aid in decision making. Decision making is a central feature on all levels of program administration, including the counseling level. Program evaluation can be structured to provide the information necessary to decision makers.

Types of research

Basic and applied research

Perhaps the simplest way to classify research is to identify it as basic or applied. Basic research is theoretical in orientation, and as such, is concerned with the development of new knowledge. Applied research is concerned with testing applications of existing knowledge. An example of a basic-research project in counseling might be a study designed to determine how people learn.

Applied research is more practical in application than basic research. It often takes basic research and finds ways of using it. For example, once basic research has determined the major factors required for one to learn, applied research would then develop ways to help people learn better and more efficiently. Behavior modification techniques are an example of applied research having been developed from learning-theory principles, which are derived from basic research.

Laboratory and field research

A similar classification divides research into laboratory or field research. Laboratory research is often associated with basic research because findings derived from laboratory research are viewed as theoretical until they can be tested in the field. Although laboratory studies in counseling are not usually done in laboratories in the same way that research is done in chemistry, for example, laboratory research in counseling attempts to accomplish a similar level of control. Laboratory research in counseling, which may be conducted in classrooms and similar situations, tries to examine those factors thought to be most influential in carefully controlled settings. The element of control is a particularly distinguishing feature of laboratory research. In counseling, laboratory research might be done to determine the effect of certain counselor attributes and styles on the counseling relationship.

Field studies are research done in noncontrolled situations. The myriad events and elements of everyday counseling may shed new light on theories that have been developed in laboratory research. For example, if laboratory research revealed that counselees of certain backgrounds prefer counselors from similar backgrounds, field research might be used to uncover whether systematic case load assignments on the basis of counselee/counselor background is actually an effective way to assign counselors to counselees.

Methodological classifications of research

There are also methodological ways of classifying research. A methodological classification is not a mutually exclusive one, since any research study may combine several methodologies. Several major classifications are described in the following pages.

Survey research is usually used to find out information about certain people. Information is typically obtained by questionnaire or interview. Once a certain group, which is referred to as the target population, is identified for study, samples are drawn and contacted. On the basis of responses from the samples, inferences are made about the characteristics of the target population. In counseling, survey research often is used to define the needs of certain groups from which counselees are likely to come.

Other methods are designed to enable the researcher to make certain comparisons. For example, is one group of counselees different from another group? Does one counseling technique work better than others? Ex post facto research describes comparisons that are made among several factors that naturally exist, that is, are not manipulated or set up by the researchers. In counseling, ex post facto research is usually done to examine the interacting relationships of counselor and counselee attributes. For example, research might be conducted to determine if counseling effectiveness is associated more with certain characteristics of counselees or the experience of counselors.

Experimental research, on the other hand, describes studies in which researchers determine the type and degree of the factors being scrutinized. In experimental research in counseling, a researcher may vary the types of counseling methods offered to counselees to determine which are most effective. The researcher would then attempt to measure the effectiveness of each. A requirement of experimental research is that the subjects of any study be randomly selected and assigned to the different comparison groups. This is done so that any eventual differences cannot be attributed to other factors that may have governed the rules for selecting and assigning subjects. In counseling, random selection is difficult to achieve for many reasons. Many counselors find that permitting random selection and assignment of counselees is ethically hard. They feel that services should not be offered or withheld on the basis of randomness. Others feel that the added value of the knowledge gained from true experimental research benefits so many counselees over the long run that the risk is worth taking. Much careful thought has been given to this matter, and ethical principles have been developed to guide research methods when people are involved as subjects.[3] In addition, compromise methodology has been developed. It uses techniques that increase the general value of knowledge gained without using randomness. This type of research has been quite prominent in counseling and is called quasi-experimental research.[4]

Many interesting quasi-experimental techniques have been developed to overcome the deficits created by not being able to use true experimental methods. Although these techniques are too technical to describe here, it is useful to know that alternatives exist, and that viable compromises are available to permit the steady development of counseling research. These techniques are particularly valuable for conducting important research in field settings.

Single-subject research

Another important method in counseling research is referred to as the intensive design[5] or single-subject research.[6] The case study, which has long been a part of counseling research, has been criticized often for its lack of generalizability. It is also suspect because the researcher's biases are not controlled. Still, it is a highly useful

3. Ad Hoc Committee on Ethical Standards in Psychological Research, *Ethical Principles in the Conduct of Research with Human Participants* (Washington, D.C.: American Psychological Association, 1973).

4. Donald T. Campbell and Julian C. Stanley, *Experimental and Quasi-Experimental Designs for Research* (Chicago: Rand McNally, 1966). Thomas D. Cook and Donald T. Campbell, *Quasi-Experimentation: Design and Analysis Issues for Field Settings* (Chicago: Rand McNally, 1979).

5. Carl E. Thoresen and J. L. Anton, "Intensive Experimental Research in Counseling," *Journal of Counseling Psychology* 21 (1974): 553–59.

6. Edith Miller and Richard W. Warner, "Single Subject Research and Evaluation," *Personnel and Guidance Journal* 54, (1975): 130–33.

method that is valued by many counselors. Single-subject design permits the researcher to overcome many of the problems associated with the case-study method. These designs are also not difficult and may be accessible to practitioners. Counselors may want to consider applying single-subject research designs to some or all of their cases. The knowledge and accountability gained could prove to be quite important for counseling other clients and for program development.

Choosing the best method

There has been much debate over the worth and validity of various research methods. It is helpful to note that information needs can and do vary. Some information needs are more critical and more exacting than others. The question to be answered or the information needed should determine the type of research to be employed. Because it has implications for human lives, counseling deserves research that is as appropriate as possible. Basic laboratory research is as important as applied field research in its proper place. Regardless of the method used, information is crucial to counseling because it forms the stuff communication is made of. Counselors may not need to be researchers, but it is wise for them to recognize valid research and how to use the information gained from it. In the future, it is hoped that more counselors will participate in research.

Use of statistics

Before going on to another subject, a final note about the use of statistics in research is in order. Increasingly, research has become more sophisticated as statistics have been used to develop highly detailed descriptions of behavior and other aspects of counseling. Because statistics deal in numbers, however, some persons feel that they are the final answer. Statistics themselves are nothing more than a set of mathematical facts. They can be properly used or abused. The possibilities for abuse are particularly high when using statistics to measure something as ephemeral as human behavior, and great care must be employed in evaluating the use of statistics in the field of counseling. One abuse is that statistics are often used to "prove" cause-and-effect relationships that simply do not exist in the reality of life. Statistics should be used to help one draw inferences about the probable causes of effects. The research design, however, and not the statistics, enables one to draw inferences in the first place.

The evaluation of counseling programs

Although intuitive program evaluation has probably occurred for as long as programs have existed, formal procedures that systematically attend to evaluation only recently have been developed. It is evident that program evaluation is beginning to evolve into a body of knowledge unto itself. Several journals and publications that focus specifically on program-evaluation concerns have emerged. Two journals in particular provide a concentrated source of material for program evaluation in social-service programs. These are *Evaluation* and *Evaluation Review.* Also, several publications have attempted to present theoretical systematic views of program evaluations, which are intended to guide the implementation of actual program evaluation studies. Particularly good sources are Weiss' *Evaluating Action Programs,*[7] Rossi's and Williams' *Evaluating Social Programs,*[8] and an annual review called *Evaluation Studies*,[9] which was edited originally by Guttentag and most recently by Sechrest.[10] Additionally, the Evaluation Research Society is a source of information.

Models of program evaluation

Although there have been several attempts to develop general models on which to base program evaluation, there has not been much agreement regarding what the components of such a model might be. Spaniol has described many of these models, particularly with a view toward illuminating their differences.[11] However, in an effort to simplify the conceptualization of program evaluation for its relevance to counselors and to provide an overview of models in general, most models can be broken down into seven basic components.

The first basic component, clarification of purpose, must attend to the purpose for program evaluation. As an emergent process, program evaluation is continually finding more and better uses for itself. Still, it must be addressed to one or only a few specific purposes in order to be effective. Performing evaluation simply because it is currently popular is rarely of much value. Unless program evaluation is used purposefully, it may become simply another fad that will soon lose its luster. This would be unfortunate, since the basic general purpose of evaluation is to provide information that will improve the delivery of services.

Following clarification of purpose, program evaluation should consist of three basic measurement components. These include the

7. Carol H. Weiss, *Evaluating Action Programs* (Boston: Allyn & Bacon, 1972).

8. Peter H. Rossi and Walter Williams, *Evaluating Social Programs* (New York: Seminar Press, 1972).

9. Marcia Guttentag, ed., *Evaluation Studies* (Beverly Hills, Calif.: Sage, 1977), 2.

10. Lee Sechrest, *Evaluation Studies* (Beverly Hills, Calif.: Sage, 1977) 4.

11. LeRoy Spaniol, *Program Evaluation Models for Rehabilitation: A Review of the Literature* (Madison, Wis.: Regional Rehabilitation Research Institute, University of Wisconsin, 1975).

measure of program inputs, program processes or operations, and program outcomes. These are described in more detail later in the chapter.

After the measurement components, the next component is the development of an evaluation, or research, design that can be used to guide the data-collection effort. This design activity must take into account the type of information sought and the capability of the program to provide the information. The evaluation design should not disrupt the service-delivery function of the program.

After inserting the obtained measures into the appropriate design, analysis of data must occur. There are many analysis techniques, some very sophisticated, and others very simple. Basically, the type of analysis will depend on the type of data collected and the form of the research design used to organize data collection. A sophisticated analysis, by itself, is no guarantee for achieving usable results. The most sophisticated analysis cannot turn poorly collected data into reliable and valid information. Also, sophisticated analyses are difficult for people to understand. The point to recognize is that the type of analysis used should be consistent with the purposes and design of the evaluation effort. To use a complicated analysis for the sake of sophistication is not warranted if a simple one will do.

The last component of program evaluation is concerned with the organization and reporting of the evaluation results. This effort must flow from all the other components. In order for a program evaluation to be useful, its results have to be communicated in a way that addresses the reason for doing the evaluation in the first place and in a way understandable to those who must use the results.

It must be emphasized that whenever program evaluation is contemplated, it must be implemented in a planned manner. A careful integration of all the components is essential.

The next section describes the relationship of program evaluation to research, as well as the relationship of the counselor to research and program evaluation activities. Subsequent sections review each program evaluation component in greater detail. An attempt will be made to provide counseling applications for each of the components.

Research, program evaluation, and the counselor

Problems with program-evaluation research

The value of research to program evaluation has been debated often.[12] It has been proposed that program evaluation is a meaningless endeavor unless its products result from rigorous research de-

12. Robert S. Weiss and Martin Rein, "The Evaluation of Broad-Aim Programs: Experimental Design, Its Difficulties, and an Alternative," *Administrative Science Quarterly* 15 (1970): 97–109.

signs. Of course, the preferred design would be an experimental one that permitted comparisons from which legitimate inferences could be drawn. In the reality of implementing a social service program, though, it is rarely possible to assign counselees on a random basis to alternative programs. It is also expensive to run several types of programs at once. The alternative of a true control group, which would be a group of counselees who by random selection receive no service, is felt to be unethical. It is believed that no one should be withheld from services for such a reason. It is easy to understand why true experimental designs that use randomly selected and assigned counselors are a very difficult and rare achievement.

Others have pointed out, however, that it is still legitimate to perform evaluation activities, even if a true experiment cannot be designed. Since this has been such a problem, much attention has been given to it. Alternative evaluation designs have been formulated that attempt to add as much research rigor to evaluation as possible.[13]

Proponents of program evaluation who feel strict research rigor is not absolutely necessary also believe that strict experimental designs would force programs into an unnatural state. Programs should not be forced to conform to research standards. Rather, any research activity must attempt to measure the important variables of a program as they exist in the natural environment.[14] The reality that impinges on service delivery would be lost if forced to conform to rigorous controlled experimental standards. Therefore, any results from such research would be artificial and misleading.

It seems reasonable to expect that an accommodation is possible that will harness the good points of each argument. The substance of programs should be measured as rigorously as possible. Care must be taken, however, that the act of measurement does not drastically alter the shape and content of what is measured. There is no reason that program-evaluation methodology should be less than appropriately rigorous as long as the act of doing the evaluation does not interfere with service delivery as it is normally performed. Of course, the results of a useful evaluation would likely affect services at a later time, but the methodology itself should be as

---

13. Thomas D. Cook and Charles S. Reichardt, "Statistical Analysis of Non-Equivalent Control Group Designs: A Guide to Some Current Literature," *Evaluation* 3 (1976): 136–38.

14. Carol H. Weiss, *Evaluation Research* (Englewood Cliffs, N.J.: Prentice-Hall, 1972).

Counselors need to meet formally and informally to discuss their work and evaluate their effectiveness.

unobtrusive as possible. This is a difficult undertaking and to accomplish program evaluation properly, specialists should be consulted in the development of some of the components of evaluation research, particularly the measurement and design components.

Need to involve counselors in program evaluation

Even though consultants may be necessary at times, counselors should be intimately involved in program evaluation. Probably the most important reason is that most counselors, particularly those employed in public service programs, will experience an actual program evaluation. An understanding of the purposes of evaluation will greatly reduce the implied threat. Also, even if consultants are used, program evaluation requires that persons who are intimately familiar with a program be highly involved in planning. Consultants can only work with the content that is provided them. They may be experts in program evaluation, but they probably know little about counseling. Unless counselors can provide detailed descriptions of important program variables, consultants will not be able to develop an evaluation adequately. Counselors should be sure their input is carefully considered before any evaluation is begun. Counselors will be able to provide appropriate input if they understand the value of their expertise for program-evaluation planning.

Also, since program evaluation is another form of research, counselors should become involved to fulfill their research obligations. Counselors, as members of a profession, are expected to develop and contribute to a body of knowledge that withstands careful scrutiny. The public trust demands that counseling services be based on confirmed evidence of effectiveness. Counselors should be consumers of research by becoming familiar with relevant research literature as found in journals, texts, and conference presentations. They should also be participants in research itself by supporting program evaluation and other research activity within their own settings. Counseling research and program evaluation is being carried out in many communities, primarily through universities. The value of research would greatly increase, though, if more counseling practitioners would invite the participation of university researchers within their own counseling settings. Research and evaluation can become a rewarding experience when it is seen as an activity that creates knowledge that will have an impact directly on the lives of counselees. For counselors to know that their own contributions to research have this kind of impact is an important reward that can greatly contribute to their own personal satisfaction.

The purposes of program evaluation

As program evaluation has become more prevalent, more and more purposes for it have been discovered. Freeman has outlined several important reasons for developing program evaluation.[15] Others have contributed useful concepts. These are basically information gathering and are as follows:

Information-gathering purposes of program evaluation

1. To document the extent to which a program has achieved its stated goals and objectives. This has been described elsewhere as a means of determining the effectiveness of a program.[16]
2. To attribute any changes in the target population to the services of the program by ruling out any other possible explanations for the changes.
3. To determine the conditions under which a program is most efficient. This considers the costs of achieving the objectives of the program.
4. To document any other effects, positive or negative, that might result from a program. This has been described in another way as an attempt to measure what the overall impact of a program may be beyond even what a program has established as goals for itself.[17]

15. Howard E. Freeman, "The Present Status of Evaluation Research," in Guttentag, ed., *Evaluation Studies*, 2: Chapter 1.

16. Eleanor C. Bennett and Marvin Weisinger, *Program Evaluation: A Resource Handbook for Vocational Rehabilitation* (New York: ICD Rehabilitation and Research Center, 1974), p. 8.

17. Eleanor C. Bennett and Marvin Weisinger, *Program Evaluation,* p. 8.

Once information like this is available, many uses can be found for it. The most obvious, of course, is to decide whether or not a program is adequately meeting its objectives. Possibly, service patterns can be changed to deliver the most effective combination of services. Problems may exist with the adequacy of resources, and remedial steps could be taken to develop more resources or to allocate them more effectively.

Program-evaluation data could also indicate whether the intended target population of the program is really being served. If deficiencies in this area are uncovered, new and more appropriate referral sources may have to be developed.

A program's objectives may be achieved regularly, but the overall impact of a program might be negligible or even harmful. In such instances, a program may elect to revise its objectives, its target population, or even its services. In short, program evaluation can provide a counseling program with the means to be flexible and adapt to the changing needs of the persons it seeks to serve. This is particularly true if the evaluation component is an ongoing activity of the program and the means are available to implement the recommendations of the evaluation effort.

Role of accountability

A program needs to have the capability to adapt internally to what it perceives as its needs. Moreover, external demands are ever more frequently made of social-service programs to justify their continued existence. The demand upon programs for justification comes from the supporting agents of the program and, as was noted earlier in the book, is referred to as a demand for accountability. Accountability is usually required of programs that are funded, in whole or in part, by public funds. Private funding sources, such as endowment foundations, are also seeking accountability to a much greater extent than before. As competition for these funds mounts, more and more demands for accountability can be expected. For this reason alone, counseling programs should recognize the need for program evaluation.

Accountability questions primarily revolve around the effectiveness of a program. In this sense, the purposes of accountability evaluation are more limited than for ongoing program evaluations. Funds are expended for a program's support in order to achieve the goals of the funding agent. Therefore, accountability concerns have to attend to how well the funding agent's goals are being met.

For program evaluation to be most effective, the administrators of a program, along with other concerned groups such as staff and service consumers, must first delineate the questions that need to be answered. Regardless of whether the evaluation is to be a one-time event or an ongoing activity, it should not proceed until precise

Figure 13–1 The components of program evaluation

questions are formed. Of course, programs with ongoing evaluation components will have more information to use in forming such questions. If used in this manner, ongoing evaluations can greatly decrease costs by providing timely information for decision making.

The measurement components of program evaluation

Once the appropriate questions have been asked and a purpose has been defined, the next step of program evaluation requires a selection of the relevant variables to be measured. There are basically three categories that need to be considered. These are input, process, and outcome variables.

One of the major weaknesses of program-evaluation literature is its failure to attend to the problem of how to plan for a thorough program assessment. In part, this failure probably rests with the fact that systematic program evaluation is such a recent enterprise. There is not yet enough knowledge available that can be applied to the problem of how to know which are the most important variables to measure. Given that most counseling programs can only afford to expend limited resources on program evaluation, a trial-and-error approach to variable selection can be too costly.

Selection of variables in program-evaluation design

Fairweather made an effort to delineate the major types of variables that must be measured in order to collect the proper data for the assessment of social-service programs.[18] Although Fairweather did not call his variables inputs, processes, and outcomes, these terms are a reasonable approximation to the terms he used. Figure 13–1 describes the stages. As a program evaluation matures, more evidence is available to guide variable selection.

18. George W. Fairweather, *Methods for Experimental Social Innovation* (New York: Wiley, 1967).

Fairweather suggests that one class of important input variables is that associated with the program participants. This includes both staff and counselee characteristics. Counselees form the target population of counseling programs.

Fairweather has two other classifications of variables, which he calls social situation variables. These include internal and external process variables. Internal process variables are similar to what are usually referred to as process variables. These include the services offered and the activities through which services are delivered. Fairweather's external process variables may be linked to input variables. These variables refer to external inputs over which a program has little control, such as economic factors, new technology, and community support.

Finally, Fairweather describes a set of variables that he refers to as the socially desired outcomes for which a program exists. For example, rehabilitation programs usually exist to provide sufficient services to persons with impairments so that they can enter the labor force. Correctional programs attempt to help offenders learn to live in society in an essentially crime-free manner.

In Fairweather's scheme, participant and social situation variables would be selected and related to the degree to which the target population was achieving the socially desired outcome. This scheme is an appropriate and helpful beginning, but much more remains to be achieved in the selection of critical variables.

Other resources can be brought to bear on this problem. Counselors and representatives of the target population can identify the relevant variables to include because of their personal experience with the program. Another important source is the body of theoretical and research-oriented counseling literature. Many variables identified by past research could be important for a specific program-evaluation effort. An additional value of the theoretical and research literature is the potential for uncovering how variables were measured. Selection of variables is important, but actual measurement procedures also need to be planned. Every effort should be made to find existing instruments and methods that could be applied in the needed program evaluation. Previously used methods are useful. They have been field-tested, implying that a reasonable expectation exists that they will be useful again. Also, the psychometric properties of these methods may be better defined, giving the evaluation personnel a better understanding of the meaningfulness of the information. If previously existing instruments are not available, the evaluation will require newly developed ones.

Another resource that will aid the selection and measurement of relevant variables will be other evaluations done at other counseling settings. As time goes on, the counseling field will have a better understanding of which variables to measure and a better supply of instruments and methods with which to measure them. Until such supplies are available, much work will need to be done to develop instruments and methods for data collection. Program evaluation consultants can be useful in the preparation of the necessary instruments and techniques when none are readily available.

The evaluation design component of program evaluation

Once a clear understanding exists regarding the variables to be measured, the evaluation design can be planned. This design defines the procedures with which the data are to be collected. This design should be constructed to hold constant or account for the effects of extraneous variables, which will permit inferences to be drawn on the basis of the intended variables only.

Even though this is the intention of any research or evaluation design, it is virtually impossible to eliminate the effects of other variables that could explain some of the observed results of the program. Even though a design cannot achieve complete control of all variables, it is still helpful because it indicates which variables are controlled and offers ideas regarding which other variables are also having an effect. In this manner, subsequent designs can be developed to account for more variables, and gradually, evaluation designs may become available that will permit program evaluation to achieve the same rigor as experimental research. Chope and Reagles provide a checklist for the development of evaluation designs, which is particularly useful for persons not regularly involved with program evaluation.[19]

It will often be necessary to consider using a consultant to help with the evaluation design. There are technical considerations, particularly when the link must be made between design and analysis, that justify the use of specialists. Still, there is a basic process in the construction of an evaluation, or research design, with which counselors should be familiar.

Development of evaluation design

The first step is to determine from the list of selected variables which ones are to be independent variables and which are to be dependent variables. Independent variables are those factors that have an influence on the results of a program; dependent variables are those factors that occur as results of a program. In other words, the dependent variables, or program results, are defined as such

19. Robert C. Chope and Kenneth W. Reagles, "A Checklist for Planning and Evaluating Follow-Up Studies in Vocational Rehabilitation," *Rehabilitation Counseling Bulletin* 20 (1976): 97–104.

Size of Population	Percent of Population in Sample
1–10	Entire population
10–100	50–100 percent
100–250	25–50 percent
250–500	10–25 percent
500–1000	5–10 percent
1000–5000	2–5 percent
Over 5000	1–2 percent

Figure 13–2 Guidelines for sample sizes

because they depend on the independent variables. In the evaluation of counseling programs, independent variables would include the characteristics of the target population as it enters the program, program services and any combination of services, staff characteristics, and external events and processes. It is usually hoped that a program evaluation will reveal that the independent variables having the most beneficial effect are those that the program can control most successfully, namely, services and staff.

Selection of the sample

The second step in design is the selection of the sample from which measurements are to be taken. There are several important considerations here. The first is to decide how big a sample should be selected. If a program has relatively few counselees, all of them might be included. As the numbers of counselees increase, cost factors might have to determine how large the sample should be. Of course, it is preferable to have an entire population included, but samples from a population usually have to be drawn. It has been suggested that the guidelines in Figure 13–2 be used to determine preferable sample sizes, given the overall size of the population of counselees.[20]

A decision must also be made as to how the sample will be selected. A random procedure should be used. A table of random numbers or even a coin toss can be used to determine if any one counselee should be included or not. It might also be possible to divide the population of counselees into several groups on the basis of one or more distinguishing characteristics that are mutually exclusive. Counselees could be grouped according to referral source, age, or any other similar characteristic. Once such groupings are determined, the same type of random selection should be done. This type of stratified sampling can provide information regarding

20. Kathyrn B. Greever, Elizabeth S. Minton, and M. S. Tseng, *Follow-Up Study of Rehabilitation Clients: A Step-By-Step Guide* (Institute, W. Va.: West Virginia Research and Training Center, 1974): Appendix D, Part III.

how influential the characteristic is that was used to determine the stratification.

An excellent sampling technique that will rarely be available to counseling program evaluators is random selection of the target population prior to their entry into the program. Those not selected would not be given services and would be a control group. This would enable the evaluation to speak directly to the value of the program, since all variables except program participation would be randomly distributed, thus allowing program variables to be the major difference. For ethical considerations, this technique is often frowned upon. Strong feelings usually result when services are withheld from people on the basis of a random decision for program-evaluation purposes. To accommodate this problem, an attempt is sometimes made to identify a group of persons who closely resemble the target population but who would not actually be eligible or available to receive services. This provides for a portion of the control that could be achieved by random selection from the target population.

Another way to handle this problem is available when a program has a waiting list. If the list of eligible persons is large enough and no one objects, counselees can be admitted to the program on a random basis, allowing the remaining counselees to serve as a control group until there is room in the program for them. It would be necessary to take the same measurements of this group as for the ones already in the program for comparison purposes. Thus, their consent would have to be obtained.

Another step to consider is the possibility of assigning the sample to various conditions, such as two different service combinations. This would permit a comparison to be made of various service patterns. If random assignment can be made, then the inferences about the relative worth of the service patterns can be much stronger. Again, if the assignment is not random, than a question can be raised as to whether any observed effects are due to service patterns or other factors that dictated the actual assignments. This indicates how important sampling considerations are in providing important controls of variables. The more control that is achieved, the better chance that the information gained from evaluation will be based on the essential factors that are operating within the program.

The final design consideration is with how the data are to be collected. When variables were being selected, attention was also given to how the measurements could be taken. During the design phase, decisions must be made as to how the data will be collected. An important factor here is the available resources, both in staff and funds, that can be used.

Methods of data gathering

There are many ways data can be gathered. A primary consideration should be given to the records routinely kept by the counseling setting. Counseling-rating scales, work-adjustment scales, counseling progress notes, occupational status of program graduates, and other important items may all be part of the file records. These should be included in the design whenever possible.

New measurement methods might be introduced. If so, these should complement service delivery and not burden it. If the instruments chosen are paper-and-pencil tests, attention should be given to the psychometric qualities of the tests, primarily reliability and validity qualities. Reliability is concerned with how stable and consistent the measurements of the instruments are. Validity is an indication of how well the instrument actually measures what it purports to measure. If an instrument is developed especially for the evaluation at hand, efforts should be made to explore these psychometric qualities. Cost considerations could preclude this, though.

Another type of measurement method that should be considered are behaviorally based measures. Since most counseling programs have as an objective the hope that their counselees will behave differently as a result of their program experiences, these measures have the potential for being valid indicators. Even behavioral measures, though, should have evidence to support their reliability and validity. Examples of behavior-based indicators are grades, production rates, wages, number of new friends, and weight lost or gained. Although these are not direct measures of behavior, they permit strong inference regarding any behavior that might produce a change.

Questionnaires and interviews are often used in program evaluations. Cost and efficiency considerations must be taken into account when deciding to use questionnaires and interviews.[21] Mailed questionnaires are much cheaper than interviews, but there is little control over whether or not they are returned. Also, the respondent might choose to answer in a way that is less than genuine, or there may be a misunderstanding of what was asked in the questionnaire. There is also the question of how to interpret nonresponses. Those who do not return the questionnaires may differ radically from those who do, yet there is no way of knowing this. At any rate, caution must be taken in making judgments from the information gained from questionnaires.

Interviews remove many of these problems. The cost becomes much greater, however, since more staff time is needed to collect

21. J. A. Bitter, J. T. Kunce, D. L. Lawyer, D. E. Miller, and C. C. Ray, "Follow-Up: A Methodological Note," *Rehabilitation Counseling Bulletin* 16 (1972): 64–70.

the same amount of information. Telephone interviews seem to be a good compromise that deserves more use.

These design considerations are only examples of some of the important factors involved. The development of a design must be done thoroughly and carefully. Decisions that can affect the structure and perhaps the existence of a program can be expected on the basis of evaluation results. The design component dictates the quality of the information to be analyzed and must not be taken lightly.

Need to involve all program consumers

Counselors should be certain in any evaluation effort that all the important consumers of a program are considered in the data-collection design. Consumers of counseling services, of course, include counselees. Program graduates, as well as those still receiving services, should be contacted. Staff should also be allowed to provide input. Significant others, such as family members, teachers, or employers of counselees, could also be approached. If this is done, it should be with the knowledge and consent of the counselees. Also, funding sources might be contacted to see what their impressions of the program are. If feasible, the local community in which the program resides might also be given the opportunity to provide input. Local residents may perceive the impact a program is having on the community-at-large. This might be particularly important when the program is a controversial one, such as a residential rehabilitation center for criminal offenders. All of these groups can provide valuable information.

The analysis component

The analysis of the data should depend on the type of design. The selection of the sample, its size, and whether or not there was any assignment of the sample to different conditions will all affect the type of analysis that is most appropriate. The data can be simply tallied, or it can be run through a computer. Sophisticated analyses should be reserved for sophisticated designs, such as a comprehensive cost-benefits study. Tallies might be useful for case study or participant-observation methods.[22] Again, caution must be taken that the analysis component does not serve as a substitute for proper evaluation design.

The reporting component of evaluation design

A program evaluation, no matter how good, is worthless unless the information it uncovers is adequately communicated. The evaluation report is linked directly to the purpose of the evaluation.

22. Edward M. Glaser and Thomas E. Backer, "A Look At Participant Observation," *Evaluation I* (1973): 46–49.

The initial questions posed must be addressed. And, of course, the report must be communicated to those persons who initiated the request for the evaluation. In many instances, the report will be directed to program administrators. In addition, thought should be given to other persons or groups of persons who might also have use of the information. Consumer groups, as well as community members, would be interested in the information. Sharing this with them indicates that the program is sensitive to the concept that service providers as well as consumers are to be linked in the effort to develop a quality program.

Uses of program evaluations

Often, program evaluations will be requested by external authorities, such as government funding or regulatory agencies. The evaluation report will, of course, be directed toward them, but thought should be given to determine if, for political reasons, other governmental or private agencies might also be interested in the performance of the program. New funding sources might be uncovered in this way. Recent evaluation literature strongly emphasizes that political use be made of evaluation findings. It is recommended that attempts be made to influence important decision makers.[23]

The evaluation results could also be used to develop new referral sources. An effective program might be able to enlarge its target population, and thereby, increase its impact on the community.

It might be important to consider how the results of the evaluation are to be communicated. Different forms might be explored for various groups. The format for reporting should be the one that has the most potential for fulfilling the purpose of the evaluation. Written reports and follow-up contact may be sufficient for external authority agents. Demonstrations and testimonies might be more suitable for consumer groups and potential referral sources. When the evaluation is intended to develop internal program change, mechanisms should be established between evaluators, administrators, and staff in order to ensure that the evaluation report will do more than merely collect dust on a shelf.

In order to promote the use of evaluation findings, the appropriate target audience will have to be identified. Evaluation results should be reported to these individuals in a way that will meet their needs and therefore, be reenforcing to them. There is a built-in temptation for evaluators to report results with certain biases—either their own or what they perceive to be those of the target audience. This is not what is meant by reporting results that will be reenforcing to the user. All results must be reported without alteration. It is appropriate, however, to address different audiences differently. For example,

23. Carol H. Weiss, "Where Politics and Evaluation Meet," *Evaluation I* (1973): 37–45.

consumers may be most interested in certain kinds of information such as the program's accessibility to public transportation. These data may be of secondary interest to program administrators who are more concerned about cost data.

Evaluators have a responsibility to disseminate their findings to all interested parties. Program personnel should encourage and support the efforts of evaluators to do this. It is justifiable to write or disseminate evaluation findings that permit interested persons to recognize and understand those results that are most pertinent to them. This requires that the evaluator, as well as other evaluation users, identify all groups who might be influenced by the program and the evaluation results and include them in the evaluation process.

Counselor participation in research and program evaluation

There are different levels of research activity on which counselors can choose to involve themselves. Some are quite passive, while others involve a lot of activity. On a very basic level, counselors can review the research literature available in such journals as *The Counseling Psychologist, Personnel and Guidance Journal,* and *The Journal of Counseling Psychology*. Other journals, published by the various divisions of the American Personnel and Guidance Association, are more specific in terms of interest area and serve the needs of counselors who work with special populations and special settings.

Counselors can participate in research by cooperating with researchers who want to do research in their work settings and with their counselees. Counselors can contribute to the development of new knowledge by being open to the requests of researchers, something they have not always done. Counselors are often quite busy with necessary work tasks and see research as an intrusion. Then, too, many researchers come from academic settings, which is a stigma as far as practicing counselors are concerned. To busy counselors, university-based researchers seem nonreality oriented and unable to perceive the real needs of people in the field. Researchers, in turn, respond with the attitude that counselors have no appreciation of a theoretical and systematic approach to guide their activities. and instead, operate on a trial-and-error, seat-of-the-pants approach. This description may be somewhat exaggerated, but contention between field counselors and researchers exists and continues to be a problem. This is unfortunate because both groups share a common goal of wanting to know more about how counseling can be made more effective. Researchers can help counselors see the value of having a framework that can provide structure to various counseling processes, and field counselors can help researchers understand how research methods can be adapted to fit within the realities of program structures and processes. Field counselors can also help define the areas that require research attention.

Counselors' obligations

When collaborating with researchers, counselors have an obligation to be certain that their own rights and safety as well as those of counselees are carefully protected. Appendix 1 describes ethical principles that counselors can use to evaluate the appropriateness of research activities.

Counselors also can strive to become researchers and program evaluators on their own. The combination of research and counseling functions is natural. Research and evaluation techniques are not all so sophisticated as to prohibit counselors from conducting their own studies. Intensive, single-subject research designs, developed to improve the usefulness of information gained from case studies, appear useful in program evaluation as well. These designs seem accessible to field counselors. Other research and evaluation methods, although more complicated, do not necessarily require a high level of expertise. Usually, university faculty and students would welcome the opportunity to collaborate, particularly if publication of the results might be possible. A university staff could be an excellent resource for field-based counselors who want to do their own research.

A final way for counselors to participate in research and evaluation is to use the findings of research in their work. There are many forms of research utilization. Certainly, reading research articles is one form. Demonstration programs, seminars, and training programs for counselors show counselors how to use new information, Funding agencies often publish research monographs and articles that mostly collect dust on shelves when they could be used by field counselors. Counselors should make serious attempts to stay up-to-date on research.

Summary

This chapter contains an overview on research and program evaluation. Program evaluation is becoming increasingly more important for a variety of reasons. In the future, counseling programs will be more involved in evaluation efforts. It is important that counselors understand program evaluation and use it to their own advantage, as well as for their counselees' advantage. This chapter presented a general overview of the components of an evaluation model. The evaluation field is a new one, and new developments in method and technology will rapidly occur within it. For this reason, counselors should not feel compelled to plan program evaluation efforts without the benefit of a consultant who specializes in evaluation and research.

This implies evaluation activities are costly in time, as well as in funds. Neither cost should be minimized. Still, these costs can be viewed as investments that will bring returns in terms of better services for counselees and more professional standing for counselors. Evaluation is, therefore, an important activity that deserves investment. It should not be done haphazardly since decisions are likely to be made on the basis of evaluation results. The information used to make these decisions should be valid and credible. To accomplish this, some costs of necessity will be incurred. As stated, counselors should equip themselves with as much capability in evaluation as possible, and participate in evaluation whenever possible. Perhaps they might also consider initiating formal evaluation where none exists within their own programs. The field of counseling is recognizing the value of evaluation as a task equal to any other in counseling practice.[24] Since many counselors cannot be expected to plan and implement evaluations due to lack of training and experience, the use of consultants should be considered until such expertise can be obtained by staff personnel. In order to defray costs, it has also been suggested that where counselors lack expertise or funds, university faculty and counseling students might be a ready and inexpensive resource.[25] The energy, expertise, and need for research and publication activity of university personnel make them likely participants in program evaluation.

The general model, presented in this chapter to familiarize counselors with program evaluation, consists of the following components:

1. Determine purpose of evaluation.
2. Select relevant input variables.
3. Select relevant process variables.
4. Select relevant outcome variables.
5. Design evaluation, including sample selection, sample assignment, and measurement methodology.
6. Analyze data.
7. Report results of evaluation.

24. H. R. Bardo, J. J. Cody, and S. L. Bryson, "Evaluation of Guidance Programs: Call the Question," *Personnel and Guidance Journal* 57 (1978): 204–8.

25. Bardo, Cody, and Bryson, "Evaluation of Guidance Programs," p. 206.

Program evaluation in counseling settings can be expected to evolve into various formats and models. Evaluation technology will be improved in coming years. Counselors should keep abreast of developments in this area, and as professionals, support and promote program evaluation in counseling.

Special emphasis has been given to the value of research and evaluation activities to the field of counseling and to the ways that counselors might become more active in research and evaluation. It is to be hoped that the future will result in more emphasis being placed on research and evaluation as important functions of field counselors. A good beginning would be for more attention to be given to research and evaluation in counselor preparation and training programs. Eventually, counselors can become increasingly independent in the performance of their research and evaluation responsibilities.

Questions

1. What is the difference between research and evaluation?

2. What are some of the misgivings counselors have about researchers and evaluators? Are these well-founded? Give reasons for your answers.

3. What are some ways that field counselors can cooperate or even initiate research projects?

4. Describe the ways that research can be of value to counselors.

5. Describe the ways that evaluation can be of value to counselors.

6. Describe the various kinds of methodological classification of research. Is any one method superior to or exclusive of another?

7. Describe the goals or objectives of program evaluation.

8. What are some resources that can be drawn upon to aid in the selection of variables for a program evaluation?

Projects

1. Write a report on the evaluation needs of a program that you have observed for several weeks or longer.

2. Collect as many examples as possible of evaluation materials for educational and noneducational counseling settings. Review these and report to the class on their value and the ways in which they might be improved.

3. Invite a panel of counselors to discuss their attitudes about evaluation.

4. Invite a research expert to discuss the possibilities for combining field counseling and research.

Appendices

Appendix A Ethical standards

From Guidepost, *American Personnel and Guidance Association, vol. 17 (Extra), July 4, 1974, pp. 4–5.*

Preamble

The American Personnel and Guidance Association is an educational, scientific, and professional organization whose members are dedicated to the enhancement of the worth, dignity, potential, and uniqueness of each individual and thus to the service of society.

The Association recognizes that the role definitions and work settings of its members include a wide variety of academic disciplines, levels of academic preparation, and agency services. This diversity reflects the breadth of the Association's interest and influence. It also poses challenging complexities in efforts to set standards for the performance of members, desired requisite preparation or practice, and supporting social, legal, and ethical controls.

The specification of ethical standards enables the Association to clarify to present and future members and to those served by members the nature of ethical responsibilities held in common by its members.

The existence of such standards serves to stimulate greater concern by members for their own professional functioning and for the conduct of fellow professionals such as counselors, guidance and student personnel workers, and others in the helping professions. As the ethical code of the Association, this document establishes principles which define the ethical behavior of Association members.

Section A: General

1. The member influences the development of the profession by continuous efforts to improve professional practices, teaching, services, and research. Professional growth is continuous throughout the member's career and is exemplified by the development of a philosophy that explains why and how a member functions in the helping relationship. Members are expected to gather data on their effectiveness and to be guided by the findings.

2. The member has a responsibility both to the individual who is served and to the institution within which the service is performed. The acceptance of employment in an institution implies that the member is in substantial agreement with the general policies and principles of the institution. Therefore the professional activities of the member are also in accord with the objectives of the institution.

If, despite concerted efforts, the member cannot reach agreement with the employer as to acceptable standards of conduct that allow for changes in institutional policy conducive to the positive growth and development of counselees, then terminating the affiliation should be seriously considered.

3. Ethical behavior among professional associates, members and nonmembers, is expected at all times. When information is possessed which raises serious doubt as to the ethical behavior of professional colleagues, whether Association members or not, the member is obligated to take action to attempt to rectify such a condition. Such action shall utilize the institution's channels first and then utilize procedures established by the state, division, or Association.

The member can take action in a variety of ways: conferring with the individual in question, gathering further information as to the allegation, conferring with local or national ethics committees, and so forth.

4. The member must not seek self-enhancement through expressing evaluations or comparisons that are damaging to others.

5. The member neither claims nor implies professional qualifications exceeding those possessed and is responsible for correcting any misrepresentations of these qualifications by others.

6. In establishing fees for professional services, members should take into consideration the fees charged by other professions delivering comparable services, as well as the ability of the counselee to pay. Members are willing to provide some services for which they receive little or no financial remuneration, or remuneration in food, lodging, and materials. When fees include charges for items other than professional services, that portion of the total which is for the professional services should be clearly indicated.

7. When members provide information to the public or to subordinates, peers, or supervisors, they have a clear responsibility to ensure that the content is accurate, unbiased, and consists of objective, factual data.

8. The member shall make a careful distinction between the offering of counseling services as opposed to public information services. Counseling may be offered only in the context of a reciprocal or face-to-face relationship. Information services may be offered through the media.

9. With regard to professional employment, members are expected to accept only positions that they are prepared to assume and then to comply with established practices of the particular type of employment setting in which they are employed in order to ensure the continuity of services.

Section B: Counselor-counselee relationship

This section refers to practices involving individual and/or group counseling relationships, and it is not intended to be applicable to practices involving administrative relationships.

To the extent that the counselee's choice of action is not imminently self- or other-destructive, the counselee must retain freedom of choice. When the counselee does not have full autonomy for reasons of age, mental incompetency, criminal incarceration, or similar legal restrictions, the member may have to work with others who exercise significant control and direction over the counselee. Under these circumstances the member must apprise counselees of restrictions that may limit their freedom of choice.

1. The member's *primary* obligation is to respect the integrity and promote the welfare of the counselee(s), whether the counselee(s) is (are) assisted individually or in a group relationship. In a group setting, the member-leader is also responsible for protecting individuals from physical and/or psychological trauma resulting from interaction within the group.
2. The counseling relationship and information resulting therefrom must be kept confidential, consistent with the obligations of the member as a professional person. In a group counseling setting the member is expected to set a norm of confidentiality regarding all group participants' disclosures.
3. If an individual is already in a counseling/therapy relationship with another professional person, the member does not begin a counseling relationship without first contacting and receiving the approval of that other professional. If the member discovers that the counselee is in another counseling/therapy relationship after the counseling relationship begins, the member is obligated to gain the consent of the other professional or terminate the relationship, unless the counselee elects to terminate the other relationship.
4. When the counselee's condition indicates that there is clear and imminent danger to the counselee or others, the member is expected to take direct personal action or to inform responsible authorities. Consultation with other professionals should be utilized where possible. Direct interventions, especially the assumption of responsibility for the counselee, should be taken only after careful deliberation. The counselee should be involved in the resumption of responsibility for his actions as quickly as possible.
5. Records of the counseling relationship including interview notes, test data, correspondence, tape recordings, and other documents are to be considered professional information for use in counseling, and they are not part of the public or official records of the institution or agency in which the counselor is employed. Revela-

tion to others of counseling material should occur only upon the express consent of the counselee.

6. Use of data derived from a counseling relationship for purposes of counselor training or research shall be confined to content that can be sufficiently disguised to ensure full protection of the identity of the counselee involved.

7. Counselees shall be informed of the conditions under which they may receive counseling assistance at or before the time when the counseling relationship is entered. This is particularly so when conditions exist of which the counselee would be unaware. In individual and group situations, particularly those oriented to self-understanding or growth, the member-leader is obligated to make clear the purposes, goals, techniques, rules of procedure, and limitations that may affect the continuance of the relationship.

8. The member has the responsibility to screen prospective group participants, especially when the emphasis is on self-understanding and growth through self-disclosure. The member should maintain an awareness of the group participants' compatibility throughout the life of the group.

9. The member reserves the right to consult with any other professionally competent person about a counselee. In choosing a consultant, the member avoids placing the consultant in a conflict of interest situation that would preclude the consultant's being a proper party to the member's efforts to help the counselee.

10. If the member is unable to be of professional assistance to the counselee, the member avoids initiating the counseling relationship or the member terminates it. In either event, the member is obligated to refer the counselee to an appropriate specialist. (It is incumbent upon the member to be knowledgable about referral resources so that a satisfactory referral can be initiated.) In the event the counselee declines the suggested referral, the member is not obligated to continue the relationship.

11. When the member learns from counseling relationships of conditions that are likely to harm others, the member should report *the condition* to the responsible authority. This should be done in such a manner as to conceal the identity of the counselee.

12. When the member has other relationships, particularly of an administrative, supervisory, and/or evaluative nature, with an individual seeking counseling services, the member should not serve as the counselor but should refer the individual to another professional. Only in instances where such an alternative is unavailable and where the individual's condition definitely warrants counseling intervention should the member enter into and/or maintain a counseling relationship.

13. All experimental methods of treatment must be clearly indi-

cated to prospective recipients, and safety precautions are to be adhered to by the member.

14. When the member is engaged in short-term group treatment/training programs, e.g., marathons and other encounter-type or growth groups, the member ensures that there is professional assistance available during and following the group experience.

15. Should the member be engaged in a work setting that calls for any variation from the above statements, the member is obligated to consult with other professionals whenever possible to consider justifiable alternatives. The variations that may be necessary should be clearly communicated to other professionals and prospective counselees.

Section C: Measurement and evaluation

The primary purpose of educational and psychological testing is to provide descriptive measures that are objective and interpretable in either comparative or absolute terms. The member must recognize the need to interpret the statements that follow as applying to the whole range of appraisal techniques including test and nontest data. Test results constitute only one of a variety of pertinent sources of information for personnel, guidance, and counseling decisions.

1. It is the member's responsibility to provide adequate orientation or information to the examinee(s) prior to and following the test administration so that the results of testing may be placed in proper perspective with other relevant factors. In so doing, the member must recognize the effects of socioeconomic, ethnic, and cultural factors on test scores. It is the member's professional responsibility to use additional unvalidated information cautiously in modifying interpretation of the test results.
2. In selecting tests for use in a given situation or with a particular counselee, the member must consider carefully the specific validity, reliability, and appropriateness of the test(s). "General" validity, reliability, and the like may be questioned legally as well as ethically when tests are used for vocational and educational selection, placement, or counseling.
3. When making any statements to the public about tests and testing, the member is expected to give accurate information and to avoid false claims or misconceptions. Special efforts are often required to avoid unwarranted connotations of such terms as IQ and grade equivalent scores.
4. Different tests demand different levels of competence for administration, scoring, and interpretation. Members have a responsi-

bility to recognize the limits of their competence and to perform only those functions for which they are prepared.

5. Tests should be administered under the same conditions that were established in their standardization. When tests are not administered under standard conditions or when unusual behavior or irregularities occur during the testing session, those conditions should be noted and the results designated as invalid or of questionable validity. Unsupervised or inadequately supervised test-taking, such as the use of tests through the mails, is considered unethical. On the other hand, the use of instruments that are so designed or standardized to be self-administered and self-scored, such as interest inventories, is to be encouraged.

6. The meaningfulness of test results used in personnel, guidance, and counseling functions generally depends on the examinee's unfamiliarity with the specific items on the test. Any prior coaching or dissemination of the test materials can invalidate test results. Therefore, test security is one of the professional obligations of the member. Conditions that produce most favorable test results should be made known to the examinee.

7. The purpose of testing and the explicit use of the results should be made known to the examinee prior to testing. The counselor has a responsibility to ensure that instrument limitations are not exceeded and that periodic review and/or retesting are made to prevent counselee stereotyping.

8. The examinee's welfare and explicit prior understanding should be the criteria for determining the recipients of the test results. The member is obligated to see that adequate interpretation accompanies any release of individual or group test data. The interpretation of test data should be related to the examinee's particular concerns.

9. The member is expected to be cautious when interpreting the results of research instruments possessing insufficient technical data. The specific purposes for the use of such instruments must be stated explicitly to examinees.

10. The member must proceed with extreme caution when attempting to evaluate and interpret the performance of minority group members or other persons who are not represented in the norm group on which the instrument was standardized.

11. The member is obligated to guard against the appropriation, reproduction, or modifications of published tests or parts thereof without the express permission and adequate recognition of the original author or publisher.

12. Regarding the preparation, publication, and distribution of tests, reference should be made to:

a. *Standards for Educational and Psychological Tests and Man-*

uals, revised edition, 1973; published by the American Psychological Association on behalf of itself, the American Educational Research Association, and the National Council on Measurement in Education.

b. "The Responsible Use of Tests: A Position Paper of AMEG, APGA, and NCME," published in *Measurement and Evaluation in Guidance*, Vol. 5, No. 2, July 1972, pp. 385–388.

Section D: Research and publication

1. Current American Psychological Association guidelines on research with human subjects shall be adhered to (*Ethical Principles in the Conduct of Research with Human Participants.* Washington, D.C.: American Psychological Association, Inc., 1973).
2. In planning any research activity dealing with human subjects, the member is expected to be aware of and responsive to all pertinent ethical principles and to ensure that the research problem, design, and execution are in full compliance with them.
3. Responsibility for ethical research practice lies with the principal researcher, while others involved in the research activities share ethical obligation and full responsibility for their own actions.
4. In research with human subjects, researchers are responsible for their subjects' welfare throughout the experiment, and they must take all reasonable precautions to avoid causing injurious psychological, physical, or social effects on their subjects.
5. It is expected that all research subjects be informed of the purpose of the study except when withholding information or providing misinformation to them is essential to the investigation. In such research, the member is responsible for corrective action as soon as possible following the research.
6. Participation in research is expected to be voluntary. Involuntary participation is appropriate only when it can be demonstrated that participation will have no harmful effects on subjects.
7. When reporting research results, explicit mention must be made of all variables and conditions known to the investigator that might affect the outcome of the investigation or the interpretation of the data.
8. The member is responsible for conducting and reporting investigations in a manner that minimizes the possibility that results will be misleading.
9. The member has an obligation to make available sufficient original research data to qualified others who may wish to replicate the study.
10. When supplying data, aiding in the research of another person, reporting research of another person, reporting research re-

sults, or in making original data available, due care must be taken to disguise the identity of the subjects in the absence of specific authorization from such subjects to do otherwise.

11. When conducting and reporting research, the member is expected to be familiar with and to give recognition to previous work on the topic, as well as to observe all copyright laws and follow the principle of giving full credit to all to whom credit is due.

12. The member has the obligation to give due credit through joint authorship, acknowledgement, footnote statements, or other appropriate means to those who have contributed significantly to the research, in accordance with such contributions.

13. The member is expected to communicate to other members the results of any research judged to be of professional or scientific value. Results reflecting unfavorably on institutions, programs, services, or vested interests should not be withheld for such reasons.

14. If members agree to cooperate with another individual in research and/or publication, they incur an obligation to cooperate as promised in terms of punctuality of performance and with full regard to the completeness and accuracy of the information provided.

Section E: Consulting and private practice

Consulting refers to a voluntary relationship between a professional helper and help-needing social unit (industry, business, school, college, etc.) in which the consultant is attempting to give help to the client in the solution of some current or potential problem. When "client" is used in this section it refers to an individual, group, or organization served by the consultant. (This definition of "consulting" is adapted from "Dimensions of the Consultant's Job" by Ronald Lippitt, *Journal of Social Issues,* Vol. 15, No. 2, 1959.)

1. Members who act as consultants must have a high degree of self-awareness of their own values and needs in entering helping relationships that involve change in social units.

2. There should be understanding and agreement between consultant and client as to the task, the directions or goals, and the function of the consultant.

3. Members are expected to accept only those consulting roles for which they possess or have access to the necessary skills and resources for giving the kind of help that is needed.

4. The consulting relationship is defined as being one in which the client's adaptability and growth toward self-direction are encouraged and cultivated. For this reason, the consultant is obligated to maintain consistently the role of a consultant and to avoid becoming a decision maker for the client.

5. In announcing one's availability for professional services as a consultant, the member follows professional rather than commercial standards in describing services with accuracy, dignity, and caution.

6. For private practice in testing, counseling, or consulting, all ethical principles defined in this document are pertinent. In addition, any individual, agency, or institution offering educational, personal, or vocational counseling should meet the standards of the International Association of Counseling Services, Inc.

7. The member is expected to refuse a private fee or other remuneration for consultation with persons who are entitled to these services through the member's employing institution or agency. The policies of a particular agency may make explicit provisions for private practice with agency counselees by members of its staff. In such instances, the counselees must be apprised of other options open to them should they seek private counseling services.

8. It is unethical to use one's institutional affiliation to recruit counselees for one's private practice.

Section F: Personnel administration

It is recognized that most members are employed in public or quasi-public institutions. The functioning of a member within an institution must contribute to the goals of the institution and vice versa if either is to accomplish their respective goals or objectives. It is therefore essential that the member and the institution function in ways to: (a) make the institution's goals explicit and public; (b) make the member's contribution to institutional goals specific; and (c) foster mutual accountability for goal achievement.

To accomplish these objectives it is recognized that the member and the employer must share responsibilities in the formulation and implementation of personnel policies.

1. Members should define and describe the parameters and levels of their professional competency.

2. Members should establish interpersonal relations and working agreements with supervisors and subordinates regarding counseling or clinical relationships, confidentiality, distinction between public and private material, maintenance and dissemination of recorded information, work load, and accountability. Working agreements in each instance should be specified and made known to those concerned.

3. Members are responsible for alerting their employers to conditions that may be potentially disruptive or damaging.

4. Members are responsible for informing employers of conditions that may limit their effectiveness.

5. Members are expected to submit regularly to review and evaluation.

6. Members are responsible for in-service development of self and/or staff.

7. Members are responsible for informing their staff of goals and programs.

8. Members are responsible for providing personnel practices that guarantee and enhance the rights and welfare of each recipient of their service.

9. Members are expected to select competent persons and assign responsibilities compatible with their skills and experiences.

Section G: Preparation standards

Members who are responsible for training others should be guided by the preparation standards of the Association and relevant division(s). The member who functions in the capacity of trainer assumes unique ethical responsibilities that frequently go beyond that of the member who does not function in a training capacity. These ethical responsibilities are outlined as follows:

1. Members are expected to orient trainees to program expectations, basic skills development, and employment prospects prior to admission to the program.

2. Members in charge of training are expected to establish programs that integrate academic study and supervised practice.

3. Members are expected to establish a program directed toward developing the trainees' skills, knowledge, and self-understanding, stated whenever possible in competency or performance terms.

4. Members are expected to identify the level of competency of their trainees. These levels of competency should accommodate the paraprofessional as well as the professional.

5. Members, through continual trainee evaluation and appraisal, are expected to be aware of the personal limitations of the trainee that might impede future performance. The trainer has the responsibility of not only assisting the trainee in securing remedial assistance, but also screening from the program those trainees who are unable to provide competent services.

6. Members are expected to provide a program that includes training in research commensurate with levels of role functioning. Paraprofessional and technician-level personnel should be trained as consumers of research. In addition, these personnel should learn how to evaluate their own and their program effectiveness. Advanced graduate training, especially at the doctoral level, should include preparation for original research by the member.

7. Members are expected to make trainees aware of the ethical responsibilities and standards of the profession.

8. Training programs are expected to encourage trainees to value the ideals of service to individuals and to society. In this regard, direct financial remuneration or lack thereof should not influence the quality of service rendered. Monetary considerations should not be allowed to overshadow professional and humanitarian needs.

9. Members responsible for training are expected to be skilled as teachers and practitioners.

10. Members are expected to present thoroughly varied theoretical positions so that trainees may make comparisons and have the opportunity to select a position.

11. Members are obligated to develop clear policies within their training institution regarding field placement and the roles of the trainee and the trainer in such placements.

12. Members are expected to ensure that forms of training focusing on self-understanding or growth are voluntary, or if required as part of the training program, are made known to prospective trainees prior to entering the program. When the training program offers a growth experience with an emphasis on self-disclosure or other relatively intimate or personal involvement, the member should have no administrative, supervisory, or evaluative authority regarding the participant.

13. Members are obligated to conduct a training program in keeping with the most current guidelines of the American Personnel and Guidance Association and its various divisions.

Appendix B Ethical standards of psychologists (1977 Revision)

Climaxing nine years of work by several task forces and the Committee on Scientific and Professional Ethics and Conduct (CSPEC), draft #11 of the Ethical Standards of Psychologists went to the Council of Representatives at its January 28–30, 1977 meeting. A number of changes were made in the document by Council, resulting in draft #12, which was adopted on January 30th as printed below.

Because the Council could not agree on several sections of Principle 5 (Confidentiality), the final action was to approve the final revised draft with the exception of this principle. The old principle (formerly Principle 6 in the Ethical Standards as printed in the 1975 *Biographical Directory*) will hold until a revision has been adopted by Council.

Council commitments and suggestions applicable to this section are now being solicited by CSPEC. Council also directed the Committee to take into account the forthcoming report of the Task Force on Privacy and Confidentiality, as well as upcoming federal regulations covering similar matters. APA members having specific wording changes to suggest may send them to Brenda Gurel, Secretary CSPEC, APA, 1200 Seventeenth Street, N.W., Washington, D.C. 20036.

Preamble

Psychologists[1,2] respect the dignity and worth of the individual and honor the preservation and protection of fundamental human rights. They are committed to increasing knowledge of human behavior and of people's understanding of themselves and others and to the utilization of such knowledge for the promotion of human welfare. While pursuing these endeavors, they make every effort to protect the welfare of those who seek their services or of any human being or animal that may be the object of study. They use their skills only for purposes consistent with these values and do not knowingly permit their misuse by others. While demanding for themselves free-

1. Approved by the Council of Representatives, January 30, 1977. Reprinted from the APA "Monitor," March 1977.

2. A student of psychology who assumes the role of a psychologist shall be considered a psychologist for the purpose of this code of ethics.

dom of inquiry and communication, psychologists accept the responsibility this freedom requires: competence, objectivity in the application of skills and concern for the best interests of clients, colleagues, and society in general. In the pursuit of these ideals, psychologists subscribe to principles in the following areas: 1. Responsibility, 2. Competence, 3. Moral and Legal Standards, 4. Public Statements, 5. Confidentiality, 6. Welfare of the Consumer, 7. Professional Relationships, 8. Utilization of Assessment Techniques, and 9. Pursuit of Research Activities.

Principle 1:
Responsibility

In their commitment to the understanding of human behavior, psychologists value objectivity and integrity, and in providing services they maintain the highest standards of their profession. They accept responsibility for the consequences of their work and make every effort to insure that their services are used appropriately.

a. As scientists, psychologists accept the ultimate responsibility for selecting appropriate areas and methods most relevant to these areas. They plan their research in ways to minimize the possibility that their findings will be misleading. They provide thorough discussion of the limitations of their data and alternative hypotheses, especially where their work touches on social policy or might be construed to the detriment of persons in specific age, sex, ethnic, socioeconomic or other social groups. In publishing reports of their work, they never suppress disconfirming data. Psychologists take credit only for the work they have actually done.

Psychologists clarify in advance with all appropriate persons or agencies the expectations for sharing and utilizing research data. They avoid dual relationships which may limit objectivity, whether political or monetary, so that interference with data, human participants, and milieu is kept to a minimum.

b. As employees of an institution or agency, psychologists have the responsibility of remaining alert to and attempting to moderate institutional pressures that may distort reports of psychological findings or impede their proper use.

c. As members of governmental or other organizational bodies, psychologists remain accountable as individuals to the highest standards of their profession.

d. As teachers, psychologists recognize their primary obligation to help others acquire knowledge and skill. They maintain high standards of scholarship and objectivity by presenting psychological information fully and accurately.

e. As practitioners, psychologists know that they bear a heavy social responsibility because their recommendations and professional actions may alter the lives of others. They are alert to personal, social, organizational, financial, or political situations or pressures that might lead to misuse of their influence.

f. Psychologists provide adequate and timely evaluations to employees, trainees, students, and others whose work they supervise.

Principle 2:
Competence

The maintenance of high standards of professional competence is a responsibility shared by all psychologists in the interest of the public and the profession as a whole. Psychologists recognize the boundaries of their competence and the limitations of their techniques and only provide services, use techniques, or offer opinions as professionals that meet recognized standards. Psychologists maintain knowledge of current scientific and professional information related to the services they render.

a. Psychologists accurately represent their competence, education, training and experience. Psychologists claim as evidence of professional qualifications only those degrees obtained from institutions acceptable under the Bylaws and Rules of Council of the American Psychological Association.

b. As teachers, psychologists perform their duties on the basis of careful preparation so that their instruction is accurate, current and scholarly.

c. Psychologists recognize the need for continuing education and are open to new procedures and changes in expectations and values over time. They recognize differences among people, such as those that may be associated with age, sex, socioeconomic, and ethnic backgrounds. Where relevant, they obtain training, experience, or counsel to assure competent service or research relating to such persons.

e. Psychologists recognize that their effectiveness depends in part upon their ability to maintain effective interpersonal relations, and that aberrations on their part may interfere with their abilities. They refrain from undertaking any activity in which their personal problems are likely to lead to inadequate professional services or harm to a client; or, if engaged in such activity when they become aware of their personal problems, they seek competent professional assistance to determine whether they should suspend, terminate or limit the scope of their professional and/or scientific activities.

Principle 3:
Moral and legal standards

Psychologists' moral, ethical and legal standards of behavior are a personal matter to the same degree as they are for any other citizen, except as these may compromise the fulfillment of their professional responsibilities, or reduce the trust in psychology or psychologists held by the general public. Regarding their own behavior, psychologists should be aware of the prevailing community standards and of the possible impact upon the quality of professional services provided by their conformity to or deviation from these standards. Psychologists are also aware of the possible impact of their public behavior upon the ability of colleagues to perform their professional duties.

a. Psychologists as teachers are aware of the diverse backgrounds of students and, when dealing with topics that may give offense, treat the material objectively and present it in a manner for which the student is prepared.

b. As employees, psychologists refuse to participate in practices inconsistent with legal, moral and ethical standards regarding the treatment of employees or of the public. For example, psychologists will not condone practices that are inhuman or that result in illegal or otherwise unjustifiable discrimination on the basis of race, age, sex, religion, or national origin in hiring, promotion, or training.

c. In providing psychological services, psychologists avoid any action that will violate or diminish the legal and civil rights of clients or of others who may be affected by their actions.

As practitioners, psychologists remain abreast of relevant federal, state, local, and agency regulations and Association standards of practice concerning the conduct of their practice. They are concerned with developing such legal and quasi-legal regulations as best serve the public interest and in changing such existing regulations as are not beneficial to the interests of the public and the profession.

d. As researchers, psychologists remain abreast of relevant federal and state regulations concerning the conduct of research with human participants or animals.

Principle 4:
Public statements

Public statements, announcements of services, and promotional activities of psychologists serve the purpose of providing sufficient information to aid the consumer public in making informed judgments and choices. Psychologists represent accurately and objec-

tively their professional qualifications, affiliations, and functions, as well as those of the institutions or organizations with which they or the statements may be associated. In public statements providing psychological information or professional opinions or providing information about the availability of psychological products and services, psychologists take full account of the limits and uncertainties of present psychological knowledge and techniques.

a. When announcing professional services, psychologists limit the information to: name, highest relevant academic degree conferred, date and type of certification or licensure, diplomate status, address, telephone number, office hours, and a brief listing of the type of psychological services offered. Such statements are descriptive of services provided but not evaluative as to their quality or uniqueness. They do not contain testimonials by quotation or by implication. They do not claim uniqueness of skills or methods unless determined by acceptable and public scientific evidence.

b. In announcing the availability of psychological services or products, psychologists do not display any affiliations with an organization in a manner that falsely implies the sponsorship or certification of that organization. In particular and for example, psychologists do not offer APA membership or fellowship as evidence of qualification. They do not name their employer or professional associations unless the services are in fact to be provided by or under the responsible, direct supervision and continuing control of such organizations or agencies.

c. Announcements of "personal growth groups" give a clear statement of purpose and the nature of the experiences to be provided. The education, training and experience of the psychologists are appropriately specified.

d. Psychologists associated with the development or promotion of psychological devices, books, or other products offered for commercial sale make every effort to insure that announcements and advertisements are presented in a professional, scientifically acceptable, and factually informative manner.

e. Psychologists do not participate for personal gain in commercial announcements recommending to the general public the purchase or use of any proprietary or single-source product or service.

f. Psychologists who interpret the science of psychology or the services of psychologists to the general public accept the obligation to present the material fairly and accurately, avoiding misrepresentation through sensationalism, exaggeration or superficiality. Psychologists are guided by the primary obligation to aid the public in forming their own informed judgments, opinions and choices.

g. As teachers, psychologists insure that statements in catalogs and course outlines are accurate and sufficient, particularly in terms of subject matter to be covered, bases for evaluating progress, and nature of course experiences. Announcements or brochures describing workshops, seminars, or other educational programs accurately represent intended audience and eligibility requirements, educational objectives, and nature of the material to be covered, as well as the education, training and experience of the psychologists presenting the programs, and any fees involved. Public announcements soliciting subjects for research, and in which clinical services or other professional services are offered as an inducement, make clear the nature of the services as well as the costs and other obligations to be accepted by the human participants of the research.

h. Psychologists accept the obligation to correct others who may represent the psychologist's professional qualifications or associations with products or services in a manner incompatible with these guidelines.

i. Psychological services for the purpose of diagnosis, treatment or personal advice are provided only in the context of a professional relationship, and are not given by means of public lectures or demonstrations, newspaper or magazine articles, radio or television programs, mail, or similar media.

Principle 5:
Confidentiality

Safeguarding information about an individual that has been obtained by the psychologist in the course of his teaching, practice, or investigation is a primary obligation of the psychologist. Such information is not communicated to others unless certain important conditions are not met.

a. Information received in confidence is revealed only after most careful deliberation and when there is clear and imminent danger to an individual or to society, and then only to appropriate professional workers or public authorities.

b. Information obtained in clinical or consulting relationships, or evaluative data concerning children, students, employees, and others are discussed only for professional purposes and only with persons clearly concerned with the case. Written and oral reports should present only data germane to the purposes of the evaluation and every effort should be made to avoid undue invasion of privacy.

c. Clinical and other materials are used in classroom teaching and writing only when the identity of the persons involved is adequately disguised.

d. The confidentiality of professional communications about individuals is maintained. Only when the originator and other persons involved give their express permission is a confidential professional communication shown to the individual concerned. The psychologist is responsible for informing the client of the limits of the confidentiality.

e. Only after explicit permission has been granted is the identity of research subjects published. When data have been published without permission for identification, the psychologist assumes responsibility for adequately disguising their sources.

f. The psychologist makes provisions for the maintenance of confidentiality in the prevention and ultimate disposition of confidential records.

Principle 6:
Welfare of the consumer

Psychologists respect the integrity and protect the welfare of the people and groups with whom they work. When there is a conflict of interest between the client and the psychologist's employing institution, psychologists clarify the nature and direction of their loyalties and responsibilities and keep all parties informed of their commitments. Psychologists fully inform consumers as to the purpose and nature of an evaluative, treatment, educational or training procedure, and they freely acknowledge that clients, students, or participants in research have freedom of choice with regard to participation.

a. Psychologists are continually cognizant of their own needs and of their inherently powerful position *vis a vis* clients, in order to avoid exploiting their trust and dependency. Psychologists make every effort to avoid dual relationships with clients and/or relationships which might impair their professional judgment or increase the risk of client exploitation. Examples of such dual relationships include treating employees, supervisees, close friends or relatives. Sexual intimacies with clients are unethical.

b. Where demands of an organization on psychologists go beyond reasonable conditions of employment, psychologists recognize possible conflicts of interest that may arise. When such conflicts occur, psychologists clarify the nature of the conflict and inform all parties of the nature and direction of the loyalties and responsibilities involved.

c. When acting as a supervisor, trainer, researcher, or employer, psychologists accord informed choice, confidentiality, due process, and protection from physical and mental harm to their subordinates in such relationships.

d. Financial arrangements in professional practice are in accord with professional standards that safeguard the best interests of the client and that are clearly understood by the client in advance of billing. Psychologists are responsible for assisting clients in finding needed services in those instances where payment of the usual fee would be a hardship. No commission, rebate, or other form of remuneration may be given or received for referral of clients for professional services, whether by an individual or by an agency. Psychologists willingly contribute a portion of their services to work for which they receive little or no financial return.

e. The psychologist attempts to terminate a clinical or consulting relationship when it is reasonably clear that the consumer is not benefiting from it. Psychologists who find that their services are being used by employers in a way that is not beneficial to the participants or to employees who may be affected, or to significant others, have the responsibility to make their observations known to the responsible persons and to propose modification or termination of the engagement.

Principle 7:
Professional relationships

Psychologists act with due regard for the needs, special competencies and obligations of their colleagues in psychology and other professions. Psychologists respect the prerogatives and obligations of the institutions or organizations with which they are associated.

a. Psychologists understand the areas of competence of related professions, and make full use of all the professional, technical, and administrative resources that best serve the interests of consumers. The absence of formal relationships with other professional workers does not relieve psychologists from the responsibility of securing for their clients the best possible professional service nor does it relieve them from the exercise of foresight, diligence, and tact in obtaining the complementary or alternative assistance needed by clients.

b. Psychologists know and take into account the traditions and practices of other professional groups with which they work and cooperate fully with members of such groups. If a consumer is receiving services from another professional, psychologists do not offer their services directly to the consumer without first informing the professional person already involved so that the risk of confusion and conflict for the consumer can be avoided.

c. Psychologists who employ or supervise other professionals or professionals in training accept the obligation to facilitate their further professional development by providing suitable working conditions, consultation, and experience opportunities.

d. As employees of organizations providing psychological services, or as independent psychologists serving clients in an organizational context, psychologists seek to support the integrity, reputation and proprietary rights of the host organization. When it is judged necessary in a client's interest to question the organization's programs or policies, psychologists attempt to effect change by constructive action within the organization before disclosing confidential information acquired in their professional roles.

e. In the pursuit of research, psychologists give sponsoring agencies, host institutions, and publication channels the same respect and opportunity for giving informed consent that they accord to individual research participants. They are aware of their obligation to future research workers and insure that host institutions are given adequate information about the research and proper acknowledgement of their contributions.

f. Publication credit is assigned to all those who have contributed to a publication in proportion to their contribution. Major contributions of a professional character made by several persons to a common project are recognized by joint authorship, with the experimenter or author who made the principal contribution identified and listed first. Minor contributions of a professional character, extensive clerical or similar nonprofessional assistance, and other minor contributions are acknowledged in footnotes or in an introductory statement. Acknowledgement through specific citations is made for unpublished as well as published material that has directly influenced the research or writing. A psychologist who compiles and edits material of others for publication publishes the material in the name of the originating group, if any, and with his/her own name appearing as chairperson or editor. All contributors are to be acknowledged and named.

g. When a psychologist violates ethical standards, psychologists who know first-hand of such activities should, if possible, attempt to rectify the situation. Failing an informal solution, psychologists bring such unethical activities to the attention of the appropriate local, state, and/or national committee on professional ethics, standards, and practices.

h. Members of the Association cooperate with duly constituted committees of the Association, in particular and for example, the Committee on Scientific and Professional Ethics and Conduct, and the Committee on Professional Standards Review, by responding to inquiries promptly and completely. Members taking longer than 30 days to respond to such inquiries shall have the burden of demonstrating that they acted with "reasonable promptness." Members also have a similar responsibility to respond with reasonable promptness to inquiries from duly constituted state association ethics committees and professional standards review committees.

Principle 8:
Utilization of assessment techniques

In the development, publication, and utilization of psychological assessment techniques, psychologists observe relevant APA standards. Persons examined have the right to know the results, the interpretations made, and, where appropriate, the original data on which final judgments were based. Test users avoid imparting unnecessary information which would compromise test security, but they provide requested information that explains the basis for decisions that may adversely affect that person or that person's dependents.

a. The client has the right to have and the psychologist has the responsibility to provide explanations of the nature and the purposes of the test and the test results in language that the client can understand, unless, as in some employment or school settings, there is an explicit exception to this right agreed upon in advance. When the explanations are to be provided by others, the psychologist establishes procedures for providing adequate explanations.

b. When a test is published or otherwise made available for operational use, it is accompanied by a manual (or other published or readily available information) that fully describes the development of the test, the rationale, and evidence of validity and reliability. The test manual explicitly states the purposes and applications for which the test is recommended and identifies special qualifications required to administer the test and to interpret it properly. Test manuals provide complete information regarding the characteristics of the normative population.

c. In reporting test results, psychologists indicate any reservations regarding validity or reliability resulting from testing circumstances or inappropriateness of the test norms for the person tested. Psychologists strive to insure that the test results and their interpretations are not misused by others.

d. Psychologists accept responsibility for removing from clients' files test score information that has become obsolete, lest such information be misused or misconstrued to the disadvantage of the person tested.

e. Psychologists offering test scoring and interpretation services are able to demonstrate that the validity of the programs and procedures used in arriving at interpretations are based on appropriate evidence. The public offering of an automated test interpretation service is considered as a professional-to-professional consultation. The psychologist makes every effort to avoid misuse of test reports.

Principle 9:
Pursuit of research activities

The decision to undertake research should rest upon a considered judgment by the individual psychologist about how best to contribute to psychological science and to human welfare. Psychologists carry out their investigations with respect for the people who participate and with concern for their dignity and welfare.

a. In planning a study the investigator has the responsibility to make a careful evaluation of its ethical acceptability, taking into account the following additional principles for research with human beings. To the extent that this appraisal, weighing scientific and humane values, suggests a compromise of any principle, the investigator incurs an increasingly serious obligation to seek ethical advice and to observe stringent safeguards to protect the rights of the human research participants.

b. Responsibility for the establishment and maintenance of acceptable ethical practice in research always remains with the individual investigator. The investigator is also responsible for the ethical treatment of research participants by collaborators, assistants, students, and employees, all of whom, however, incur parallel obligations.

c. Ethical practice requires the investigator to inform the participant of all features of the research that might reasonably be expected to influence willingness to participate, and to explain all other aspects of the research about which the participant inquires. Failure to make full disclosure imposes additional force to the investigator's abiding responsibility to protect the welfare and dignity of the research participant.

d. Openness and honesty are essential characteristics of the relationship between investigator and research participant. When the methodological requirements of a study necessitate concealment or deception, the investigator is required to insure as soon as possible the participant's understanding of the reasons for this action and of a sufficient justification for the procedures employed.

e. Ethical practice requires the investigator to respect the individual's freedom to decline to participate in or withdraw from research. The obligation to protect this freedom requires special vigilance when the investigator is in a position of power over the participant, as, for example, when the participant is a student, client, employee, or otherwise is in a dual relationship with the investigator.

f. Ethically acceptable research begins with the establishment of a clear and fair agreement between the investigator and the research participant that clarifies the responsibilities of each. The investigator has the obligation to honor all promises and commitments included in that agreement.

g. The ethical investigator protects participants from physical and mental discomfort, harm, and danger. If a risk of such consequences exists, the investigator is required to inform the participant of that fact, secure consent before proceeding, and take all possible measures to minimize distress. A research procedure must not be used if it is likely to cause serious or lasting harm to a participant.

h. After the data are collected, the investigator provides the participant with information about the nature of the study and to remove any misconceptions that may have arisen. Where scientific or human values justify delaying or withholding information, the investigator acquires a special responsibility to assure that there are not damaging consequences for the participant.

i. When research procedures may result in undesirable consequences for the individual participant, the investigator has the responsibility to detect and remove or correct these consequences, including, where relevant, long-term after effects.

j. Information obtained about the individual research participants during the course of an investigation is confidential unless otherwise agreed in advance. When the possibility exists that others may obtain access to such information, this possibility, together with the plans for protecting confidentiality, be explained to the participants as part of the procedure for obtaining informed consent.

k. A psychologist using animals in research adheres to the provisions of the Rules Regarding Animals, drawn up by the Committee on Precautions and Standards in Animal Experimentation and adopted by the American Psychological Association.

l. Investigations of human participants using drugs should be conducted only in such settings as clinics, hospitals, or research facilities maintaining appropriate safeguards for the participants.

References

Psychologists are responsible for knowing about and acting in accord with the standards and positions of the APA, as represented in such official documents as the following:

American Association of University Professors. Statement on Principles on Academic Freedom and Tenure. *Policy Documents & Report*, 1977, 1–4.

American Psychological Association. *Guidelines for Psychologists for the Use of Drugs in Research.* Washington, D.C.: Author, 1971.

American Psychological Association. *Principles for the Care and Use of Animals.* Washington, D.C.: Author, 1971.

American Psychological Association. Guidelines for conditions of employment of psychologists. *American Psychologist,* 1972, 27, 331–334.

American Psychological Association. Guidelines for psychologists conducting growth groups. *American Psychologist,* 1973, 28, 933.

American Psychological Association. *Ethical Principles in the Conduct of Research with Human Participants.* Washington, D.C.: Author, 1973.

American Psychological Association. *Standards for Educational and Psychological Tests.* Washington, D.C.: Author, 1974.

American Psychological Association. *Standards for Providers of Psychological Services.* Washington, D.C.: Author, 1977.

Committee on Scientific and Professional Ethics and Conduct. Guidelines for telephone directory listings. *American Psychologist,* 1969, 24, 70–71.

Appendix C The education for all handicapped children act public law 94–142

Paper delivered by the Council for Exceptional Children 1977–78.

Does P.L. 94–142 replace the earlier Federal Education of the Handicapped Act?

No. P.L. 94–142 is a complete revision of Part B *only* of the Education of the Handicapped Act. Part B was formerly that portion of the act addressing the basic state grant program. The other components of EHA (Parts A–G) remain substantially unchanged and continue in operation. Parenthetically, all programs under the aegis of the EHA, including the P. L. 94–142 revision of Part B, are administered through the Bureau of Education for the Handicapped (USOE–HEW).

How are handicapped children defined for the purposes of P.L. 94–142?

Handicapped children are defined as mentally retarded, hard of hearing, deaf, speech impaired, visually handicapped, seriously emotionally disturbed, orthopedically impaired, or other health impaired, or children with specific learning disabilities, who by reason thereof require special education and related services (Sec. 602).

P.L. 94–142 is intended to help pay for special education and related services for handicapped children as defined above. How are special education and related services defined?

The term "special education" means specially designed instruction, at no cost to parents or guardians, to meet the unique needs of a handicapped child, including classroom instruction, instruction in physical education, home instruction, and instruction in hospitals and institutions.

The term "related services" means transportation, and such developmental, corrective, and other supportive services (including speech pathology and audiology, psychological services, physical and occupational therapy, recreation, and medical and counseling services, except that such medical services shall be for diagnostic and evaluation purposes only) as may be required to assist a handicapped child to benefit from special education. This includes the early identification and assessment of handicapping conditions in children.

What age groups may benefit from this act?

P.L. 94–142 stipulates that all handicapped children, aged 3 to 21 years, may enjoy the special education and related services provided through this measure. There is also provision for the use of federal monies for programs of early identification and screening.

Are there priorities in the expenditure of funds?

Yes. The given state must have established priorities for providing a free, appropriate public education in the following manner:

First priority to children who are not receiving an education

Second priority to children inadequately served with the most severe handicaps (within each disability)

Correspondingly, there must be a priority in the expenditure of federal dollars received under this act which conforms to those same priorities. Moreover, these priorities must be adhered to by both the state education agency and its local education agencies.

What is the formula for distribution of funds among the states?

P.L. 94–142 establishes a payment formula based upon a gradually escalating percentage of the national average expenditure-per-public-school child times the number of handicapped children being served in the school districts of each state in the nation. That percentage will escalate on a yearly basis until 1982, when it will become a permanent 40 percent for that year and all subsequent years.

Formula Scale	
fiscal 1978	5 percent
fiscal 1979	10 percent
fiscal 1980	20 percent
fiscal 1981	30 percent
fiscal 1982	40 percent

It should be carefully noted that such a formula carries an inflation factor, i.e., the actual money figure fluctuates with inflationary-deflationary adjustments in the national average-per-pupil expenditure.

What are the currently estimated dollar totals thus generated by this formula?

On the basis of the national average per-pupil expenditure at the time action on this legislation in the Congress was being finalized (approximately $1250, autumn 1975), Congressional sources drew up the following estimates for the first years under this new formula:

fiscal 1978	$387 million (on the 5 percent factor)
fiscal 1979	$775 million (on the 10 percent factor)
fiscal 1980	$1.2 billion (on the 20 percent factor)
fiscal 1981	$2.32 billion (on the 30 percent factor)
fiscal 1982	$3.16 billion (on the 40 percent factor)

Does the preceding guarantee actual appropriations?

No. This is the "authorizing" mechanism only. In other words, this formula will determine the absolute ceiling, beyond which ceiling no further dollars can be appropriated. But the dollars must still, in fact, be appropriated by the Congress.

Is there a limit on the number of children who can be counted as handicapped for purposes of the federal formula?

P.L. 94–142 addresses the potential threat of "overcounting" children as handicapped in order to generate the largest possible federal allocation. The measure requires that the total number of children counted should not be greater than that number which equals 12 percent of the total school age population of the state between the ages of 5 and 17, inclusive. It must be emphasized that this limitation relates to the federal entitlement *only*, and in no way places a limitation on the number of children assessed as handicapped by the states and their localities *for their own* purposes. Furthermore, this limitation has no relation to the mandates for serving all handicapped children contained in this act.

Is there a limitation on the number of children with specific learning disabilities (SLD) who may be counted for purposes of the federal funding formula?

The U.S. Commissioner of Education may, within one year, provide detailed regulations relative to SLD, including the development of a more precise federal definition, the prescription of comprehensive diagnostic criteria and procedures, and the prescription of procedures for monitoring of said regulations by the commissioner. If the authorizing committees of the House and Senate disapprove the commissioner's regulations, then a ceiling on the number of children with learning disabilities who may be counted by the state for purposes of the formula will be included when the new formula takes effect. The ceiling would provide that not more than one-sixth of the 12 percent of school-age children aged 5 to 17 inclusive who may be counted as handicapped children served may be children with specific learning disabilities.

What is the relationship of this act to P.L. 89–313?

Children counted for purposes of generating an entitlement under this act may not also be counted under the formula for P.L. 89–313, the program of supplemental educational services for handicapped children in state operated or supported facilities.

How does a local education agency participate under this act?

P.L. 94–142 contains a substantial pass-through to the local school districts. In the first year of the new formula, 50 percent of the monies going to each state would be allocated to the state education agency, and 50 percent would be allocated to the local education agencies. In the following year, fiscal 1979, the LEA entitlement would be enlarged to 75 percent of the total allocation to a given state, with the SEA retaining 25 percent. This 75–25 arrangement commencing in fiscal 1979 becomes the permanent distribution arrangement. The current state control of all funds is retained for the remainder of fiscal 1976 and fiscal 1977.

Are there constraints upon this pass-through?

Though P.L. 94–142 authorizes a substantial local entitlement, there are numerous "strings attached." The state education agency must refuse to pass-through federal monies generated when:

the school district does not conform to the overall state plan requirements contained in this act and in existing law (such as "full service" goal, confidentiality, etc.);

the school district fails to meet the local application requirements;

the state deems the local district unable to make effective use of its entitlement unless it consolidates its entitlement with the entitlement of one or more other school districts (thus allowing great flexibility in funding arrangements);

when the program for handicapped children within the school district is of insufficient size and scope;

when the school district is adequately providing a free appropriate public education for all handicapped children with state and local funds. (This provision is permissive. The state education agency does not have to do so.);

when the state determines that one or more children in a local school district can best be served by a regional or state center.

Furthermore, P.L. 94–142 sets a flat monetary minimum. If a school district, after counting all of its handicapped children served, cannot generate an allocation for itself of at least $7,500, a pass-through to that school district does not occur. This provision is, of course, also aimed at encouraging various sorts of special education consortia in order to make a meaningful use of the federal dollars.

What are the major requirements under this act?

P.L. 94–142 makes a number of critical stipulations which must be adhered to by *both* the state and its localities. These stipulations include:

assurance of extensive child identification procedures;

assurance of "full service" goal and detailed timetable;

a guarantee of complete due process procedures;

the assurance of regular parent or guardian consultation;

maintenance of programs and procedures for comprehensive personnel development including in-service training;

assurance of special education being provided to all handicapped children in the "least restrictive" environment;

assurance of nondiscriminatory testing and evaluation;

a guarantee of policies and procedures to protect the confidentiality of data and information;

assurance of the maintenance of an individualized program for all handicapped children;

assurance of an effective policy guaranteeing the right of all handicapped children to a free, appropriate public education, *at no cost* to parents or guardian;

assurance of a surrogate to act for any child when parents or guardians are either unknown or unavailable, or when said child is a legal ward of the state.

It is most important to observe that an official, written document containing all of these assurances is now required (in the form of an application) of *every* school district receiving its federal entitlement under P.L. 94–142. Correspondingly, such a public document also exists at the state level in the form of the annual state plan, which must be submitted to the U.S. Commissioner.

Parenthetically, the state education agency is responsible for monitoring compliance by its local school districts with respect to these stipulations. The U.S. Commissioner has corresponding monitoring responsibilities with respect to state education agency compliance.

What if a school district is too small to qualify or cannot offer programs of sufficient size and scope?

Provision is made in the act for a type of educational unit larger than the local education agency. An intermediate educational unit is defined as a public authority established by state law to provide free public education on a regional basis to handicapped children. Unlike the other consolidated arrangements allowed under this act, where authority is shared equally among the local districts thus consolidated, the intermediate educational unit is self-governing.

Such an intermediate educational unit, when so determined by the state education agency, may have all of the rights and responsibilities under this act of a local education agency and may receive a federal entitlement.

What are the supplanting provisions?

In the use of the federal dollars generated under this formula, both the state agency and the local education agencies must maintain their own expenditure levels. In other words, they may not supplant state and local dollars with federal dollars.

However, if the state agency provides convincing evidence to the U.S. Commissioner that the state is making available a free, appropriate public education to all handicapped children within the state, and if the U.S. Commissioner certifies that declaration, then the U.S. Commissioner may waive the nonsupplanting provision in whole or in part.

What is the "excess cost" feature?

P.L. 94–142 provides that federal monies must be spent only for those "excess cost" factors attendant to the higher costs of educating handicapped children. A given school district must determine its average annual per-pupil expenditure for all children being served, and then apply the federal dollars only to those additional cost factors for handicapped children beyond the average annual per-pupil expenditure. Such a requirement does not obtain for the state education agency in the utilization of its allocation under this act. However, the state education agency is required to match its allocation on a "program basis," but is not required to match with new monies.

When must all handicapped children be served?

P.L. 94–142 requires that every state and its localities, if they are to continue to receive funds under this act, must be affording a free public education to all handicapped children aged 3 to 18 by the beginning of the school year (September 1) in 1978, and further orders the availability of such education to all children aged 3 to 21 by September 1, 1980. However, for children in the 3 to 5 and 18 to 21 age ranges, such mandate does not apply if such a requirement is inconsistent with state law or practice, or any court decree.

Is there a requirement for individualized instruction?

The state education agency must guarantee that there is a written individualized education program for each and every handicapped child in the state, developed jointly with the parents or guardian of each child, and reviewed at least annually and revised where necessary. The local agencies must guarantee the same individualized program for all children within their educational jurisdiction.

What procedures are contained in the act to protect the educational rights of handicapped children and their parents?

Those provisions of previously existing law (P.L. 93–380, the Education Amendments of 1974) toward the guarantee of due process rights are further refined in P.L. 94–142, and their scope is substantially enlarged.

Basically, the state education agency must guarantee the maintenance of full due process procedures for all handicapped children within the state and their parents or guardian with respect to all matters of identification, evaluation, and educational placement, whether it be the initiation or change of such placement, or the refusal to initiate or change. Interested individuals are strongly urged to read Section 615 of the act ("Procedural Safeguards") in its entirety.

It should be observed that the P.L. 94–142 refinements take effect in the first year under the new formula, i.e., fiscal 1978. In the meantime, those basic features of due process as authorized in the prior act (P.L. 93–380) must be maintained by the states.

It should be further noted that when the parents or guardian of a child are not known, are unavailable, or when the child is a legal ward of the state, the state education agency, local education agency, or intermediate education agency (as appropriate) must assign an individual to act as a *surrogate* for the child in all due process proceedings. Moreover, such assigned individual may not be an employee of the state educational agency, local educational agency, or intermediate educational unit *involved in* the education or care of the particular child.

Can federal money under this act be withheld?

The U.S. Commissioner must cut off funds to a given state education agency if that agency is in substantial noncompliance with any of the major requirements of this act. In such an instance, the commissioner must also cut off funding for those programs specifically designed for handicapped children under the following titles:

Part A of Title I of the Elementary and Secondary Education Act

Title III of the Elementary and Secondary Education Act (innovative programs) and its successor, Part C, Educational Innovation and Support, Section 431 of P.L. 93–380

The Vocational Education Act

Moreover, the U.S. Commissioner may order the state education agency to cut off the flow through to a given school district if the U.S. Commissioner evidences substantial noncompliance by a school district.

What are the parameters of state education agency authority and responsibility under this act?

P.L. 94–142 requires that the state educational agency be responsible for ensuring that all requirements of the act are carried out. Moreover, all education programs within the state for all handicapped children, including all such programs administered by any other state or local agency, must meet state educational agency standards and be under the general supervision of the state education agency. This provision establishes a single line of authority within one state agency for the education of all handicapped children within each state.

Is there special encouragement to serve preschool handicapped children?

P.L. 94–142 carries a special incentive grant aimed at encouraging the states to provide special education and related services to its preschool handicapped children. Each handicapped child in the state aged 3 through 5 who is counted as served will generate a special $300 entitlement. It should be noted that this incentive entitlement goes to the state education agency and must be used by the state education agency to provide further preschool services. Additionally, this entitlement requires a separate "line item" appropriation, independent of the larger P.L. 94–142 appropriation.

Is there special encouragement for the removal of architectural barriers within existing school systems?

P.L. 94–142 authorizes such sums as may be necessary for the U.S. Commissioner to award grants to pay all or part of the cost of altering existing buildings and equipment to eliminate architectural barriers in educational facilities. Such provision is aimed at assuring certain handicapped children an appropriate public education in the least restrictive environment. As in the case of the previous heading on preschool incentive, the actual money for this component must be separately appropriated by the Congress.

Are private facilities eligible to receive funds under this act?

Children in private elementary and secondary schools may receive assistance for their special education under this act if:

such children are placed in or referred to such schools by the state or local education agency *as a means of carrying out public policy;*

an individualized education program, as required by this act, is maintained for such children in private facilities;

the special education is at no cost to the parents;

the state education agency determines that participating schools meet the standards that apply to state and local education agencies;

the children served in such facilities are accorded all of the educational rights they would have if served directly by public agencies.

Is a formal advisory panel mandated in P.L. 94–142?

P.L. 94–142 orders that each state shall have an advisory panel to be appointed by the governor or any other official authorized under state law to make such appointments. This panel must be composed of individuals involved in or concerned with the education of handicapped children, including handicapped individuals, teachers, parents or guardians of handicapped children, state and local education officials, and administrators of programs for handicapped children. The panel shall have the following duties:

advise the state education agency on unmet needs relative to the education of all handicapped children within the state;

comment publicly on rules and regulations issued by the state and procedures proposed by the state for distribution of funds;

assist the state in developing and reporting such data and evaluations as may assist the U.S. Commissioner.

Are the states allowed to reserve monies for administration of the act?

The state education agency is permitted to reserve to itself from the total allotment to the state under this act—in any given year—5 percent or $200,000, whichever is greater, to support its administrative responsibilities. This administrative reservation must be taken from the overall state education agency allocation, i.e., from the 50 percent state education agency allocation in fiscal 1978, and from the 25 percent state education agency allocation of fiscal 1979 and thereafter.

What national evaluations are mandated?

The U.S. Commissioner must evaluate the impact of this act on an annual basis and provide a full report to the Congress not later than 120 days after the close of each fiscal year. That annual evaluation shall include the following special evaluations:

an evaluation of the effectiveness of individualized instruction;

an evaluation of the effectiveness of educating handicapped children in the least restrictive environment;

an evaluation of the effectiveness of procedures to prevent the erroneous classification of children.

Will vital data be generated on a regular basis?

The U.S. Commissioner is required to provide to the Congress and the public at least annually—and is required to update annually—data and information on the educational status of the nation's handicapped children, such as the number of children served and unserved within each disability, the kinds and number of educational personnel employed, etc.

Are the nation's educational systems encouraged to employ the handicapped?

P.L. 94–142 stipulates that recipients of federal assistance under this act shall make positive efforts to employ and advance in employment qualified handicapped individuals.

How long will this act be in force?

P.L. 94–142 is established as a permanent authority with no expiration date.

Appendix D Standards for the preparation of counselors and other personnel services specialists

Prepared by the Association for Counselor Education and Supervision

Introduction

These Standards are intended as guidelines for the graduate preparation of counselors and other personnel services specialists. They should be beneficial to college and university staff who are involved in initiating programs of preparation or in evaluating existing programs. The Standards can also be helpful to state, regional and national accrediting agencies. While the Standards are designed to serve as guidelines for minimum preparation, they are flexible enough to allow for creative approaches to counselor education. The Standards do not include guidelines for the preparation of support personnel or professional personnel at the doctoral level.

These Standards recognize that:

The faculty has developed a written statement of philosophy for the counselor education program and that this statement has been accepted by the institution.

The trend toward the development of competency based/performance based counselor education programs is likely to continue. However, whether or not a counselor education program is developed upon such a base, the Standards reflect the concern that all programs should give to the assessment of demonstrated competencies by students during various stages of their development.

Students take varying rates of time to demonstrate the competencies and professional maturation demanded in the complexities of counseling and personnel services work. While the Standards recommend minimum hours of study in certain areas, these stated minimum hours should be interpreted in the context that some students will demonstrate the desired competency and professional maturation levels in a shorter time than indicated while others may take substantially longer.

The need of counselors and other personnel services specialists for self-renewal and in-service education beyond minimum preparation or certification will increase. Therefore, the counselor education program should provide enriching experiences for those who have already completed the minimum program.

Minimum study in counselor education will increasingly extend beyond the one year program of graduate preparation. Such programs might include (1) a combination of an undergraduate major in guidance and a year of graduate study in counselor education, (2) two years of graduate study in counselor education, or (3) other models which include a minimum of one year of graduate study.

All counselor education programs are not expected to prepare counselors and other personnel services specialists for all the work settings encompassed by the Standards. Institutions should offer preparation programs only in those areas where sufficient qualified full-time staff and other resources are available.

The Standards reflect current thinking concerning the preparation of counselors and other personnel services specialists and combine the three existing statements on counselor preparation previously adopted by the Association for Counselor Education and Supervision (ACES). "Standards for the Preparation of Secondary School Counselors—1967"; "Standards for the Preparation of Elementary School Counselors," February, 1968; and "Guidelines for Graduate Programs in the Preparation of Student Personnel Workers in Higher Education—1969."

In addition to acknowledging the similarity of preparation among the various specialists, the Standards also provide for different goals which may exist in various work settings. While this single document has been developed for the entire profession, the respective divisions of the American Personnel and Guidance Association and other professional groups are encouraged to develop jointly with ACES, specific statements concerning the specialized needs of counselors and their personnel services specialists who work in different settings in this respect, attention is called to Section II, B.2 of the Standards, "Environmental and Specialized Studies."

Leadership for the development of these Standards was assumed by the ACES Commission on Standards and Accreditation, working under the supervision of the Executive Council of ACES. The Standards were adopted by the membership of ACES in 1973.

Standards
Section 1: Objectives

A. Objectives of the Program to Prepare Counselors and Other Personnel Services Specialists

1. *The faculty has developed program objectives.*
    a. Objectives reflect a knowledge of studies and recommendations of local, state, regional, and national lay and professional groups concerned with counseling and personal services needs of society.
    b. Objectives reflect the needs in society which are represented by different ethnic and cultural groups served by counselors and other personnel services specialists.
    c. Objectives are reviewed and revised continuously throughout student as well as faculty participation.

d. Objectives are developed and reviewed with the assistance of personnel in cooperating agencies.
e. Objectives are written in such a way that evaluation of a student can be based on demonstrated competencies as he progresses through the program.

2. *Objectives are implemented on a planned basis in all areas of the program including selection, retention and endorsement of students; curriculum; instructional methods; research activities; and administrative policies, procedures, and execution.*
3. *Personnel in cooperating agencies and faculty members with primary assignments in other disciplines are aware of and are encouraged to work toward the objectives of the counselor education program.*
4. *There is a planned procedure for a continued evaluation of the outcomes of the program.*
   a. The program is evaluated in terms of demonstrated competencies of each student as he or she progresses through the program.
   b. Evaluation of the effectiveness of preparation is accomplished through evidence obtained from: (1) former students, (2) supervisors in agencies employing graduates of the program, and (3) personnel in state and national licensing and accrediting agencies.

Section II: Curriculum—Program of studies and supervised experiences

A. General Program Characteristics
   1. *The institution provides a graduate program in counselor education designed for the preparation of counselors and other personnel services specialists.*
      a. The opportunity for full-time study throughout the academic year is provided and actively encouraged.
      b. Flexibility is provided within the curriculum to allow for individual differences in competencies and understandings developed before entering the program.
      c. Descriptions of the various program options and requirements for graduate studies are published and distributed to prospective students.
      d. Concepts relating to differentiated staffing and preparation in counseling and personnel services are reflected in the program. The faculty is aware of lifetime opportunities for development and advancement in the field of counseling and personnel services. There is

also an emphasis on the use of support personnel to free more professionally prepared personnel for the performance of higher level functions.

2. *Continuing and/or in-service education offerings in counselor education meet all of the criteria in faculty qualifications, faculty load, physical facilities, faculty-student ratios, etc. as described in these Standards.*
3. *There is evidence of high quality instruction in all aspects of the program.*
   a. Syllabi or other evidence of organized and coordinated instructional units of the curriculum are available.
   b. Resource materials are provided.
   c. Responsibilities are assigned to, or assumed by, faculty members only in those areas of the counselor education program for which they have demonstrated professional competency.
   d. Provisions are made for periodic evaluation by students and staff of all aspects of the program, i.e., course content, methods of instruction, and supervised experience, both on and off campus.
4. *Planned sequences of educational experiences are provided.*
   a. Within the minimum counselor education program a sequence of basic and advanced graduate studies and other associated learning experiences is defined and provided.
   b. The program provides for the integration of didactic studies and supervised experiences.
   c. All prerequisite studies and other experiences are identified.
   d. Representatives of departments offering studies in related fields are regularly consulted regarding how related studies can be made more useful to counselor education majors.
   e. The faculty has identified performance indicators to determine whether the professional competencies to be developed by the sequence of educational experiences are achieved.
5. *A close relationship exists between the faculty of the counselor education program and the staff members in work settings.*
   a. The staff in the work settings is consulted in the design and implementation of all aspects of the program including practicum and internship experiences.

   b. The faculty of the preparation program is consulted in the design and implementation of in-service preparation of staff in work settings.
6. *Within the framework of the total program, there are opportunities for the student to develop understandings and skills beyond the minimum requirements of the program.*
   a. Elective courses and related experiences are available.
   b. Supervised individual study is available.
   c. Enrichment opportunities are provided and faculty encourage students to take part in them.
7. *The spirit of inquiry and the production and utilization of research data are encouraged among both faculty and students.*
   a. The statement of objectives of the program reflects an awareness of the role of research in the counseling and personnel services field.
   b. Instructional procedures make frequent use of, and reference to, research findings. Areas in which research is needed are identified.
8. *Opportunities for planned periodic self-evaluation and the development of greater self-understanding are provided for both students and faculty.*
   a. Self-analysis is encouraged through such activities as laboratory experiences, including audio and/or video tape recordings.
   b. Opportunities for improvement of interpersonal relationships are provided through small group activities.
   c. Counseling services for students are available and are provided by qualified persons other than counselor education faculty.

B. Program of Studies
   1. *Common core: The common core is composed of general areas considered to be necessary in the preparation of all counselors and other personnel services specialists.*
      a. Human growth and development: Includes studies that provide a broad understanding of the nature and needs of individuals at all developmental levels. Emphasis is placed on psychological, sociological, and physiological approaches. Also included are such areas as human behavior (normal and abnormal), personality theory, and learning theory.
      b. Social and cultural foundations: Includes studies of changes, ethnic groups, sub-cultures, changing roles

of women, sexism, urban and rural societies, population patterns, cultural mores, use of leisure time, and differing life patterns. Such disciplines as the behavioral sciences, economics, and political science are involved.

c. The helping relationship: Includes (a) philosophic bases of the helping relationship; (b) counseling theory, supervised practice, and application; (c) consultation theory, supervised practice, and application, and (d) an emphasis upon development of counselor and client (or consultee) self-awareness and self-understanding.
d. Groups: Includes theory and types of groups, as well as descriptions of group practices, methods, dynamics, and facilitative skills. It also includes supervised practice.
e. Life style and career development: Includes such areas as vocational choice theory, relationship between career choice and life style, sources of occupational and educational information, approaches to career decision-making processes, and career development exploration techniques.
f. Appraisal of the individual: Includes the development of a framework for understanding the individual including methods of data gathering and interpretation, individual and group testing, case study approaches, and study of individual differences. Ethnic, cultural, and sex factors are also considered.
g. Research and evaluation: Includes such areas as statistics, research design, development of research and demonstration proposals. It also includes understanding legislation relating to the development of research, program development, and demonstration proposals, as well as the development and evaluation of program objectives.
h. Professional orientation: Includes goals and objectives of professional organizations, codes of ethics, legal considerations, standards of preparation, certification, licensing, and role identity of counselors and other personnel services specialists.

2. *Environmental and Specialized Studies: The counselor education program includes those specialized studies necessary for practice in different work settings. There is evidence that the faculty, in planning and evaluating the counselor curriculum, has taken into consideration*

statements made by other professional groups relating to role, function, and preparation.

a. Environmental studies: Includes the study of the environment in which the student is planning to practice. This includes history, philosophy, trends, purposes, ethics, legal aspects, standards, and roles within the institution or work setting where the student will practice.

b. Specialized studies: Includes the specialized knowledge and skills needed to work effectively in the professional setting where the student plans to practice. For example, the student preparing to be an elementary school counselor may need to take, among other specialized courses, work in diagnosis of reading dysfunction; the student preparing to be a personnel services educator in higher education might need, among other specialized work, both course work and supervised experiences in student financial aid; or the student preparing to work in employment counseling may need additional information about employment trends as well as the sociology and psychology of work.

The different professional associations jointly concerned with the preparation of counselors and other personnel services specialists are encouraged to develop statements concerning environmental and specialized studies, and make these statements available to the ACES Commission on Standards and Accreditation and to the profession in general.

C. Supervised Experiences

1. *Appropriate supervised experiences provide for the integration and application of knowledge and skills gained in didactic study.*
   a. Students' supervised experiences are in settings which are compatible with their career goals.
   b. Supervised experiences include observation and direct work with individuals and groups within the appropriate work setting.
   c. Opportunities are provided for professional relationships with staff members in the work settings.
2. *Supervised experiences include laboratory, practicum, and internship.*
   a. Laboratory experiences, providing both observation and participation in specific activites, are offered

throughout the preparatory program. This might include role-playing, listening to tapes, viewing video tape playbacks, testing, organizing and using personnel records, interviews with field practitioners, preparing and examining case studies, and using career information materials.

b. Supervised counseling practicum experiences provide interaction with individuals and groups actually seeking services from counselors and other personnel services specialists. Some of these individuals and groups should come from the environments in which the counselor education student is preparing to work.
   (1) Specific counseling practica have sufficient duration and continuity to assure optimum professional development. The minimum recommended amount of actual contact with individuals and groups is 60 clock hours extending over a minimum nine-month period.
   (2) Supervision in consultation is also provided.
   (3) The supervisor's role is clearly identified and sufficient time for supervision is allocated. The recommended weekly minimum of supervision is one hour of individual supervision and one hour of supervision in a group for the duration of the practicum experiences. Supervisory responsibilities include critiquing of counseling, either observed or recorded on audio or video tape.

c. Internship is a post-practicum experience that provides an actual on-the-job experience, and should be given central importance for each student.
   (1) The internship placement is selected on the basis of the student's career goals.
   (2) The internship includes all activities that a regularly employed staff member would be expected to perform. In the setting the intern is expected to behave as a professional and should be treated as one.
   (3) For those students who have no prior work experience in their particular setting, an intensified or expanded internship is provided.
   (4) The intern spends a minimum of 300 clock hours on the job. It is desirable that the internship be a paid experience.
   (5) Supervision is performed by a qualified staff in the

field placement setting who have released time from other regular duties.

(6) The counselor education faculty provides these field supervisors opportunities for in-service education in counseling and personnel services supervision.

(7) There should be close cooperative working relationships between staff in field placement setting and the counselor education faculty.

3. *A qualified faculty and staff with adequate time allocated to supervision is provided for laboratory, practicum, and internship experiences.*
   a. Members of the on-campus faculty responsible for supervision include those who:
      (1) have earned doctoral degrees, perferably in counselor education, from accredited institutions.
      (2) have had experience and demonstrate competencies in counseling and other personnel services at the level appropriate for the students supervised.
   b. Doctoral students serving as supervisors of practicum experiences are themselves supervised by qualified faculty.
   c. The practicum and internship experiences are tutorial forms of instruction; therefore, the supervision of five students is considered equivalent to the teaching of one three-semester-hour course. Such a ratio is considered maximum.
4. *Facilities, equipment, and materials are provided for supervised experiences in both on- and off-campus settings. (See also Section IV).*

D. Program Development Outreach
1. *The counselor education faculty assists individual counselors and other personnel services specialists in off-campus agencies providing supervised experiences in the program of preparation.*
   a. The institution encourages agency personnel to seek the counselor education faculty's assistance in planning and conducting in-service education and in developing program improvement models
   b. The counselor education faculty is provided a teaching-work load recognition for their part in in-service and program development activities in cooperating agencies.
   c. The counselor education faculty involves advanced

graduate students in programs of in-service education and in program development planning and implementation at the agency level.

2. *The counselor education faculty provides on-campus assistance to agency personnel in resolving unique problems or difficulties.*
   a. The faculty encourages agency personnel to seek assistance through the use of such techniques as personal appointments, telephone access programs, information storage and retrieval, position papers, and various audio and/or visual media.
3. *The counselor education faculty integrates the experiences of the out-reach activity into its counselor education program by adapting or modifying the counselor education program as may be appropriate. Outreach activities are viewed as a significant function in the preparation program.*

Section III: Responsibilities concerning students in the program

A. Information
   1. *Information concerning major aspects of the counselor education program and the faculty is available in a variety of media for prospective students.*
      a. The academic areas in which the program offers preparation and the degrees offered are clearly stated.
      b. Counselor education faculty are available to discuss the program of preparation.
      c. Personnel in various counseling and related job settings have been designated as referral sources for discussion of their areas of interest with prospective students.

B. Selection
   1. *Applicants accepted meet the institution's standards for admission to graduate study.*
      a. There is evidence that staff in cooperating agencies have been consulted relative to admission policies and procedures.
      b. Students in the program reflect an effort, on the part of the faculty, to select individuals who represent a variety of subcultures and subgroups within our society.
      c. A committee of faculty members makes the decisions concerning admission of applicants to the program based upon established criteria such as:
         (1) Potential effectiveness in close interpersonal relationships.

(2) Aptitude for counseling and related human development responsibilities.
(3) Commitment to a career in counseling and personnel work.
(4) Potential for establishing facilitative relationships with people at various levels of development.
(5) Openness to self-examination and commitment to self-growth.

C. Retention
1. *A continuing evaluation through systematic review is made of students as they progress through the program.*
2. *In situations where evaluations of a student indicates an inappropriateness for the counseling field, faculty members assist in facilitating change to an area more appropriate for the student.*

D. *Endorsement*
1. *A statement of policy relating to the institution's procedure for formal endorsement has been adopted and approved by the faculty and administrative authorities.*
   a. Each candidate is informed of procedures of endorsement for certification, licensing, and employment.
   b. Insofar as possible, all faculty members acquainted with the student, including supervisors of practicum and internship experiences, should participate in the endorsement process.
2. *Endorsement is given by the counselor education faculty only for the particular job setting for which the student has been prepared.*
3. *Endorsement is given only on the basis of evidence of demonstrated proficiency. The candidate should have completed a substantial part of his graduate work in counselor education, including supervised counseling experience, at the endorsing institution.*

E. Placement
1. *The institution has a placement service with policies and procedures consistent with recognized placement practices.*
   a. The faculty assist the student with the preparation of placement papers and the selection and securing of a suitable position.
   b. Placement services are available to graduates of the program throughout their professional careers.
   c. Opportunities are provided for students to participate

in local, state, and federal examinations for employment opportunities.

F. Research and Evaluation

1. *Policies and procedures relating to recruitment, selection, retention, and placement are continually studied through various research and evaluative methods.*
   a. Regular follow-up studies are made of former students, including dropouts, students removed from the program, and graduates.
   b. Evaluation is followed by appropriate revisions and improvements in the preparation program.

Section IV: Support for the counselor education program, administrative relations, and institutional resources

1. *Administrative organization and procedures provide recognition and designated responsibilities for a counselor education program.*
   a. The program is a clearly identified part of the institution's graduate program.
      (1) There is preferably only one unit directly responsible for the preparation of counselors and other personnel services specialists.
      (2) If more than one unit in the institution is directly involved in the preparation of counselors and other personnel services specialists, there is evidence of close cooperation and coordination.
   b. Cooperative relationships exist between the counselor education program and other units of the institution related to the program.
      (1) Contributions of other units to the program as defined.
      (2) Channels of communication with faculty members in other units are identified and maintained.
   c. Use is made of a wide range of professional and community resources. Evidence of positive working relationships exists with agencies off campus that have the potential for contributing to the preparation of counselors and other personnel services specialists. They may be potential employers of graduates of the program.
2. *The institution provides for the professional development of the counselor education faculty as well as students in the counselor education program.*

a. Faculty are involved in professional activities on local, state, regional, and national levels.
b. Faculty participate in voluntary professional service capacities.
c. The institution provides encouragement and financial support for the faculty to participate in professional activities.
d. Faculty engage in programs of research and contribute to literature of the field.
e. Students participate in the activities of professional organizations.

3. *The institution provides adequate faculty and supporting staff for all aspects of the counselor education program.*
   a. An individual is designated as the professional leader of the counselor education program.
      (1) This individual is an experienced counselor and possesses an earned doctorate in counselor education from an accredited institution.
      (2) This individual has full-time assignment to the counselor education program.
      (3) This individual is recognized for his leadership in the counseling profession.
      (4) This individual is qualified by preparation and experience to conduct and to supervise research activities.
4. *In addition to the designated leader there are at least two full-time faculty members with comparable qualifications.*
   a. Additional faculty are provided at the ratio of one full-time staff member for every ten full-time graduate students or their equivalent in part-time graduate students. This ratio should be reduced in institutions where a large percentage of the counselor education students are enrolled on a part-time basis and/or when program changes create the need for the faculty to spend more time in the evaluation of each student.
5. *The full-time teaching load of faculty members is consistent with that of other graduate units in the institution which require intensive supervision as an integral part of professional preparation.*
   a. The faculty load is modified in proportion to assigned responsibilities for graduate advisement and research supervision on a formula that is consistent with established graduate school policy in the institution.

b. Time is provided within the total faculty work load for cooperative interdisciplinary activities with teaching faculty in related fields.
c. The total work load of faculty members includes a recognition of time needed for professional research.

6. *Faculty in closely related disciplines are qualified in their respective areas and also are informed about the objectives of the counselor education program.*
7. *Off-campus agency personnel who supervise students are qualified through academic preparation and professional experience.*
   a. Such staff members have two or more years of appropriate professional experience.
   b. These staff members have at least two years of graduate work in counselor education or can demonstrate equivalent preparation.
8. *Graduate assistantships are provided to assist the faculty and to provide additional experiences for students in the program.*
   a. Regular procedures are established for the identification and assignment of qualified students to assistantships.
   b. A minimum of one half-time graduate student is assigned to the counselor education program for each 30 full-time equivalent students.
   c. Assignments are made in such a way as to enrich the professional learning experiences of the graduate assistants.
9. *Secretarial, clerical, and other supportive staff are provided in the counselor education program.*
   a. A minimum of one full-time secretary or equivalent is provided for the clerical work of the counselor education program.
   b. Additional clerical service is provided at the ratio of one full-time clerical assistant for the equivalent of every three faculty members.
   c. Responsibilities of secretarial, clerical and other supportive staff are defined and adequate supervision is provided.
10. *The institution provides facilities and a budget that insures continuous operation of all aspects of the counselor education program.*
    a. The institution provides a designated headquarters for the counselor education program.

(1) The headquarters is located near the classroom and laboratory facilities used in the counselor education program.
(2) The headquarters area includes a private office for each faculty member.
(3) The headquarters area includes office space for secretarial, clerical, and other supportive staff.
(4) The headquarters provides appropriate work space equipment and supplies for graduate assistants.

b. Facilities for supervised experiences are provided in a coordinated laboratory setting on campus. Consideration is given to:
(1) Facilities for individual counseling in rooms with assured privacy and adequate space for related equipment.
(2) Facilities for small group work. The area provides for small group counseling, testing, staffing, meetings, and so forth.
(3) Classroom and seminar meeting rooms.
(4) Facilities appropriately equipped with the following:
(a) recording and listening devices, both portable and permanent
(b) one-way vision glass
(c) video-tape recording and playing devices, both portable and permanent
(5) Technical assistance for both operational and maintenance services.
(6) Acoustical treatment throughout the facility.
(7) Facilities that are conducive to modeling and demonstrating exemplary environments and practices in counseling and personnel services. The facilities should include a "model" counseling laboratory with related resource materials and audio-visual equipment. Included as resources in the "model" laboratory are:
(a) career occupational and educational information materials
(b) standardized tests and interpretation data
(c) a variety of media, equipment, and materials
(d) space for teaching and laboratory experiences
(8) Data processing assistance and equipment that

are available for both teaching and research.

(9) Facilities that are located in close approximation to the counselor education faculty offices and away from centers of extreme noise and confusion.

c. Library facilities provide an appropriate supply of resource materials for study and research in counselor education.

(1) The facilities include basic resources, both books and periodicals, in areas in which the counselor education program provides preparation. Resources in related areas such as psychology, sociology, and economics are also available.

(2) Both current and historical materials are available.

(3) Library resources are available during evening and weekend hours.

(4) Inter-library loans, ERIC services, microfilm, and photocopy services are available.

(5) Multiple copies of frequently used publications are available.

11. *Research facilities are available to faculty and students in counselor education.*

a. Facilities include offices and laboratories equipped to provide opportunities for the collection, analysis, and synthesis of data.

b. Consultant services are available from research specialists on the institution's faculty.

c. Campus computer centers and other data-processing facilities are available.

d. Appropriate settings, for research both off and on campus, are provided.

12. *The institution recognizes the individual needs of graduate students and provides services for personal as well as professional development.*

a. Since full-time academic-year attendance is possible for most graduate students only if some form of financial assistance is available, efforts are made to develop financial assistance for students in the counselor education program.

(1) The counselor education program is assigned a proportionate share of the institution's funds for student assistance.

(2) Part-time work opportunities appropriate for stu-

dents in the program are identified and efforts are made to secure assignments for those desiring such opportunities.

(3) Loan resources are available to students in counselor education.

(4) Prospective students are provided information about possible sources of financial assistance.

b. Personal counseling services are available to all counselor education students.

(1) A counseling service is available from professionals other than the members of the counselor education faculty.

(2) Procedures for referral are known by all faculty members.

Appendix E Ethical principles involved in research

From Ethical Principles in the Conduct of Research with Human Participants *by the Ad Hoc Committee on Ethical Standards, Washington, D.C., 1973, pp. 1–2.*

The decision to undertake research should rest upon a considered judgment by the individual psychologist about how best to contribute to psychological science and to human welfare. The responsible psychologist weighs alternative directions in which personal energies and resources might be invested. Having made the decision to conduct research, psychologists must carry out their investigations with respect for the people who participate and with concern for their dignity and welfare. The principles that follow make explicit the investigator's ethical responsibilities toward participants over the course of research, from the initial decision to pursue a study to the steps necessary to protect the confidentiality of research data. These principles should be interpreted in terms of the context provided in the complete document offered as a supplement to these principles.

1. In planning a study the investigator has the personal responsibility to make a careful evaluation of its ethical acceptability, taking into account these principles for research with human beings. To the extent that this appraisal, weighing scientific and humane values, suggests a deviation from any principle, the investigator incurs an increasingly serious obligation to seek ethical advice and to observe more stringent safeguards to protect the rights of the human research participant.
2. Responsibility for the establishment and maintenance of acceptable ethical practice in research always remains with the individual investigator. The investigator is also responsible for the ethical treatment of research participants by collaborators, assistants, students, and employees, all of whom, however, incur parallel obligations.
3. Ethical practice requires the investigator to inform the participant of all features of the research that reasonably might be expected to influence willingness to participate and to explain all other aspects of the research about which the participant inquires. Failure to make full disclosure gives added emphasis to the investigator's responsibility to protect the welfare and dignity of the research participant.
4. Openness and honesty are essential characteristics of the relationship between investigator and research participant. When the methodological requirements of a study necessitate concealment or

deception, the investigator is required to ensure the participant's understanding of the reasons for this action and to restore the quality of the relationship with the investigator.

5. Ethical research practice requires the investigator to respect the individual's freedom to decline to participate in research or to discontinue participation at any time. The obligation to protect this freedom requires special vigilance when the investigator is in a position of power over the participant. The decision to limit this freedom increases the investigator's responsibility to protect the participant's dignity and welfare.

6. Ethically acceptable research begins with the establishment of a clear and fair agreement between the investigator and the research participant that clarifies the responsibilities of each. The investigator has the obligation to honor all promises and commitments included in that agreement.

7. The ethical investigator protects participants from physical and mental discomfort, harm, and danger. If the risk of such consequences exists, the investigator is required to inform the participant of that fact, secure consent before proceeding, and take all possible measures to minimize distress. A research procedure may not be used if it is likely to cause serious and lasting harm to participants.

8. After the data are collected, ethical practice requires the investigator to provide the participant with a full clarification of the nature of the study and to remove any misconceptions that may have arisen. Where scientific or humane values justify delaying or withholding information, the investigator acquires a special responsibility to assure that there are no damaging consequences for the participant.

9. Where research procedures may result in undesirable consequences for the participant, the investigator has the responsibility to detect and remove or correct these consequences, including, where relevant, long-term aftereffects.

10. Information obtained about the research participants during the course of an investigation is confidential. When the possibility exists that others may obtain access to such information, ethical research practice requires that this possibility, together with the plans for protecting confidentiality, be explained to the participants as a part of the procedure for obtaining informed consent.

Name Index

Subject Index

ABCDEFGHIJ-RM-898765432I